THE GREAT
PHILOSOPHERS

THE GREAT PHILOSOPHERS

Series editors
Frederic Raphael and Ray Monk

Routledge

NEW YORK

Published in the United States
by Routledge in 2000
Routledge
29 West 35th Street
New York, NY 10001

First published in Great Britain in 2000
by Weidenfeld & Nicolson

© 2000
The moral right of Anthony Gottlieb,
Bernard Williams, John Cottingham, Roger Scruton,
David Berman, Anthony Quinton, Terry Eagleton,
Jonathan Rée, Peter Hacker, Andrew Hodges, Ray Monk,
Frederic Raphael to be identified as the authors of
this work has been asserted in accordance with the
Copyright, Designs and Patents Act of 1988.

A CIP catalog record for this book
is available from the Library of Congress.

ISBN 0 415 928176

Typeset by Deltatype Limited, Birkenhead Merseyside

Set in Linotype Sabon

Printed in Great Britain by
Clays Ltd, St Ives plc

Contents

THE GREAT PHILOSOPHERS

INTRODUCTION

The twelve essays in this collection were originally published, separately, in the ongoing series of monographs entitled *The Great Philosophers*. They were planned not only as introductions to the work of individual philosophers but also as demonstrations of philosophy in action. Their authors were invited first to give a brief account of the life and thought of their subjects and then to select and examine in critical detail some key aspect of their ideas.

'As a result,' Julian Baggini observed in *The Philosopher's Magazine*, 'you get a strong impression that . . . the writers have really enjoyed the challenge of trying to get over what they really care about in their subjects . . . there's no sense that they are begrudgingly reducing their cherished subjects to mere soundbites in the name of popularisation.'

Through inciting our contributors to explore a specific aspect of a philosopher's work, we hoped to avoid the blandness and superficiality that can mark introductory surveys. By choosing contributors who were both experts in their fields and accomplished writers, we sought to sponsor studies that would be at once accessible and authoritative.

Our tally of philosophers to feature in the series was deliberately eclectic. We had, of course, to include the indisputably great names, whose canon is uncontested: Socrates, Plato, Descartes, Spinoza, Berkeley and Hume have to be seeded players in any general introduction. However, we also wanted to include those such as Alan Turing and Karl Marx who might, at first sight, seem improbable selections.

In general, what distinguishes our contributors from those who figure in a hundred encyclopaedias and general summaries is their determination to engage the reader by emphasising just one – and not the most obvious – aspect of their subject's thought. David Berman, for example, chose to focus on Berkeley's interest in scientific experimental method. This not only liberated him from plodding through the well-worn arguments for and against Berkeley's Absolute Idealism; it also enabled him to display the philosopher in a fresh light. What is true of Berman on Berkeley is, we believe, true of the other essays in the collection: philosophers are treated as proponents of ideas which retain their vitality, not as the sources of antiquated curiosities.

If Alan Turing's work is little known to most academic philosophers, its importance is established by Andrew Hodges' masterly introduction to his ideas on artificial intelligence. Turing not only laid the foundations of the computer-based technology which will dominate the world in the next century, he also had significant things to say on issues relating to the philosophy of mind. As a somewhat tart counter to Hodges' advocacy of Turing's ideas, Peter Hacker reminds us, with cool eloquence, of Wittgenstein's dismissal of the notion of thoughtful machines. He takes this view not because it is *false* to ascribe thought to machines, but because it is *meaningless*. 'Thinking,' Hacker reminds us, 'is a phenomenon of life.' Wittgenstein's view was that, while we need not fear that machines will out-think us, 'we might well fear that they will lead us to cease to think for ourselves.'

Contrasting views of this kind are abrasive reminders that great philosophers, whatever their genius, rarely provide definitive answers to problems. They are more likely to stimulate a continuation, perhaps a refinement, of the eternal debates. Nietzsche once said, 'you say there can be no argument about matters of taste? All life is an argument about matters of taste!' Logic, it may seem, it *not* a matter of taste, but by *which* logic to read the world is finally a question as much of selection as of inevitability.

The same lesson can be learned from Ray Monk's concise explanation of Russell's philosophy of mathematics. In one way, Monk's is a sorry tale of disappointed hopes (for ultimate certainties), but seen in another way, it clarifies some of the deepest reflections of our time on the nature of mathematics. In this department, as in many others, Russell's achievement was not in providing answers but in articulating, more precisely and more elegantly than before, not only where the difficulties lay but also what *kind* of issues they raised.

The inclusion of Karl Marx may seem provocative. No one denies the great influence that Marx had on the politics of his time, and ours, but many could, and most do, refuse him any importance as a pure, and moral, philosopher. Through concentrating on Marx's views on freedom, Terry Eagleton can maintain that we should regard Marx's uncertain place in the philosophical register as evidence less of his inadequacies than of a systematic deficiency in traditional attitudes to the subject.

Martin Heidegger has often been regarded by conventional philosophers (especially on this side of the Channel) with something of the same suspicion as Marx. Heidegger's key work, *Being and Time*, has been denounced as more or less unintelligible. Jonathan Rée's exposition is both elegant and unambiguous; it renders Heidegger's masterpiece accessible without denying its knotty idiosyncrasy.

Frederic Raphael's account, and partial endorsement, of Karl Popper's assault on philosophical historicism could be said to stand to Eagleton on Marx, and Rée on Heidegger, as Hacker's Wittgenstein does to Hodges' Turing. 'Compare and contrast', as the examiners used so often to require, is an enduring and vital habit in human thought. No one can believe without contradiction *everything* that is said in this anthology. What more salutary introduction could there be to philosophy's endless, and sometimes all too human, search for the truth, or truths?

Ray Monk
Frederic Raphael

Anthony Gottlieb

SOCRATES

Philosophy's Martyr

PHILOSOPHY'S MARTYR: SOCRATES

Socrates is the saint and martyr of philosophy. No other great philosopher has been so obsessed with righteous living. Like many martyrs, Socrates chose not to try to save his life when he probably could have done so by changing his ways. According to Plato, who was there at the time, Socrates told the judges at his trial that '[y]ou are mistaken . . . if you think that a man who is worth anything ought to spend his time weighing up the prospects of life and death. He has only one thing to consider in performing any action – that is, whether he is acting rightly or wrongly.' But, unlike many saints, Socrates had a lively sense of humour; this sometimes appeared as playful wit, sometimes as pregnant irony. And, unlike the saints of any and every religion, his faith consisted not in a reliance on revelation or blind hope but in a devotion to argumentative reason. He would not be swayed by anything less.

His friends told stories about how strange he was. After dinner one night, according to a dialogue of Plato's, a young man who had been on military service with Socrates recounted how Socrates had

> started wrestling with some problem or other about sunrise one morning, and stood there lost in thought, and when the answer wouldn't come he still stood there thinking and refused to give it up. Time went on, and by about midday the troops . . . began telling each other how Socrates had been standing there thinking ever since daybreak. And at last, toward nightfall, some of the Ionians brought out their bedding after supper . . . partly to see whether he was going to stay there all night. Well, there he stood till morning, and then at sunrise he said his prayers to the sun and went away.

Despite such uses of his spare time, Socrates had by all accounts an honourable military record.

Another friend described how, on the way to the dinner party at which the above story is told, Socrates 'fell into a fit of abstraction and began to lag behind'. Socrates then lurked in a neighbour's porch to continue thinking. 'It's quite a habit of his, you know; off he goes and there he stands, no matter where it is.' His other regular habits did not include washing; even his best friends admitted that it was unusual to see him freshly bathed and with his shoes on. He was shabby and unkempt, never had any money or cared where his next meal was coming from. He admitted to the court that 'I have never lived an ordinary quiet life. I did not care for the things that most people care about – making money, having a comfortable home, high military or civil rank, and all the other activities . . . which go on in our city.' But Socrates did not think that any of these trappings of a conventionally successful life were bad in themselves. Neither was he an ascetic in the ordinary sense of the term. He never preached abstinence (he could, said his friends, drink any of them under the table, though he was never seen to be drunk), nor did he urge others to live as simply as he did. A hardy and preoccupied man, he was just too busy to pay much attention to such things as clothing, food or money.

For most of the time he was busy talking to others, not just contemplating by himself. His discussions, it seems, were as intense as his fits of solitary abstraction. A distinguished general who knew him once said:

> anyone who is close to Socrates and enters into conversation with him is liable to be drawn into an argument, and whatever subject he may start, he will be continually carried round and round by him, until at last he finds that he has to give an account both of his present and past life, and when he is once entangled, Socrates will not let him go until he has completely and thoroughly sifted him.

Socrates was poor, had no conventional achievements to his name and was of humble birth – his father was a stonemason and his mother was a midwife. The fact that he nevertheless had an entrée to Athenian high society attests to his remarkable conversation. Alcibiades, who told the story of Socrates' vigil at camp, compared his speech to the music of Marsyas, the river god 'who had only to put his flute to his lips to bewitch mankind'. The 'difference between you and Marsyas,' Alcibiades tells Socrates, 'is that you can get just the same effect without any instrument at all – with nothing but a few simple words, not even poetry.' And:

> speaking for myself, gentlemen, if I wasn't afraid you'd tell me I was completely bottled, I'd swear on oath what an extraordinary effect his words have had on me . . . For the moment I hear him speak I am smitten with a kind of sacred rage . . . and my heart jumps into my mouth and the tears start into my eyes – oh, and not only me, but lots of other men . . .
> This latter-day Marsyas, here, has often left me in such a state of mind that I've felt I simply couldn't go on living the way I did . . . He

makes me admit that while I'm spending my time on politics I am neglecting all the things that are crying for attention in myself.

The young Alcibiades was indeed 'bottled' at this stage of the dinner, so no doubt he was getting carried away. It is a telling fact that everyone got carried away when they talked about Socrates, whether it was Alcidiades singing his praises or his enemies ranting against him.

Alcibiades also wanted Socrates to love him. It was fairly usual for dealings between Athenian philosphers and young men to be tinged with homo-eroticism, especially among Plato's circle. Attracted by the youthful beauty of boys, an older man would happily hold their attention by spooning them wisdom. But both Plato and Socrates criticized homosexual intercourse; Alcibiades had at first been mortified when Socrates refused to return his physical affections. As Socrates had tactfully explained at the time, he resisted the advances of Alcibiades for ethical reasons, not because he was not attracted to him. Alcibiades was famously handsome and Socrates was famously ugly. It was an inner beauty that Alcibiades saw in him: 'I've been bitten in the heart, or the mind, or whatever you like to call it, by Socrates' philosophy, which clings like an adder to any young and gifted mind it can get hold of.'

Socrates poked fun at his own ugliness, and he could make something more than half-serious out of even such a lighthearted subject as that. Critobulus, a friend of Socrates, apparently once challenged him to a 'beauty contest' in which each man was to try to convince a mock jury that he was better looking than the other. Socrates begins the contest:

Socrates The first step, then, in my suit, is to summon you to the preliminary hearing; be so kind as to answer my questions . . . Do you hold . . . that beauty is to be found only in man, or is it also in other objects?

Critobulus In faith, my opinion is that beauty is to be found quite as well in a horse or an ox or in any number of inanimate things. I know, at any rate, that a shield may be beautiful, or a sword, or a spear.

Soc. How can it be that all these things are beautiful when they are entirely dissimilar?

Crit. Why, they are beautiful and fine if they are well made for the respective functions for which we obtain them or if they are naturally well constituted to serve our needs.

Soc. Do you know the reason why we need eyes?

Crit. Obviously to see with.

Soc. In that case it would appear without further ado that my eyes are finer ones than yours.

Crit. How so?

Soc. Because, while yours see only straight ahead, mine, by bulging out as they do, see also to the sides.

Crit. Do you mean to say that a crab is better equipped visually than any other creature?

Soc. Absolutely . . .

Crit. Well, let that pass; but whose nose is finer, yours or mine?

Soc. Mine, I consider, granting that Providence made us noses to smell with. For your nostrils look down toward the ground, but mine are wide open and turned outward so that I can catch scents from all about.

Crit. But how do you make a snub nose handsomer than a straight one?

Soc. For the reason that it does not put a barricade between the eyes but allows them unobstructed vision of whatever they desire to see; whereas a high nose, as if in despite, has walled the eyes off one from the other.

Crit. As for the mouth, I concede that point. For if it is created for the purpose of biting off food, you could bite off a far bigger mouthful than I could. And don't you think that your kiss is also the more tender because you have thick lips?

Soc. According to your argument, it would seem that I have a mouth more ugly even than an ass's . . .

Crit. I cannot argue any longer with you, let them distribute the ballots . . .

Of course Socrates lost. He knew he could not really be said to be good-looking, and they were only having fun. This exchange (from a dialogue by another admirer, Xenophon) is not the sort of thing that would bring tears to the eyes of Alcibiades, unless perhaps they were tears of laughter. Nor yet does it show Socrates at his most sophisticated. Far from it: this is the Beginner's Socrates. But it is interesting to see how this simple banter has much of the Socrates that one meets in the weightier and better-known philosophical exchanges in Plato's dialogues.

First there is his characteristic method of interrogation. Instead of proposing a thesis himself, Socrates lets the other man do so and then draws out its consequences. As always with Socrates, the business begins with a request for an enlightening definition of whatever is being discussed – in this case, of beauty. Critobulus takes the bait and offers as his definition: '[things are] beautiful and fine if they are well made for the

respective functions for which we obtain them or if they are naturally well
consituted to serve our needs'. Then Socrates reels him in. He has no
difficulty in showing that if this is what beauty is, then he himself is
beautiful. Unravelling the accounts of others is how Socrates always
played the game of dialectic.

The contest also shows Socrates' complex irony. He knows that he is
ugly. He knows that Critobulus' definition of beauty is faulty. Yet he
proceeds as if neither of these things were so: he seems perfectly happy to
adopt the definition and to use it to prove that he is in fact good-looking.
But he is not just trying to exploit Critobulus' words to win the beauty
contest by foul means. He is not really trying to win it at all. While
pretending to fight the contest, Socrates is in fact doing something else. By
playfully adopting Critobulus' definition, Socrates demonstrates that
Critobulus has failed to get to the bottom of what beauty is. It cannot be
defined in terms of fitness and usefulness alone, since this would imply
that Socrates' features are beautiful, which everybody knows they are not.
Thus, while ironically pretending to convince Critobulus of his beauty,
Socrates has in fact established the negative result that beauty cannot be
what Critobulus says it is.

Socrates frequently and tiresomely denied that he knew anything about
beauty or virtue or justice, or whatever else was being discussed. Such
avowed ignorance was his trademark. Like his playful claim to personal
beauty, these denials were partly ironic, though with a more serious
purpose. Although he always claimed to have nothing to teach, his
activities looked very much like teaching – enough so to get him hauled
before the courts as a teacher with a malign influence. I shall now turn to
the trial of Socrates and his defence, which show just what it was that
made him so unpopular with some conservative Athenians, and so
popular with most subsequent philosophers.

The trial of Socrates took place in 399 BC when he was nearly seventy.
The charges were that he refused to recognize the official gods of the
state, that he introduced new gods and that he corrupted the young.
There was a vivid political background to the trial, but this does not mean
that the charges were a sham and that the trial was really a political one.
Politics, religion and education were all intertwined in the matter, and,
however you looked at it, Socrates was saying the wrong things at the
wrong time.

In 404 BC, five years before the trial, a twenty-seven-year war between
Athens and Sparta had ended with the defeat of Athens. The Athenian
democracy was overthrown and replaced by a group of men, subsequently known as the Thirty Tyrants, who were installed by Sparta. In the

course of earning their name, the Tyrants murdered so many people that they lasted for only a year, though it was not until 401 BC that democracy was fully restored. Understandably, the democrats were still feeling rather insecure in 399 BC. There were plenty of reasons to be uneasy about the presence of Socrates in the city.

Two close former associates of his had been involved in the tyranny. One, Critias, was the leader of the Thirty and a particularly bloodthirsty man. The other, Charmides, was one of their deputies (both men were, incidentally, relations of Plato's). Alcibiades had also turned out to be rather a liability. A headstrong and arrogant aristocrat, he was accused of sacrilegious high-jinks and profanity – committed, perhaps, while 'bottled'. Alcibiades heard about these charges while he was on a military expedition to Sicily. Rather than return to face them, he defected and treacherously fought on the side of Sparta instead. None of this looked good for these men's former mentor, Socrates.

In 403 BC, however, a political amnesty had been declared in Athens, so it would not have been possible to indict Socrates on explicitly political charges, even if anyone had wanted to. Besides, there were deeper causes for concern about his influence. During the long war with Sparta, Athenians had grown increasingly nervous about the home front. It was felt that intellectuals were weakening Athenian society by undermining its traditional views and values. Well might a man who captivated idle youths with his questioning about justice have aroused suspicion. The fact that there had been a hilarious caricature of Socrates as a bumbling but subversive teacher in a play by Aristophanes, staged in Athens twenty-four years earlier, did not help matters. And whatever truth there was to the rumour that Socrates disbelieved in the traditional gods – he seemed to deny the charge, but not convincingly – there was no doubt that he had an unorthodox approach to divinity. The way he talked about his *daimonion*, his 'guardian spirit' or personal 'divine sign', gave reasonable cause for concern that he did indeed 'introduce new gods', as the indictment put it. That would have been a grievous sin against the shaky democracy. The state alone had the power to say what was a suitable object for religious veneration; it had its own procedures for officially recognizing gods, and anyone who ignored them was in effect challenging the legitimacy of the democratic state. All of this Socrates was up against when he faced the 500 Athenian citizens who were to judge him.

Plato was at the trial; the *Apology* (or 'defence-speech') *of Socrates* which he wrote a few years afterwards was probably his first work. There are reasons to believe that in this work Plato tried harder to represent the real Socrates than he subsequently did elsewhere, though he did not necessarily try to reproduce his exact words. So I shall rely on Plato (as I have done for much of the information about Socrates provided so far). There is no alternative. The Socrates of Plato's *Apology* is the only Socrates there is, or has been for nearly all of the history of philosophy.

From a legal point of view, Socrates' speech is a miserable performance. He begins by saying that he has no skill as a speaker; this is a standard rhetorical first move, but in this case one would have to agree with him, if his aim in speaking were simply to get himself acquitted. Almost everything he says to rebut the official charges is either irrelevant or else unpersuasive. For example, on the subject of religion he confines himself to mocking his accuser. He gets him to contradict himself by provoking him into saying that Socrates is a complete atheist who believes in no gods at all. But if that were so, Socrates points out, how could he also be guilty of introducing new gods? To the charge that he has corrupted the young, Socrates makes the unconvincingly convoluted reply that he cannot intentionally have done any such thing, since this would have been against his own interests. To corrupt someone is to harm him, he says, and if you harm someone then that person will try to harm you back. So clearly he would not have risked that. This argument will have persuaded nobody.

Socrates knew that his judges were already prejudiced against him by the slanders of Aristophanes, and set out to correct these false impressions. He is not, he says, a man who teaches for money, like the professional 'Sophists' with whom Aristophanes has confused him. This seems to have been true enough: he did not charge a fee. But he did sing for his supper. He accepted hospitality in a tacit bargain for his edifying conversation, and apparently did no other sort of work. So the way he earned his living was not really different from that of the Sophists – not that either way of life would be regarded as inherently suspicious today. He also tried to dismiss the slander that he taught people how to win arguments by trickery when they were in the wrong. Far from it, he protested, for he did not know enough to teach anybody anything.

This is the main theme of the *Apology*, which is more of a general defence of his way of life than a rebuttal of the official charges. The nub of this defence is Socrates' claim that he has positively benefited the Athenians by subjecting them to his philosophical cross-examinations, but that they have failed to realize this and merely been angered by it, which is why he has ended up on trial for his life.

Socrates says that he is fulfilling the wishes of the gods when he goes about and argues with people. A friend of his once went to the oracle at Delphi and asked if there was any man wiser than Socrates. No, came back the answer, which threw Socrates into a frightful confusion – or so he says. For he always held that he was not wise at all. 'After puzzling about it for some time, I set myself at last with considerable reluctance to check the truth of it.' He did so by interrogating all sorts of people who had a reputation for wisdom or specialized knowledge. But he was always disappointed, because it seemed that there was nobody whose alleged wisdom could stand up to his questioning. He was always able to refute the efforts of others to establish some thesis of theirs, usually by highlighting some unwelcome and unexpected consequences of their views. He also questioned poets, but they could not even elucidate their poems to his satisfaction. After one such encounter:

> I reflected as I walked away, Well, I am certainly wiser than this man. It is only too likely that neither of us has any knowledge to boast of, but he thinks that he knows something which he does not know, whereas I am quite conscious of my ignorance. At any rate it seems that I am wiser than he is to this small extent, that I do not think that I know what I do not know.

Then it dawned on him what the oracle must have meant:

> whenever I succeed in disproving another person's claim to wisdom in a given subject, the bystanders assume that I know everything about that subject myself. But the truth of the matter, gentleman, is pretty certainly this, that real wisdom is the property of God, and this oracle is his way of telling us that human wisdom has little or no value. It seems to me that he is not referring to Socrates, but has merely taken my name as an example, as if he would say to us, The wisest of you men is he who has realized, like Socrates, that in respect of wisdom, he is really worthless.

In other words, the superior wisdom of Socrates lies in the fact that he alone is aware of how little he knows. Of course, there is a little more to Socrates' wisdom than just that, as he is made to admit elsewhere in Plato's dialogues. Although, he claims, 'the arguments never come out of me; they always come from the person I am talking with', he acknowledges that he is 'at a slight advantage in having the skill to get some account of the matter from another's wisdom and entertain it with fair treatment'. He aptly describes himself as an intellectual midwife, whose questioning delivers the thoughts of others into the light of day. But this skill in elucidation and debate, which he obviously has in abundance, is not a form of real wisdom so far as Socrates is concerned. Real wisdom is perfect knowledge about ethical subjects, about how to live. When

Socrates claims ignorance, he means ignorance about the foundations of morality; he is not asserting any general sort of scepticism about everyday matters of fact. His concern is solely with ethical reflection, and he cannot with a clear conscience abandon his mission to encourage it in others:

> If I say that this would be disobedience to God, and that is why I cannot 'mind my own business', you will not believe that I am serious. If on the other hand I tell you that to let no day pass without discussing goodness and all other subjects about which you hear me talking and examining both myself and others is really the very best thing that a man can do, and that life without this sort of examination is not worth living, you will be even less inclined to believe me. Nevertheless that is how it is.

His pious references to the wisdom of God (sometimes he speaks of a single God, sometimes of the gods) are apt to disguise how unconventional his attitude to divinity was. When he says that only God has wisdom, he seems to mean this figuratively, just as one might shrug and say, 'God knows!'. For consider how he sets about interpreting 'God's' words and trying to tease out hints of 'His' wisdom. The Delphic oracle was as authentic a voice of God as any available: yet Socrates did not just accept what it says but instead set out 'to check the truth of it'. He says elsewhere that 'it has always been my nature never to accept advice from any of my friends unless reflection shows that it is the best course that reason offers; he seems to have adopted exactly the same approach to the advice of God. Presented with the divine pronouncement that no man is wiser than Socrates, he refuses to take this at face value until he has satisfied himself that a true meaning can be found for it.

He seems to be speaking in a roundabout way when he refers to his mission as divine, because the Delphic oracle did not explicitly tell him to go forth and philosophize. He does at one point say that his mission to argue and question was undertaken 'in obedience to God's commands given in oracles and dreams and in every other way that any divine dispensation has ever impressed a duty upon man'. But when he continues by saying that this is a true statement 'and easy to verify', his verification consists merely in arguing that his mission is a morally good thing. He does not give any evidence that God told him to do it. He probably came closest to the heart of the matter when he said, 'I want you to think of my adventures as a sort of pilgrimage undertaken to establish the truth of the oracle once for all.' It was his conscience and intelligence which told him to interrogate those who believed themselves to be wise. He could claim that this 'helps the cause of God' because such activities do help to confirm the Delphic pronouncement that nobody is wiser than Socrates. But the talk of God is largely a gloss, which serves to mark Socrates' high moral purpose and to win the approval of his hearers. His basic motive for philosophizing was simply that it seemed to him the right thing to do.

Socrates says he is influenced in his actions by what he calls his *daimonion*, a guardian spirit or voice which has been with him since childhood. This seems to have been the unorthodox divinity or 'new gods' referred to in the charges against him. Once again the advice of the *daimonion* is treated as advice to be reasoned with before it is endorsed, like the counsel of friends or the words of the Delphic oracle. The voice of the *daimonion* is pretty clearly what we would call the voice of cautious conscience. He says that 'when it comes it always dissuades me from what I am proposing to do, and never urges me on'.

The guardian spirit warned him off any involvement in politics, he says, because if he had made a public figure of himself, he would have been killed long before he could have done much good. That is why he chose to minister to the people privately:

> I spend all my time going about trying to persuade you, young and old, to make your first and chief concern not for your bodies nor for your possessions, but for the highest welfare of your souls, proclaiming as I go, wealth does not bring goodness, but goodness brings wealth and every other blessing, both to the individual and to the state.

This persuasion seems to have been rather strident at times. He implies that the Athenians should be 'ashamed that you give your attention to acquiring as much money as possible, and similarly with reputation and honour, and give no attention or thought to truth and understanding and the perfection of your soul'. He must have particularly annoyed them when he said, during his trial, that he thought he was doing the Athenians 'the greatest possible service' in showing them the errors of their ways. This was at a stage of the proceedings when he had already been voted guilty and was required to argue for a suitable penalty, to counter the prosecution's proposal that he be put to death. Typically, he treats this responsibility with irony. What he actually deserves for doing the Athenians such a service, he says, is not a punishment but a reward. He suggests free meals for life at the expense of the state. Such an honour was usually reserved for victors at the Olympic games and suchlike; he has earned it even more than they have, he says, because 'these people give you the semblance of success, but I give you the reality'. He ends this part of the speech by suggesting a fine instead, at the instigation of Plato and other friends who offer to pay it for him. But the Athenians had already lost their patience. They voted for the death penalty by a larger majority than that by which they had found him guilty. This means that some of them, having previously found him innocent, were so enraged by his cheek that they either changed their minds or else decided to get rid of him anyway.

One story has it that as Socrates was leaving the court, a devoted but dim admirer called Apollodorus moaned that the hardest thing for him to bear was that Socrates was being put to death unjustly. What? said Socrates, trying to comfort him. Would you rather I was put to death justly?

As for the prospect of death itself, he was already very old and close to death anyway, so he says, and he had had a good and useful life. Besides:

> to be afraid of death is only another form of thinking that one is wise when one is not . . . No one knows with regard to death whether it is really the greatest blessing that can happen to a man, but people dread it as though they were certain that it is the greatest evil, and this ignorance, which thinks that it knows what it does not, must surely be ignorance most culpable . . . and if I were to claim to be wiser than my neighbour in any respect, it would be in this . . . that not possessing any real knowledge of what comes after death, I am also conscious that I do not possess it.

If there were an afterlife, he added, he would get the chance to meet 'heroes of the old days who met their death through an unfair trial, and to compare my fortunes with theirs – it would be rather amusing'.

For all his talk of ignorance, and his insistence that he merely acted as a midwife for the ideas of others, Socrates did have strong beliefs of his own. Unfortunately he never wrote them down. For one of these beliefs was that philosophy is an intimate and collaborative activity; it is a matter for discussions among small groups of people who argue together in order that each might find the truth for himself. The spirit of such a pastime cannot accurately be captured in a lecture or a treatise. That is one reason why Plato and Xenophon (and several of their contemporaries whose works are now lost) chose to present Socrates' teaching in the form of dialogues. Dialogue had been his *métier* and dialogue would be his monument.

There are four main witnesses for the intimate thoughts of Socrates: Plato, Xenophon, Aristophanes and Aristotle. None of these men is quite what a historian might have wished for. Plato has by far the most to say on the subject, but as an objective guide to Socrates he suffers from the disability of having practically worshipped him. He is therefore likely to have exaggerated what he took to be his finest qualities. Also, in the course of some forty years of thinking and teaching, during which Plato's ideas naturally changed quite a lot, he paid Socrates the tribute of using him as a mouthpiece. To Plato, Socrates was pre-eminently wise, so whenever something seemed to Plato to be wise, he put it in the mouth of Socrates. Plato himself – or else a close associate – once described his dialogues as 'the work of a Socrates embellished and modernized'. This is double trouble, because not only does the Socrates in Plato's dialogues often speak for Plato rather than for himself, but he is also made to say rather different things at the various stages of Plato's literary career.

What about the other three witnesses? Xenophon's failings as a source are quite different. He was not (like Plato) too much of a philosopher to act as a guide to Socrates, but rather too little of one. It is no crime to be a retired general turned gentleman-farmer, but such a man is perhaps not the safest custodian of the key to one of the world's great thinkers. Xenophon implausibly uses the figure of Socrates to pass on his own tips about farming and military tactics. He also depicts him as a boringly conventional goody-goody: 'All his private conduct was lawful and helpful: to public authority he rendered such scrupulous obedience in all that the laws required, both in civil life and in military service, that he was a pattern of good discipline to all.' A leading scholar of ancient philosophy has understandably referred to Xenophon as 'that stuffy old prig'. In fairness to Xenophon it must be said that anyone who admired an eccentric like Socrates as much as he did cannot have been all that stuffy. But Xenophon was certainly no Socrates himself, and he may often have failed to grasp both the strangeness of his character and what he was getting at. If Xenophon tried too hard to make Socrates respectable and a sound chap, then the playwright Aristophanes tried too hard to do the opposite. His Socrates is a slapstick fool who is intrigued by such questions as from which end a gnat breaks wind. Aristotle's disability in describing Socrates is simply stated: he was born fifteen years too late.

Yet it is Aristotle who holds a vital clue. Although he never heard Socrates' opinions at first hand, he studied for some twenty years in Plato's Academy and had plenty of opportunity to hear Plato's views from Plato himself. He was therefore in a position to disentangle the thinking of the two men. To a considerable extent, Aristotle's testimony lets one subtract Plato from his own dialogues and see the Socratic remainder. Aristotle was also much less in awe of Socrates than Plato was, and therefore managed to take a more dispassionate approach to his teachings.

The fact that the four main sources for Socrates were so different turns out to be something of a boon. It means that the features which are common to their various accounts are all the more likely to be authentic. And the more we know about each of the four and what he was up to, the easier it is to discount his bias and see the true Socrates loitering behind. By following up such clues, modern scholars have pieced together much of the philosophy of the man who literally argued himself to death.

It is simplest to consider the views of Socrates in relation to those of Plato. The approximate dating of Plato's dialogues, plus some information about his life, make it possible to retrace his steps on an intellectual journey that started in the company of Socrates but eventually left him far behind. At first Plato largely limited himself to re-creating the conversations of his revered teacher. Gradually, Pythagorean and other mystical glosses were put on Socrates' ideas as Plato came increasingly under the influence of Italian Pythagoreans. And eventually Plato reached a point where he invoked the name of Socrates to expound on all sorts of subjects.

The important discussions of the real Socrates were exclusively concerned with how one ought to live. They were mostly about the virtues, of which there were conventionally held to be five: courage, moderation, piety, wisdom and justice. His mission was to urge people to care for their souls by trying to understand and acquire these qualities. This task was enough to keep Socrates busy, but Plato was much more ambitious on his master's behalf. He wrote many dialogues that do not focus on morality at all but which usually still have Socrates as the main speaker. For example, Plato's *Republic* starts out as a discussion of justice but ends up touching on practically everything that interested Plato.

Even when the real Socrates made a point of saying that he did not have a clue, Plato often plunged ahead and credited him with firm opinions. For instance, Socrates thought that what happens after death is an open question. But in the *Phaedo*, which purports to give Socrates' last words before he drank hemlock in prison, Plato makes him produce a whole barrage of proofs for the immortality of the soul.

Plato seems to have had few doubts about what would happen after death. He thought that the soul was separable from the body, that it existed before birth and that it would definitely continue to exist after death. Under Pythagorean influence, he held that while it was tied to a physical body during life it led a defiled and inferior existence from which it needed to be 'purified' and 'freed from the shackles of the body'. According to Plato in this dialogue, what the good man can hope to enjoy after death is reunification, or at least communion, with those incorporeal higher forms of existence that are conventionally called 'the divine'. The philosopher, in particular, should regard the whole of his life as a preparation for the blissful release of death. As we have seen, Socrates lived a shambling, poor and unconventional life that was certainly unworldly. But Plato was positively other-worldly, which is a rather different thing (and actually he led a mostly comfortable existence until escaping the shackles of his amply fed body).

Socrates pursued the virtues because he felt morally obliged to, here and now. Earthly life imposed its own duties, brought its own blessings and was not simply a preparation for something else. Plato's motives were less straightforward because he had at least one eye fixed on something beyond. One belief about virtue that the two men held in common is that the pursuit of goodness is not only a matter of acting in certain ways but also an intellectual project. Yet they saw this project differently. Socrates believed that coming to understand the virtues was a necessary precondition for possessing them. A man could not be truly virtuous unless he knew what virtue was, and the only way he might be able to get this knowledge was by examining accounts of the particular virtues. That is why Socrates went around questioning people and arguing with them. Plato believed in this argumentative search too, but he also interpreted it as something almost mystical. While Socrates saw the search for definitions as a means to an end, namely the exercise of virtue, Plato saw the search as an end in itself. To look for a definition was, for Plato, to seek the ideal, eternal, unchanging Form of whatever was under discussion; the contemplation of such Forms was itself the highest good. That is what he thought Socrates' questioning really amounted to and what it ought to aim at.

For Plato, philosophy was the ladder to this elevated world of the Forms, but not everyone could climb it. Its higher rungs were reserved for those who were especially talented in dialectical argument, an élite, like the initiates of cult religions, or the followers of Pythagoras who had been privy to the master's secrets. Socrates had a more egalitarian approach to knowledge and virtue. The unexamined life, as he famously said in his defence-speech, is not worth living, and this is not a fate to which he meant to condemn all but a chosen few. Anybody could examine his own life and ideas and thus lead a worthwhile existence. Socrates would happily question and argue with anybody, cobbler or king, and for him this was all that philosophy was. He would have had little use for Plato's Forms or the rare skills needed to find them.

One thing which led Plato to the mysterious Forms was his fascination with mathematics, again a Pythagorean matter and again a point of difference between him and Socrates. Above its gates, Plato's Academy was said to have had the words 'No one ignorant of geometry admitted here'; Aristotle later complained that for Plato's followers, 'mathematics has come to be the whole of philosophy' – a petulant exaggeration, but a pointed one. What struck Plato about the objects dealt with in mathematics, such as numbers and triangles, is that they are ideal, eternal, unchanging and pleasingly independent of earthly, visible things. Plainly one cannot see or touch the number four: it therefore exists in a different sort of realm, according to Plato. And the lines, triangles and other sorts of objects that figure in mathematical proofs cannot be identified with anything physical either. Particular physical lines and triangles are nothing more than approximations to ideal mathematical ones. A perfect line, for example, would have no thickness; but any visible line, or rim of a physical object, always will. Given the impressiveness of mathematics, Plato reasoned, other sorts of knowledge ought to copy it and be about ideal and incorporeal objects too. These objects of knowledge were the Forms.

In one of his dialogues, Plato used a geometrical example to argue that knowledge of the Forms, which for him meant all the important sorts of knowledge, is acquired before birth. The truths of pure reason, such as those of mathematics, are not discovered afresh but are painstakingly recollected from a previous existence in which the soul was disembodied and could encounter the Forms directly. Thus one does not strictly speaking learn these truths at all: one works to remember them. When a soul is born into a body, the knowledge which it previously enjoyed slips from memory: as Wordsworth wrote in his *Intimations of Immortality*, 'our birth is but a sleep and a forgetting'. Wordsworth was not particularly thinking about geometry, but he liked the general idea. To illustrate this theory, Plato makes 'Socrates' elicit some apparent knowledge of geometry from an uneducated slave-boy. This is supposed both to confirm the Platonic idea that some knowledge is recollected from an earlier existence and to show why the teaching of Socrates is indeed, as Socrates had claimed, really like midwifery.

The problem which 'Socrates' sets the slave is that of determining the sides of a square of a given area. He starts by drawing a square whose sides are two feet long, and whose area is thus four square feet, and asks how long the sides would have to be if its area were instead eight square feet. At first the slave ignorantly reasons that the sides would have to be twice as long as those of the original square, i.e., four feet. By drawing another diagram, 'Socrates' soon shows him that this must be wrong, since the area of such a square would be not eight but sixteen square feet. The slave is surprised to learn that he does not know as much as he thought he did. 'Socrates' notes that at this point, 'we have helped him to some extent toward finding the right answer, for now not only is he ignorant of it but he will be quite glad to look for it.' Next, with the aid of further diagrams and by asking the right questions about them, Socrates gradually leads the slave to work out the answer for himself: the sides of a triangle with twice the area of the original one would have to be the same length as a diagonal drawn across the original square – which, in effect, boils down to the famous theorem of Pythagoras. Bingo: since Socrates never actually told him this, the slave must have 'known' it already.

This little episode does not really prove Plato's theory of recollection, as Plato himself acknowledged. But the story does illustrate a distinctly Socratic thesis about knowledge and how it can be imparted. Socrates' questions to the slave are indeed leading ones (and the diagrams help, too), yet it is nevertheless true that the slave comes to see the answer for himself. He has not simply been told it as one might be told how many feet there are in a yard or what the capital of Greece is. He has come to appreciate something through his own intellectual faculties. So Socrates can modestly make his usual claim that he has not handed over any knowledge himself but has just acted as a midwife to bring it out of somebody else. And there is another thing: as Socrates points out, in order for the slave to know this piece of mathematics properly, it is not quite enough for him to work through the example just once:

> At present these opinions [of the slave's], being newly aroused, have a dreamlike quality. But if the same questions are put to him on many occasions and in different ways, you can see that in the end he will have a knowledge on the subject as accurate as anybody's . . .
>
> This knowledge will not come from teaching but from questioning. He will recover it for himself.

Repeated doses of Socratic questioning are called for. In other words, what the slave needs is exactly the sort of treatment that the real Socrates offered the largely ungrateful Athenians. As he says in the *Apology*, if anyone claims to know about goodness, 'I shall question him and examine him and test him.' Thus, in his fanciful story of assisted recollection, Plato has given us a striking illustration of the sort of thing Socrates was doing when he claimed to help other people deliver their own opinions. It is as if Socrates were drawing out and firming up some knowledge that was already there.

This is all very well for Plato's example of his beloved triangles and squares. It is not hard to believe that a skilled questioner can bring a pupil to appreciate a mathematical truth without explicitly stating this truth for him – anyone who has had a good teacher will recognize this experience. But what about matters of justice and the other virtues, which is what the real Socrates was interested in? Ethics is messier than mathematics; it does not, for one thing, seem to have any proofs to offer. So presumably the business of learning about virtue will be quite different from the business of learning about mathematics.

Socrates knew this. He had no illusions about being able conclusively to prove any ethical doctrines. Quite the contrary, in fact, for he was forever insisting on his own uncertainty and the tentativeness of his enquiries. For example, before starting a defence of one thesis, he admits that, 'Sometimes, however, I am of the opposite opinion, for I am all abroad in my ideas about this matter, a condition obviously occasioned by ignorance.' No doubt he is wrong to maintain this thesis now, he says to his interlocutor, but let us follow the argument wherever it leads and perhaps you will be able to put me right. When Socrates says earlier on in this dialogue that, 'I am full of defects, and always getting things wrong in some way or other', he is partly just being modest. But he was quite clear that he had no mathematical-style proofs about virtue.

Does he ever get anywhere, then? Does he really succeed in delivering any knowledge about virtue? In one sense, yes. He does, albeit indirectly, lay out several pronounced and rather extraordinary views about virtue, which all slot together to form a theory of human life. As for whether he succeeds in convincing his hearers of this theory, the answer is generally no. But he does not really aim to do that anyway because he is not absolutely sure that the theory is right and, besides, people must find their own way to the truth about such matters. What he aims to do is to put opinions about virtue to the test, and this applies both to his own opinions and to those of the people he is talking to. The test is to be trial by dialectical ordeal: definitions or accounts of various matters are to be queried and thereby elucidated, and whatever seems to survive such questioning is provisionally to be accepted. The results yielded by this approach fall short of true wisdom in various ways, but it is nevertheless the best approach available. Such enquiry does lead to a sort of knowledge, so Socrates' bare-faced denials that he knows anything are partly ironic.

Most of the authentically Socratic investigations in Plato's dialogues wind up without settling on a final conclusion. Socrates ambitiously sets off to find out what, say, justice is; he argues away for a while; and then usually has to go home apparently empty handed. But he is not really empty handed. The discussions usually succeed at least in showing up something important along the way. For example, in one early Platonic dialogue, Socrates quizzes a man called Euthyphro on the nature of piety or holiness. Although Socrates does not manage to establish exactly what piety is, he does manage to show something interesting about what it is not.

The two men meet outside the law courts, where Euthyphro is about to prosecute his own father for unintentionally (though perhaps culpably) causing the death of a slave who had himself murdered another slave. Socrates is surprised that Euthyphro should want to pursue such a case. Euthyphro insists that although his family think it impious for a son to prosecute his father as a murderer, he knows what he is about. His family are ignorant about what is holy, whereas he has 'an accurate knowledge of all that'. He therefore has no doubts about the rightness of his action. Socrates wonders at Euthyphro's confident wisdom and asks him to share it and tell him what holiness is. At first Euthyphro says that it is what the gods love. But Socrates gets him to see that since the gods are commonly represented as having fierce disagreements, they presumably do not always love or approve the same things. This means that whether or not a god approves something cannot be the criterion of whether or not it is holy: one god might approve it and another not, in which case one would be none the wiser as to its holiness. So Socrates and Euthyphro amend the proposed definition and say that the holy is what all the gods agree in approving. But now a question occurs to Socrates: 'Is what is holy holy because the gods approve it, or do they approve it because it is holy?'

This is an excellent question, so good in fact that at first Euthyphro does not understand it. It comes down to this: would absolutely anything that the gods approved of count as holy, just because they approved of it, or are they bound to approve only of certain things, namely those which would count as holy whether they approved of them or not? Unfortunately Plato did not have the vocabulary to make this distinction absolutely clear. So when Socrates tries to explain it, his account gets tangled in irrelevant grammatical matters and is not altogether compelling. Yet Socrates does seem to have uncovered a dilemma about the relationship between religion and morality. If we ask the same sort of question about what is morally good instead of about what is holy, we can see that we are faced with a revealing choice: either goodness cannot be explained simply by reference to what the gods want, or else it is an empty tautology to say that the gods are good – in which case the praise of the gods would simply be a matter of power-worship. As Leibniz put it, at the start of the eighteenth century (by which time the gods had long ago dwindled to one God):

Those who believe that God has established good and evil by an arbitrary decree ... deprive God of the designation *good*: for what cause could one have to praise him for what he does, if in doing something quite different he would have done equally well?

The Socrates in Plato's dialogue did not develop the argument that far. But he does appear to have seen that moral values cannot simply be derived from considerations about what the gods want, since to do so would rob the gods (or God) of any distinctively moral authority. Euthyphro apparently accepts the point, though later he wavers and hurries into court before he can be pinned down. Thus Socrates does succeed in making useful progress even though he does not finally settle the matter at hand.

Yet there is still something unconvincing about what Socrates says he is up to in arguments like this. Can his questioning, or indeed any sort of intellectual enterprise, really have the sort of practical benefits he claims? Even though he never professes to establish the whole truth about virtue, and although we can agree that he nevertheless manages to make some intellectual headway, it is hard to see how his interrogations can have the power with which he seems to credit them. The problem lies in his belief that discussing the virtues can lead one actually to become a better person. This is no casual aside: it is this very idea which Socrates invokes to justify subjecting people to his trying examinations. It is all for their own good, he thinks, not only because such discussions are worthwhile in themselves but mainly because having them is the only path to personal virtue. This sounds implausible, to say the least. Surely it is one thing to come to know that a principle of action is right and quite another to behave in accordance with it. Could not someone find out all sorts of things about virtue by talking to Socrates but still go off and be wicked? As we have seen, Critias, Charmides and maybe Alcibiades seem to have done just that.

Aristotle frequently attacked Socrates along these lines: 'We must not limit our enquiry to knowing what it [virtue] is, but extend it to how it is to be produced.' He accused Socrates of failing to distinguish between practical questions and theoretical ones:

he thought all the virtues to be kinds of knowledge, so that to know justice and to be just came simultaneously . . . Therefore he enquired what virtue is, not how or from what it arises. This approach is correct with regard to theoretical knowledge, for there is no other part of astronomy or physics or geometry except knowing and contemplating the nature of things which are the subjects of those sciences . . . But the aim of the practical sciences is different . . . For we do not wish to know what bravery is but to be brave, nor what justice is but to be just, just as we wish to be in health rather than to know what health is . . .

Socrates had a sort of answer to this. He could have replied along the following lines: 'You are not being fair to me. The reason why Critias, Charmides and some other troublesome pupils failed to be virtuous is simply that they had not yet learned enough about virtue. If only we had got further in our discussions, these people would indeed have become just. Thus while I agree that we not only want to know what virtue is but want to be virtuous ourselves, my point is that if we really did know what it was, virtue would follow of its own accord. As I keep saying, I do not yet know what it is; so I cannot yet produce it in myself, let alone in others. That is precisely why we must keep on looking for it.'

The main point of this reply is fair enough. We cannot say that Socrates' claim about what his methods could achieve has been refuted: it has never yet been put to the test, because he has not yet found out what virtue is. But even so, why should anyone believe him when he says that full knowledge of virtue, if we ever managed to get it, would itself produce virtuous behaviour? It sounds an implausible hypothesis when we consider how weak-willed, selfish and short-sighted people often are. People frequently think that something is morally wrong and yet do it anyway. Why should we think they would be any different if only they knew more?

Aristotle reckoned that Socrates suffered from an over-simplified picture of human psychology: 'He is doing away with the irrational part of the soul, and is thereby doing away also both with passion and character.' Socrates saw human action and emotion in largely rational or intellectual terms; he ignored impulses and wilful irrationality. 'No one, he said, acts against what he believes best – people act so only by reason of ignorance.' This explains the exaggerated importance that Socrates attached to enquiries about virtue. If the only reason why people fail to do whatever is best is that they are ignorant, then the cure for immorality would indeed be more knowledge.

On this subject, Plato seems for once to have been more down to earth and realistic than Socrates. He recognized an 'irrational part of the soul' and saw it as often in conflict with the rational part. (In his more Pythagorean moments, he described this as a conflict between soul and body.) Producing virtue was thus for Plato not just a matter of imparting knowledge but of encouraging certain behaviour. In the utopian state described in his *Republic*, this involved careful training and discipline of the young and close attention to their early environment – even to the sort of music they listened to and the sort of stories they were allowed to hear.

Socrates himself evidently had no need of such training. He was by all accounts supremely disciplined and a master of rational self-control. Maybe that was the problem. Perhaps it explains why he seems to have had such impossibly high expectations for others and to have supposed that if only they really knew what justice was they would immediately become just themselves. It has been said of Socrates that 'in the strength of his character lay the weakness of his philosophy'. This is a neat formulation, but the ideas of Socrates had rather more coherence than it suggests. Besides, it must be said that his implausibly rationalistic account of psychology was not the only problem anyway. Even if some wise person were as disciplined as he was, and had somehow been born with the irrational part of his soul missing, it is hard to see how this would automatically make such a person morally good. Could not someone be as rational as Socrates, as wise as he sought to be, but also as bad as Milton's Satan, who knowingly embraced evil with the words, 'Evil, be thou my Good'? Not according to Socrates, who held (said Aristotle) that 'No one would choose evil knowing it to be such.' Not only did Socrates conveniently ignore impulsiveness and irrationality, he apparently declared that wilful immortality was simply impossible. He seems never to have met a fallen man, let alone a fallen angel.

Was he then just naive? Nietzsche wrote of the 'divine naiveté and sureness of the Socratic way of life', but what he seems to have had in mind is the clear-eyed focus of Socrates' vision, not any merely foolish innocence. Nietzsche thought long and hard about Socrates' habit of expressing himself in apparently naive propositions, and concluded that it was in fact 'wisdom full of pranks'. Nietzsche realized that it is important to bear in mind the circumstances in which Socrates conducted his discussions. Most of the paradoxical views that can be attributed to Socrates are based on things which he said to someone, or which he agreed to, for a distinctive purpose and in a distinctive context. He sought to teach – while denying that he taught at all – by teasing, cajoling and provoking. He tried to uncover the truth about things by playfully trying out various ideas on his hearers. And intellectual pranks were no small part of it. 'This was Socrates' Muse,' wrote Galen, a doctor and philosopher of the second century AD: 'to mingle seriousness with a portion of lightheartedness.'

One cannot excuse all the implausibilities in his views by saying that he did not really mean them. This might salvage an appearance of mundane common sense for Socrates, but only at the cost of discarding almost everything he said. One can, though, often interpret Socrates better by bearing his unusual educational project in mind. I shall now piece together the theory of human life that lies behind Socrates' apparently naive and implausible pronouncements. What emerges is a set of ideas that have proved to be, at the very least, extremely fruitful, not only in edifying some of his immediate hearers but also in stimulating a great deal of subsequent moral philosophy.

Socrates' theory starts and ends with the soul; in the *Apology*, he says that the most important thing in life is to look to its welfare. The soul, he says elsewhere, is that which is 'mutilated by wrong actions and benefited by right ones'. He does not mean the actions of others, but those of oneself. To do good is to benefit one's own soul and to do wrong is to harm it. Since the soul's welfare is paramount, no other sort of harm is so important. Nothing that other people can do to you can harm you enough to cancel out the benefit you bestow on yourself by acting rightly. It follows that bad people ultimately harm only themselves: 'Nothing can harm a good man either in life or after death.'

Socrates therefore has no fear of the court which is trying him. He will not stoop to dishonourable behaviour in order to win acquittal, for 'the difficulty is not so much to escape death; the real difficulty is to escape from doing wrong, which is far more fleet of foot'. One reason why it is hard to stop evil catching up with you is that if someone tries to do you wrong, it is often tempting to try to get your own back on them. But since it is always wrong to do evil – which would harm your soul whatever your excuse for doing it might be – Socrates points out that one must never return evil for evil. In other words, one must turn the other cheek.

This conflicts with old Greek moral conventions, according to which it is acceptable to harm one's enemies, though not one's friends and especially not one's family. The rigorous ethics of Socrates removes such distinctions between people and enjoins a universal morality instead. One striking thing about it is that it does so by appealing to self-interest, not to the sort of altruistic feelings that are usually thought of as the main motive for moral behaviour. Doing good is a matter of looking after the part of yourself which matters most, namely your soul. This is not like ordinary selfishness, though, because the only way to achieve this sort of benefit for yourself is by acting justly and practising the other virtues too. It cannot be gained by greedily putting your own interests above those of other people, but only by putting moral self-improvement above any other motive. Neither does this unusual ethics rest on any hope of heavenly reward or fear of its opposite. The benefits of virtue are reaped more or less immediately, for 'to live well means the same thing as to live honourably' and 'the just [man] is happy and the unjust miserable'. In Socrates' view, happiness and virtue are linked, which is why it is in people's own interests to be moral.

This is particularly hard to swallow. For one unfair fact of life is that the wicked do sometimes seem to prosper, which rather darkens Socrates' sunny landscape. But to Socrates' mind, the successful care of the soul brings all sorts of good things that may not immediately be apparent. He argues that there are unexpected connections between some of the good things in life, and that happiness turns out to be a more complicated matter than one might at first think. It might seem that wicked people can enjoy all sorts of pleasures, but in fact there are some that they cannot enjoy, and these are important enough to cast doubt on the idea that such people can truly be said to be happy at all. Intellectual pleasures allegedly come into this class, and there are all sorts of other satisfactions which cannot be obtained without the exercise of the virtues. To take a simple example: unless you practice the virtue of moderation, you will not enjoy good health, and will probably deprive yourself of many future pleasures for the sake of a few present ones. So without exercising the virtues a man cannot be all that happy after all.

It turns out that among the aspects of the good life which are subtly and surprisingly linked are the virtues themselves. Socrates argues that they come as a package-deal or not at all. His arguments typically proceed by trying to show that some particular virtue cannot work properly unless another is present as well. Courage, for instance, requires wisdom. It is no good being daring if you are foolish, for such would-be courage will degenerate into mere rashness. And all the other virtues are intertwined in similar ways. One of them, namely the virtue of wisdom, plays a special part. For without some degree of wisdom, people will be too bad at seeing the consequences of actions to be able to tell what is right and what is wrong, which is the fundamental prerequisite for virtuous living. Without wisdom they will be unable to be truly happy either, because every benefit that has the potential to make one happy also has the potential to be misused and thus to do the opposite. One therefore needs wisdom both to reap the benefits of good things and to be virtuous.

For Socrates, the connection between virtue and wisdom was so close that he seems in some sense to have identified the two. They certainly seemed to run into one another. According to Socrates, if someone has any of the other virtues, he must have wisdom as well – because otherwise he would not have managed to be virtuous. And if he has wisdom, he must have all of the virtues – because, being wise, he will realize that he cannot be happy without practising all the other virtues too. As we have seen, Socrates thought that moral behaviour benefits the soul and that a person who acts wickedly is doing himself a spiritual mischief. If this is true, then anyone who is genuinely wise will realize this fact. Anyone who realizes it – and who values his own soul, as any wise person surely must – will therefore try to avoid doing wrong. This train of thought explains why Socrates held that nobody does evil knowingly, for if someone does wrong, the only plausible explanation for his doing so is that he does not realize that his actions will harm his soul. He is, in effect, acting out of ignorance. All in all, these sorts of considerations sup- ported Socrates' idea that if his discussions helped people towards wisdom, he would thereby be helping them towards virtue too.

In one of Plato's dialogues, Socrates encapsulates much of his theory in the course of summing up a discussion with Callicles, a young aristocrat who was about to enter public life:

> So there is every necessity, Callicles, that the sound-minded and temperate man, being, as we have demonstrated, just and brave and pious, must be completely good, and the good man must do well and finely whatever he does, and he who does well must be happy and blessed, while the evil man who does ill must be wretched.

Did Socrates really manage to demonstrate all of that? His hearers frequently shied at the logical jumps he effortlessly made himself. So much seemed questionable, particularly what he said about happiness. Aristotle was typically forthright in his objections on this point: 'Those who say that the victim on the rack or the man who falls into great misfortunes is happy if he is good, are, whether they mean to or not, talking nonsense.' At one point one of Socrates' hearers understandably remarked, in no doubt baffled tones, that 'if you are serious and what you say is true, then surely the life of us mortals must be turned upside down'.

That is precisely what Socrates aimed to do: to reshape people's moral ideas. Clearly this was not going to be easy. In order to succeed in doing it by debate, the discussions would have to be rather different from purely theoretical ones, for 'it is no ordinary matter that we are discussing, but how we ought to live'. A degree of exaggereration and simplification would sometimes be needed if the ethical point at hand was to be made forcefully. For example, when Socrates said that nothing can harm a good man, he did not mean to deny that various undesirable things can happen to the virtuous. He was trying to persuade his hearers to regard such misfortunes as less important than the misfortune of spoiling your own soul. When he said that the evil man is wretched, he did not mean that such a man could not occasionally enjoy a good night out. He was exhorting his hearers to appreciate the satisfactions of virtue, in the broadest sense of virtue, and perhaps to pity the man who could not enjoy them. And when he said that goodness brings wealth and every other blessing, he did not mean that if you behave yourself, you will get rich quick. In this context – in which he was more concerned to deny that wealth will automatically bring goodness than to persuade anyone of exactly the reverse – he was holding up a picture of the best sort of human life, in which all good things are pursued and enjoyed to the full, thanks to the exercise of practical wisdom and the other virtues.

This is indeed no ordinary set of dogmas; in fact, they are not dogmas at all. What I have called Socrates' theory of human life is not something which he explicitly expounded as such. These ideas are the ones on which he depended in his questioning of others, or which had apparently withstood trial by dialectical ordeal. The final goal, which perhaps would never be reached, was to achieve a sort of expert knowledge like the expert knowledge of skilled craftsmen, though not about shoemaking or metalwork but about the ultimate craft of living well.

What Socrates came out with in discussions should often be seen as nothing more definite than faltering steps on this road to expert moral knowledge. Sometimes the road twisted as he coaxed and prodded with irony, or tossed in an argument that seemed likely to propel his fellow-travellers in an interesting direction (or at least to make them stop and think). The result, as Nietzsche said, was wisdom full of pranks. And because it was a specifically moral sort of wisdom or knowledge that Socrates was trying to arrive at, his arguments are tinged with exhortation, idealism and appeals to the moral sentiments as well as to logic and common sense. That is why, considered in the abstract and as attempts at pure logic, they seem to have many implausible gaps of the sort Aristotle noticed.

Socrates does not just paint an inspiring picture of the ideal life. His style of talk makes an intimate marriage between exhortation and logic, which is why it stands as a contribution to argumentative philosophy rather than to preaching. Everything he says is presented in the context of an argument: reasons are demanded, inferences are examined, definitions are refined, consequences are deduced, hypotheses are rejected. This is the only approach serious enough to do justice to the matter of how one should live. Responsible exhortation must, for Socrates, be embedded in reasoned argument. A bare summary of his provisional conclusions, such as I have given here, cannot convey the strength of this marriage of idealism and down-to-earth logic. Such a summary inevitably reduces his thoughts to a shoal of beached propositions gasping out of their element. His thoughts flourished in the swim of discussion, and can be seen alive nowadays only in the setting of Plato's early dialogues.

Socrates was not an easy guru to follow, not least because a guru was one thing that he resolutely refused to be. Still, it is hardly surprising that after his death several of his friends wanted to carry on the good work somehow. Since it was, and is, no simple matter to say exactly what the good work amounted to, it should be equally unsurprising that these would-be successors of Socrates ended up championing very different causes. The greatest of his heirs was Plato. The rest were a mixed bunch. But three of them seem to have had a significant influence in one way or another.

Two of the men who were with Socrates when he died – Antisthenes of Athens, and Euclides of nearby Megara – went on to become founders or father figures of schools of thought whose traces could still be seen hundreds of years later. The school founded by a third companion of Socrates, Aristippus of Cyrene in Libya (*c*.435–*c*.355 BC), has not lived on in the same way, which was no great loss. What Aristippus and his followers made of the teachings of Socrates is of interest mainly as an instance of how easily Socrates' followers could exaggerate and twist what they had learned.

The Cyrenaics who followed Aristippus were devoted to pleasure, but in a curiously philosophical way. Impressed by the rational self-control of Socrates, Aristippus turned his own self-discipline to the single-minded pursuit of gratification. While Socrates saw no reason not to enjoy the good things in life – provided, of course, that this did not interfere with his search for virtue – Aristippus saw little reason to do anything else. After Socrates died, Aristippus became a sort of licensed court jester to Dionysius I, the tyrannical ruler of Syracuse in Sicily, who is reputed to have died in a drinking bout to celebrate winning the prize in a drama contest.

The basis of Aristippus' pursuit of enjoyment, riotous or otherwise, was apparently sincere and partly Socratic. Like most moralists, Socrates held that one must beware of becoming a slave to one's desires. Aristippus agreed. But his rather novel interpretation of this was to exert authority over his desires by getting them to work overtime for him. This made him happy; and what, after all, could be wrong with happiness? Had not Socrates dangled the promise of happiness as an incentive to virtue? There could not be much wrong with it, then.

Socrates had a somewhat highfaluting conception of happiness as a state of spiritual satisfaction obtained by noble living. Here Aristippus begged to differ. According to him, the form of happiness one should aim for was one's own physical pleasure. He regarded such pleasure as the only workable criterion of what is good and bad generally. He apparently held that it is impossible to have certain knowledge of anything but one's own sensations, a philosophical idea that had several defenders at the time. So pleasurable sensations, which were undoubtedly a good thing in some sense even if nothing else was, may have seemed the logical thing for a philosopher to concentrate on in an uncertain world.

The pursuit of pleasure was thus a serious business. The philosopher's job was to engineer his desires and his circumstances in such a way as to maximize his pleasurable sensations, and to preach the wisdom of this way of life to others (who naturally ought to pay for such valuable advice). It took the self-discipline of a Socrates to do this difficult job properly, or so Aristippus seems to have thought, and it was important not to be distracted by other pursuits that might divert one from the only practical and intelligible quest in life, namely pleasure. Mathematics and science, for example, were no help and so should be ignored. Here once more the example of Socrates could be invoked, after a fashion, for did he not relentlessly pursue the matter of how to live, at the expense of all other questions?

Socrates would have enjoyed showing Aristippus and other Cyrenaics where they had gone wrong. He would have wanted to know, for instance, what had happened to justice and the other virtues he had championed. He would also have rejected the ideas of the Cynics, though they were much more interesting. Like the Cyrenaics, Antisthenes (*c*.445–*c*.360 BC) and the later Cynics hijacked some of what they had got from Socrates and blew it out of proportion. 'A Socrates gone mad' is how Plato is supposed to have described the Cynic Diogenes, a follower of Antisthenes. But the Cynics still managed to keep more of their Socratic inheritance than did Aristippus, and indeed their main doctrine was the exact opposite of Cyrenaic indulgence.

Like Aristippus, Antisthenes thought that a Socratic strength of mind was needed for the pursuit of happiness. There the similarity with Aristippus ended. Antisthenes held that happiness was to be found not in satisfying desires, as the Cyrenaics maintained, but in losing them. He was impressed by Socrates' indifference to wealth and comfort, and turned this into an ascetic philosophy that positively embraced poverty. Socrates, after all, had said that nothing could harm a good man. Antisthenes drew the conclusion that so long as one was good, nothing else in life mattered at all. This certainly goes beyond Socrates, who never denied that wealth or possessions were, in their proper place, a better thing to have than to lack. His apparent indifference to them was largely a by-product of the demanding search for virtue and a healthy soul, not to mention mere absent-mindedness.

While Socrates was quite prepared to ignore ordinary ways and values when his principles demanded it, Antis-thenes appeared to pursue unconventionality for its own sake. If something was neither virtuous nor wicked, then it did not make the slightest difference whether one did it or not. As can be imagined, this was a powerful recipe for eccentricity. Freed of the desire for possessions, and liberated from conventional behaviour, the wise man could wander around declaiming against society's foolish ways and generally making a spectacle of himself. He would console himself with the knowledge that conventional values are worthless and quite different from the natural values of the genuinely good life. Unfortunately, it was never made clear what natural values and true virtue actually involved. Antisthenes was much better at loudly saying what they were not.

Diogenes of Sinope, on the Black Sea (*c.*400–*c.*325 BC) came to Athens and was taken by the ideas of Antisthenes. But he thought that Antisthenes had failed to live up to his own teachings, which would not have been surprising. Diogenes made up for this magnificently, especially in eccentricity and unconventional living. One of the best-known tales about early philosophers says that Diogenes lived in an earthenware tub; another says that he set a fashion among the Cynics for public masturbation. True or not, the scores of stories about his wacky words and deeds show what a disconcerting impression he made. He revelled in the nickname of 'the dog' (*kyon*), which is how the Cynics, or 'dog-men', got their name. It was given to him because he sought the uncomplicated, instinctive and shameless life of an animal – animals being the true exponents of 'natural' values. He had a sharp tongue and was quick to savage those he disagreed with, which may also have contributed to his nickname. He was particularly hostile to Plato and liked to play practical jokes on him. He apparently turned up at one of Plato's lectures brandishing a plucked chicken in order to heckle him contemptuously on a point of definition – a low-life echo of Socrates' 'wisdom full of pranks'.

Diogenes' disturbing renunciation of conventional life evidently did not go so far as to make a hermit of this 'Socrates gone mad'. Life was too busy for that. There were people to be persuaded, examples to be set, there was preaching to be done and practical advice to be given. His activities seem to have made him quite popular. When his tub was destroyed, the citizens of Athens are said to have clubbed together and bought him a new one. His sincerity and the simplicity of his life seem to have been respectfully admired from a safe distance, although his teachings were far too radical to attract more than a small number of committed followers or to have any direct political effect. He taught that happiness consisted in satisfying only the most basic needs and in disciplining oneself not to want any more. Everything else was to be renounced – riches, comfort, ordinary family life – because none of it made one a morally better person. All the restrictive trappings of civilization in the city-state, from taboos against incest or eating human flesh to the institution of marriage, social-class barriers and traditional religion, were to be overcome for the same reason. The ideal society would be a loose community of spartan, self-sufficient, rational beings who indulged in any and every form of relationship to which all parties consented, unbound by conventional prohibitions.

Much of what Diogenes said was meant to shock; he probably did not make a regular habit of breaking all the taboos he condemned. But he did not want to jolt people into examining their lives. Over the years, and especially in the first two centuries of the Christian era, Cynicism attracted all sorts of wandering hippies and free-loving, back-packing beggars, who were keener on general denunciation and on ridiculing society than on philosophy or doing good. Such people, and the satirical and sarcastic literature that was influenced by the movement, gave rise to the modern meaning of 'cynical'. But the earliest Cynics, Bohemian though they were, earnestly saw themselves as moral teachers and seem to have performed a useful service. Crates of Thebes (c.365–c.285 BC), for example, gave away his sizeable fortune to become a pupil of Diogenes. He apparently made house calls as a sort of therapist or pastor, offering a service of moral guidance that was not available to ordinary people from any other source – certainly not from the formal schools of philosophical research set up by Plato and Aristotle. Hipparchia, the sister of a pupil of Crates, was desperate to join Crates in his unconventional life, but had to threaten her well-off parents with suicide before they would let her go. They eventually consented, and she 'travelled around with her husband and had intercourse publicly and went out to dinners'.

Euclides, the last of the followers of Socrates to be considered here, was so devoted to the master that when Athens banned the citizens of Megara from entering the city, he is said to have dressed up in women's clothes and slunk in under cover of darkness to be with him. Euclides shared not only Socrates' interest in the nature of moral goodness but also his passion for argument. While Socrates often seemed prepared to follow a promising line of reasoning wherever it led to, Euclides was interested in logical arguments for their own sake, especially paradoxical ones. One opponent spoke of 'wrangling Euclides, who inspired the Megarians with a frenzied love of controversy'.

Frenzied or not, the intellectual curiosity of the Megarians led them to come up with some of the most enduring riddles about logic and language. Eubulides, a pupil of Euclides, is credited with several, including the most famous one, commonly known as the Liar. This is the paradox presented by someone who says, 'This statement is false.' The problem is what to say about such a statement; arguments about its truth tend to go round in a dizzying circle. For example, if it is false, then the speaker spoke truly because that is what he said it was. On the other hand, if he spoke truly, then it must be false because what he said is that it was false. Thus if it is false, it follows that it is true; and if it is true, it follows that it is false. This riddle is easier to make fun of than it is to solve. It has a remarkable ability to bounce back in the face of any proposed solution. One can sympathize with the poet Philetas of Cos, who is said to have worried about it so much that he wasted away, becoming so thin that he had to put lead weights in his shoes to stop himself blowing over. The epitaph on his gravestone read:

> O Stranger: Philetas of Cos am I,
> 'Twas the Liar who made me die,
> And the bad nights caused thereby.

It may be hard to see the puzzle itself as profound, but attempts to get to the bottom of it certainly have been. The Liar has stimulated a great deal of work on the nature of truth and linguistic meaning, by mathematical logicians and by linguists who look at the formal structure of languages. It seems, however, to have caused no further casualties. One eventual by-product of an interest in the sort of 'self-reference' involved in the paradox – the paradoxical statement is curiously about itself – was Gödel's Theorem, one of the most significant results of modern mathematics, which shows that there are certain limits to mathematical proof.

The pupils and successors of Euclides turned Megara into a real-life version of the farcically exaggerated 'logic factory' portrayed in Aristophanes' play about Socrates. The fact that to some sceptics their work seemed like mere 'wrangling' and controversy for its own sake, which no doubt some of it was, recalls the reception that Socrates' incessant arguments about virtue got from some of the less intellectual citizens of Athens. One reason why Euclides would have felt it was his task as a philosopher both to hold forth about moral goodness and to get involved in abstruse logical questions was his admiration for Socrates' view that knowledge is the path to virtue. Socrates may not himself have discussed logic, but Euclides probably felt that doing so was one way to continue the search for wisdom. In particular, if one understood the process of argument, then this would presumably help one to carry on the good work of Socratic examination.

All these schools of philosophy that flowed from Socrates shared his idea that wisdom brings virtue and virtue brings happiness. They evidently differed over what they took happiness to involve – indulgent pleasure in the case of the Cyrenaics, ascetic discipline in the case of the Cynics. But they agreed that philosophical reflection of some sort was the way to find it, and that such an occupation amounted to the good life. The ethical views of these philosophers were all rather individualistic (to an extreme, in the case of Diogenes) and one can see how the unusual example of Socrates' life could have led to this. But in the case of the Cynics, at least, there was a clear break with Socrates over the ties of social obligation and about loyalty to the values of the city-state. The Cynics stressed a contrast between the life of virtue and the life enjoined by the city in which one happens to be born or live. In one sense Socrates did this too, but in another sense he did not. He certainly would have accepted that the individual must follow his own conscience, not the city's dictates when those dictates are unjust. But he sought to better the life of the city, not to relinquish it altogether. He urged the Athenians to live justly together and to improve their laws and behaviour where necessary, not to abandon the whole enterprise of civilization and lose respect for the law.

Socrates made it clear that although you must disobey the laws if they are unjust, you must nevertheless submit to punishment if caught, which is exactly what he himself did when he was condemned. Some friends gave him the chance to escape prison and flee Athens before execution; one of Plato's early dialogues, the *Crito*, deals with this episode and gives Socrates' reasons for rejecting the offer. As well as feeling a moral obligation to the legitimate authority of the city and the due process of law, Socrates loved Athens and did not relish life anywhere else. Some of the things he is made to say in Plato's dialogues suggest that he had misgivings about democracy as a form of government; this has led to him being sometimes described as anti-democratic. But it was really Plato who had those misgivings, as he did eventually about all the forms of government he came across. Socrates himself showed every sign of deep loyalty to the constitution of Athens. He often praised the city and its institutions, and seems never to have left it except on its military service. On the question of whether he approved its type of democracy, Socrates voted with his feet – or rather, showed his preference by failing to do so. There were many other states with non-democratic governments to which he could have emigrated. Perhaps most embarrassingly for those of his opponents in his own time who would have liked to cast him as an enemy of democracy, it was well known that he had risked death under the anti-democratic Tyrants by refusing to take part in the arrest of an innocent man.

Socrates was, if anything, too democratic for the Athenians. It was this aspect of his character and teaching which led to the exaggerated individualism of some of his imitators. His attitude to religion and morality can be seen as ultra-democratic. Nothing is to be taken for granted, especially not if it is handed down by an authority which puts itself above the moral reasoning of the people, be that putative authority in the form of Zeus or of a human tyrant. Every man must work out for himself what is good and right, and nobody can escape the obligation of examining himself and his life. The result of such discussions between citizens should ideally be a just society with just laws, arrived at through such collective self-examination. In the Socratic dream of democracy, individual conviction would lead to collective agreement – not about everything, presumably, but at least about the outlines of how to live.

Socrates was no politician. He felt he could play his part only by debating with individuals, one by one or in small groups: 'I know how to produce one witness to the truth of what I say, the man with whom I am debating, but the others I ignore. I know how to secure one man's vote, but with the many I will not even enter into discussion.'

Over the years, the votes for Socrates have steadily accumulated as Plato's dialogues have carried his debating, or a semblance of it, far beyond fifth-century Athens and its dinner parties. There are now at any rate few who would disagree with one thing that Socrates told his judges: 'If you put me to death, you will not easily find anyone to take my place.'

Bernard Williams

PLATO

The Invention of Philosophy

Plato invented the subject of philosophy as we know it. He lived from 427 to 347 BC,[1] and he is the first philosopher whose works have come down to us complete. He is also the first to have written on the full range of philosophical questions: knowledge, perception, politics, ethics, art; language and its relations to the world; death, immortality and the nature of the mind; necessity, change and the underlying order of things. A. N. Whitehead said that the European philosophical tradition consisted of 'a series of footnotes to Plato'[2], and his remark makes a point. Of course, the content of the questions has changed in all sorts of ways, with the development of the sciences and radical transformations in society and culture. It is important, too, that we, unlike Plato, have a strong sense of the importance of history in understanding human life, but this sense has come about quite recently, and is absent not only from Plato but from most other philosophers before the nineteenth century, who tended, like him and under his influence, to think of the most important truths as timeless.[3]

Western philosophy not only started with Plato, but has spent most of its life in his company. There was a period in the Middle Ages when almost all his works were unknown, but before that, and after the rediscovery of his texts (Petrarch in the fourteenth century had a manuscript of Plato), he has been read and has been a point of reference. Some thinkers, in various different styles, have thought of themselves as 'Platonists'; most others have not, and many reject every one of his distinctive positions, but they are all indirectly under his influence. We are all under the influence of thinkers we do not read, but in Plato's case, people also turn back continually to his work itself. He is in any case a great writer, who can command extraordinary ingenuity, charm, and power, but beyond that, his genius as a philosophical writer is expressed in a special way. Many philosophers write treatises, analysing the problem, arguing with other positions, and setting out their own solutions. Plato did not: he wrote dialogues. With the exception of some *Letters*, which are doubtfully genuine,[4] all Plato's works are in this form. Because they are dialogues, there is always something more and different to be drawn from them, not just in the way that this is true of all great works of philosophy, but because Plato specially intends it to be so. The dialogue form is not, for most part, just an artful way of his telling one something. It is an entry and an invitation to thought.

Plato never appears in the dialogues himself.[5] In most of them, a major part is taken by the striking figure of Socrates, Plato's teacher. They are by far our most important source for what Socrates was like.[6] Socrates is the inspiration of the dialogues in more than one way. He himself wrote nothing, and indeed claimed to know nothing, devoting himself, it seems, to engaging people in conversations in which he questioned their most basic beliefs and showed that they had no basis for them. This method is described in several of Plato's dialogues, and many of them display it in action. But Socrates' legacy was not just a matter of method. His life, and more particularly his death, left Plato with some of his deepest concerns. Socrates was tried by the Athenian courts in 399 BC and executed, on charges, among other things, of 'corrupting the youth', and this disaster starkly raised a range of questions: what the evil was in a political order that could do this; how it was that Socrates' presence had not made his fellow citizens (including some of his associates) better people; and how much it mattered – whether in the end it mattered at all – that Socrates' life was lost, granted that his character was uncorrupted. All these were to be central themes of Plato's philosophy, a philosophy expressed through the dialogue form which was itself a tribute in writing to Socrates' style of life and talk.[*]

In some of the dialogues, particularly some that can be dated to late in Plato's life, the conversational form withers away, and they do function almost as treatises. In a few, characters other than Socrates do not express much more than puzzlement, agreement, or admiration. But for the most part, the dialogue form is an active presence, and this affects in more than one way our relations to Plato's ideas. In some dialogues, no one offers a definite conclusion, and we find that we have been presented with a question, a refutation, or a puzzle. This particularly applies to those which we can take to have been written in Plato's earlier years, but it is also true, to a considerable extent, of a notably powerful later dialogue, the *Theaetetus*.[7] Even when an authoritative figure in a dialogue, usually Socrates, seems to leave us with a conclusion or theory to be taken away from it, we should not necessarily suppose that this is what Plato is telling us to believe.[8]

Not everything asserted in a dialogue, even by Socrates, has been asserted by Plato: Socrates asserting may be Plato suggesting. Because an immensely serious philosopher, who indeed set philosophy on the path of claiming to address our deepest concerns by means of argument, orderly enquiry, and intellectual imagination, and because we project on to him images of seriousness which are drawn from other philosophy[9] and from later experience, we may well underestimate the extent to which he could

---

[*] As a help in identifying the various dialogues mentioned in this book, there is a list of them, with brief descriptions, at p. 74

combine intensity, pessimism, and even a certain religious solemnity, with an ironical gaiety and an incapacity to take all his own ideas equally seriously. It is a weakness of scholars who study philosophers to think that philosophers are just like scholars, and it is particularly a mistake in the case of Plato. Plato gathered about him a group of people who pursued philosophical discussion, teaching and enquiries into mathematics and astronomy. This gave rise, eventually, to a new kind of institution, a place for what we would now call 'research'. From the public space on the edge of Athens in which Plato carried on his discussions, it was called the Academy[10], and in this way Plato gave the word 'academic' to the world, but it is an irony that he should have done so. We should not be trapped into thinking of him as a professor.

This point bears on a passage which itself raises a question of how far we should trust his written works. Towards the end of the *Phaedrus*[11], there is this conversation:

Socrates Well, then, someone who thinks that he can set down an art in writing, and equally someone who accepts something from writing as though it were going to be clear and reliable, must be very simple-minded . . . how can they possibly think that words which have been written down can do more than serve as a reminder to those who already know what the writing is about?

Phaedrus Quite right.

Socrates You know, Phaedrus, writing shares a strange feature with painting. The offspring of painting stand there as if they were alive, but if anyone asks them anything, they are solemnly silent. The same is true of written words. You'd think they were speaking as if they had some understanding, but if you question anything that has been said because you want to learn more, it gives just the same message over and over. Once it has been written down, every discourse rolls about everywhere, reaching just as much those with understanding as those who have no business with it, and it does not know to whom it should speak and to whom not. And when it is faulted and attacked unfairly, it always needs its father's support; alone, it cannot defend itself or come to its own support.

Phaedrus You are quite right about that too.

Socrates Now tell me, can we discern another kind of discourse, a legitimate brother of this one? Can we say how it comes about, and how much better and more capable it naturally is?

Phaedrus Which one is that? How do you say it comes about?

Socrates It is a discourse that is written down, with knowledge, in the

soul of the listener; it can defend itself, and it knows to whom it
should speak, and with whom it should remain silent.

Phaedrus You mean the living, breathing discourse of the man who
knows, of which the written one can fairly be called an image.

Socrates Exactly – and tell me this. Would a farmer who was sensible
and cared about his seeds and wanted them to yield fruit plant them
in all seriousness in the gardens of Adonis in the middle of summer
and enjoy watching them become fine plants in a week? Or would he
do this as an amusement and in honour of the holiday, if he did it at
all? Wouldn't he use his knowledge of farming to plant the seeds he
cared for when it was appropriate, and be satisfied if they bore fruit
eight months later?

Phaedrus That's how he would handle those he was serious about,
Socrates, quite differently from the others, as you say.

Socrates Now what about the man who knows what is just, noble and
good? Shall we say that he is less sensible with his seeds than the
farmer is with his?

Phaedrus Certainly not.

Socrates Therefore he wouldn't be serious if he wrote them in ink,
sowing them, through a pen, with words that are unable to speak in
their own defence and unable to teach the truth properly.

Phaedrus He surely wouldn't.

Socrates No – he is likely to sow gardens of writing just for fun, and to
write, when he writes, to store up reminders for himself when he arrives
at old age and forgetfulness, and for other people who follow in his
footsteps, and he will like to see them sweetly blooming; and while
others take up other amusements, refreshing themselves with drinking
parties and such things, he is likely to enjoy himself, rather, like this.

Phaedrus Socrates, you are contrasting a vulgar amusement with a
very fine one – with the amusement of a man who can while away his
time telling stories of justice and the other things you mentioned.

Socrates That's just how it is, Phaedrus. But there is a much finer
concern about these things – that of someone who uses the art of
dialectic, and takes a suitable soul and plants and sows discourse
accompanied with knowledge: discourse which is capable of helping
itself and the sower, which is not barren but produces a seed from
which other discourse grows in other lives, and in turn can go on to
make the seed immortal, making the man who has it as happy as any
man can be.   (*Phaedrus*, *275c–277a*)

By 'the art of dialectic' here Socrates means argument in speech, teaching
through conversation. There has been discussion of why Plato, after this,

should have gone on writing. But even if we take Socrates' remarks (a little stolidly, perhaps) entirely at their face value, they do not mean that Plato should not write – they give him a reason to write, and that reason is obviously only one among similar reasons we might imagine. This passage does not mean the end of philosophical writing. But it does expect an important idea about the limitations of philosophical writing, an idea which, I shall suggest, is important in relation to the spirit in which Plato wrote his works and the spirit in which we should read them.

PLATO'S DEVELOPMENT

A complication in trying to extract Plato's philosophy from the dialogues is that they do not all present the same philosophy, and his views and interests, not surprisingly, changed over time. It is thus very important to establish, if we can, the order in which the dialogues were written. There are various sorts of evidence that can be brought to bear on this. There are occasionally references to historical events. Some dialogues refer explicitly or by implication to others. There is a technique called 'stylometry', which treats certain features of Plato's style statistically to establish gradual changes in them over time. In addition, there is the content of the various dialogues, in terms of which we can try to make sense of Plato's philosophical development. Here there is an obvious danger that we shall fall into a circle, dating the dialogues in terms of their ideas, and working out the development of the ideas from the order of the dialogues. However, with the help of all these methods together, scholars have arrived at a fair measure of agreement.[12]

The earliest is a group of short dialogues often called 'Socratic' because the role played by Socrates does not go beyond what, it is generally thought, can reasonably be ascribed to the historical Socrates himself. There is then a pair of dialogues, the *Gorgias* and the *Meno*, which, as we shall see, seem to mark a transition from the concerns of the Socratic dialogues to those of Plato's Middle Period, in which, as everyone now agrees, he goes beyond the interests of the historical Socrates, and develops very distinctive ideas of his own. The Middle Period contains what may be the most famous of his dialogues, the *Phaedo*, the *Symposium*, and the *Republic*.[13] These dialogues have particularly helped to form the traditional picture of 'the Platonic philosophy', which contrasts with the everyday physical world of appearance a realm of intellectual, eternal objects, which are the objects of real knowledge and can be directly attained, in some sense, by the immortal soul. These objects are called 'Forms', and we shall be concerned later with questions of what Plato thought they could explain, and how far he had a consistent theory of them.

These famous dialogues of the Middle Period were not by any means Plato's last word, and among the hardest questions in Platonic scholarship is to decide exactly which dialogues are later than the Middle Period, and to form a picture of how much, and in what ways, Plato may have changed his mind and his approach as he got older. The late dialogues include the *Theaetetus, Sophist, Statesman, Philebus* and *Laws*.[14] The last (from which Socrates has finally disappeared) is probably the least read of Plato's major dialogues: it is a long discussion, in twelve books, of political and social arrangements, in a more realistic but also much darker tone than that of the *Republic*.

There are two dialogues that, together, give rise to problems of dating in a particularly acute form. On stylometric grounds, the *Timaeus* seems to be a late dialogue. However, it gives an elaborate account of the creation of things by a 'demiurge' who imposes form on matter (there is no question in Plato of a divine creation of the world from nothing, as in the Christian tradition), and it refers to the Forms in terms very similar to those used in Middle Period works such as, above all, the *Republic*. On the other hand, the *Parmenides*, which cannot be distinguished stylistically from Middle Period dialogues, contains a number of extremely serious criticisms of those ways of talking about Forms, criticisms which many, including Aristotle, have regarded as fatal. They occur in the first part of the dialogue, where a very young Socrates is represented conversing with the old and sage figure of Parmenides, who in fact wrote a bold metaphysical poem claiming the unity of everything and the impossibility of change, and who was held in great respect by Plato.[15] (It is just possible, in terms of dates, that Socrates should have met Parmenides, very unlikely that he did so, and quite certain that they could not have had such a conversation.) Socrates advances an account of Forms to which Parmenides (virtually quoting from the *Phaedo*), makes a series of objections which Socrates cannot answer. Parmenides says that he needs training in 'dialectic' (which was, significantly, Plato's favourite term for more than one method in philosophy which, at various times, he found most promising), and suggests that he listen to a demonstration from Parmenides' companion and pupil, Zeno.[16] The second part of the dialogue consists of a very elaborate set of entirely abstract arguments, the content, and indeed the whole point, of which are still not agreed.

On one picture of Plato's development, he started with the modest methods of enquiry that he acquired from Socrates. He then developed a 'theory of Forms', with the very ambitious doctrines, particularly about immortality, that are associated with it in the *Republic*, the *Phaedo*, and the *Symposium*. He then became convinced that there were deep difficulties with the theory, difficulties which are expressed in the *Parmenides*. Then, in later works, notably the *Theaetetus*, *Sophist*, and *Statesman*, which are without doubt more technical, he pursued in much more severely analytical detail problems that had been latent in the grand theories of the Middle Period.

I think that there is some truth in this schema[17] and some of what I say about Plato's outlook will be in this spirit, but we should not be tied to any simple version of it. In particular, we should not ask whether or when Plato gave up 'the Theory of Forms', because, as we shall see, there is no Theory of Forms. In any case, it is artificial[18] to discuss these matters as though Plato wrote his dialogues in an order, in the sense that he always finished one before starting another. He may have had more than one unfinished at once; still more, the ideas that appeared in various dialogues were at work in his head at the same time.

Above all, it is a mistake to suppose that Plato spends his time in the various dialogues adding to or subtracting from his system. Each dialogue is about whatever it is about, and Plato pursues what seems interesting and fruitful in that connection. We often cannot know, in fact, exactly what made a consideration seem to him interesting and fruitful at a given point. Plato was recognizably, I think, one of those creative thinkers and artists – it is not true of all, including some of the greatest – who are an immensely rich source of thoughts and images, too many, perhaps, for them all to have their place and use. We may think of him as driven forward by his ideas, curious at any given point to see what will happen if some striking conjunction of them is given its head. We should not think of him as constantly keeping his accounts, anxious of how his system will look in the history of philosophy.

THE SOCRATIC DIALOGUES

In the early dialogues Socrates typically appears discussing with one or more characters a question about the nature of the virtues, and refutes some claim to knowledge which they have made, while offering his habitual disclaimer to the effect that he himself knows nothing. To this extent, the dialogues are 'aporetic', that is to say, negative in their outcome, but there is often some significant suggestion in the offing. In the *Laches*, a characteristic example, Socrates is asked by two distinguished citizens, Nikias and Laches, whether young men should be trained to fight in armour; he draws them into a discussion about the

nature of courage. Their common-sensical suggestions are refuted, and no
conclusion is reached. By the end, however, Socrates has implicitly
advanced a distinctive view, by associating the virtue of courage with
knowledge, as he does elsewhere with other virtues. Moreover, the
dramatic frame of the dialogue introduces a theme which was to be of
constant concern to Plato, and which is brought to focus later in the
Meno: how is it that worthy people in an earlier generation, who
basically, if unreflectively, lived by decent values, were unable, as Plato
believed, to pass them on to their children?[19]

One of the dialogues that is assigned to the early group on grounds of
its style and, in general terms, its content, is the *Protagoras*, but it is a
strikingly special case. Socrates tells how he was woken early in the
morning by an enthusiastic friend wanting him to come to a house where
they could see the great teacher, Protagoras, who is visiting Athens.
Protagoras is a 'sophist', someone who takes fees for teaching, in
particular for teaching young people how to be successful and happy.
Plato repeatedly attacks such people, and it is to him, principally, that
they owe their bad reputation, but he clearly had a genuine respect for
Protagoras. He comes out very well from this dialogue, and later, in the
Theaetetus, though he does not appear himself, Plato discusses as his
invention a sophisticated theory based on his well-known saying, 'man is
the measure of all things.'

Admitted to the house, Socrates and his friend find Protagoras
surrounded by admirers, and there is also a notable group of other
sophists, sketched by Plato with a lightly malicious touch. Socrates raises
the question whether virtue can be taught. Protagoras gives a long and
brilliant speech in which he tells a story about the natural defencelessness
of human beings and their survival through their intelligence and
inventiveness, and he lays out what may be seen as a theory of knowledge
for democracy:[20] virtue can be taught, but, unlike the arts, where there is a
division of labour and conspicuous experts, in the matter of virtue citizens
teach their children and each other.

Plato gives Protagoras a compelling and thoughtful expression of such
an outlook, though it is exactly what he himself rejected. He himself came
to believe that there were distinctive kinds of knowledge that must
underlie virtue, and the project of the *Republic* is to design a social order
which will indeed be authoritarian, because it will use political power to
express the authority of knowledge. There is no place in this for
democracy. Plato typically compares a democratic city to a ship navigated
by majority vote of the passengers, and in the *Republic* it is represented in
hostile and embittered terms, as, in the *Gorgias*, the greatest of Athenian
democratic leaders, Pericles[21], is brutally attacked as a demagogue. Here,

however, Protagoras is allowed to offer a different and more benign conception. It is an example of something that is one of Plato's strengths, even if his polemics sometimes conceal it – that he can understand, not just the force of contrary arguments, but the power of an opposing vision.

In the course of the exchanges that follow, Socrates demands, as he often does in the presence of sophists and teachers of rhetoric, that there should be a real conversation, proceeding by question and answer, and that there should be no long speeches. The idea (which no doubt came from the historical Socrates himself) is that only through question and answer is it possible to construct and follow a logical argument, which will actually prove or disprove a definite conclusion: speeches allow irrelevance, bad logic, and misleading emotional appeals. Quite often, characters in the dialogues complain about Socrates' method. Even if they do not put it in quite these terms, they might be said to see the question and answer form as itself a rhetorical contrivance, one that helps Socrates to force his opponents down a favoured train of thought, often a chain of misleading analogies, instead of giving them a chance to stand back and ask what other kinds of consideration might bear on the issue. The criticism certainly occurs to many of Plato's readers.

When Socrates' procedure invites that criticism, one must in any case ask, as I suggested earlier, whether Plato necessarily expects the reader to accept his argument or to question it. But there is a further point, that we should not assume that 'the force of argument' is an entirely fixed and determinate notion. It is not so anyway, and it is less so in Plato, for the special reason that he more or less invented the idea.[22] What one sees in his dialogues is a process, of his seeking in many different ways to distinguish sound argument from the mere power of persuasive speech, as it might be heard in an Athenian law court, for instance. Ancient Greeks, and particularly, perhaps, the notoriously litigious and political Athenians, were very impressed by the power of speech. It is significant that the common Greek word *logos* had semantic roots in both speech and reason; it can mean 'word', 'utterance', 'story', 'account', 'explanation', 'reason', and 'ratio', among other things. One of Plato's major and ongoing undertakings was to construct models of what it is for an utterance not just to tell a story but to give a reason.

In the *Protagoras*, after his protests against speeches, Socrates makes a long one himself, which is an engaging parody of another sophistic method, that of advancing a view by commencing on a poem, a method which he shows, in effect, can be used to prove anything you like.[23] He then turns to refuting Protagoras's position, but this, too, takes a strange turn, since he claims as the basis of his argument that the only good is pleasure, something that Plato himself quite certainly did not believe. At the end of this brilliantly inventive dialogue, the two protagonists, Socrates and Protagoras, find themselves in a puzzling situation, with great respect for each other, and much work still to be done:

—I have only one more question to ask you. Do you still believe, as you did at first, that some men are extremely ignorant and yet still very courageous?

—I think you just want to win the argument, Socrates, and that is why you are forcing me to answer. So I will gratify you and say that on the basis of what we have agreed upon, it seems to me to be impossible.

—I have no other reason for asking these things than my desire to answer these questions about virtue, especially what virtue is in itself. For I know that if we could get clear on that, then we would be able to settle the question about which we both have had much to say: I, that virtue cannot be taught, you, that it can. It seems to me that the recent outcome of our argument has turned on us like a person making fun of us, and that if it had a voice it would say 'Socrates and Protagoras, how strange you are, both of you. Socrates, you said earlier that virtue cannot be taught, but now you are insisting on the opposite, trying to show that everything is knowledge – justice, temperance, courage – in which case virtue would appear to be eminently teachable. On the other hand, if virtue is something other than knowledge, as Progatoras has been trying to say, then clearly it would not be teachable. But if it turns out to be wholly knowledge, as you are now insisting, Socrates, it would be very surprising indeed if virtue could not be taught. Protagoras maintained at first that it could be taught, but now he thinks the opposite, urging that hardly any of the virtues turn out to be knowledge. On that view, it hardly could be true that it was teachable.'

Now, Protagoras, seeing that everything is upside down and in a terrible confusion, I am most eager to clear it all up, and I would like us, having come this far, to continue until we come through to what virtue is in itself, and then to enquire once more whether it can or cannot be taught . . . If you are willing, as I said at the beginning, I would be pleased to investigate these things along with you.

—Socrates, I commend your enthusiasm and your ability to find your way through an argument. I really don't think I am a bad man, and certainly I am the last man to be envious. Indeed, I have told many people that I admire you more than anyone I have met, certainly more than anyone in your generation. And I say that I would not be surprised if you came to be very well regarded for wisdom. We shall examine these matters later, whenever you wish. But now the time has come to turn to other things.   (*Protagoras*, 360e–361e)

VIRTUE IS NOT YET KNOWLEDGE

The question whether virtue can be taught is taken up in the *Meno*, and again it leads to another: how can one answer this question if one does not already know what virtue is? To ask what a particular virtue is, is a standard Socratic move, as he asked about courage in the *Laches*, but now Plato explains rather more fully than he had earlier what the answer to any such question might be like. It cannot consist of a list of examples – that will not show what the examples have in common. It cannot merely be a characteristic that necessarily goes with the item in question: we cannot say, for instance, that shape is 'the only thing that always accompanies colour'[24] – that is true, perhaps, but it does not explain what shape is. This discussion of method gives us some ideas that were implicit in Socratic questioning, but were not all clearly recognized. One is that the account we are looking for (in this case, of virtue) must be explanatory – it must not simply capture an adequate definition of the word, but must give us insight into what virtue is. This in turn raises the possibility that the account may have to be part of a larger theory.

A further idea is that the account will not leave everything where it was. It may revise the ideas that people typically have of the virtues. Indeed, it may well require them to change their lives. That, certainly, was part of Socrates' project, even if it was not clear how it could be so. The distinctively Platonic idea, which begins to grow in the *Meno*, is that it is theory that, in one way or another, must change one's life.

But now Meno finds an obstacle to the search for what virtue is:

Meno How will you look for something, Socrates, when you do not know at all what it is? What sort of thing will you set as the target of your search, among the things you do not know? If you did meet with it, how would you know that this was the thing that you did not know?

Socrates I understand what you want to say, Meno. Do you realize that this is a debater's argument you are bringing up: that a man cannot search either for what he knows or for what he does not know? He cannot search for what he knows – since he knows it, there is no need for a search; nor for what he does not know, since he does not know what to look for.

Meno Does that argument not seem sound to you, Socrates?

Socrates Not to me.

Meno Can you tell me why?

Socrates I can.

And he goes on to say something which in terms of the earlier dialogues is extraordinary:

> *Socrates* I have heard from men and women who are wise about divine things . . .
> *Meno* What do they say?
> *Socrates* Something, I thought, both true and beautiful.
> *Meno* What is it, and who are they?
> *Socrates* Those who say it are among the priests and priestesses whose care it is to be able to give an account of their practices. Pindar too says it, and many other poets, those who are divine. What they say is this; see whether you think they speak the truth. They say that the human soul is immortal; at times it comes to an end, which they call dying, at times it is reborn, but it is never destroyed. So one must live as holy a life as possible:[25]
> > Persephone will receive the debt of ancient wrong;
> > In the ninth year she will give back their souls to the sun above,
> > And from these there will grow noble kings, and men great in strength and skill,
> > And for the rest of time they shall be called sacred heroes.
>
> As the soul is immortal and has been born often and has seen everything here and in the underworld, there is nothing that it has not learned; so it is not surprising that it can recollect the things it knew before, about virtue and about other things. As the whole of nature is akin, and the soul has learned everything, nothing prevents a man, after he has recalled just one thing – the process that people call learning – discovering everything else for himself, if he is brave and does not tire of the search; for searching and learning are simply recollection. (*Meno* 80d–81d)

These are stories, Socrates admits, not demonstrations, but perhaps there can be a demonstration. He summons a slave boy, and, in a famous scene, gets him, merely by questioning him, to see the solution to a geometrical problem which he had never even heard of at the beginning of their conversation. How can this be possible? Socrates' suggestion is that the demonstration reminded the boy of the answer; he knew it already, but until now had forgotten it. Since he knew it already, he must have learned it already; but he did not learn it in this life, so he learned it in an earlier life. The soul is immortal.

It is not much of an argument. There is in any case an objection, that even if we have been shown by this episode that the boy's soul existed earlier, there is nothing here to show that it will exist later – pre-existence is less than immortality. Plato fills in the missing piece by pure sleight of hand.[26] But there is a deeper and more interesting problem. It is often objected to in this scene that Socrates leads the boy in the demonstration. This misses the point. If the question had been one in history or geography, the boy could not, in any comparable way, have come to see the answer: in such subjects, if one does not know, one does not know. It is essential that the exercise is in mathematics and involves what is called *a priori* knowledge, knowledge which is independent of experience. Plato offers here the first theory of such knowledge.

The demonstration may well show something about how we become conscious of *a priori* knowledge. Indeed, many philosophers have agreed with Plato to this extent, that such knowledge is in some sense innate. Very few, however, have agreed that this has anything to do with an earlier existence. For why should we say that there was some more direct way in which the boy must have originally learned it? Learning in the way that the boy has just learned, the way displayed in the demonstration, is how we learn mathematics: how could there be some more direct, original, way of doing so? Plato thinks, or will come to think, that there is an answer to this question, that the naked soul once saw mathematical objects directly by the eye of the intellect. But how could such a process possibly be a way of coming to know mathematics? It is a strange, and typically metaphysical, reversal; Plato praises reason over sense perception, the intellectual over the material, but, trying to give an account of *a priori* knowledge, he straight off interprets it as an intellectual version of sense perception.

Socrates says that the boy does not yet properly know this mathematical truth (in this life), because he has no secure hold on it, will no doubt forget it, and, most importantly, cannot explain it. At the moment it is a mere belief, which will become knowledge only if it is 'tied down by a chain of reasoning'. Later on in the *Meno*, he illustrates this important distinction between knowledge and true belief by a different sort of example. He contrasts a man who knows the way to Larissa,[27] because he has been there, with one who simply happens to have got it right. Put like this, the distinction is not confined to any particular subject matter: if you have a true belief, and you have the reasons, the backing, or the experience appropriate to that kind of belief, then you have knowledge. This does not suggest, as the experiment with the geometry problem might perhaps suggest, that only *a priori* knowledge is really knowledge. Still less does it suggest – indeed, it contradicts the suggestion – that knowledge might have one subject matter and belief another. As we shall see, Plato does come to some such position in the *Republic*, but that is to move a long way, and in a rather perverse direction, from what is first offered in the *Meno*.

Socrates uses the *Meno's* distinction between knowledge and true belief to answer the familiar question: how can decent men have failed to teach their sons to have their own virtues? He and Meno, even though they do not know what virtue is, have agreed to conduct their argument on an assumption, which if virtue is knowledge, then it must be teachable. Certainly virtue has not been taught. The sophists claim to do so, but if they have any effect at all, it is to make their pupils worse people. More significantly, worthy men, who care above all that their sons should share their virtues, have failed to bring this about. So, it seems, virtue is not teachable, and therefore, on the assumption which they have accepted, it is not knowledge. That is, in a way, correct, but given the *Meno's* distinction, it does not mean that virtue could not become knowledge. What we learn from the worthy men's experience is only that *their* virtue was not knowledge. It was not nothing, however: they did have virtue, but it took the form of true belief. That worked all right for them in practice, just as a true belief about the road to Larissa will get you there, and will enable you to lead others there if they are actually with you. It does not enable you to teach another to get there by himself. But if we could find the right chains of reasoning to tie these beliefs down, so they do not run away, then they might become knowledge, and then they could be taught. Philosophy will provide those chains of reasoning, and this is how it will change our lives.

That Plato should present Socrates as making this point has a special pathos about it, for the most striking instance of someone who failed to teach his virtue was Socrates himself. Socrates had a pupil and a lover,[28] Alcibiades, who was very talented and, it seems, very beautiful. His life was a disaster: vain and petulant, he betrayed Athens and others as well, and died a ruined man. The case of Alcibiades was a reproach to Socrates as a teacher, and Plato's recurrent and developing concern with the issues discussed in the *Meno* is a response to that reproach, an ongoing apology. In the *Symposium* Plato confronts squarely the relations between Socrates and Alcibiades, and one of the less obvious features of that wonderful dialogue is the ethical assurance with which he does so. In his own contribution to the series of speeches, Socrates had already said that the goddess Diotima had told him[29] that he himself would not reach the highest level of intellectual love, which in outline she describes to him, love in the presence of the Form of beauty; this signals the metaphysical deficit, so to speak, which Plato diagnosed in Socrates' experience. Alcibiades, drunk, bursts into the party after the speeches (his part has to be something separate, dramatic, not a contribution under the rules of the occasion). He gives a vivid account of Socrates, and of their strange relations. It is an encomium, and we are to take it as true; it reveals some understanding; but at the same time it shows that, whatever might possibly be learned from Socrates, Alcibiades, inside an invincible vanity, could not learn it.

THE ETHICAL CHALLENGE

It was not merely that decent people did not manage to pass on their values, because they did not grasp and could not explain reasons for leading a decent life. There were also people who argued that there was no reason to lead a decent life, and that the best idea would be a life of ruthless self-interest. How many people argued this as a philosophic position we do not know but certainly there was a social attitude, to the effect that the conventional values of justice – to behave fairly and co-operatively, keep one's word, consider others' interests – were a racket, which was encouraged by people who were intelligent and powerful and did not need to live like this themselves.

There are two characters in the dialogues who express this view. One, the more colourful and formidable, is Callicles in the *Gorgias*. Callicles' first speech offers a powerfully expressed challenge both to the life of justice and to the activity of philosophy, as contrasted with a political life in which one can exercise power. Besides the reference to Socrates' trial and execution, perhaps one can hear, too, what Plato knew might be said of himself if he had got it wrong about applying his talents to philosophy:

> We mould the best and the most powerful among us, taking them while they're still young, like lion cubs, and with charms and incantations we subdue them into slavery, telling them that one is supposed to get no more than his fair share, and that this is what is fair and just. But I believe that if there were to be a man whose nature was up to it, one who had shaken off, torn apart, and escaped all this, who had trampled under foot our documents, our trickery and charms, and all those laws that are against nature – he, the slave, would rise up and be revealed as our master, and then the justice of nature would shine out . . .
>
> Philosophy is no doubt a charming thing, Socrates, if someone is exposed to it in moderation at the appropriate time of life. But if one spends more time on it than he should, it is the undoing of mankind. For even if someone has great natural advantages, if he engages in philosophy far beyond the appropriate time of life, he will inevitably turn out to be inexperienced in all those things in which a man has to

be experienced if he is to be admirable and good and well thought of. Such people have no experience of the laws of their city or of the kind of speech one must use to deal with people on matters of business, public or private; they have no experience in human pleasures and appetites; no experience, in short, of human character altogether. So when they venture into some private or political activity, they become a laughing stock . . .

So when I see an older man still engaging in philosophy and not giving it up, I think such a man by this time needs a flogging. As I was just saying, such a man, even with natural advantages, will end up becoming unmanly and avoiding the middle of the city and its meeting places – where, as the poet said, men become really distinguished – and will slink away for the rest of his life, whispering with three or four boys in a corner, never coming out with anything free-spirited, important, or worth anyone's attention . . .

As it is, if someone got hold of you or of anyone else like you and took you off to prison on the charge that you're doing something unjust when you're not, be assured that you wouldn't be able to do yourself any good. You would get dizzy, your mouth would hang open, and you would not know what to say. You would come up for trial and face some no-good wretch of an accuser and be put to death, if death is what he wanted as your sentence. How can this be a wise thing, Socrates, 'the craft which took a well-favoured man and made him worse', not able to protect himself or to rescue himself or anyone else from the gravest dangers, to be robbed by his enemies, and to live a life without honour in the city? To put it rather crudely, you could give such a man a smack on the jaw and get away with it. Listen to me, friend, and stop this refuting. 'Practise the sweet music of an active life and do it where you'll get a reputation for being intelligent. Leave these subtleties to others' – whether we call them merely silly, or outright nonsense – 'which will cause you to live in empty houses', and do not envy those who go in for these fiddling refutations, but those who have a life, and fame, and many other good things as well.

                                   (*Gorgias*, 483e–486d (with omissions))

Socrates has already had two conversations before Callicles appears, and they are carefully structured to show how radical Callicles' outlook is. The first speaker is Gorgias, a famous orator and teacher of rhetoric, who gives a defence of his profession. Plato believes that this profession is dangerous and its claims to any expertise hollow, and in this notably angry dialogue he goes on to denounce the rhetorician as a technician of mere appearances, like someone who serves the sick with rich and unhealthy pastries or paints the face of the dying. But Gorgias himself is treated with some respect. He indeed gives a respectable defence: he thinks that his skills serve the cause of justice, that the life of justice is worth living, and that to be a just person is *kalon* – a significant ethical term for the Greeks, which means that it is worthy of admiration, and that a person would properly be well regarded and would have self-respect for living such a life.

He is succeeded in the conversation (as, Plato believes, also in social reality) by a younger and more belligerent figure, who is called Polus. He thinks that the life of justice is not reasonable; given an alternative, it is not worth pursuing. Under Socrates' questioning,[30] however, he makes the mistake of admitting both that justice is *kalon*, worth admiring, and also (reasonably) that something worth admiring is worth pursuing. Having said that justice is not worth pursuing, he is faced, Socrates shows him, with a contradiction. Granted that he thinks that we have reason to do what will make us admired, and no reason to do what will make us feel foolish or ashamed of ourselves – that is to say, he still attaches value to the *kalon* – he should not go on saying that just behaviour is to be admired and injustice is something to be ashamed of. This is what Callicles, stormily breaking into the conversation, points out. It is a purely conventional idea, he insists, which must be given up if we are going to have a realistic view of what is worth doing. Callicles himself does still subscribe to the value of the *kalon*, but he does not apply it to justice. He thinks that a reasonable person will want to be admired and envied, to think well of himself, and not to be an object of contempt, but the way to bring this about is through power and the exploitation of others, having no concern for justice. Implicit in this, indeed very near the surface of it, is the idea that people do secretly admire the successful exploiter and despise the virtuously exploited, whatever they say about the value of justice.

Socrates does refute Callicles, but only by forcing him into a position which, critics have thought, he has no reason to accept. He ends up[31] defending a crudely gluttonous form of hedonism, which not many people are likely to envy. But this, surely, was not supposed to be the idea. The successfully unjust man was supposed to be a rather grand and powerful figure, whom others, if they were honest, would admire and envy, but he has ended up in Socrates' refutation as a squalid addict whom anyone with any taste would despise. It is easy to think that Socrates wins the argument only because Plato has changed the subject. But Plato does not suppose that he has changed the subject. His point is that without some idea of values that apply to people generally, there will be no basis for any kind of admiration, and if Callicles wants still to think of himself in terms of the *kalon*, he will have to hold on to something more than bare egoism, which by itself offers nothing for admiration and really does lead only to an unstructured and unrewarding hedonism. Plato himself, of course, believes something that goes beyond this, that only a life of justice can offer the structure and order that are needed to make any life worth living.

This is what the *Republic* is meant to show: 'It is not a trivial question we are discussing,' Socrates says towards the end of the first book of that dialogue: 'what we are talking about is how one should live.'[32] He says it to Thrasymachus, Plato's other (and rhetorically less impressive) representative of the enemies of justice. Thrasymachus has been defending the idea that if a person has a reason to act justly, it will always be because it does somebody else some good.[33] It is not very hard for Socrates to refute this in the version that Thrasymachus offers; attached as he is to the rather flashy formula 'justice is the interest of the stronger', Thrasymachus has not noticed that the 'stronger' typically take the form of a group, a collective agent (such as the people in the Athenian democracy), and that they can be a collective agent only because they individually follow rules of justice.

This leads naturally to the idea that justice is not so much a device of the strong to exploit the weak, as a device of the weak to make themselves strong. This idea is spelled out in Book II by two further speakers, Glaukon and Adeimantus, who say that they do not want to believe it themselves, but that they need to have it refuted by Socrates. It is bound to seem to us ethically a lot more attractive than Thrasymachus's proposition: it is the origin, in fact, of the social contract theories that have played an important part in later political philosophy. It is interesting, then, that Glaukon and Adeimantus, as much as Socrates himself, regard this position as only a more effective variant of Thrasymachus's.[34] The reason for this is that on this account justice still comes out as a second best. Just as much as in Thrasymachus's cruder account, it is an instrument or device for satisfying one's desires. An adequate defence of justice, Plato thought, must show that it is rational for each person to want to be just, whatever his circumstances, and the suggestion of Glaukon and Adeimantus fails this test: if someone were powerful and intelligent and well enough placed, he would reasonably have no interest in justice. What Socrates must show is that justice is prized not simply for its effects, but for its own sake.

But why is this the demand? Why is the standard for a defence of justice raised so high? The answer fully emerges only after one has followed the whole long discussion of the *Republic*. That discussion takes the form of considering justice both in an individual and in a city, and

Plato constructs a complex analogy between the two. He discusses in great detail what the institutions of a just city must be. He pursues this, as indeed Socrates makes clear, for its own sake, but the main features of the analogy are needed to answer the question about the value of justice 'in itself', and indeed to show why that has to be the question in the first place. A just person is one in whom reason rules, as opposed to the other two 'parts' of the soul that Plato distinguishes,[35] a 'spirited', combative and competitive, part, and a part that consists of hedonistic desires. Just people, who will have this balance and stability in their soul, need to be brought up in a just city, one that is governed by its own rational element; that is to say, by a class of people who are themselves like this. Those people certainly need to see justice as a good in itself; there is nothing to make them pursue it except their own understanding of justice and of the good. They will be able to do this, since their education will give them a philosophical understanding of the good, and of why justice represents the proper development of the rational soul. So, Plato hoped, the *Republic* would have answered the question about the transmission of virtue from one generation to another: it could be brought about only in a just city, and a just city must be one in which the authority of reason is represented politically, by the unquestioned authority of a class of Guardians who – and Socrates recognizes that it will be seen as a very surprising solution – have been educated in philosophy.

In one sense, the foundation of a just city is supposed to be the final, the only, answer to the question of how to keep justice alive. But even in the *Republic* Plato does not suppose that it could in practice be a final answer, for no earthly institution can last uncorrupted, and even if we imagine the city coming about, it will ultimately degenerate, in a process which Plato lays out in Books VIII and IX. There is a parallel story about the effects of the ethical degeneration among individual people, and together they give an opportunity, not only for an evaluation of different kinds of society, but for a good deal of social and psychological observation.

OUT OF THE CAVE

Books V to VII of the *Republic* are devoted for the most part to the education of the Guardians, and they also express some of Plato's highest metaphysical ambitions. This is because the further reaches of what the Guardians learn extend to a reality which in some sense lies beyond everyday experience, and it is only an encounter with this reality that secures the firm hold on the good that underlies the stability of their own characters and their just governance of the city. (It is worth mentioning that Plato says that women should not, as such, be excluded from the highest and most abstract studies, an idea that sets him apart from most of his contemporaries and, as often, from the more conventional Aristotle.[36])

Plato pictures the progress of the soul under education in terms of an ascent from what, in a vivid and very famous image, he represents as the ordinary condition of human beings:

—Next, compare our nature, and the effect of its having or not having education, to this experience. Picture human beings living in an underground dwelling like a cave, with a long entrance open to the light, as wide as the cave. They are there from childhood, with chains on their legs and their necks so that they stay where they are and can only see in front of them, unable to turn their heads because of the fetters. Light comes from a fire which is burning higher up and some way behind them; and also higher up, between the fire and the prisoners, there is a road along which a low wall is built, like the screen in front of puppeteers above which they show their puppets.
—I can picture it.
—Now imagine that there are men along this wall, carrying all sorts of implements which reach above the wall, and figures of men and animals in stone and wood and every material, and some of the men who are doing this speak, presumably, and others remain silent.
—It is a strange image you are describing, and strange prisoners.
—They are like us: for do you think that they would see anything of themselves or each other except the shadows that were cast by the fire on the wall in front of them?
—How could they, if they are forced to keep their heads motionless for all their lives?
—And what about the objects that are being carried along the wall? Wouldn't it be the same?
—Of course.
—And if they could talk to each other, don't you think they would suppose that the names they used applied to the things passing before them?
—Certainly.
—And if the prison had an echo from the wall facing them? Wouldn't they suppose that it was the shadow going by that was speaking, whenever one of those carrying the objects spoke?
—Of course.

—Altogether then, they would believe that the truth was nothing other than the shadows of those objects.

—They would indeed.

—But now consider what it would be like for them to be released from their bonds and cured of their illusions, if such a thing could happen to them. When one of them was freed and forced suddenly to stand up and turn his head and walk and look up towards the light, doing all these things he would be in pain, and because he was dazzled he would not be able to see the things of which he had earlier seen the shadows. What do you think he would reply if someone said to him that what he had seen earlier was empty illusion, but that now he is rather closer to reality, and turned to things that are more real, and sees more correctly? Don't you think he would be at a loss and would think that the things he saw earlier were truer than the things he was now being shown?

—Much truer.

—And if he were forced to look at the light itself, wouldn't his eyes hurt, and wouldn't he turn away and run back to the things he was able to see, and think that they were really clearer than the things that he had been shown?

—Yes.

—And if someone dragged him by force up the rough steep path, and did not let him go until he had been dragged out into the light of the sun, wouldn't he be in pain and complain at being dragged like this, and when he got to the light, with the sun filling his eyes, wouldn't he be unable to see a single one of the things now said to be true?

—He would, at least at first.

—He would need practice, if he were going to see the things above. First he would most easily see shadows, and then the images of men and other things reflected in water, and then those things themselves; and the things in the heavens and the heavens themselves he would see more easily at night, looking at the light of the moon and the stars, than he could see the sun and its light by day.

—Certainly.

—Finally he would be able to look at the sun itself, not reflected in water or in anything else, but as it is in itself and in its own place: to look at it and see what kind of thing it is.   (*Republic*, 514a–516b)

This image brings together two different ideas of what is wrong with the empirical world and with the skills, such as rhetoric, that live off it and its politics of illusion: that it is all empty appearance, and that nevertheless it involves coercive forces (symbolized by the chains) from which people need to be freed. The everyday world, with its sensations, desires, and inducements, is at once flimsy and powerful. In this it resembles what later times would understand as magic: the world that Prospero brings into being in *The Tempest* is merely the baseless fabric of a vision, and yet he can claim

> graves at my command
> Have wak'd their sleepers, op'd, and let 'em forth
> By my so potent Art.[37]

It is just this profound ambivalence, about its power and its emptiness, that inspires Plato's attack on painting, poetry, and the other arts, an attack which is expressed at various points in the *Republic* but most concentratedly in Book X.

When the future Guardians go up from the cave into the open air, they may eventually even be able to look directly at the sun. The sun, in Plato's story, stands for the Good, and the analogy is a complex one. As the sun makes living things grow, so the existence of everything is explained by the Good; as the sun enables everything to be seen, including itself, so the Good enables everything, including itself, to be known. What this means is that explanation and understanding must reveal why it is 'for the best' that things should be so rather than otherwise.[38] Plato's conception of 'the best' must be understood in a very abstract way: he is concerned with such matters as the mathematical beauty and simplicity of the ultimate relations between things, an interest which he seems to have derived (together, probably, with his belief in immortality) from the mystical and mathematical tradition of the Pythagoreans, which he encountered on his visits to Greek communities in Italy, first in about 387 BC.

When Plato talks of things being 'for the best', we should not think of him as like Dr Pangloss in Voltaire's *Candide*, who claims that this is the best of all possible worlds and that if we knew enough we would see that everything, however disastrous, is ultimately for the best in humanly recognizable terms such as happiness and welfare. That outlook is a shallow version of Christianity, a religion which is committed (at least after Augustine) to believing that human history and everyday human experience do matter in the ultimate scale of things. Plato, in the *Republic* and, notably, in the *Phaedo* (but by no means everywhere else), expresses something different, the aspiration to be released and distanced from finite human concerns altogether, and this is reflected in his conception of what is 'for the best'. Dr Pangloss and his metaphysically more distinguished model, Leibniz, are regarded as optimists,[39] but even in the Utopian *Republic* Plato is pessimistic about everyday life, and although these Middle Period works frequently remind us of finite and fleeting happiness, particularly through friendship, the ascent from the cave into the sunlight signals a departure from human concerns altogether.

Plato offers us in the *Republic* another model of the relation between everyday experience and the 'higher' reality. We are to imagine a line, divided into two sections. The top part corresponds to knowledge, and also, therefore, to those things that we can know; the lower part corresponds to belief, and to those things about which we can have no better than belief. These two parts are each divided again into two sub-sections. When we consider these sub-sections the emphasis is not so much on different things about which we may have knowledge or belief, but rather on more or less direct methods[40] of acquiring knowledge or belief. The lowest sub-section is said to relate to shadows and reflections, while the sub-section above relates to ordinary, three-dimensional, things. Plato can hardly think that there is a special state of mind involved simply in looking at shadows and reflections. The point is that relying on shadows and reflections is a poor or second-best way of acquiring beliefs about ordinary solid objects. The sub-sections of the upper part of the line make a similar point, one that is also expressed in the story of the cave. There is a state of mind that is a poor or second-best way of getting to know about unchanging reality. This, according to Plato, is the state of mind of mathematicians in his time.

He saw two limitations to that mathematics. One was that although it understood, of course, that its propositions were not literally true of any physical diagram – no line is quite straight, no equalities are really equal, no units are unequivocally units – nevertheless, it relied on diagrams. Moreover, it relied on unproved assumptions or axioms, and Plato takes the opportunity of describing the Guardians' education to sketch an ultimately ambitious research programme, which will derive all mathematical assumptions from some higher or more general truths, arriving ultimately at an entirely rational and perspicuous structure which in some sense depends on the self-explanatory starting point[41] of the Good. It is made quite clear that Socrates cannot explain what this will be like, not just because his hearers will not understand it but because he does not understand it himself. It involves an intellectual project and a vision that lay beyond the historical Socrates, obviously enough, but also beyond Plato when he wrote the *Republic*. In fact, it was a project that was never to be carried out on such a grandiose scale.

The reality that corresponds to the highest section of the line[42] consists of Forms, objects which are – whatever else – eternal, immaterial, unchanging, and the objects of rational, *a priori*, knowledge (which, in the *Republic*'s scheme of things, is the only knowledge there is).

Commentators discuss 'the Theory of Forms', but there is really no such thing (which is why there is no question to be answered of whether or when Plato gave it up). It is more helpful to see Plato as having a general conception of a Form, in the sense of some such abstract, intellectual, object; having also a set of philosophical questions; and as continually asking how such objects might contribute, in various ways, to answering those various questions. The *Republic* represents the boldest version of the idea that one and the same set of objects could answer all those questions. Plato did not cease to think that there were abstract objects of rational understanding, existing independently of the material world, but he came to see that one and the same kind of object could not serve in all the roles demanded of it by the *Republic*.

Aristotle[43] says that Socrates was interested in questions of definition, but that Plato was the first to make Forms 'separate'. In this connection, a Form can be understood as the quality or character in virtue of which many particular things are of the same kind; and to say that it is 'separate' marks the point that the quality would exist even if there were no particulars that possessed it, as one might say that there would be a virtue of courage even if there were no courageous people. (As we shall see, Plato also wants to say that, for more than one reason, particulars cannot properly, perfectly, or without qualification instantiate Forms.) This is the approach to Forms from the theory of meaning; in the *Republic* Plato seems to give an entirely general formulation of this idea when he says: 'Shall we start the enquiry with our usual procedure? We are in the habit, I take it, of positing a single idea or Form for each case in which we give the same name to many things.'[44]

Aristotle also says[45] that Plato, 'Having in his youth first become familiar with Cratylus and the Heracleitean doctrines (that all sensible things are always in a state of flux and there is no knowledge about them), these views he held even in later years.' In this connection, Forms are, or are very closely associated with, the objects of mathematical study. As the image of the divided line makes clear, geometers use material, particular, diagrams, but they cannot be talking directly about those diagrams, or what they say ('the line AB is equal to the line AC' and so on) would be simply untrue. They must be talking about something else, triangles formed of absolutely straight lines with no breadth. This is the approach from the possibility of *a priori* knowledge. It is in this role that Forms can also be naturally taken to be those objects of intellectual vision that the argument of the *Meno* needed as the archetypal source of the beliefs recovered in recollection.

The geometers' triangles, unlike scrawled or carpentered triangles of everyday life, are perfect. This is an idea that Plato applied to some other kinds of objects as well: a Form was a paradigm. So when a craftsman makes an artefact, his aim is to approximate to the best that such a thing could be, an ideal which, it may well be, neither he nor anyone else will ever adequately express in a particular material form. So it is with a couch in Book X of the *Republic* and a shuttle in the *Cratylus*.[46] The conceptions of a Form as a paradigm, and of a Form as a general quality or characteristic, come together with special force when there is a quality that we find in particular things, but which occurs in them in a way that is imperfect in the strong sense that our experience of them carries with it an aspiration, a yearning, for an ideal. The most powerful example of this, for Plato, is beauty.

The geometers' triangles, on the one hand, and qualities or characteristics such as courage or dampness, on the other, are all uncreated and unchanging. The world changes: damp things dry out, particular people become courageous or cease to be so. But dampness and courage and such things do not themselves change, except in the boring sense that beauty changes if at one time it characterizes Alcibiades and at a later time it does not, and this is not a change *in it* (any more than it is a change in Socrates that young Theaetetus, who is growing, is shorter than him one year and taller the next year).[47] So there is a fundamental contrast between Forms and the world in which things change, our everyday world.

Sometimes, Plato invokes Forms to explain change. This is notably so in the *Phaedo*, which uses conceptions that are hard to fit together with the discussions, particularly in the *Republic*, which emphasize the metaphysical distance between Forms and particulars. It treats Forms as though parts of them could be transitory ingredients or occupants of material things (as we speak of the dampness in the wall). It is relevant that this discussion has a very special aim, to support a curious proof of the immortality of the soul (which Plato nowhere else uses or relies on). This proof requires the indestructible Form, life, in the sense of 'aliveness', to join with a particular, Socrates, in such a way that there will be an item, 'Socrates' aliveness', which is as indestructible as the Form but as individual as Socrates. This is Socrates' soul; indeed, it is Socrates himself, when he is freed of the irrelevance of his body.[48]

When Plato says that, in contrast to the Forms, particulars in the material world are 'changing', he means more than that they are changing in time. He also means that when we say that a material thing is round or red, for instance, what we say is only relatively or qualifiedly true: it is round or red from one point of view but not another, to one observer rather than another, by comparison with one thing and not another. So what we say about material things is only relatively or qualifiedly true. Indeed, if our statements mean what they seem to say, for instance that this surface is red without qualification, then they are not true at all – not *really* true. Only what we say about Forms can be absolutely or unqualifiedly true.

This gives a broader sense in which things in the material world are imperfect compared with Forms. Only in some cases, such as beauty, does the imperfection of particular things evoke the pathos of incompleteness, of regret, indeed (given Plato's idea of recollection) of nostalgia. But in the sense that nothing is unqualifiedly or absolutely what we say it is, but is so only for a time, to an observer, or from a point of view – in that sense, everything in the material world is imperfect. In the *Republic* this contrast is expressed in the strongest terms, which we have already encountered in the image of the line. Only what is in the world of Forms 'really is'; the world of everyday perception is 'between being and not being', and is mere appearance or like a dream; only 'being' can be the object of knowledge, while the world of 'becoming' is the object of mere belief or conjecture.

There has been much discussion of what exactly Plato meant by these formulations. We should certainly try to make the best sense we can of them, but we should not expect an overall interpretation that is fully intelligible in our terms. To do so is to ignore a vital point, that, however exactly his thought developed, he himself certainly came to think that the *Republic*'s formulations would not do. There are many ways in which the later dialogues acknowledge this. Most generally, Plato came to recognize the tensions that the various approaches to the Forms, taken together, must create. The approach from the theory of meaning implies, unless it is restricted, that there should be a Form for every general term we can use, but other approaches imply that Forms, being perfect, have something particularly grand and beautiful about them. So are there Forms for general terms which stand for low and unlovely things, such as mud and hair? Again, some approaches imply that a Form itself has the quality it imparts. The Form of beauty is itself beautiful, paradigmatically so; the *Phaedo*'s theory of explanation seems to imply that the dampness in an object is indeed damp. The theory of meaning approach, on the other hand, and perhaps others, imply that this had better not be so, or we may be confronted with a regress: shall we need another Form to explain how the first Form has the properties that it has? All these are among the questions that are put to the embarrassed Socrates in the first part of the *Parmenides*.[49]

In the *Sophist*, Plato explores with very great care the complex relations between five particularly abstract concepts, which he calls 'the greatest kinds' rather than Forms – being, sameness, difference, motion and rest – and reaches subtle conclusions about the ways in which they apply to each other and to themselves. In the course of this, he distinguishes various ways in which a thing 'is' something or other, and invents powerful instruments for solving the logical and semantic problems that underlie some of the central formulations of the *Republic*. He also recognizes there, gravely dissociating himself from the admired Parmenides, that there cannot be two worlds of appearance and reality. If something appears to be so, then it really does so appear: appearance must itself be part of reality.[50] This conclusion in itself represents a direct repudiation of the detailed metaphysics of the *Republic*.

The *Theaetetus*, which offers a most powerful and subtle discussion of knowledge, develops a theory of sense perception which at least refines the *Republic*'s view out of all recognition, and on one reading, is opposed to it.[51] In the same dialogue, and in the *Sophist*, Plato advances in discussion of false belief, and of being and not being, to a point at which it is clear that many things said in the *Republic* need revision. Moreover, he goes back in the *Theaetetus* to the point acknowledged in the *Meno*, that it must be possible for one person merely to believe what another person knows. The ideas of knowledge and belief that are articulated in the *Republic* and expressed in the images of the line and the cave are controlled by consideration of subject matter, of what might be or become a body of systematic *a priori* knowledge. The *Republic* is not interested, for example, in the state of mind of someone who makes a mathematical mistake (it cannot be belief, because he is thinking about the eternal, and it cannot be knowledge, because he is wrong.) This would not matter if Plato were concerned only with the nature of the sciences, but, as he recognizes, we must be able to talk about knowledge and belief as states of individual people. The ascent from the cave must be a story of personal enlightenment, if the *Republic* is to fulfil its promise of helping us to understand how to live, and this needs a psychology of belief which can bridge the metaphysical gulf beween the eternal and the changing.

PLATO'S PHILOSOPHY AND THE DENIAL OF LIFE

The sharp oppositions of the *Republic* between eternal reality and the illusions of the changing material world not only left deep problems of philosophical theory; they defeated Plato's ethical purposes. The problem of how justice is to be preserved in the world was solved by the return of the Guardians to rule, unwillingly, in the cave. There is a question, touched on in the *Republic*, of why they should do this. Certainly, Plato thinks that it is better that the just and wise should rule unwillingly, rather than that those who actually want power should have it. But that must mean, *better for the world*, and Plato must acknowledge the reality of the material world to this extent, that Socrates' fate and other injustices, and the horrors described in the degeneration of the city, are real evils, which are better prevented. Although the just city (and only the just city) suits the Guardians' nature, even there the activity of philosophy is more satisfying than ruling. Returning to the cave is good for them only because it is a good thing to do.

But why is it a good thing to do, and why is it better 'for the world' that it should be ruled justly? The returning Guardians cannot abolish the cave and its apparatus, as Parsifal with the sign of the cross destroys Klingsor's magic garden. Do they release its prisoners? (Here again we meet the ambivalence between power and mere illusion.) Most of the prisoners could not be released, for the ascent to the light is reserved for those special people in whom reason is strong and who are capable of becoming Guardians themselves. But those who are not like this will at least be saved from exploitation, and they can be helped by the laws and institutions of the city not to become unjust exploiters themselves, making others and themselves miserable. So it does matter, a great deal, what happens in this world, and the sense, which it is easy to get from the *Republic*, that in being required to rule, the Guardians are displaced or sentenced to it, like intellectual imperialists in a dark place, cannot really be adequate to Plato's conception of them and of society's need for justice.

The same tensions surface, differently, in the *Gorgias*. There, Socrates asserts the paradoxes that it is better to have injustice done to one than to do injustice, and that the good man 'cannot be harmed', because the only thing that really matters to him is his virtue and that is inviolate against the assaults of the world.[52] This outlook (which was to be developed by some philosophers in later antiquity into an extreme asceticism) leaves an impossible gap between the motivations that it offers for an ethical life, and what one is supposed to do if one leads it. The motivations to justice are said to lie in the care of the soul, and, along with that, in the belief that what happens to one's body or one's possessions does not really matter; but, if we have that belief, why do we suppose, as justice requires us to suppose, that it matters whether other people's bodies and possessions are assaulted or appropriated?[53]

In the *Phaedo*, Plato seems to present in the strongest terms the idea that the good person is better off outside the world. We are told that Socrates' very last words[54], as the hemlock took its effect, were, 'Crito, we owe a cockerel to Asclepius', and since Asclepius was a god of healing, this has been taken to mean that life is a disease, a 'terrible and ridiculous "last word"', as Nietzsche put it, a 'veiled, gruesome, pious and blasphemous saying'.[55] Spinoza, equally, rejected the *Phaedo*'s suggestion that philosophy should be a 'meditation' or preparation of death, urging that it should be a 'meditation of life'. It might be said that the dialogue's disparagement of this life as opposed to the metaphysical beyond is forgivable granted the occasion. Yet that is not right either, since the end of the *Phaedo* is, hardly surprisingly, run through with a deep sorrow, and we are not supposed to think that Socrates' friends are grieving simply because they have not been convinced by the arguments for immortality. It registers, rather, that, even given immortality and the world of Forms, this world and its friendships are of real value, and that its losses are at some level as bad as they seem.

Plato's will to transcend mortal life, to reach for the 'higher', is part of the traditional image of his philosophy, and is one element in the equally traditional contrast between him and the more empirically rooted Aristotle, a contrast expressed most famously, perhaps, in Raphael's fresco in the Vatican, *The School of Athens*, which displays at its centre the figures of Plato and Aristotle, the one turning his hand towards heaven, the other downwards towards earth. In our own century, Yeats wrote:

> Plato thought nature but a spume that plays
> Upon a ghostly paradigm of things;
> Solider Aristotle played the taws
> Upon the bottom of a king of kings . . .[56]

But Plato is not always drawing us beyond the concerns of this world. Even those works in which 'the higher' is celebrated do not always take the tone of the *Phaedo*'s official message, or of the *Republic*. In the case of the *Republic*, we spoke first in terms of ascent, the journey out of the cave, but in fact it is the Guardians' return that lends its colour to the work as a whole, an impression strengthened as it goes on by the long story of social and personal decline. The world of desire, politics, and material bodies is essentially seen from above, from outside the cave, and we are left with a sense of it as denatured and unreal or as powerfully corrupting. But elsewhere, and above all in the *Symposium*, the picture really is of ascent, and the material world is seen with the light behind it, as it were, giving an image not of failure and dereliction but of promise.

The participants in the dinner party which the *Symposium* describes, talk about what *eros* is, what it is to be a lover. The lover and his desires have some relation to beauty, or beautiful things; in particular, beautiful young men. We learn more precisely what these desires are. His desire is not a desire for the beautiful, at least in an obvious sense:

—Love is not love of the beautiful, as you think.

—What is it, then?

—Of reproduction and birth in the beautiful.   (*Symposium*, 206e)

This desire itself turns out to be an expression, or form, of a desire to be immortal.

Now this provides a schema, to put it in rather formal terms, which can be filled out differently for different types of love. A man's love for a woman defines 'birth' literally; 'in', 'in association with', is sexual; and the immortality in question is genetic. A man may bring forth or generate not babies but ideas or poems, and live for ever (or at least for longer) through those. The beauty in question may now be that of a particular youth, or something more general – as we might say, youthful beauty; again, it may be beauty of soul rather than of body. There is nothing to imply that the various abstractions, as we might call them, necessarily keep step with one another. Socrates has been disposed to generate ideas and good thoughts but in association with youths who had beautiful bodies. Conversely, Alcibiades, we learn later,[57] is drawn to Socrates' beautiful soul, but he has little idea of what an appropriate birth would be.

Then Diotima gives her account of the end of the progress, to the 'final and highest mysteries of love', which she doubts that Socrates can achieve. Here, in a famous passage, the lover is said to turn to the great sea of beauty, and will come to see something 'wonderfully beautiful in its nature', which

> always is and neither comes to be nor passes away, neither waxes nor wanes; it is not beautiful in one way and ugly in another, nor beautiful at one time and not at another, nor beautiful in relation to one thing and ugly in relation to another, nor beautiful in one place and ugly in another, as it would be if it were beautiful to some people and ugly to others . . .   (*Symposium*, 210e–211a)

and it is not embodied in any face or body, or idea, or knowledge, or, indeed, in anything at all. This culminating, ultimately fulfilling, encounter still fits the original schema. This would indeed be a worthwhile life for a man; he would bring forth, not images of virtue, but true virtue, and his relation to the Form of beauty, which is what has just been described, would be that of seeing it and being with it, words reminiscent of the language originally applied to sexual relations with a beautiful person.

Diotima's account of this progress or ascent does not imply, as some have thought, that no one ever really loves a particular person, but only the beauty in that person, or beauty itself. On the contrary, one can love a particular person in any of the various ways that count as bringing something to birth in the presence of that person's beauty. The account directly denies, in fact, that all love is love of beauty. Moreover, it does not suggest that the particulars, sights and sounds and bodies, were only seemingly or illusorily beautiful. They are not unconditionally, or unqualifiedly, or absolutely, beautiful, which is what the item of the final vision is. Indeed, Diotima can say that from the vantage point of the vision, colours and human bodies and other such things are merely 'mortal nonsense', but that is only by comparison with the vision, and it does not imply that the mortals who thought that those things were beautiful were simply mistaken, or that they were mistaken to have pursued them. The undertaking she teaches is something like a growth in aesthetic taste, from kitschy music, say, to more interesting music. It does not deny the point or the object of the earlier taste, and indeed the earlier taste is a condition of the process, which is a progress rather than the mere detection of error or the elimination of a misunderstanding.

Diotima says that the earlier pursuits were 'for the sake of' the final secrets. This does not mean that unless the ultimate state is reached the earlier states are pointless. It means that from the latter perspective we can see a point to them which they do not reveal at all to some people, and reveal only imperfectly even to those who are going about them in the right way. For those who do go about them in the right way, that imperfection is expressed in an obscure unsatisfactoriness or incompleteness in those earlier relationships, which can be traced to their failure to express adequately the desire to be immortal, to have the Good for ever. How far such a feeling may come even to those who are not going about the erotic in the right way and could never reach the vision, is something about which the earlier speeches have things to say.

All of this, certainly, expresses a discontent with the finite, and a sense of a greater splendour that lies beyond our ordinary passions, but it does so in way that, far more than the *Republic* or the rather dismal *Phaedo*, allows those passions to have their own life and to promise more. This effect is achieved in the dialogue by the later intervention of Alcibiades, and by the earlier speeches, which are variously funny and idiosyncratic and one of which, that of Aristophanes, tells a suitably absurd and touching story about the origins of sexual attraction. The sense that the *Symposium* knows what it is talking about in its dealings with desire – in this respect it is like some other less sunny dialogues – lends colour to another comment of Nietzsche's: 'All philosophical idealism to date was something like a disease, unless it was, as in Plato's case, the caution of an over-rich and dangerous health, the fear of over-powerful senses . . .'[58]

Plato set higher than almost any other thinker the aspirations of philosophy, and, as we have seen, its hopes to change one's life through theory. Granted the distrust and even the rejection of the empirical world which do play a significant role in his outlook; granted, too, the fact that his politics are far removed from any that could serve us now, not only in time but by an unashamedly aristocratic temperament; we may ask how his dialogues can remain so vividly alive. They are, indeed, sometimes sententious, and Socrates speaking on behalf of virtue can be tiring and high-minded, just as his affectation of ignorance and simplicity, the famous 'irony', can be irritatingly coy. But their faults are almost always those of a real person. They speak with a recognizable human voice, or more than one, and they do not fall into the stilted, remote complacency or quaint formalism to which moral philosophy is so liable. In part this is because of the dialogue form. In part, it is because (as Nietzsche's remark implies) Plato is constantly aware of the forces – of desire, of aesthetic seduction, of political exploitation – against which his ideals are a reaction. The dialogues preserve a sense of urgency and of the social and psychological insecurity of the ethical. Plato never forgets that the human mind is a very hostile environment for goodness, and he takes it for granted that some new device, some idea or imaginative stroke, may be needed to keep it alive there and to give it a hold on us. A treatise which supposedly offered in reader-friendly form the truth about goodness could not do anything that really needed doing.

The dialogues are never closed or final. They do not offer the ultimate results of Plato's great enquiry. They contain stories, descriptions, jokes, arguments, harangues, streams of free intellectual invention, powerful and sometimes violent rhetoric, and much else. Nothing in them straightforwardly reports those theoretical findings on which everything was supposed to turn, and they never take the tone that now you have mastered this, your life will be changed. There are theoretical discussions, often very complex, subtle, and original. There are many statements of how our lives need to be changed and of how philosophy may help to change them. But the action is always somewhere else, in a place where we, and typically Socrates himself, have not been. The results are never in the text before us. They could not be. The passage from the *Phaedrus* from which we started was true to Plato's outlook, as it seems to me, in claiming that what most importantly might come from philosophy cannot be written down.

This does not mean that it could be written down, but somewhere else. Nor does it mean, I think, that it could not be written down but could be spoken as a secret lore among initiates. The Pythagoreans in Italy from whom Plato may have got some initial inspiration seem to have had esoteric doctrines, and some scholars have thought that the same was true of Plato's Academy, but there is not much reason to believe it. The limitations of writing do not apply only to writing. Rather, Plato seems to have thought that the final significance of philosophy for one's life does not lie in anything that could be embodied in its findings, but emerges, rather, from its activities. One will find one's life changed through doing something other than researching the changes that one's life needs – through mathematics, Plato thought, or through dialectical discussion of such things as the metaphysical problems of not being, conducted not with the aim of reaching edifying moral conclusions, but the aim of *getting it right* (particularly if one has got it wrong before, and intellectual honesty, or – come to that – a most powerful curiosity, demand that one try again).

Plato did think that if you devoted yourself to theory, this could change your life. He did think, at least at one period, that pure studies might lead one to a transforming vision. But he never thought that the materials or conditions of such a transformation could be set down in a theory, or that a theory would, at some suitably advanced level, explain the vital thing you needed to know. So the dialogues do not present us with a statement of what might be most significantly drawn from philosophy, but that is not a peculiarity of them or of us; nothing could present us with that, because it cannot be stated anywhere, but can only, with luck and in favourable surroundings, emerge. Plato probably did think himself that the most favourable surroundings would be a group of people entirely dedicated to philosophy, but clearly he supposed that reading the dialogues, thinking about them, entering into them, were activities that could offer something to people outside such a group. He acknowledged, as Socrates makes clear in the *Phaedrus*, that they could not be the vehicles of one determinate message, and it is just because they are not intended to control the minds of his readers, but to open them, that they go on having so much to offer.

It is pointless to ask who is the world's greatest philosopher: for one thing, there are many different ways of doing philosophy. But we can say what the various qualities of great philosophers are: intellectual power and depth; a grasp of the sciences; a sense of the political, and of human destructiveness as well as creativity; a broad range and a fertile imagination; an unwillingness to settle for the superficially reassuring; and, in an unusually lucky case, the gifts of a great writer. If we ask which philosopher has, more than any other, combined all these qualities – to that question there is certainly an answer, Plato.

A quick reference list of Plato's dialogues that are mentioned in this book.
E(arly), M(iddle), L(ate): represent datings. In most cases there is a fair consensus, but some remain controversial.

Apology [E] a speech that Socrates might have given at his trial.

Cratylus [?M] on language, critically discussing certain theories of names.

Gorgias [E/M] on rhetoric and the good life; Socrates argues successively with Gorgias, Polus and Callicles.

Laches [E] on courage.

Laws [L] probably Plato's last work; in twelve books, on desirable political and social arrangements. Socrates does not appear, and the main speaker is 'an Athenian'.

Meno [E/M] whether virtue can be taught; Socrates invokes 'recollection' and immortality.

Parmenides [?L] Parmenides raises problems about Forms, and Zeno gives a demonstration of dialectic.

Phaedo [M] the scene of Socrates' death; they discuss immortality.

Phaedrus [M] during a walk in the country, Phaedrus and Socrates have a conversation about love, beauty, poetry, philosophy and writing.

Philebus [L] on pleasure, but with an opening discussion of 'limit' and the 'unlimited'.

Protagoras [E] brilliant exchanges between Socrates and Protagoras, on virtue, knowledge and politics.

Republic [M] in ten books, on justice in the individual and in the city, and many other matters.

Socratic dialogues [E] dialogues in which the discussion does not go beyond the interests and methods of the historical Socrates. Besides the **Laches**, among those of particular interest are the *Euthyphro*, which discusses the relations of ethics to the gods, and the *Crito*, in which Socrates argues that he must stay and face the death penalty.

Sophist [L] complex and sophisticated argument in metaphysics and the philosophy of language. Socrates is present, but the argument is entirely conducted by an 'Eleatic stranger'.

Statesman (Politicus) [L] also conducted by the Eleatic stranger, the discussion develops a classificatory form of dialectic by 'division', which also appears in the *Sophist*.

Symposium [M] a dinner party, at which the guests entertain themselves with a series of speeches about love.

Theaetetus [L] exceptionally powerful and concentrated philosophical enquiry, in which three accounts of knowledge are considered and rejected; the first, in terms of perception, is the most developed.

Timaeus [?L] elaborate, if tentative, speculations about the creation of the world. Socrates is present but five-sixths of the work consists of uninterrupted exposition by Timaeus.

John Cottingham

DESCARTES

Descartes' Philosophy of Mind

Descartes the scientist

The name of René Descartes is synonymous with the birth of the modern age. The 'new' philosophers, as he and his followers were called in the seventeenth century, inaugurated a fundamental shift in scientific thinking, the effects of which are still with us today. Indeed, Descartes was one of the principal architects of the very notion of 'scientific thinking' as we now understand it. All scientific explanation, Descartes insists, must be expressed in terms of precise, mathematically defined *quantities*:

> I recognize no matter in corporeal things apart from that which the geometers call *quantity*, and take as the object of their demonstrations, i.e. that to which every kind of *division, shape and motion* is applicable. Moreover, my consideration of such matter involves absolutely nothing apart from these divisions, shapes and motions . . . And since all natural phenomena can be explained in this way, I do not think that any other principles are either admissible or desirable in physics   (*Principles of Philosophy* [1644], Pt II, art. 64).

Our ordinary everyday picture of the world is of course very far from purely quantitative: it involves, apart from size, shape and motion, a host of different qualities – all the various colours, tastes, smells, textures and sounds we are aware of through our five senses. And the traditional 'scholastic' philosophy that had dominated the European universities for many centuries had tended to explain the natural world in terms of just such 'real qualities' ('heaviness', 'moistness', 'dryness', and so on) that were supposed to inhere in things. Today, by contrast, all scientists take it for granted that to try to explain things purely at this 'common sense' level is not enough: we need to probe deeper, to the micro-level, and investigate the interactions between the various particles out of which our ordinary world of medium-sized objects is composed. Descartes' resounding declaration of his scientific principles underlines just this need. Physics, from henceforth, becomes the investigation of explanatory mechanisms operating at the micro-level; and the operations of those mechanisms have to be described in the exact language of mathematics.

But Descartes' vision of science was yet more ambitious. He insisted that the same underlying explanatory schema held good for all observable phenomena, ranging from the vast revolutions of the heavenly bodies down to events in the atmosphere and on the earth's surface, and even the microscopic processes going on inside our own bodies. He was, in short, a *reductionist*; that is, he claimed that all natural phenomena, terrestrial or celestial, organic or inorganic, no matter how striking their surface differences, can be reduced to, or fully explained in terms of, the elementary mechanics of the particles out of which the relevant objects are made up:

> Consider how amazing are the properties of magnets and of fire, and how different they are from the properties we commonly observe in other bodies: how a huge and massively powerful flame can be instantaneously kindled from a tiny spark when it falls on a large quantity of powder; or how the stars radiate their light instantly in every direction over such an enormous distance. In this volume I have deduced the causes – which I believe to be quite evident – of these and many other phenomena from principles which are known to all and admitted by all, namely the *shape, size, position and motion of particles of matter*. And anyone who considers all this will readily be convinced that there are no powers in stones and plants that are so mysterious, and no marvels attributed to 'sympathetic' and 'antipathetic' influences that are so astonishing, that they cannot be explained in this way. In short there is nothing in the whole of nature . . . which is incapable of being deductively explained on the basis of these self-same principles
>
> (*Principles of Philosophy*, Pt IV, art. 187).

All of science becomes, for Descartes, an integrated whole – a great *tree* of knowledge (to use one metaphor he favoured), where the solid trunk of physics branches off into all sorts of particular sciences (like medicine), but without departing from the same fundamental set of explanatory principles (cf. *Principles of Philosophy*, Preface to French edition of 1647).

But there is one exception. In the triumphant exposition of the Cartesian scientific creed just quoted, one crucial phrase has been omitted from the final sentence. What Descartes in fact added was the vital caveat which, in some form or another, he always inserted when extolling the scope and range of his new scientific programme:

> In short there is nothing in the whole of nature, *nothing, that is, which should be referred to purely corporeal causes, i.e. those devoid of thought and mind*, which is incapable of being explained on the basis of these self-same principles.

With the phenomena of 'thought and mind' the grand Cartesian project of explanatory science grinds to a halt. For Descartes divides reality into two fundamental categories: in addition to *res extensa* ('extended substance') – the three-dimensional world of physics, a world explicable entirely in terms of moving particles of a specified size and shape – there is the quite distinct realm of *thought*. Each conscious mind is a *res cogitans* or 'thinking substance', a being whose essential characteristics are entirely independent of matter and wholly *in*explicable via the quantitative language of physics.

Descartes' 'dualistic' division of reality into two fundamentally distinct kinds of entity – thinking stuff and extended stuff – bequeathed a massive conundrum for philosophy that has been with us ever since: what exactly is the nature of consciousness, and what is its relationship to the physical world? Not many modern philosophers are much enamoured with Descartes' own position (that thought is the property of an entirely immaterial substance); but all agree that the 'mind–body problem', as it has come to be known, is a philosophical-cum-scientific puzzle of enormous importance, and that Descartes' ideas on the subject have had, for good or ill, an extraordinarily pervasive influence on subsequent ways of approaching it.

Descartes' famous, or infamous, theory of the mind is the subject of this essay. The next chapter will explain his arguments for the non-material nature of the thinking self, and the paradoxes and tensions which his 'dualistic' theory creates. The final chapter will discuss the fascinating insights arising from his (much lesser known) attempts to resolve those paradoxes and to show how, despite their distinctness, the spiritual self and the mechanical body are intimately *united*, so as to constitute what Descartes called a 'genuine human being'. But first it will be useful to give a brief account of the life and work of that remarkable Frenchman who is so aptly known as 'the father of modern philosophy'.

Life and works

Descartes was born on 31 March 1596 in a small town between Tours and Poitiers, then called La Haye, but now renamed after its greatest son. His mother died when he was thirteen months old, and he was brought up by his maternal grandmother; his father remarried when he was four. At the age of ten, he was sent away to boarding school at the Jesuit college of La Flèche (between Angers and Le Mans). A sickly child, he was given the privilege of 'lying in' in the mornings, a habit that remained with him all his life. In 1610 (aged fourteen) he took part in a lavish ceremony commemorating the death of the college's founder, Henry IV, and among the recitations arranged for the occasion was a poem heralding Galileo's discovery, earlier that same year, of the moons of Jupiter. That the Earth was the centre of all motion had been a central doctrine of the scholastic philosophy, based on a synthesis of Aristotle and the Bible, which had long formed the basis of the curriculum in most schools and universities. But the old order was beginning to crumble.

As a young man, Descartes used the opportunity of volunteering for military service to travel around Europe, and one of the most important experiences of this formative period was his friendship with the Dutch mathematician Isaac Beeckman, whom he met by chance in Breda, in the Netherlands, in 1618. Beeckman, who called himself a 'physico-mathematician', was working on micro-mechanical models of scientific explanation, and he inspired Descartes with enthusiasm for the idea that mathematics, so far from being a purely abstract subject unconnected with the real world, could be employed in the solution of countless problems in physics. Here are some extracts from the letters Descartes wrote to Beeckman early the following year:

I have received your letter, which I was expecting. On first glancing over it, I was delighted to see your notes on music. What clearer evidence could there be that you had not forgotten me? But there was something else I was looking for, and that the most important, namely news about what you have been doing, what you are doing, and how you are. You ought not to think that all I care about is science; I care about you – and not just your intellect, even if that is the greatest part of you, but the whole man . . .

Let me be quite open with you about my project. What I want to produce is . . . a completely new science, which would provide a general solution of all possible equations involving any sort of quantity, whether continuous or discrete, each according to its nature . . . I am hoping to demonstrate what sort of problems can be solved exclusively in this . . . way, so that almost nothing in geometry will remain to be discovered. This is of course a gigantic task, one hardly suitable for a single person; indeed, it is an incredibly ambitious project. But through the confusing darkness I have caught a glimpse of some sort of light, and with the aid of this I think I shall be able to dispel even the thickest obscurities . . .

Do not expect anything from my Muse at the moment, for while I am preparing for the journey about to begin tomorrow, my mind has already set out on the voyage. I am still uncertain 'where fate may take me, where my foot may rest'. The preparations for war have not yet led to my being summoned to Germany, but I suspect that many men will be called to arms . . . If I should stop somewhere, as I hope I shall, I promise to see that my *Mechanics* or *Geometry* is put in order, and I will salute you as the promoter and prime author of my studies.

For it was you alone who roused me from my state of indolence and reawakened the learning which by then had almost disappeared from my memory; and when my mind strayed from serious pursuits it was you who led it back to worthier things. Thus, if perhaps I should produce something not wholly to be despised, you can rightly claim it all as your own ...   (AT X 151–64: CSMK 1–4).

The impending journey to which Descartes refers took him to southern Germany, where on the night of 10 November 1619, he found himself in lodgings at Ulm, on the Danube. It was the eve of St Martin's day, a time of painful childhood memories for Descartes; every year on that evening, in his native region of France, crowds would process though the darkened streets to commemorate the souls of the departed – surely a distressing experience for a small boy who had lost his mother very early in life. Now aged twenty-three, Descartes suffered what some have interpreted as a nervous breakdown, while others, taking their cue from his own more positive interpretation of events, have construed as the real start of his philosophical career. This is how his seventeenth-century biographer, Adrien Baillet, describes it, drawing on records based on Descartes' own notes:

He went to bed 'quite filled with mental excitement' and preoccupied with the thought that that day he had 'discovered the foundations of a wonderful system of knowledge'. He then had three consecutive dreams, which he imagined could only have come from above. First he was assailed with the impression of several phantoms, which came up to him and terrified him to such an extent that (thinking himself to be walking along a street) he was obliged to cross over onto the left side, in order to get to where he wanted to go; for he felt such a great weakness on his right side that he could not stand up. Being embarrassed to walk in such a fashion, he made an effort to stand upright, but he felt a violent wind which swept him round in a kind of whirlpool, making him spin round three or four times on his left foot. But this was still not what terrified him most. The difficulty which he had in standing made him believe that he would fall down at each step, until he noticed a College that opened onto his road, and went in to find a refuge and a remedy for his trouble. He tried to reach the college chapel, where his first thought was to go and pray; but noticing that he had passed someone whom he knew without greeting him, he decided to turn back to pay his respects, and was violently pushed back by the

wind which blew against the chapel. At the same time, he saw in the
middle of the college quadrangle someone else, who addressed him by
name in very civil and obliging terms, and told him that if he wanted to
look for Monsieur N., he had something to give him. He imagined that
this was a melon brought from some foreign country. But what
surprised him more was to see that the people who gathered round the
man to talk were upright and steady on their feet, while, on the same
ground, he was still bent double and reeling, although the wind which
had tried to blow him over several times had much lessened . . .

Another dream came to him in which he thought he heard a loud and
violent noise which he took for a thunderclap. The terror which he felt
at this woke him up at once, and opening his eyes he saw many fiery
sparks scattered throughout the room . . .

Shortly afterwards he had a third dream, which contained nothing
terrible like the first two. He found a book on his table, though without
knowing who had put it there. He opened it and, seeing that it was an
encyclopedia, he was struck with the hope that it might be very useful
to him. At the same instant he found another book . . . a collection of
the poems of different authors entitled *Corpus Poetarum*. He was
curious to read something, and opening the book he came to the verse
Quod vitae sectabor iter? ['What road in life shall I follow?'] At the
same instant he saw a man whom he did not know, but who gave him a
piece of verse beginning *Est et Non* . . . The first book then appeared
once more at the other end of the table, but he found that the
Encylopedia was no longer complete, as it had been when he saw it
before.

Beginning to interpret the dream while still asleep, he considered that
the encyclopedia signified all the sciences collected together, and that
the anthology of poetry indicated philosophy and wisdom combined . . . He then woke up quite calmly and continued the interpretation of his dream. The collected poets he took to signify revelation and
enthusiasm, with which he had some hope of seeing himself blessed.
The piece of verse *Estet Non* – the 'yes and no' of Pythagoras – he took
to stand for truth and falsity in human knowledge . . .

(Adrien Baillet, *La Vie de Monsieur Des-Cartes* [1691], Bk I, ch. 1).

Many rival interpretations have been offered of these strange dreams,
including psychoanalytic ones (in some of which, unsurprisingly, the
'melon' figures as a sexual symbol); but from a philosophical point of
view it is not hard to see in the whirlpool-like wind of the first dream the
kind of disorientation associated with the collapse of confidence in
previously accepted certainties. This is precisely the scenario of the

philosophical masterpiece Descartes was to compose some twenty years later – the *Meditations* – at the start of which the author decides to doubt all his previous beliefs in a search for the foundations of a new system of knowledge. 'So serious are the doubts into which I have been thrown', he declares at the start of the Second Meditation, 'that I can neither put them out of my mind nor see any way of resolving them. It feels as if I have fallen unexpectedly into a deep whirlpool which tumbles me around so that I can neither stand on the bottom nor swim up to the top' (AT VII 16: CSM II 23–4). As for the 'revelation and enthusiasm' of the poets, this is not normally an image associated with philosophical inquiry; but Descartes clearly believed as a result of his final dream that he was destined to complete the unfinished 'encyclopedia' of the sciences, starting with the 'gigantic project' he had outlined in his earlier letter to Beeckman. In his *Discourse on the Method*, when reflecting some fourteen years later on the thoughts that came to him in the 'stove-heated room', Descartes wrote that 'those long chains of very simple and easy reasonings, which geometers use to arrive at their most difficult demonstrations, gave me occasion to suppose that all the things which come within human knowledge are interconnected in the same way' (*Discourse*, Pt II, AT VI 19: CSM I 120). And just as the poet traditionally claimed divine inspiration, so the clear guiding light of divine truth – always a central feature of Descartes' mature metaphysics – will illuminate the mind of the philosopher. The 'light of reason', or 'natural light' as Descartes came to call it, is nothing 'revelatory' in the biblical sense; on the contrary, it is the austerely intellectual faculty bestowed on us by God which enables us to grasp as self-evident the fundamental mathematical and logical truths that are the key to understanding the universe:

> I always remained firm in the resolution I had taken . . . to accept nothing as true which did not seem to me clearer and more certain than the demonstrations of the geometers . . . And I noticed certain laws which God has so established in nature, and of which he has implanted such notions in our minds, that after adequate reflection we cannot doubt that they are exactly observed in everything that exists or occurs in the world (*Discourse*, Pt V, AT VI 41: CSM I 131).

After his travels, Descartes lived for a time in Paris, but decided at the age of thirty-two to settle in the Netherlands, where he lived for the next twenty years, though without staying in any one place for very long. His residences included Franeker, Amsterdam, Deventer, Leiden, Haarlem, Utrecht and Endegeest; his favourite retreat was the countryside in the northern coastal area around Egmond, between Haarlem and Alkmaar. His first major work, the *Regulae ad directionem ingenii* (*Rules for the Direction of our Native Intelligence*) was written before he left for Holland, but abandoned unfinished and not published in his lifetime. Also unpublished was his treatise on cosmology and physics *Le Monde* (*The World*), which was ready for the press by 1633, when Descartes suffered an unexpected blow. As he explained in a letter written at the end of November that year to his friend and chief correspondent Marin Mersenne:

> I had intended to send you my *World* as a New Year gift, and only two weeks ago I was quite determined to send you at least a part of it, if the whole work could not be copied in time. But I have to say that in the meantime I took the trouble to inquire in Leiden and Amsterdam whether Galileo's *World System* was available, for I thought I had heard that it was published in Italy last year. I was told that it had indeed been published, but that all the copies had immediately been burnt at Rome, and that Galileo had been convicted and fined. I was so astonished at this that I almost decided to burn all my papers, or at least to let no one see them. For I could not imagine that he – an Italian and, as I understand, in the good graces of the Pope – could have been made a criminal for any other reason than that he tried, as he no doubt did, to establish that the Earth moves. I know that some Cardinals had already censured this view, but I thought I had heard it said that all the same it was being taught publicly even in Rome. I must admit that if the view is false, so too are the entire foundations of my philosophy, for it can be demonstrated from them quite clearly. And it is so closely interwoven in every part of my treatise that I could not remove it without rendering the whole work defective. But for all the world I did not want to publish a discourse in which a single word could be found that the Church would have disapproved of; so I preferred to suppress it rather than to publish it in a mutilated form . . .
>
> (AT I 270–2: CSMK 40–1).

Other works, however, followed thick and fast, beginning with the *Discourse on the Method*, published (in French) together with three scientific essays in 1637, and followed closely by the *Meditations*, which appeared (in Latin) in 1641. The *Principles of Philosophy*, a massive compendium of Cartesian metaphysics and science, came out (in Latin) in 1644. These works, as we shall see, contain Descartes' central arguments for the distinction between mind and body. During the middle 1640s, however, Descartes became increasingly interested in the *interaction* between mind and body, prompted by the acute questions put to him in a long correspondence with Princess Elizabeth of Bohemia (who first wrote to him about his theory of the mind in May 1643). In his replies to Elizabeth, Descartes explores the paradox that while philosophical reason teaches us that mind and body are distinct, our everyday human experience shows us they are united. It is that human experience, and its characteristic modes of awareness, the emotions and passions (such as fear, anger, and love), that forms the subject of Descartes' last work, the *Passions of the Soul*, published in French in 1649.

The same year Descartes accepted, after much hesitation, an invitation by Queen Christina of Sweden to visit her court in Stockholm and instruct her in his philosophy. The decision proved disastrous. In one of his last letters, written in Stockholm on 15 January 1650 to a recently acquired friend, the Comte de Brégy, the philosopher gives voice to his gloom:

> I have seen the Queen only four or five times, always in the morning in her library ... A fortnight ago she went to Uppsala, but I did not go with her, nor have I seen her since she returned on Thursday evening. I know also that our ambassador saw her only once before her visit to Uppsala, apart from his first audience at which I was present. I have not made any other visits, nor have I heard about any. This makes me think that during the winters men's thoughts are frozen here, like the water ... I swear to you that my desire to return to my solitude grows stronger with each passing day ... It is not that I do not still fervently wish to serve the Queen, or that she does not show me as much goodwill as I may reasonably hope for. But I am not in my element here. I desire only peace and quiet, which are benefits that the most powerful monarchs on earth cannot give to those who are unable to acquire them for themselves. I pray God that you are granted the good things that you desire, and I beg you to be assured that I am, Sir, your most humble and obedient servant, Descartes
>
> (AT V 466–7: CSMK 383–4).

Within less than a month of writing the letter, just short of his fifty-fourth birthday, Descartes was dead, from a flu-like illness which rapidly produced pneumonia – something the medical resources of the day were utterly unable to cope with. His last words, encapsulating the mind–body dualism which he had so long maintained, were 'Now my soul, 'tis time to depart.'

THE INCORPOREAL MIND

Systematic doubt and the nature of the self

Descartes first expounded his theory of mind, and indeed his metaphysics in general, in the context of an engaging personal narrative, where he describes his intellectual development following the momentous day and night in the 'stove-heated room':

> Throughout the next nine years, I did nothing but roam about in the world, trying to be a spectator rather than an actor in all the comedies that are played out there. Reflecting especially upon the points in every subject which might make it suspect and give occasion for us to make mistakes, I kept uprooting from my mind any errors that might previously have slipped into it. In doing this, I was not copying the sceptics, who doubt only for the sake of doubting and pretend to be always undecided; on the contrary, my whole aim was to reach certainty – to cast aside the loose earth and sand so as to come upon rock or clay.
>
> In this I think I was quite successful. For I tried to expose the falsity or uncertainty of the propositions I was examining by clear and certain argument, not by weak conjectures . . . And just as in pulling down an old house we usually keep the remnants for use in building a new one, so in destroying all those opinions of mine that I judged ill-founded, I made various observations and acquired many experiences which I have since used in establishing more certain opinions . . .
>
> Those nine years passed by, however, without my taking any side regarding the questions which are commonly debated among the learned, or beginning to search for the foundations of any philosophy more certain than the commonly accepted one . . . Exactly eight years ago . . . [I resolved] to move away from any place where I might have acquaintances and retire to this country [Holland] . . . Living here amidst this great mass of busy people who are more concerned with their own affairs than curious about those of others, I have been able to lead a life as solitary and withdrawn as if I were in the most removed desert, while lacking none of the comforts found in the most populous cities   (AT VI 28–31: CSM I 125–6).

Thus ends Part Three of the *Discours de la méthode* (*Discourse on the Method*), published anonymously in 1637. The passage that immediately follows, at the start of Part Four, is one of the most famous in all philosophy, containing the celebrated dictum *je pense donc je suis* – 'I think therefore I am' – or (perhaps closer to Descartes' meaning) 'I am thinking, therefore I exist.' The *Discourse* was translated into Latin seven years later (Latin, in the seventeenth century, still being the best way to reach an international audience), and there the dictum appears in what is probably still its best known form: *Cogito ergo sum.*

The full title of the *Discourse* is 'Discourse on the Method of rightly conducting one's reason and seeking the truth in the sciences', and one key to the 'method' in question is Descartes' deliberate use of the techniques (though not the philosophical outlook) of scepticism, pushing doubt as far as it will go. The purpose is to see whether there is anything at all that *survives* the doubt: if so, it will serve as the foundation stone for the new reliable edifice of science that Descartes is seeking to construct. The first truth that Descartes proceeds to discover is, of course, the famous *Cogito* – so long as I am thinking, I must exist – and commentators have endlessly analysed and debated the precise significance of the 'Archimedian point' on which Descartes proposes to rely in order to launch the rest of his system. But more interesting for our purposes is the move Descartes makes immediately following the Cogito, where he goes on to dicuss the *nature* of this thinking being of whose existence he is so sure. Here is the opening of Part Four of the *Discourse* in full:

> I do not know whether I should tell you of the first meditations that I had there, for they are perhaps too metaphysical and uncommon for everyone's taste. And yet, to make it possible to judge whether the foundations I have chosen are firm enough, I am in a way obliged to speak of them. For a long time I had observed . . . that in practical life it is sometimes necessary to follow opinions which one knows to be quite uncertain, just as one would if they were indubitable. But since I now wished to devote myself solely to the search for truth, I thought it necessary to do the very opposite and reject, treating as absolutely false, everything in which I could imagine the least doubt, in order to see if I was left believing anything that was entirely indubitable.
>
> Thus, because our senses sometimes deceive us, I decided to suppose that nothing was such as they had led us to imagine. And because there are people who make mistakes in reasoning and commit logical fallacies even about the simplest matters in geometry, judging that I was as prone to error as anyone else I rejected as unsound all the arguments I had previously taken as demonstrative proofs. Lastly, considering that the very thoughts we have while awake may also occur while we are asleep, without any of them being, at the time, true, I resolved to pretend that all the things that had ever entered my mind

were no truer than the illusions of my dreams. But immediately I noticed that while I was trying in this way to think that everything was false, it was necessary that I, who was thinking this, was something. And observing that this truth '*I am thinking, therefore I exist*' was so firm and sure that even the most extravagant suppositions of the sceptics were incapable of shaking it, I decided I could accept it without scruple as the first principle of the philosophy I was seeking.

Next, I examined attentively *what* I was. I saw that while I could pretend I had no body and that there was no world and no place for me to be in, I could not for all that pretend that *I* did not exist. I saw on the contrary that from the mere fact that I thought of doubting the truth of other things, it followed quite evidently and certainly that I existed; yet if I had but ceased to think, even if everything else I had ever imagined were true, this would have left me no reason whatever to believe I existed. From this I recognized that I was a substance whose whole essence or nature is solely to think, and which does not require any place, or depend on any material thing, in order to exist. Accordingly this 'I' – that is, the soul by which I am what I am – is entirely distinct from the body, and indeed is easier to know than the body, and would not cease to be everything it is even if the body did not exist

(AT VI 31–3: CSM I 126–7).

The final paragraph contains Descartes' first attempt (he produced other arguments in later works) to prove the immaterial nature of the mind. It is important, incidentally, not to be put off by the faintly religious or 'spiritual' modern overtones of the term 'soul', which appears in the concluding sentence. Descartes uses *l'âme* ('soul') and *l'esprit* ('mind') more or less interchangeably, simply to refer to whatever it is that is conscious, or thinks – the 'thinking thing' (*res cogitans*) as he later calls it in the *Meditations*. And his conclusion, here in the *Discourse* as in the later works, is that the conscious thinking self – 'This "I"' (*ce moi*) by which I am what I am' – is entirely independent of anything physical, and indeed could survive the complete destruction of the body (including, let us be clear, the brain).

At the turn of the twentieth century, when scientists are almost every month discovering more about the chemical and electrical processes going on in the brain during thought, Descartes' position may initially strike some people as bizarre or even ridiculous. But Descartes does not deny that thought in human beings may be *accompanied* by brain processes (indeed, he spent a great deal of time discussing the physiology of the brain and nervous system); what he insists is that thought is not to be *identified* with these or any other physical processes, since it is, in its essential nature, distinct from the material realm, and indeed is in principle capable of existing without any physical substrate whatsoever.

The key premise for understanding Descartes' argument is the statement, 'I could pretend I had no body.' This clearly links up with the technique of doubt Descartes has described earlier on. Consider a proposition about a bodily movement, for example, 'I am stretching out my hand.' Well, however simple and obvious truths such as this may seem, they can, with enough determination and ingenuity, be doubted: I might be asleep and dreaming, in which case I am not stretching out my hand at all, but (for example) lying in bed with my hands pillowed under my ear. This level of 'the dreaming argument', however, still admits that I have a body. Yet Descartes is prepared to push the doubt one stage further: maybe 'all the things that have *ever entered my mind*' are 'no truer than the illusions of my dreams' (middle paragraph of passage quoted above). Perhaps, in other words, the whole of life might be some sort of dream, including the belief that I have a body. Or to use the more dramatic scenario which Descartes introduced four years later, in the *Meditations*:

> I will suppose that . . . some malicious demon of the utmost power and cunning has employed all his energies in order to deceive me. I shall think that the sky, the air, the earth, colours, shapes, sounds and *all external things* are merely the delusions of dreams which he has devised to ensnare my judgement. I shall consider myself as not having hands or eyes or flesh or blood or senses, but as falsely believing that I have all these things . . . (AT VII 22–3: CSM II 15).

This extreme form of doubt enables me to suspend belief in all 'external' things – that is, everything apart from the direct and immediate flow of my thoughts. Conclusion: I may not have a body at all; I may be some kind of bodiless spirit mercilessly tricked by the wicked demon into thinking I am a creature of flesh and blood living on planet Earth. Yet even pushing doubt to these exaggerated or 'hyperbolical' limits (as Descartes himself called them), I nevertheless cannot doubt that *I* exist. Even if I am the dupe of the demon, I must exist for him to be able to deceive me. This is how Descartes takes up the story in the Second Meditation:

> I will suppose that everything I see is spurious. I will believe that my memory tells me lies, and that none of the things that it reports ever happened. I have no senses. Body, shape, extension, movement and place are chimeras. So what remains true? . . .

I have just said that I have no senses and no body. This is the sticking point: what follows from this? Am I not so bound up with a body and with senses that I cannot exist without them? But I have convinced myself that there is absolutely nothing in the world, no sky, no earth, no minds, no bodies. Does it follow that I too do not exist? No! If I convinced myself of something then I certainly existed. But there is a deceiver of supreme power and cunning who is deliberately and constantly deceiving me. In that case I too undoubtedly exist, if he is deceiving me. And let him deceive me as much as he can, he will never bring it about that I am nothing so long as I think I am something

(AT VII 24–5: CSM II 16–17).

So the existence of my own conscious self is utterly indubitable: unlike the body, it is immune even to the most extreme doubts that can be devised.

But even if we go along with Descartes here, can we accept the result he deduces from all this? He has established that I can doubt the existence of my body, but not that of my mind or my conscious self: very well, but does it follow, in the words of the *Discourse*, that this 'I' is 'entirely distinct from the body' and could exist without it? To answer this we must look at the *logical form* of Descartes' argument, which appears to be as follows:

> I can doubt the existence of B
> But I cannot doubt the existence of M
> So M could exist without B

Now if this form of argument were valid, it would be valid not just for Mind and Body, but for all substitutions of M and B. Yet consider the following analogy. Let M be Mashed potato, and B be carBohydrate. Suppose (being utterly ignorant of chemistry) I can doubt the existence of carbohydrate; yet suppose also, for the sake of argument, that I am incapable of doubting the existence of this mashed potato that is being rammed down my throat. Does it follow, to parody Descartes, that the mashed potato could still exist, and 'would not fail to be what it is', even if carbohydrate did not exist?

Descartes' mistake seems to be to try to read off truth about ontology from epistemological truth – or, to put the matter less portentously, to try to deduce conclusions about the *real nature* of the mind or thinking self from premises about what he can or cannot be *certain* of, or can or cannot *doubt*. Yet what I am capable of doubting about any given item seems to depend partly on the extent of my own familiarity with that item. And the extent of my own familiarity, with minds, or potatoes, or anything else, seems a poor basis for reaching firm conclusions about what is really essential or inessential to their existence.

As to the inherent plausibility of Descartes' conclusion, in identifying 'this "I"' with an incorporeal entity he is certainly departing from what might be called the 'common sense' position. Most people asked the question 'What are you?' would presumably reply 'a human being'; and a human being, plainly, is not something incorporeal but, as Aristotle put it, a 'rational animal', a certain sort of biological creature, and therefore very much a creature of flesh and blood. Descartes acknowledges, in the Second Meditation, that his view is a departure from the 'first thought to come to mind':

I do not yet have a sufficient understanding of what this 'I' is that now necessarily exists. So I must be on my guard against carelessly taking something else to be this 'I' and so making a mistake in the very item of knowledge that I maintain is the most certain and evident of all. I will therefore go back and meditate on what I originally believed myself to be, before I embarked on this present train of thought. I will then subtract anything capable of being weakened, even minimally, by the arguments now introduced, so that what is left at the end may be exactly and only what is certain and unshakeable.

What then did I formerly think I was . . . Well, the first thought to come to mind was that I had a face, hands, arms, and the whole mechanical structure of limbs which can be seen in a corpse and which I called 'the body'. The next thought was that I was nourished, that I moved about, and that I engaged in sense perception and thinking . . .

But what shall I now say that I am, when I am supposing that there is some supremely powerful and . . . malicious deceiver who is deliberately trying to trick me in every way he can? Can I now assert that I possess even the most insignificant of all the attributes which I have just said belong to the nature of a body? I scrutinize them, think about them, go over them again, but nothing suggests itself; it is tiresome and pointless to repeat the list once more. But what about . . . nutrition and movement? Since now I do not have a body, these are mere fabrications. Sense perception? This surely does not occur without a body, and besides, when asleep I have appeared to perceive through the senses many things which I have afterwards realized I did not perceive through the senses at all. Thinking? At last I have discovered it – thought. *This alone is inseparable from me.* I am, I exist – that is certain. But for how long? For as long as I am thinking. For it could be that were I totally to cease from thinking, I should totally cease to exist. At present I am not admitting anything except what is necessarily true.

I am, then, in the strict sense only a thing that thinks; that is, I am a mind, or intelligence, or intellect or reason – words whose meaning I have been ignorant of until now. But for all that I am a thing which is real and which truly exists. But what kind of a thing? As I have just said, a thinking thing   (AT VII 25–7: CSM II 17–18).

Thought, this reasoning claims, is the only attribute that cannot be separated from me by the extreme doubts raised in the demon scenario: it is the only thing that cannot be 'torn away from me' (*divelli*), as the original Latin has it. Yet this seems to beg some questions. If, as many people now believe, brain activity is in fact essential to thought, then how does this affect the imaginary scenario where I am supposed to be a bodiless creature deceived by the demon into thinking I have a body? The answer must surely be that the alleged scenario is incoherent; for in 'tearing off' the brain and all the other bodily attributes, one would thereby be 'tearing off' thought as well. As Descartes' acute contemporary Antoine Arnauld put it, summing up his enduring worries about the argument, for all Descartes has shown it could still be that the body is, after all, essential to what makes me 'me':

So far as I can see, the only result that follows is that I can obtain some knowledge of myself without knowledge of the body. But it is not yet transparently clear to me that this knowledge is complete and adequate, *so as to enable me to be certain that I am not mistaken in excluding body from my essence* (Fourth Replies, AT VII 201: CSM II 141).

'Clear and distinct perception' and the logical possibility of disembodied minds

Soon after writing the *Discourse*, Descartes became all too aware of problems in his argument from doubt for the immateriality of the mind. As he explained in the Preface to the *Meditations*, published in 1641:

In the *Discourse*, I asked anyone who found anything worth criticizing in what I had written to be kind enough to point it out to me. In the case of my remarks concerning . . . the soul, only [one objection] worth mentioning was put to me, which I shall now briefly answer . . .

The . . . objection is this. From the fact that the human mind, when directed towards itself, does not perceive itself to be anything other than a thinking thing, it does not follow that its nature or essence consists *only* in its being a thinking thing, where the word 'only' excludes everything else that could be said to belong to the nature of the soul. My answer to this objection is that in that passage it was not my intention to make those exclusions in an order corresponding to the actual truth of the matter (which I was not dealing with at that stage) but merely in an order corresponding to my own perception. So the sense of the passage was that I was aware of nothing at all that I *knew* belonged to my essence, except that I was a thinking thing, or a thing possessing within itself the faculty of thinking. I shall, however, show below how it follows from the fact that I am unaware of nothing else belonging to my essence, that *nothing else does in fact belong to it*

(AT VII 7–8: CSM II 7).

Although, as we have already seen, the Second Meditation repeats much of the reasoning of the *Discourse*, the promised additional argument makes its appearance in the Sixth (and final) Meditation. The argument, as Descartes presents it, depends heavily on his proofs of God's existence, and hence (since the proofs in question are widely regarded as invalid) has not perhaps received as much attention as it deserves; as we shall see shortly, however, there is what might be called a 'secular analogue' of the argument, which many present-day philosophers, even anti-Cartesian ones, tend to accept.

To explain how Descartes' argument works some brief stage-setting will be necessary. By the time we reach the Sixth Meditation, the meditator has established, to his own satisfaction, the existence of a perfect creator who has bestowed on the mind its faculty of 'clear and distinct perception', a faculty which, if we use it carefully, cannot lead us astray:

The cause of error must surely be the one I have explained [viz. misusing my free will in rashly giving assent to propositions I do not clearly perceive]. For if, whenever I have to make a judgement, I restrain my will so that it extends to what the intellect clearly and distinctly reveals, and no further, then it is quite impossible for me to go wrong. This is because every clear and distinct perception is undoubtedly something real and positive, and hence cannot come from nothing, but must necessarily have God for its author. Its author, I say, is God, who is supremely perfect and who cannot be a deceiver on pain of contradiction; hence the perception is undoubtedly true. So today I have learned not only what precautions to take to avoid ever going wrong, but also what to do to arrive at the truth. For I shall unquestionably reach the truth if only I give sufficient attention to all the things which I perfectly understand, and separate these from all the other cases where my apprehension is more confused and obscure. And this is just what I shall take good care to do from now on

(Fourth Meditation, AT VII 62: CSM II 43).

God, in Descartes' metaphysics, is the bridge from the subjective world of thought to the objective world of scientific truth. The mind, owing its existence to God, is innately programmed with certain ideas that correspond to reality; hence the importance, in Descartes' system, of proving the existence of God, the perfect guarantor of our ideas, so that the meditator can move from isolated flashes of cognition (I am thinking, I exist . . .) to systematic knowledge of the nature of reality:

> I see plainly that the certainty and truth of all knowledge depends uniquely on my awareness of the true God, to such an extent that I was incapable of perfect knowledge about anything else until I became aware of him. And now it is possible for me to achieve full and certain knowledge of countless matters, both concerning God himself and other things whose nature is intellectual, and also concerning that whole of that corporeal nature which is the subject matter of pure mathematics   (Fifth Meditation, AT VII 71: CSM II 49).

Having opened up the possibility of systematic knowledge of the real natures of things, via the (divinely guaranteed) clear and distinct perceptions of the intellect, this is how Descartes proceeds in the Sixth Meditation to argue for the distinctness of mind and body.

> I know that everything which I clearly and distinctly understand is capable of being created by God so as to correspond exactly with my understanding of it. Hence the fact that I can clearly and distinctly understand one thing apart from another is enough to make me certain that the two things are distinct, since they are *capable of being separated*, at least by God. The question of what kind of power is required to bring about such a separation does not affect the judgement that the two things are distinct.
>   Thus, simply by knowing that I exist, and noticing at the same time that absolutely nothing else belongs to my nature of essence except that I am a thinking thing, I can infer correctly that my essence consists solely in the fact that I am a thinking thing. It is true that I may have (or, to anticipate, certainly have) a body that is very closely joined to me. But nevertheless, on the one hand I have a clear and distinct idea of *myself, in so far as I am simply a thinking, non-extended thing*; and on the other hand I have a distinct idea of *body, in so far as this is simply an extended, non-thinking thing*. And accordingly it is certain that I am really distinct from my body, and can exist without it.
>   (AT VII 78: CSM II 54).

'Extended' things (as explained in the previous chapter) are the subject matter of Cartesian physics; they are defined as whatever has spatial dimensions and hence can be *quantified* or measured in terms of size, shape and motion. The body, and all its organs, including the brain, is clearly 'extended' in this sense; indeed, it seems a contradiction to call anything a 'body' unless it has measurable dimensions. Descartes' premise that he has a clear and distinct idea of body as extended thus seems unexceptionable. Many, moreover, would agree with his further premise that we have a clear and distinct idea of mind as something *un*extended. Certainly, thoughts do not seem to occupy space in the way in which molecules or tables or planets do. Consciousness – the flow of sensations and reflections and desires and cogitations that make up our mental life – seems on the face of it to belong to an entirely separate category from the particles of measurable shape and motion that make up the universe as studied by the physicist. So the notions of mind and of body, let us agree with Descartes, are distinct notions.

Can we get from here to the conclusion that 'I am really distinct from the body and could exist without it?' Descartes' reasoning seems to be that if I can clearly understand the notion of mind without reference to anything extended, and if I can clearly understand the notion of body without reference to anything conscious, then it is at least logically possible that a mind could exist apart from a body. As Descartes puts it, 'they are *capable* of being separated, at least by God'. And if they *can* exist apart, then mind does not depend for its existence on the body, and hence the body is not part of its essential nature.

Notice (to come back to the 'secular analogue' of Descartes' argument hinted at earlier) that this reasoning does not in fact depend on there being a God who creates disembodied souls. The real point of the argument is not that minds *do* exist apart from bodies, but that they are *capable* of so doing. And anyone who concedes this has really conceded the basic plank of Descartes' mind–body dualism. Thus those philosophers nowadays who maintain that in our actual universe all consciousness is embodied in some physical or organic system, but allow that it is at least *logically possible* that there could be purely spiritual entities, existing free from any bodily structure – such philosophers are in fact going along with the main thrust of Cartesian dualism. And it is a very short step from this to agreeing with Descartes that, though your present human life involves both mental and physical attributes, it is possible that your body could be destroyed, and yet the real essential 'you' still survive.

There is, however, another perspective from which Descartes' argument appears more suspect. To approach the question 'Can thought exist without a brain (or some analogous physical structure)?', consider the parallel question: 'Can digestion exist without a stomach (or appropriate alternative physical organs)?' The answer to the second question is surely: no. For although the concepts of digestion and stomach are quite distinct concepts, and we can, as it were, separate them out in our thought, the two are nevertheless intimately related as function is related to structure: the function of digestion, if it is actually to *operate*, must be embodied in a physical structure with the appropriate causal powers (e.g. the ability to process food). And similarly, it seems plausible to argue that although the concept of thought is quite distinct from the concept of brain activity, thought is nonetheless a *functional* process, which cannot operate without some sort of hardware (either a brain or something analogous). Software engineers, to be sure, design their programs in purely abstract terms, without any reference to the physical world; but they know, nonetheless, that for their programs actually to *operate*, they must be physically embodied (e.g. on a hard disk). For there to be an operating software program in the absence of a physical substrate is, ultimately, an incoherent notion: it is not just that it does not occur in our universe, but that there is no possible world in which it is found (any more than there is a possible world in which there are functioning digestive processes in the absence of some kind of physical organs capable of doing the job). If this is right, then however plausible it might appear at first sight to suppose it is logically possible for there to be minds existing apart from bodies, the notion turns out ultimately to be incoherent, and Descartes' argument thus fails.

The indivisibility of consciousness

Descartes has one more string to his bow in arguing for the distinctness of mind and body. Towards the end of the Sixth Meditation, he makes the following observation:

> There is a great difference between the mind and the body, inasmuch as the body is by its very nature always divisible, while the mind is utterly indivisible. For when I consider the mind, or myself in so far as I am merely a thinking thing, I am unable to distinguish any parts within myself; I understand myself to be something quite single and complete. Although the whole mind seems to be united to the whole body, I recognize that if a foot or arm or any other part of the body is cut off, nothing has thereby been taken away from the mind. (As for the faculties of willing, of understanding, of sensory perception and so on, these cannot be termed *parts* of the mind, since it is one and the same mind that wills, and understands, and has sensory perceptions.) By contrast there is no corporeal or extended thing that I can think of

which in my thought I cannot easily divide into parts; and this very fact makes me understand that it is divisible. This one argument would be enough to show me that the mind is completely different from the body, even if I did not already know as much from other considerations

(AT VII 85–6: CSM II 59).

Some of this seems rather inept, as when Descartes talks of the removal of a foot or arm not taking anything from the mind, to which his modern opponents will immediately retort, 'What about the removal of the brain or the nervous system?' Other recent critics have cast doubt on the alleged 'indivisibility' of the mind, pointing out that contemporary research has shown that the alleged unity of consciousness may be an illusion, our mental functioning being in reality an uneasy amalgam of a host of semi-autonomous and often quite loosely co-operating subsystems. But perhaps the most questionable aspect of Descartes' argument is that he already seems tacitly to be 'reifying' the mind – assuming it is an entity or substance in its own right. If, instead, the mind is the name for a set of *functions*, or *attributes*, rather than a substance, then the fact that we cannot divide up and weigh and measure those functions in the way we can divide up and measure portions of the brain is ultimately beside the point. We cannot divide up, measure and weigh the spell-checking function in a wordprocessor, in the way we can divide up, measure and weigh the hardware; but for all that the wordprocessing function cannot operate except in virtue of the properties of a physical system.

Descartes' arguments, flawed though they may be, do succeed in underlining an important fact about mental phenomena, namely that the quantitative language of physics, involving terms like size, shape, extension, motion and so on, seems wholly inadequate to describe the inner dimension of our mental life. It is this subjective dimension that makes many modern philosophers retain what might be called 'quasi-Cartesian' leanings, even though they have little truck with the notion of independent spiritual substances. However complete our physical science, will it ever be able to encompass what it is like to smell new-mown hay, or to taste a ripe raspberry, or to hear the bagpipes? Such subjective qualitative impressions, or 'qualia', as the jargon now dubs them, are felt by many to be destined to elude for ever the clutches of even the most advanced physics we can conceive of.

It is interesting that examples of such allegedly recalcitrant 'qualia' are generally drawn not from the domain of 'pure thought' – e.g. the thought that two plus two makes four, which seems relatively abstract and 'colourless' from the standpoint of the experiencing subject – but rather from the warm-blooded world of human sensation and emotion. It is to

Descartes' treatment of this characteristically human dimension to our mental life that we must now turn.

THE TRUE HUMAN BEING

Descartes' rebuttal of 'angelism'

It is one of the great paradoxes of Descartes' philosophical development that, having expended so much energy arguing that mind and body are two distinct and mutually *independent* substances, he spent a large part of the final decade of his life insisting on their *interdependence* – an interdependence so close and intimate as to amount to what he called a 'real substantial union'. This is not, however, as abrupt a *volte face* as it might seem, since the basic fact of the 'union' between mind and body was something Descartes had already asserted quite unequivocally in the *Meditations*:

> There is nothing that my own nature teaches me more vividly than that I have a body, and that when I feel pain there is something wrong with the body, and that when I am hungry or thirsty the body needs food and drink, and so on . . .
> Nature also teaches me, by these sensations of pain, hunger, thirst and so on, that I am not merely *present* in my body as a sailor is present in a ship, but that I am *very closely joined and, as it were, intermingled with it, so that I and the body form a unit*. If this were not so, I, who am nothing but a thinking thing, would not feel pain when the body was hurt, but would perceive the damage purely by the intellect, just as a sailor perceives by sight if anything in his ship is broken. Similarly, when the body needed food or drink, I should have an explicit understanding of the fact, instead of having confused sensations of hunger and thirst. For the sensations of hunger, thirst, pain and so on are nothing but confused modes of thinking which arise from the *union and, as it were, intermingling* of the mind with the body
> (Sixth Meditation, AT VII 80–1: CSM II 56).

What would life be like for a pure disembodied spirit that happened to be implanted into a body? The body, being alien to its essential nature, would simply be a piece of apparatus, or a vehicle, Descartes suggests; and hence damage to the body would be perceived rather as I perceive that my car has been dented, or the roof of my house is leaking: the mind would simply record these facts as 'external' to itself – inconvenient, to be sure, but not directly and immediately involving its very being, as happens when a human feels bodily distress as the result of illness or injury. In the latter case, it is not just that I make the judgement: 'What a nuisance, this body I am using is damaged'; rather I *feel*, in a peculiarly direct and intimate way, that acute and obtrusive sensation we all know as pain. And it is this 'confused mode of thinking', Descartes argues, that is a sure sign that mind and body are not just related as sailor to ship, or passenger to vehicle, but are closely 'united' and 'intermingled'.

Why does Descartes call sensations like pain *confused* thoughts? Part of the reason is that they lack the clarity and distinctness of which intellectual perceptions are capable. When I judge that two and two make four, or that a triangle has three sides, the content of my thought is transparently clear to the understanding, and I have – right in front of me as it were – everything that is necessary for me to be certain of the truth of the proposition in question. By contrast, there is for Descartes something inherently opaque about the sensory data we receive when the body is stimulated in various ways. The feelings are vivid and intense enough, but there are not the same transparent logical connections that are manifest when the intellect is contemplating clear and distinct propositions like those of mathamatics:

> As for the body which by some special right I called 'mine', my belief that this body, more than any other, belonged to me has some justification. For I could never be separated from it, as I could from other bodies; and I felt all my appetites and emotions in, and on account of, this body; and finally, I was aware of pain and pleasurable tickling in parts of this body, but not in other bodies external to it. But why should that curious sensation of pain give rise to a particular distress of mind; or why should a certain kind of delight follow on a tickling sensation? Again, why should that curious tugging in the stomach which I call hunger tell me that I should eat, or a dryness of the throat tell me to drink, and so on? I was not able to give any explanation of all this, except that nature taught me so. For there is absolutely no connection (at least that I can understand) between the tugging sensation and the decision to take food, or between the sensation of something causing pain and the mental apprehension of distress that arises from that sensation . . . (AT VII 76: CSM II 52–3).

It is the *strangeness* of psycho-physical sensations like hunger and pain, their inherent dissimilarity from the transparent perceptions of the intellect, that shows us that we are not simply pure minds annexed to bodies. Instead, this particular body is *mine* in a peculiar, yet undeniable and vividly manifested way. This is the characteristic 'signature', as it were, of my existence not just as a 'thinking thing' plugged into a mechanical body, but as that unique amalgam of mind and body, a *human being*.

Commentators, at least the anglophone tradition, have tended to ignore this crucial aspect of Descartes' philosophy, preferring instead to focus on his arguments for the distinctness of mind and body. In the celebrated phrase of the English philosopher Gilbert Ryle (in *The Concept of Mind*, 1949), the Cartesian approach has become synonymous with the doctrine of the 'ghost in the machine' – an immaterial spirit controlling an alien, mechanical body. The charge is not a new one, but is found among Descartes' own contemporaries, who often accused him of reverting to a Platonic-style 'angelism'. Antoine Arnauld, author of the Fourth Set of Objections to the *Meditations*, put it this way:

> It seems that the argument [that mind can exist apart from body] proves too much, and takes us back to the Platonic view ... that nothing corporeal belongs to our essence, so that man is merely a rational soul, and the body merely a vehicle to the soul – a view which gives rise to the definition of a human being as *anima corpore utens* ('a soul which makes use of a body')   (AT VII 203: CSM II 143).

Descartes briskly replied:

> I do not see why the argument 'proves too much' . . . I thought I was very careful to guard against anyone inferring that a human being is simply 'a soul which makes use of a body'. For in the Sixth Meditation, where I dealt with the distinction between the mind and the body, I also proved at the same time that the mind is substantially united with the body. And the arguments which I have used to prove this are as strong as any I can remember ever having read. Now someone who says that a man's arm is a substance that is really distinct from the rest of his body does not thereby deny that the arm belongs to the nature of the whole man. And saying that the arm belongs to the nature of the whole man does not give rise to the suspicion that it cannot subsist in its own right. In the same way, I do not think I proved too much in showing that the mind can exist apart from the body. Nor do I think I proved too little in saying that the mind is substantially united with the body, since that substantial union does not prevent our having a clear and distinct concept of the mind on its own, as a complete thing
> (AT VII 227–8: CSM II 160).

Descartes' reply is not perhaps as perspicuous as it might be; but the nub of the issue boils down to whether Descartes has a genuine 'anthropology' (Greek *anthropos*, 'human being') – whether he has a theory which does justice to our essential nature as human beings. Following the publication of the *Meditations*, Descartes' over-enthusiastic disciple Regius put it forward as the Cartesian view that the human being was simply a contingent or accidental entity – in the jargon, an *ens per accidens* – something, as it were, that merely happens to come into existence when a soul is joined to a body, but which lacks the status of something with a genuine essence of its own. In a stern letter to him, Descartes thundered, 'You could scarcely have said anything more objectionable and provocative' (AT III 460: CSMK 200). A month later he wrote again in more detail, adamantly rejecting Regius' interpretation, and insisting that the human being is indeed an *ens per se*, a genuine entity in its own right:

> The mind is united in real and substantial manner to the body . . . As I said in my *Meditations*, we perceive that sensations such as pain are not pure thoughts of a mind distinct from a body, but confused perceptions of a mind really united to a body. For if an angel were in a human body, it would not have sensations as we do, but would simply perceive the motions which are caused by external objects, and in this way would differ from a *genuine human being* (AT III 493: CSMK 206).

Emphatic though Descartes' reply is, it leaves many questions unanswered. If mind and body are indeed distinct and independent substances, how is it that they can interact and combine; and what exactly is meant by the 'real substantial union' between them? These are questions to which Descartes did not give systematic further attention until he was challenged to explain himself more fully by perhaps his most famous correspondent, the Princess Elizabeth, daughter of Frederick, the exiled King of Bohemia, and niece of the ill-fated Charles I of England.

'Primitive notions' and the substantial union

Princess Elizabeth wrote to Descartes in May 1642 asking him how the soul, being simply a 'thinking substance', can initiate the relevant events in the nervous system so as to produce voluntary movements of the limbs (a highly pertinent question, anticipating Gilbert Ryle's attack, three hundred years later, on the idea of a Cartesian 'ghost' supposedly able to move a corporeal 'machine'). Descartes replied with unusual candour:

> I may truly say that the question Your Highness poses seems to me the one which can most properly be put to me in view of my published

writings. There are two facts about the human soul on which depend all the knowledge we can have of its nature. The first is that it thinks; the second is that, being united to the body, it can act and be acted upon along with it. About the second I have said hardly anything; I have tried only to make the first well understood. For my principal aim was to prove the *distinction* between the soul and the body, and to this end only the first was useful, and the second might have been harmful. But because Your Highness's vision is so clear that nothing can be concealed from her, I will try now to explain how I conceive the *union* of the soul and the body, and how the soul has the power to move the body.

First, I consider that there are in us certain primitive notions which are as it were the patterns on the basis of which we form all our other conceptions ... As regards body in particular we have only the notion of extension, which entails the notions of shape and motion; as regards the soul on its own, we have only the notion of thought, which includes the perceptions of the intellect and the inclinations of the will. Lastly, as regards the soul and the body together, we have only the notion of their *union*, on which depends our notion of the soul's power to move the body and the body's power to act on the soul and cause its sensations and passions   (letter of 21 May 1643, AT 664–5: CSMK 217–18).

This does not do much to explain how mind and body are able to interact, but Descartes was later to deny that this was, in itself, a problem: 'It is a false supposition ... that if the soul and the body are two substances whose nature is different, this prevents them from being able to act on each other' (AT IXA 213: CSM II 275). The most striking aspect of his comments to Elizabeth, however, is that Descartes makes no attempt to use the somewhat obscure jargon he had employed in dealing with Regius ('accidental entity' versus 'entity in its own right'), but instead makes the remarkable claim that the concept of the human being, the mind–body union, is a *primitive notion*. On the face of it this is quite mysterious: 'primitive' suggests 'basic', or 'not further analysable'; yet if the union is made up of body plus soul, elsewhere declared to be the fundamental categories of Cartesian metaphysics, how can the amalgam of the two be apprehended by a 'primitive notion'? It is as if a chemist were to say the concept of water is a 'primitive' one, but then go on to add that water is made up of the more basic substances, hydrogen and oxygen.

In response to further probing by Elizabeth, Descartes wrote to her again a month later:

I observe one great difference between these three kinds of notion. The soul is conceived only by the pure intellect; body (i.e. extension, shapes and motions) can likewise be known by the intellect alone, but much better by the intellect aided by the imagination; and finally what belongs to the union of the soul and the body is known only obscurely by the intellect alone, or even by the intellect aided by the imagination, but it is known very clearly by the senses. That is why people who never philosophize and use only their senses have no doubt that the soul moves the body and that the body acts on the soul. They regard both of them as a single thing, that is to say, they conceive their union; because to conceive the union between two things is to conceive them as one single thing. Metaphysical thoughts, which exercise the pure intellect, help to familiarise us with the notion of the soul; and the study of mathematics, which exercises mainly the imagination in the consideration of shapes and motions, accustoms us to form very distinct notions of body. But it is the ordinary course of life and conversation, and abstention from meditation and from the study of the things which exercise the imagination, that teaches us how to conceive the union of the soul and the body

        (letter of 28 June 1643, AT III 691–2: CSMK 226–7).

The passage is a strange one, since it almost seems to abdicate the role of the philosopher: stop trying to *analyse* the union, Descartes seems to be telling Elizabeth; it is enough that we *feel* it, in our day-to-day sensory experience. The difficulty here is what seems to be an admission that our ordinary experience is actually inconsistent with Descartes' official mind–body dualism: his philosophical arguments have purported to show that there are two distinct entities here, but he now appears to concede that our ordinary experience reveals a single, united being. The impression of a serious philosophical impasse is reinforced in the following paragraph:

I think it was [philosophical meditations] rather than thoughts requiring less attention that have made Your Highness find obscurity in the notion we have of the union of the mind and the body. It does not seem to me that the human mind is capable of forming a very distinct conception of both the distinction between the soul and the body, and their union; for to do this it is necessary to conceive of them as a single thing and at the same time to conceive of them as two things, and the two conceptions are mutually opposed   (AT III 693: CSMK 227).

*

Some have taken this to be throwing in the towel and admitting the whole theory of the union of distinct substances is incoherent. The way forward, however, is to focus on those attributes which Descartes always refers to when discussing the mind–body union: the emotions, feelings and passions. These are modalities of awareness that are unique to the human mind–body composite, and it is here, it seems to me, that the 'primitiveness' of the notion of the union is to be explained.

In insisting that we have a 'primitive notion' of the union of mind and body, alongside our primitive notions of thought and of extension, Descartes should be understood as asserting that the mind–body complex is something which is the bearer of *distinctive and irreducible properties in its own right*. In this sense we might say that water is a 'primitive' notion, meaning that it is not a mere mixture but a genuine compound, possessing attributes 'in its own right' (distinctive 'watery' characteristics that cannot be reduced to the properties of the hydrogen or oxygen which make it up). In the same way, Descartes regards the sensations and passions as not reducible either to pure thought, on the one hand, or to events in the extended world of physics, on the other. That he is on to something important here may be seen from the fact that to experience *hunger* is not reducible either to (i) making the purely intellectual judgement 'I need nourishment', on the one hand, or to (ii) the occurrence of the purely physiological events (stomach contractions, fall in blood sugar) on the other. For example, (i) someone could be drugged into not feeling hungry, yet still make the judgement that he needs to eat, e.g. as a result of calculating the time elapsed since the last meal, or by measuring his blood sugar. And (ii) the physiological events could obviously occur without the experience of hunger – for example, in an anaesthetized patient.

If Descartes' theory of the 'three primitive notions' is supported by the irreducibility of psycho-physical attributes like hunger either to pure thought or to extension, this need not imply any logical clash with his official doctrine of two and only two substances, mind and body. For the 'trialistic' division found in the letters to Elizabeth can, along the lines just suggested, be construed as an *attributive* rather than substantival trialism: the human being is not an additional *substance* alongside mind and body (any more than water is an additional substance in the universe, to be listed alongside hydrogen and oxygen); but what is true is that in virtue of our embodied state, as creatures of flesh and blood, human beings enjoy modes of awareness which (to use Descartes' own language) 'must not be referred either to the mind alone or to the body alone'. This is how Descartes sums it up in Part I article 48 of his *Principles of Philosophy*, published in 1644:

I recognize only *two* ultimate classes of things: first, intellectual or thinking things, i.e. those which pertain to mind or thinking substance; and secondly, material things, i.e. those which pertain to extended substance or body. [Intellectual] perception, volition, and all the modes both of perceiving and of willing are to be referred to thinking substance; while to extended substance belong size (that is extension in length, breadth and depth), shape, motion, position, divisibility of component parts and the like. But we also experience within ourselves certain other things which *must not be referred either to the mind alone or to the body alone*. These arise . . . from the close and intimate union of our mind with the body. This list includes, first, appetites like hunger and thirst; secondly, the emotions or passions of the mind which do not consist of thought alone, such as the emotions of anger, joy, sadness and love; and finally all the sensations such as those of pain, pleasure, light, colours, sounds, smells, tastes, heat, hardness and the other tactile qualities (AT VIIIA 23: CSM I 208–9).

Human nature and the passions

As its title implies, Descartes' last work, *Les passions de l'âme*, completed just before his ill-fated visit to Sweden in 1649, was a detailed study of the passions, modalities of experience that are unique to the mind–body union, and which testify to the fact that we are not pure *res cogitantes* or 'thinking things', but are *humans*, whose day-to-day lives are intimately bound up with bodily states and events. One can, presumably, imagine beings whose lives operated on a purely intellectual level, who calmly contemplated those propositions that rational analysis reveals to be true, and calmly pursued those goals that are rationally perceived to be beneficial. Such a life would perhaps be 'superior' to ours, in the sense of being free from the tensions and turmoil that often arise from the bodily side to our nature; but it would also be strangely 'colourless' in comparison with the vivid interplay of emotion and feeling that characterizes human existence.

Some of these contrasts were explored by Descartes in a letter written to the French ambassador to Sweden, who had asked him, on behalf of Queen Christina, to explain his views on the subject of love:

In answer to your question I make a distinction between the love which is purely intellectual or rational, and the love which is a passion. The first, in my view, consists simply in the fact that when our soul perceives some present or absent good, which it judges to be fitting for itself, it joins itself to it willingly . . .

But when our soul is joined to the body, this rational love is commonly accompanied by the other kind of love, which can be called sensual or sensuous. This . . . is nothing but a confused thought aroused in the soul by some motion of the nerves . . . Just as in thirst the sensation of the dryness of the throat is a confused thought which disposes the soul to desire to drink, but is not identical with that desire, so in love a mysterious heat is felt around the heart, and a great abundance of blood in the lungs which makes us open our arms as if to embrace something, and this inclines the soul willingly to join to itself the object presented to it. There is no reason to be surprised that certain motions of the heart should be naturally connected in this way with certain thoughts, which they in no way resemble. The soul's natural capacity for union with a body brings with it the possibility of an association between each of its thoughts and certain motions or conditions of this body, so that when the same conditions recur in the body, they induce the soul to have the same thought . . .

(AT IV 601–4: CSMK 306–7).

The idea of psycho-physical *associations* which Descartes alludes to here is the key to his view of what it is like to be a human being. Some of the associations are 'natural', or, as he sometimes says, 'divinely ordained', such as the sensation of thirst which we feel when the throat is dry. We might now say that these are genetically programmed into the species, as a result of their obvious survival value in the struggle for existence; what Descartes says, in pre-Darwinian mode, is that

any given movement occurring in the part of the brain that immediately affects the mind produces just one corresponding sensation; and hence the best system that could be devised is that it should produce the one sensation which of all possible sensations is most especially and most frequently conducive to the preservation of the healthy man. And experience shows that the sensations which nature has given us are all of this kind; and so there is absolutely nothing to be found in them that does not bear witness to the power and goodness of God

(AT VII 87: CSM II 60).

Other associations are generated environmentally, as a result of repeated patterns of stimulus and response. Descartes here uses the example of animal training (strikingly anticipating the much later Pavlovian theory of conditioned reflexes):

I reckon that if you whipped a dog five or six times to the sound of a violin, it would begin to howl and run away as soon as it heard that music again

(letter to Mersenne of 18 March 1630, AT I 134: CSMK 20).

And, finally, there are beneficial associations that we can decide to set up not in animals but in ourselves; we can, in short, 'reprogram' the operation of the passions to enable us to lead a better and more fulfilled life:

When a dog sees a partridge it is naturally disposed to run towards it; and when it hears a gun fired, the noise naturally impels it to run away. Nevertheless, setters are commonly trained so that the sight of partridge makes them stop, and the noise they hear afterwards, when someone fires at the bird, makes them run towards it. These things are worth noting in order to encourage each of us to make a point of controlling our passions. For since we are able, with a little effort, to change the movements of the brain in animals devoid of reason, it is evident that we can do so still more effectively in the case of human beings. Even those who have the weakest souls could acquire absolute mastery over all their passions, if we employed sufficient ingenuity in training and guiding them.

(*Passions of the Soul*, art. 50, AT XI 370: CSM I 348).

The 'substantial union' of soul and body that constitutes a human being requires, for its survival and wellbeing, not just intellect and volition, but the whole range of sensory and affective states. All sensory states, as we have seen, are attributable to us not *qua* pure 'thinking things', but *qua* embodied creatures – human beings. And it is clear that many of the psycho-physical correlations involved are crucial for our survival, both as individuals and as a species: that we feel a characteristic kind of discomfort when the stomach is empty and the blood sugar is low has obvious survival value in impelling us to eat (and thus relieving the feeling of hunger); that I feel pain when I tread on a thorn has evident utility in encouraging me to avoid such noxious stimuli in future. The susceptibility of the passions to reprogramming, moreover, opens the possibility of our using the mind–body associations to our own advantage; unlike the animals, who are 'lumbered' with genetically and environmentally determined patterns of response, the human being is in the unique position of being able to put the associative patterns to the service of a rationally planned vision of the good life.

Descartes' conclusion is that the passions that arise from our bodily inheritance are to be embraced, since their operation, in general, is intimately related to our human welfare. This is not to say that they are always and uncontroversially good. Because of the relatively rigid way innate physiological mechanisms and environmentally conditioned responses operate, we may become locked into behaviour that leads to

distress, misery or harm. The dropsical man, to use one of Descartes'
instances, feels a strong desire to drink, even when fluid is the last thing
his health requires (Sixth Meditation, AT VII 89: CSM II 61); or, to take
an intriguing example from Descartes' own life, the philosopher found
himself in the grip of an unfortunate attraction to all cross-eyed women,
just because as a boy he had fallen in love with a girl with a squint (letter
to Chanut of 6 June 1647, AT V 57: CSMK 323). But the appropriate
way to cope with such irrational impulses is, for Descartes, not to retreat
to an austere intellectualism, nor to suppress the passions, but rather to
use the resources of science and experience to try to understand what has
caused things to go wrong, and then to attempt to reprogram our
responses so that the direction in which we are led by the passions
corresponds to what our reason perceives as the best option:

> Often passion makes us believe certain things to be much better and
> more desirable than they are; then, when we have taken much trouble
> to acquire them, and in the process lost the chance of possessing other
> more genuine goods, possession of them brings home to us their
> defects; and thence arise dissatisfaction, regret and remorse. And so the
> true function of reason is to examine the just value of all the goods
> whose acquisition seems to depend in some way on our conduct, so
> that we never fail to devote all our efforts to trying to secure those
> which are in fact the more desirable . . .
>
> Often however the passions . . . represent the goods to which they
> tend with greater splendour than they deserve, and they make us
> imagine pleasures to be much greater before we possess them than our
> subsequent experiences show them to be . . . But the true function of
> reason in the conduct of life is to examine and consider without passion
> the value of all the perfections, both of the body and of the soul, which
> can be acquired by our conduct, so that since we are commonly obliged
> to deprive ourselves of some goods in order to acquire others, we shall
> always choose the better
> (letter to Elizabeth of 1 September 1645, AT IV 284–5, 286–7: CSMK
> 264–5).

Despite the alienation from the body which Cartesian dualism often
seems to threaten, Descartes' final vision of the human condition is
characterized by an engaging realism and, ultimately, by a humane
optimism. Strange hybrid creatures compounded of pure mind and
mechanical body, we nonetheless enjoy, at the level of our ordinary daily
experience, a whole range of sensory and emotional responses whose
operation, in the first place, is designed to conduce in general to human

fulfilment, and which, in the second place, we have the power to modify and reprogram to our own advantage. As Descartes resoundingly declared to a correspondent in 1648:

> The philosophy I cultivate is not so savage or grim as to outlaw the operation of the passions; on the contrary, it is here, in my view, that the entire sweetness and joy of life is to be found
> (letter to Silhon of March or April 1648: AT V 135).

Of course, the road ahead, as Descartes sometimes acknowledged, will often be a difficult one: the strength of the passions can lead us to put them to bad use, and the way things work out is, in any case, influenced by the external dimension of fortune, over which we have no control. There are no guarantees. But the nobility of the Cartesian vision of the human condition lies in its clear-eyed acceptance of this, and of the inherent frailty, yet possibility of joy, that arises from the inescapably corporeal side to our humanity:

> The pleasures common to soul and body depend entirely on the passions, so that persons whom the passions can move most deeply are capable of enjoying the sweetest pleasures of this life. It is true that they may also experience the most bitterness when they do not know how to put these passions to good use, and when fortune works against them. But the chief use of wisdom lies in teaching us to be masters of our passions and to control them with such skill that the evils which they cause are quite bearable, and even become a source of joy
> (*Passions of the Soul*, art. 212, AT XI 488: CSM I 404).

Roger Scruton

SPINOZA

LIFE AND CHARACTER

Benedict de Spinoza (1632–77) was born, lived and died in Holland, where his family, who were Jews from Portugal, had come as refugees from the Inquisition. He was brought up in the Jewish faith, but was anathematized for his heretical opinions, which had been acquired during a study of Descartes (1596–1649), the founding father of modern philosophy. Descartes too, although French by birth, had lived for most of his creative life in Holland. Thanks to Descartes and the Cartesians, and thanks to the intellectual freedom enjoyed by the Dutch Republic during the years following its successful revolt against Spain, seventeenth-century Holland was, for a few precious decades, a centre of intellectual life, and the first home of the Enlightenment.

Freedom of thought is more easily lost than won, and with the rise of Calvinism the tolerant regime of the Republic came to an end. In 1670 Spinoza published a *Theologico-Political Treatise*, to which he did not add his name, but which was soon discovered to be his work. This treatise defended secular government, the rule of law and freedom of opinion, and was richly illustrated by biblical examples that did not conceal the author's hostility to the government of priests and pharisees. The *Treatise* was banned, and its author briefly exiled from Amsterdam.

In response to this confrontation with authority, Spinoza went to live in retirement among dissenting Christians. He retained an interest in politics, and made several hazardous forays into public life. He also began work on a second political treatise that he never finished. But he published nothing further, and his masterpiece, the *Ethics*, which had been circulating among eager students for some years before his death, appeared posthumously, and was promptly banned.

Spinoza led a chaste and studious life, refusing the offer of a professorship at Heidelberg, and developing his thought through correspondence with other scientific and philosophical writers. He had wide-ranging interests, in politics, law, biblical scholarship and painting, as well as in mathematics and physical science. He carried out experiments in optics, and the grinding of lenses for these experiments may have exacerbated the consumption that brought him to an early but peaceful death. He was esteemed by all who knew him, and loved by many. In a letter he wrote:

> So far as in me lies, I value, above all other things out of my control, the joining hands of friendship with men who are lovers of truth. I believe that nothing in the world, of things outside our own control, brings more peace than the possibility of affectionate intercourse with such men; it is just as impossible that the love we bear them can be disturbed . . . as that truth once perceived should not be assented to.

That vision of friendship, as bound up with the pursuit of truth, radiates from all Spinoza's writings. Friendship and the pursuit of truth, he believed, contribute to our highest goal – which is *amor intellectualis Dei*, the intellectual love of God. Spinoza's philosophy was an attempt to reconcile this profoundly religious outlook with the scientific view of man.

THE ETHICS

Spinoza wrote in Latin, adopting medieval and Cartesian technicalities, and forging his own style, which was sparse and unadorned, yet solemn and imposing. The occasional aphorisms jump from the page with all the greater force, in that they emerge from arguments presented with mathematical exactitude. There is space here to consider only Spinoza's greatest work, the *Ethics*, whose argument, however, is of such intrinsic relevance to us who live three centuries after its publication that thinking people have as much reason as they had in its author's day to acquaint themselves with its main conceptions.

The *Ethics* is divided into five parts, each of which is set out in the manner of Euclid's geometry, beginning with definitions and axioms, and deducing theorems by abstract proofs. The axioms are supposed to be self-evident, and the theorems valid deductions. If this were so, then the entire philosophy would be not merely true, but necessarily true – in the way that mathematics is necessarily true. The unlikelihood of this should not deter us. Even if the proofs are shaky and the axioms obscure, there is a great intellectual treasure to be mined from them, and – judged as a whole and in terms of its underlying agenda – Spinoza's philosophy is nearer to the truth than any other that has addressed the same barely fathomable questions. These questions are just as important for us as they were for Spinoza. The difference is that we are seldom aware of them. Here they are:

1. Why does anything exist?
2. How is the world composed?

3. What are we in the scheme of things?
4. Are we free?
5. How should we live?

Our modern inability to answer these questions accounts for our modern reluctance to confront them, which in turn accounts for our deep disorientation. What is fashionably known as the 'postmodern condition' is really the condition of people who, having given up on their fundamental anxieties, find it easier to conceal them. Such people no longer know what to hope for or how. There is no better therapist for their condition than Spinoza, and no greater advocate of the spiritual life to those who have lost the desire to repossess it.

The five questions that I have listed are philosophical: they cannot be answered by observation and experiment, but only by reasoning. Cosmologists dispute over the 'origins of the Universe', some arguing for a Big Bang, others for a slow condensation. But both theories leave a crucial question unanswered. Even if we conclude that the Universe began at a certain time from nothing, there is something else that needs to be explained – the 'initial conditions' which then obtained. Something was true of the Universe at time zero – namely, that *this* great event was about to erupt into being, and to generate effects in accordance with laws that were already, at this initial instant, in place. And what is the explanation of *that*?

This is a version of the first question listed above. No scientific theory can answer it. Yet, if it has no answer, nothing really has an explanation. We can describe how the Universe works, but not why it is there. Indeed, the existence of a universe that *works*, a universe that admits of scientific explanations, is an even greater mystery than the existence of random chaos. What immortal hand or eye could frame this fearful symmetry? Or did it just *happen*? And if so, how and why?

Spinoza lived at a time when modern science was beginning to emerge from the hinterground of theological speculation. He was an accomplished scientific thinker, who anticipated many aspects of modern physics and cosmology. But he recognized no absolute divide between science and philosophy. For him, as for Descartes, physics rests upon metaphysics, and a scientist who ignores the fundamental questions does not really understand what he is doing. These fundamental questions cannot be answered by experiment; it is reason and not experience that is our guide to ultimate reality. It is because he thought in this way that Spinoza is described as a rationalist (rather than an empiricist, i.e. one who founds all knowledge on experience). And that is why he adopted the 'geometrical method', since reason knows no other. All the truths of reason are either self-evident or derived from self-evident truths by chains of deductive argument.

The adoption of the geometrical method means that Spinoza's philosophy appears at first sight intolerably austere. It is normal for philosophers to begin from local puzzles, and thereafter to advance by degrees towards an abstract picture of reality. Thus Descartes began by asking himself whether there is anything that he could not doubt, and went on to construct a metaphysical theory that would bring his doubts to an end. Spinoza begins from the point where other thinkers end – from the axioms of an abstract theory. He then *descends* by degrees to the human reality, and to the problems that his theory is supposed to solve. To accomplish this at all is a great achievement; to accomplish it in the manner of Spinoza, so as to provide solutions to the perennial questions, is little short of a miracle.

GOD

The first part of the *Ethics* is devoted to the first two of our questions: why does anything exist? and how is the world composed? Spinoza, like many of his forerunners, was convinced that the Universe lacks an explanation unless there is something which is *cause of itself* – that is, whose nature it is to exist. The explanation of such a thing will be found within itself: it *has* to exist, otherwise it would be in violation of its own definition. This thing that exists necessarily and by its very nature has traditionally been called God, and the first part of the *Ethics* is duly entitled 'On God'. Here, abridging slightly, are the definitions with which it begins:

> D1: By cause of itself I understand that whose essence involves existence, *or* that whose nature cannot be conceived except as existing.
> D2: That thing is said to be finite in its own kind that can be limited by another of the same nature.
> D3: By substance I understand what is in itself and conceived through itself, i.e., that whose concept does not require the concept of another thing, from which it must be formed.
> D4: By attribute I understand what the intellect perceives of a substance, as constituting its essence.
> D5: By mode I understand the modifications (*affectiones*) of a substance, *or* that which is in another through which it is also conceived.
> D6: By God I understand a being absolutely infinite, i.e., a substance

consisting of an infinity of attributes, each of which expresses an eternal and infinite essence.

D7: That thing is called free which exists from the necessity of its nature alone, and is determined to act by itself alone. But a thing is called necessary, or rather compelled, which is determined by another to exist and to produce an effect in a certain and determinate manner.

D8: By eternity I understand existence itself, insofar as it is conceived to follow necessarily from the definition of the eternal thing.

Seldom has a great work of philosophy begun so forbiddingly. Already a large part of Spinoza's world-view has been suggested by these eight definitions, and much of the difficulty of the *Ethics* lies in deciphering them.

The first definition is taken from Moses Maimonides, a twelfth-century Jewish thinker who was one of the greatest influences on medieval philosophy. As I remarked above, it seemed to Spinoza that there could be an answer to the riddle of existence only if there were a being whose very nature it is to exist, a being whose existence would be self-explanatory. Such a being must be self-produced, or 'cause of itself'. Hence the definition.

From the same repertoire of theological ideas comes Spinoza's distinction between the finite and the infinite. Finite things, he believes, have limits – whether in space or time or thought. And a thing with limits is limited by something: a larger or greater or more long-lasting thing can always be conceived. Not everything can be compared with (and therefore limited by) everything else. A great elephant is not larger or smaller than a great thought. In general, physical things (bodies) are limited by physical things, and mental things (ideas) by mental things. Hence the expression 'finite in its own kind'.

The third definition introduces the pivotal concept of Spinoza's philosophy – the concept on which his metaphysical arguments turn. The term 'substance' was one of the technicalities of seventeenth-century philosophy. But each thinker had his own way of using it. According to Spinoza, reality divides into those things that depend upon, or are explained through, other things, and those things that depend upon nothing but themselves. Thus the child derives from its parents, who in turn derive from their parents, who in turn ... The chain of human reproduction is a chain of dependent beings. These are not substances, since to form a true conception of their nature (an explanation of what and why they are) we must conceive them in terms of their causes. 'Substance' is the term Spinoza reserves for the things in which all else inheres or upon which all else depends. Substances are conceived not through their causes, but through themselves. Lesser, dependent, beings are 'modes' of substances. In Definition 5 he calls these lesser things '*affectiones*' – a Latin technicality, meaning, roughly, 'ways in which substances are affected', as a piece of wood is affected by being painted red or a chair by being broken. (If a chair were a substance, then its being broken would be a mode of the chair. But we can already see that, by the definition, nothing so humble and contingent as a chair could be a substance.)

Definition 4 is fraught with controversy. Roughly speaking, here is what Spinoza had in mind. When we understand or explain a substance, it is through knowledge of its essential nature. But there may be more than one way of 'perceiving' this essential nature. Imagine two people looking at a picture painted on a board, one an optician, the other a critic. And suppose you ask them to describe what they see. The optician arranges the picture on two axes, and describes it thus: 'At $x = 4$, $y = 5.2$, there is a patch of chrome yellow; this continues along the horizontal axis until $x = 5.1$, when it changes to Prussian blue.' The critic says: 'It is a man in a yellow coat, with a lowering expression, and steely blue eyes.' You could imagine these descriptions being complete – so complete that they would enable a third party to reconstruct the picture by using them as a set of instructions. But they have nothing whatever in common. One is about colours arranged on a matrix, the other about the scene that we see in them. You cannot switch from one narrative to the other and still make sense: the man is not standing next to a patch of Prussian blue, but next to the shadow of an oak tree. The Prussian blue is not situated next to a coat sleeve, but next to a patch of chrome yellow. In other words, the two descriptions are incommensurate: no fragment of the one can appear in the midst of the other without making nonsense. Yet neither description misses out any feature that is mentioned in the other. This is something like what Spinoza had in mind with his concept of an attribute: a complete account of a substance, which does not rule out other, and incommensurate, accounts of the very same thing.

Spinoza's sixth definition introduces the 'God of the philosophers': the God familiar from countless works of ancient and medieval theology, who is distinguished from all lesser things by the completeness and fullness of his being. He contains 'an infinity of attributes' – in other words, infinitely many accounts can be given of him, each of which conveys an infinite and eternal essence. The idea of the eternal is explained in the final definition, where, in an added clause, Spinoza makes the distinction between eternity and duration. Nothing that is conceived in time can be eternal – at best it endures without limit. True eternity is the eternity of mathematical objects, like numbers, and of the 'eternal truths' that describe them. To be eternal is to lie outside time. All necessary truths are eternal in that sense, like the truths of mathematics. When the existence of something is proved by deductive argument from its definition, then the result is an eternal truth: and God is eternal in just that sense.

The seventh definition tells us that dependent and determined things are not free, in the proper sense of the word. Only self-dependent things – that is, things that accord with the first definition – can be truly free.

Having given us these definitions, Spinoza moves on to the axioms, which are the supposedly self-evident premises of his philosophy. Here they are:

A1: Whatever is, is either in itself or in another.

A2: What cannot be conceived through another, must be conceived through itself.

A3: From a given determinate cause the effect follows necessarily; and conversely, if there is no determinate cause, it is impossible for an effect to follow.

A4: The knowledge of an effect depends on, and involves, the knowledge of its cause.

A5: Things which have nothing in common with one another also cannot be understood through one another, i.e. the conception of the one does not involve the conception of the other.

A6: A true idea must agree with its object.

A7: If a thing can be conceived as not existing, its essence does not involve existence.

The axioms are scarcely less forbidding than the definitions. Spinoza was aware of this, and counselled his readers to follow some of the proofs in order that the meaning and truth of the axioms should be brought gradually home to them. This is not to deny the self-evidence of the axioms, but only the difficulty in achieving the perspective from which their self-evidence will dawn. It is true of geometry and set theory, too, that the axioms are often less clear than the theorems.

The first two axioms nevertheless need elucidating. For Spinoza, 'B is *in* A' is another way of saying that A is the explanation of B. In such a case B must also be 'conceived through' A – which means that no adequate account of the nature of B can fail to mention A (hence Axiom 4). In effect, the first two axioms divide the world into two kinds of thing. The first are those that are dependent on other things (their causes), and which must be conceived through their causes. The second are things that are self-dependent and conceived through themselves. And it should be obvious from the definitions that this is the distinction between modes and substances.

To understand the axioms fully, we need to know what Spinoza wishes to prove. The first part of the *Ethics* consists of 36 propositions and their proofs, together with several extended passages of commentary. They constitute Spinoza's argument for the view that there is one and only one substance, and that this one substance is God, and therefore infinite and eternal. Everything else exists *in* God – that is, it is a mode of God, and as such is dependent upon God. The proof of this remarkable claim follows a pattern familiar from medieval philosophy – the pattern of the 'ontological argument' for God's existence, as Kant was later to call it. Since God is defined as a being with infinite attributes, then nothing exists that could limit or take away his being: in every respect he is without limits. Since non-existence is a privation, a limitation, it cannot be predicated of God. Therefore God's essence involves existence – he is, by Definition 1, 'cause of himself'. However, if we understand this traditional argument for the existence of God correctly, Spinoza reasons, we must see that it does not prove only that God exists, but that God embraces everything – that, outside God, nothing can exist or be conceived. If there is anything other than God, either it is *in* God and dependent upon him, in which case it is not a substance but simply a mode of God, or else (Axiom 1) it is outside God, in which case there is something that God is not – some respect in which God is limited, and therefore finite (Definition 2) – which is impossible (Definition 6). Hence there is in the world only one substance, and this substance is God.

All finite things follow each other in an infinite chain of cause and effect, and each is determined to be what it is by the cause that produces it. As Spinoza puts it:

> Proposition 29: In nature there is nothing contingent, but all things have been determined from the necessity of the divine nature to exist and produce an effect in a certain way.

The one substance is both God and Nature, and can be considered both as the free and self-creating creator (*Natura naturans*) and as the sum of his creation – of those things that are *in* God and conceived through him (*Natura naturata*). In the metaphysical sense, only God is free (see Definition 7). Hence:

> Proposition 32: The will cannot be called a free cause, but only a necessary one.

From all this it follows that

> Proposition 33: Things could have been produced by God in no other
> way, and in no other order, than they have been produced.

God, the infinite substance who comprehends everything, is the only free
being, in the sense defined in Part 1 of the *Ethics*, since only he fully
determines his own nature. Everything else is bound in the chain of
causation, whose ultimate ground is God.

It is easy to understand why Spinoza was regarded as such a dangerous
heretic. He offered to prove the existence and grandeur of God. But the
small print tells us that God is identical with Nature, and that nothing in
the world is free. For the bewildered believer, anxious for a philosophy
with which to counter modern science, this is the ultimate sell-out. The
inexorable machine of nature is all that there is, and we are helplessly
enslaved to it. And the fact that nature is 'cause of itself' – that is, the fact
that it exists of *necessity* and could not be other than it is – only adds to
the disaster.

GOD'S ATTRIBUTES

Spinoza would have rejected that interpretation of his philosophy. For it
overlooks the most important and original of his claims, which is that
God has infinitely many attributes, only one of which is studied by
physical science. Two of these attributes are thoroughly familiar to us –
namely, thought and extension. The term 'extension', taken from the
science of Spinoza's day, refers to space and its contents – in other words,
to the physical world. Extension is an attribute of God in the sense that a
complete theory of the physical world (of extended things) is a theory of
all that there is. And thus far modern science would agree with Spinoza.
But while physics is, when complete, the truth about the whole, it is not
the whole truth. For God can be conceived in other ways. For example, he
can be conceived under the attribute of thought. This means that God is
essentially a thinking thing, just as he is essentially an extended thing.
And by studying the nature of thought, one studies God as he is in
himself, advancing towards a complete theory of the world – just as when
one studies the nature of extension.

Another way of expressing this point is to say that everything that
exists – every mode of the divine substance – can be conceived in two
incommensurate ways, as physical or mental. In my own case I have an
inkling of what this means – for I know that I have both a mind and a

body, the first being composed of ideas (where 'idea' is a general term for all mental entities), the second being composed of particles in space. Spinoza's suggestion is that the relation between mind and body that I perceive in myself is reduplicated through the whole of nature: that everything physical has its mental correlate.

But what *is* the relation between mind and body? This problem has vexed philosophers since ancient times, and had come to a head in Spinoza's day, on account of Descartes' influential argument for the view that I am a mental substance, distinct from my body and only contingently connected with it. By contrast, the second part of the *Ethics* – 'Concerning the Nature and Origin of the Mind' – describes the relation between mind and body as one of identity:

> Part 2, Proposition 21, scholium: The mind and the body are one and the same thing, which is conceived now under the attribute of thought, now under the attribute of extension.

Spinoza thinks that his theory of the attributes enables him to say this, since it implies not only that the one substance can be known in two ways, but that the same two ways of knowing apply also to modes. The mind is a finite mode of the infinite substance conceived as thought; the body is a finite mode of the infinite substance conceived as extension. And another way of saying this (Part 2, Proposition 13) is that the mind is the 'idea of' the body – meaning that the two modes are in fact one and the same reality, conceived in two different ways.

This is a striking claim, with many surprising consequences. For Spinoza, every object in the physical world has its mental counterpart, with which it is identical, in the same way that mind and body are identical in me. The idea of every physical thing already exists – not necessarily in any human mind, but in the mind of God, which comprehends the whole of reality under the attribute of thought. Moreover, there is no interaction between mind and body, despite their identity, for interaction implies cause and effect, and A is cause of B, in Spinoza's thinking, only if B must be conceived *through* A. But nothing conceived under one attribute can be explained in terms of (that is, conceived through) something conceived under another attribute. The world may be one substance, but there is no single theory of its nature, and in particular no way of reducing the mental to the physical.

This theory looks less odd if we forget our own case and look at the minds of others. Suppose I see John waving frantically from the other end of the field. I ask Helen, one of my companions, why John is waving. She replies, 'Electrical impulses from his brain are activating the motor neurones of the arm and producing muscular spasms of a rhythmical kind.' Well yes, that is true. But it is not the answer I was seeking. I turn to Jim and repeat the question. Jim answers: 'He is trying to warn us about a danger somewhere – maybe a bull.' The answer is more pertinent, but no more true.

In this example, both Helen and Jim have given true explanations of what we observe. But one is framed in physical terms, the other in mental terms. One mentions processes in the body, the other conceptions in the mind. As we might put it, the one gives the physical causes of John's action, the other the mental *reasons* for it. And I can relate to the second explanation more readily, since it gives insight into what John *means* – in other words, into his mental states, which have a direct connection with my own intentions. Helen could be the best neurophysiologist in the world; she could give a far more complete explanation of John's waving than any broached by Jim. But the chances are we should both be dead before the explanation ended.

Moreover, the two explanations are incommensurate. You cannot add fragments of Helen's account to fragments of Jim's and achieve a complete account – or any account at all – of John's behaviour. You must take either one route or the other to an explanation of what you see. And that is what Spinoza meant by saying that 'the body cannot determine the mind to think, nor the mind the body to remain in motion or at rest' (*Ethics*, Part 3, Proposition 2).

But what of those finite modes – rocks and stones and trees, tables and chairs, typescripts and coffee cups – that we normally regard as inanimate? Spinoza must say that they are not inanimate at all, and that if I saw them as God sees them then I should be as clearly aware of their mental counterparts as I am aware of my own mind and its ideas. This is not as absurd as it sounds. Consider the following example. When I hear music, I hear a sequence of sounds, distinguished by their pitch, timbre and duration, which are events in the physical world. A physicist can give a thorough description of these sounds as vibrations in the air, and say exactly what they are, in terms of the 'motion and rest' (to use Spinoza's terminology) of things in space. And that is what I hear, when I listen to music. But I also hear these sounds in another way, a way that is not captured by their physical description. I hear a melody, which begins on the first note, rises through an unseen dimension, and falls again. Note responds to note in this melody, as thought responds to thought in consciousness. A musical movement, through musical space, carries on through the sequence, even though no sound moves in the space described by the physicist. A critic, describing the music, is describing the very same objects as the physicist who describes the sounds; and yet he is interpreting them in mental terms, seeing the *intention* that animates the musical line and drives the melody to its logical conclusion. The music is not separate from the sounds. Rather it *is* the sounds, understood through the conceptions that we use when describing the mental life of people. And that, incidentally, is why music is so important to us: it provides a sudden insight into the soul of the world. These rare glimpses into the soul of things enable us to understand what it would be like to see the world as God sees it, and know it not as extension only, but also as thought.

KNOWLEDGE AND ERROR

To understand what Spinoza is trying to say, we must turn to his theory of knowledge. This is contained in the second part of the *Ethics*, Definition 4 of which reads as follows:

> By adequate idea I understand an idea which, in so far as it is considered in itself, without relation to an object, has all the properties, or intrinsic marks of a true idea.

And he adds by way of explanation:

> I say intrinsic in order that I may exclude what is extrinsic, i.e. the agreement of the idea with its object.

This extrinsic mark of truth had been used in Axiom 6 of the first part as a definition of truth. Every idea, understood rightly, is in exact correspondence with its object, since every idea is nothing more than a conception of its object under the attribute of thought. Hence:

> Part 2, Proposition 33: There is nothing positive in ideas, whereby they could be called false.

However, we do not always grasp the relation between an idea and its object. In sense perception and other forms of 'imagination', our ideas follow each other according to the rhythm of the body, and not according to their intrinsic logic, for 'the human mind perceives no external body as actually existing save through ideas of modifications of its body' (Part 2, Proposition 26). Spinoza gives an example:

> Part 2, Proposition 35, note: . . . when we look at the Sun we imagine that it is only some two hundred feet distant from us: which error does

not consist in that imagination alone, but in the fact that while we thus imagine it we are ignorant of the cause of this imagination . . . we do not imagine the Sun to be near because we are ignorant of the true distance, but because the modification of our body involves the essence of the Sun in so far as the body is affected by it.

My image of the Sun is the mental correlate (the idea) of a physical object. But that object is not the Sun; it is a modification of my body – a brain process, perhaps. By assigning the image to the Sun I fall into error. And this is a paradigm of falsehood, which consists 'in a privation of knowledge, resulting from inadequate or mutilated and confused ideas' (Part 2, Proposition 35).

We can obtain knowledge only through adequate ideas – ideas that guarantee their own truth. The search for such ideas has been the common goal of rationalist philosophers; and it is their common failing that they do not explain quite what an 'intrinsic' mark of truth could be. Spinoza's definition merely substitutes one mysterious term ('adequate') for another ('intrinsic'), and it is only in the course of his argument that we can gain any understanding of his meaning.

However, he does have an example: that of mathematics. The proposition that two straight lines in a plane meet at most only once is an axiom of Euclidean geometry, and seems to be self-evident: its truth is apparent, just as soon as it is understood. And when setting out a mathematical proof, we proceed from proposition to proposition by steps that can be seen to be valid by anyone who understands them. In such a proof we grasp not only the truth of the propositions involved, but also their necessity. And the result is a paradigm of 'adequate' knowledge.

Spinoza argues that God, because he contains the whole of reality, has only adequate ideas, for there is, in God, no 'privation' of knowledge. We, however, are not so lucky. We must strive to amend our thinking, so as to replace our inadequate and confused perceptions (which Spinoza assigns to 'imagination or opinion') with more adequate notions of reality. To return to our example: the Sun cannot be adequately known through modifications of our body, but only through the science which aims to provide an adequate idea of the Sun. This kind of science, proceeding by reasoned reflection from first principles, involves adequate ideas and 'common notions'. A common notion is an idea of some property that is common to everything, and 'those things which are common to all and which are equally in a part and in the whole, can only be conceived adequately' (Part 2, Proposition 38). These notions are common too in another sense: namely, that we all possess them, since we all partake of the common nature that they express. For example, we have an adequate idea of extension, since extension, which runs through all things, runs also through us. And that is why we can recognize the axioms of geometry as self-evident.

Spinoza recognizes another and yet higher level of knowledge, which he calls 'intuition' (*scientia intuitiva*) (Part 2, Proposition 40, Note 2). Intuition is the immediate insight into truth that comes when we grasp a proposition and its proof in a single act of mental attention. An intuition comes to us, he argues, only when we reason from 'an adequate idea of the formal essence of God' – in other words, when we see the exact relation between a thing and the divine substance on which it depends.

For Spinoza, therefore, there are three kinds of understanding: imagination or opinion; the kind of rational science that proceeds through common notions and adequate ideas; and intuition. Understanding of the first kind 'is the only cause of falsity', whereas 'understanding of the second and third kinds is necessarily true' (Part 2, Proposition 41). From our point of view, therefore, the truth of an idea is given in its logical connectedness to the system of adequate ideas, and not merely in its extrinsic correspondence to its object. The advance of knowledge consists in the steady replacement of our confused and inadequate perceptions with adequate ideas until, at the limit, all that we think follows from an adequate idea of the essence of God.

HUMAN NATURE

In the stark metaphysical perspective of Part 1, Spinoza's *Ethics* seems to leave little room for the human being, as a distinct part of God's creation. Whether conceived as mind or as body, I am no more than a finite mode of the divine substance; in what, then, does my individuality consist?

It is only in a problematic sense that God can be spoken of as an individual – as 'one or single' – for an individual is something bounded and finite. What place is there in Spinoza's philosophy for such a thing, or for the distinction that we normally make, between an individual and its properties?

Consider the redness of this book before me. On Spinoza's theory this is a mode of God. Why then should we ascribe the redness to the *book* and not to God, and why are we reluctant to see the book as a *property* of God, in the way that redness is a property of the book? Surely, because we see the book as an independent individual, and not just as a transient state of the divine substance in which it inheres.

There is a sense in which finite modes may be self-dependent, in

Spinoza's view, in the way that God is self-dependent. Consider a snowman. This melts away, fragments, is remade and changed and mounts no resistance. There is no real reason why we should regard such a thing as an individual in its own right, rather than as a heap of snow, which in turn is no more than a solid mass of water. By contrast there are finite modes that resist damage, fracture or melting; in some cases, they restore themselves when injured and protect themselves when threatened. They endeavour, as Spinoza puts it, to persist in their own being. This endeavour (*conatus*) is the causal principle in terms of which we explain the persistence and properties of the object that possesses it. The more *conatus* a thing has, therefore, the more it is self-dependent – the more it is 'in' itself.

The obvious examples are organisms. Consider animals: unlike stones they avoid injury, protect themselves when it is threatened, and heal themselves when it is inflicted – unless the injury is so serious as to destroy their *conatus* entirely. For this reason we attribute to animals a self-dependence and an individuality that we rarely accord to insentient things. This is borne out by our way of describing them. A stone is a *lump* of stone, a lake is a *pool* of water, a snowman is a *heap* of snow. But until dead a cat is an individual cat and not a lump of cat, and when dead it is no longer strictly a cat at all, but a lump of catflesh. The individuality and self-dependence of a cat, like those of a man, are part of its *nature*, and to divide a cat in two is to create, not two half-pieces of cat, but two whole pieces of something else. The cat endeavours to persist as *one* thing, and exists just so long as that endeavour is, in Spinoza's idiom, 'granted'. By Definition 2 of Part 2, therefore, the *conatus* of a thing is also its essence:

> Part 2, Definition 2: That pertains to the essence of a thing which, when granted, necessarily involves the granting of the thing, and which, when removed, necessarily involves the removal of the thing; or that without which the thing . . . can neither exist nor be conceived.

The endeavour of the body is also an endeavour of the mind. Conceived in mental terms, this endeavour is what we mean by will. Sometimes we refer to both body and mind in describing a creature's *conatus*, and then we speak of 'appetite'; sometimes – especially when describing people – we wish to emphasize the element of consciousness that leads them not only to have appetites, but also to be aware of them: then we use the term 'desire' (*cupiditas*) (Part 3, Proposition 9). In every case, however, we are referring to the same reality: the *conatus* that causes an organism to stand apart from its surroundings, in a persistent and active self-dependence.

There is truth in this view of our condition, for if we look at the world with the dispassionate eye of science, we discover very few genuine individuals in it. Under the impact of scientific theory, things break down into the stuff from which they are composed, which further breaks down into molecules and atoms, and finally into energy distributed in space and time – the 'motion and rest' that forms the basis of Spinoza's physics. Only organisms seem to introduce, into our world, some lasting and resistant forms of individuality, and among organisms only those with conscious life and self-understanding seem to behave in God-like ways. To such things we grant proper names, an identity through time, and a self-dependent existence. And the greater their *conatus*, the more God-like they seem, since the activity through which they endeavour to persist in their being presses them to understand and take charge of their condition. Such is our nature, and such is our place in the scheme of things.

Of course, we are apt to mislead ourselves, for 'the human mind, whenever it perceives a thing in the common order of nature, has no adequate knowledge of itself, nor of its body, nor of external bodies, but only a confused and mutilated knowledge thereof' (Part 2, Proposition 29). And from these confused perceptions many of our ordinary beliefs derive, including the belief in free will. Thus:

> Part 2, Proposition 35, note: Men are mistaken in thinking themselves free; and this opinion depends on this alone, that they are conscious of their actions and ignorant of the causes by which they are determined. This, therefore, is their idea of liberty, that they should know no causes of their actions. For when they say that human actions depend on the will, these are words of which they have no idea. For none of them know what is will and how it moves the body; those who boast otherwise and feign dwellings and habitations of the soul, provoke either laughter or disgust.

Strong stuff, and not calculated to endear Spinoza to his pious readers. But an inevitable result, nevertheless, of the theory given in Part 1, and one that presented Spinoza with his supreme challenge as a moralist – how to reconstruct the moral life, in such a way that the popular notion of freedom plays no part in it. And we can already glimpse a part of his brilliant solution. The absolute freedom defined in Part 1, Definition 7, exists in God alone. But there is another, more relative idea of freedom, suggested by the theory of *conatus*. Although only God exists by the necessity of his own nature, and all else depends on him as the all-comprehending cause, finite modes may contain the causes of their activity and persistence to a greater or lesser extent *in* themselves. Even though all causation is to be traced back to the divine essence, the chains that bind us may be either external, operating on us from outside, like the causes that affect a stone, or internal, operating in and through us, like the workings of desire. And the greater the *conatus*, the more inward the chains. By gathering our chains into ourselves, and becoming conscious of their binding force, we also rid ourselves of them, and obtain the only freedom that we can or should desire.

To understand this ingenious idea, we must briefly return to the theory of knowledge.

THE GOD'S-EYE PERSPECTIVE

All ideas exist in God, as modifications of his thinking. Some ideas exist also in the human mind. Spinoza therefore says that our ideas exist in God *in so far as* he constitutes the human mind. Conversely, since God has adequate knowledge of everything, our own ideas are adequate *in so far as* we share in the infinite intellect. This 'in so far as' is a matter of degree: the more adequate my conceptions, the more I reach beyond my finite condition to the divine substance of which I am a mode.

Now it is only in a manner of speaking that we can describe God and his attributes in temporal terms. God is eternal, which means (Part 1, Definition 8) that he is outside time and change. Hence 'things are conceived as actual in two ways – either in so far as they exist in relation to a certain time and place, or in so far as we conceive them as contained in God, and following from the necessity of the divine nature' (Part 5, Proposition 29, note). To pass from the divine to the human perspective is to pass from the timeless to time, and conversely. Although the modifications of God are understood by us as 'enduring' and as succeeding each other in time, this permeation of our knowledge by the concept of time reflects only the inadequacy of our understanding. In so far as we conceive things adequately, we understand them as flowing from God's eternal nature, by a chain of explanation that is logical in form and therefore free from time's dominion in the same way as the truths of mathematics.

Hence 'it is in the nature of reason to perceive things under a certain aspect of eternity' (Part 2, Proposition 44, corollary 2). An adequate conception of the world is a conception 'under the aspect of eternity' (*sub specie aeternitatis*); that is how God sees the world (with which he is identical), and that is how we see it, *in so far as* our minds participate in the vision that is God's.

Spinoza argues that 'the human mind has an adequate knowledge of the eternal and infinite essence of God' (Part 2, Proposition 47), for what is the *Ethics*, if not a demonstration of our ability to know God as he essentially is, and to know that, apart from God, there is nothing? By achieving adequate knowledge we come to understand what is divine and eternal. On the other hand, we understand our own nature and identity under the aspect of time – *sub specie durationis* – for it is as enduring and finite modes that we enjoy the *conatus* that distinguishes us from the self-sufficient whole of things, and to know *ourselves* as separate individual existences is to be locked in the time-bound conception that leads to confused and partial knowledge. The human condition is one of conflict: reason aspires towards the eternal totality, while the concerns of sensuous existence bind us to what is temporal and partial. The remaining three parts of the *Ethics* set out to prove that our salvation consists in seeing the world *sub specie aeternitatis*, as God sees it, and in gaining thereby freedom from the bondage of time.

ACTION AND PASSION

Part 3 of the *Ethics* deals with the 'origin and nature of the emotions'. Spinoza begins by declaring that he intends to treat this topic with the same geometrical rigour as he had deployed in his discussion of God and the mind:

> Such emotions as hatred, anger, envy, etc., considered in themselves, follow from the same necessity and force of nature as other particular things. And therefore they acknowledge certain causes through which they are understood, and have certain properties as worthy of study as the properties of any other thing the contemplation of which delights us. And so I shall treat of the nature and force of the emotions, and the power of the mind over them, by the same method by which I treated of God and the mind in previous parts, and I shall consider human actions and appetites exactly as if I were dealing with lines, planes and bodies.

The argument sets out from three definitions:

> Definition 1: I call that an adequate cause whose effect can be clearly and distinctly perceived through it. I call that one inadequate or partial whose effect cannot be understood through itself alone.

> Definition 2: I say that we act when something happens in us or outside us of which we are the adequate cause . . . On the other hand I say we

are passive when something takes place in us . . . of which we are only the partial cause.

Definition 3. By emotion (*affectus*) I understand the modifications of the body by which the power of action of the body is increased or diminished, aided or restrained, and at the same time the ideas of these modifications.

The first definition brings together two key concepts: cause and adequate idea. For Spinoza, causation is another name for explanation; the relation between cause and effect is therefore an *intellectual* relation, like the relation between premise and conclusion in a mathematical proof. The perfect (adequate) explanation is also a deduction. In such an explanation, knowledge of the effect follows from knowledge of the cause.

Spinoza then defines action and passion: I am active in respect of those things that are fully explained through my own nature, passive in relation to those that must be explained through external causes. Activity and passivity, so defined, are matters of degree.

The definition of emotion reflects Spinoza's theory of the relation between mind and body. An emotion is a bodily condition, and at the same time the idea of that condition. It is what happens in us, when our activity is increased or diminished – activity being both mental and physical.

From these beginnings, Spinoza sets out his strange and forbidding theory of the moral life – a theory that also contains some of the wisest maxims that have ever issued from the pen of a philosopher. He first argues that the mind is active in so far as it has adequate ideas, passive in so far as it has inadequate ideas (Part 3, Proposition 1). The distinction between doing things and suffering things is a distinction of degree, and, since only God is the full and originating cause of anything, only he acts without being acted upon. But we can become more God-like by ascending the ladder of knowledge, replacing our confused perceptions with the adequate ideas that bring understanding and power.

Spinoza's conception of mental activity corresponds only distantly to our ordinary idea of will and agency – ideas that he dismisses in any case as confused. But consider this example: I am pushed from behind and fall on the eggs that I am carrying, so breaking them. Here we should say, not that I broke the eggs, but that the eggs were broken, as a result of someone pushing me. The effect proceeded from an external cause. If, however, I decide to cast the eggs to the ground, it is I who am the cause of their destruction. And the more deliberate my decision, the more responsible I am. Reasoning, which gives me a clear conception of what I do, makes *me* the cause of it. And that, roughly, is what Spinoza means by action – an effect that follows from an idea that clearly conceives it.

Of course, ideas do not, in Spinoza's thinking, have physical effects. But to every idea in the mind there corresponds a modification of the body. When a physical effect is described as an action, we mean that its physical cause is the correlate of a more or less adequate idea. And the more adequate the idea, the more is the cause internal to the agent – the more does it belong to the *conatus* that defines him. In a very real sense, therefore, adequacy of ideas means power. The rational person is the one who strives always to increase his power, to change passion to action, and to secure for himself the joy, independence and serenity that are the true marks of freedom. To achieve this condition, however, is to amend our emotions – to master that in our nature which otherwise might master us.

THE EMOTIONS

Emotions result from the increase or decrease of power, and power is perfection. Joy is the passion with which we proceed to a higher perfection, sadness the passion with which we sink to a lower (Part 3, Proposition 11). Our essence is the striving (*conatus*) with which we endeavour to persist in our own being. When this striving is related only to the mind, it is called will; when referred to both mind and body, it is called appetite. Desire is appetite together with the consciousness thereof (Part 3, Proposition 9). So desire is the very essence of man. As our desires are fulfilled or frustrated, so we experience joy or sadness. But since the objects of desire are various, so too are the occasions of suffering and joy. In his account of the emotions, Spinoza tries to give a systematic theory of human desires, to show how the emotions arise from them, and to warn us against the passions that will undermine our power. This enterprise occupies him in Part 3, where he describes the various emotions, and in Part 4 – 'on human servitude, or the power of the emotions' – in which he explores the paths that we may take to liberation.

For Spinoza, mind and body move in parallel. Every change in bodily power is also a change in mental power and vice versa.

> Part 3, Proposition 11: The idea of any thing that increases or diminishes, aids or restrains, our body's power of acting, increases or diminishes, aids or restrains, our mind's power of thinking.

Thus bodily injury, which reduces our body's power of acting, has its mental parallel in pain, which reduces our power of thinking. Our emotional life stems from this close complicity of mind and body. The mind strives to imagine those things that enhance the body's power, and to blot out the images of adversity and failure (Part 3, Propositions 12 and 13). But the influence is reciprocal, and the more inadequate our understanding, the more the body and the external causes that afflict it exert their control. We become passive when our ideas follow bodily processes of which we have only a partial understanding, and this passivity is what we mean by human servitude.

Underlying Spinoza's approach are two powerful insights into the emotional life. The first is that emotions derive from our nature as embodied creatures, propelled by forces that we do not wholly understand. The second is that emotion is nevertheless a form of thought, in which a greater or lesser activity of the mind is expressed. Emotional corruption is also intellectual corruption, and the person who is led by his passions is one who has a defective knowledge of the world.

Because emotions are forms of thought, they may be changed through reasoning. We can argue with the jealous person, and show that his jealousy is mistaken, exaggerated or misplaced. Moreover, we can study emotions in their mental aspect, and discover which of them are good for us, and which of them bad. In this context 'good' means 'useful' (Part 4, Definition 1), and those emotions are useful to us which enable us to flourish according to our nature – in other words, to increase our power. It is obvious, therefore, that all passions, in so far as they are passions, should be transcended, by obtaining a more adequate idea of their object and of its linkage to oneself. But some emotions resist this act of transcendence – hatred, for example, which ceases to be hatred just as soon as it is fully understood (Part 4, Proposition 46). The same is true of all those emotions that involve a downward slope in power and perfection – all those that are forms of sadness, such as envy, jealousy, lust, rage and fear. Emotions that are forms of joy, by contrast, involve a transition from a more passive to a more active frame of mind, and therefore are in agreement with reason: love is an example. (Spinoza defines love, in the appendix to Part 3, as 'joy accompanied by the idea of an external cause'.) Hence love does not demand the same emendation as hatred. Nevertheless, 'love and desire can be excessive' (Part 4, Proposition 44), since the physical correlate of joy is pleasure; love can become fixated on this pleasure, and thereby deprive the body of its versatility and power (Part 4, Proposition 43). Even in their most powerful forms, however, the passions have no power over us that is greater than the power of reason, since 'to every action to which we are compelled by an emotion which is a passion, we can be determined by reason, without such an emotion' (Part 4, Proposition 59). In such ways Spinoza contrives to justify his preferred way of life, in which a kind of godly tranquillity overcomes the turbulence of passion, as reason brings the disordered material of emotion into line with its more adequate conceptions.

The details of Spinoza's 'geometry of the passions' lie beyond our scope. But the reader will ask, nevertheless, why any of it should be accepted. From a sceptical standpoint, Spinoza's adroit definitions and slippery proofs might seem to move too easily to a foregone conclusion, without compelling us to accept it. Ever since Plato, philosophers have advocated the ascent from the world of human passion to the serene realm of reason; yet their morality comes too pat; seems too clearly designed to justify their chosen lifestyle, derives too obviously from their remoteness from the life that they despise. And why is Spinoza any more persuasive than the rest of them? Thus Nietzsche wrote of

> the hocus-pocus in mathematical form, by means of which Spinoza has as it were clad his philosophy in mail and mask – in fact, the 'love of *his* wisdom', to translate the term fairly and squarely – in order thereby to strike terror at once into the heart of the assailant who should dare to cast a glance on that invincible maiden, that Pallas Athene . . .

And he added: 'how much of personal timidity and vulnerability does this mask of a sickly recluse betray!' (*Beyond Good and Evil*, 1, 5).

Such criticism overlooks what is most striking and original in Spinoza's vision. He does not advocate a victory of mind over body, nor does he defend the ascetic way of life. Spinoza believes that mind and body are identical, and that the health of the one is inextricably bound up with the health of the other. We are essentially embodied, desiring, striving creatures. Yet we are buffeted and bruised by things outside us, and locked with them into the system of cause and effect. In such circumstances there is only one true wisdom, which is to increase our power, and to ensure that, in so far as it is possible, the things that happen to us are also produced by us.

Philosophy consists in thought. And if Spinoza is right, thought cannot directly change the body, but only the mind. At the same time, by improving the mind, we improve the body. It is a necessary truth that the philosopher's advice must be addressed to the mind of the reader, with a view to enhancing his understanding. A philosopher is a thinker, not a gymnast. Only if the enhancement of understanding is an increase in power can the philosopher's advice be useful. If we see things rightly, however, the ascent of the ladder of reason, from confused perceptions to adequate ideas, can *only* be an increase in the power of the mind. In the mental sphere, this is what power consists in – namely, completeness of knowledge. The advice that Spinoza gives, therefore, is the only advice that ever could be given by a philosopher. And the burden of his metaphysics is to show that the advice is justified.

THE FREE MAN

Spinoza tells us that we are essentially desiring, acting creatures; but he also argues that 'a desire that arises from reason cannot be excessive' (Part 4, Proposition 61). So long as we conduct our lives by the rule of reason, therefore, we shall be living in accordance with our true nature, and achieving fulfilment.

Now it is in the nature of reason to see the world *sub specie aeternitatis* – that is, without reference to time. Reason therefore makes no distinction between past, present and future, and is as much and as little affected by present things as by things in the future or the past (Part 4, Proposition 62.) Only if we see the world *sub specie durationis* are we tempted to lose ourselves in the pursuit of present temptation. But we can have only inadequate ideas of duration and enduring things, so that, in giving way to this 'life in the present moment', we lose sight of what we are doing, and become the passive instruments of external causes.

The one who lives by the dictates of reason is the 'free man' – the person who is active rather than passive in all that involves him. The illusory idea of free will stems from inadequate and confused perceptions; rightly understood, however, freedom is not the release from necessity but the *consciousness* of necessity that comes when we see the world *sub specie aeternitatis* and ourselves as bound by its immutable laws. The free man, in Spinoza's encomium, is a lofty but cheerful character, with no traces of Calvinist gloom. He 'thinks of nothing less than of death, and his wisdom is a meditation on life, not on death' (Part 4, Proposition 67). He steadfastly pursues the good and avoids evil, is robust in overcoming dangers, and also in avoiding them, and is scrupulously honest (Part 4, Proposition 72). But he is not solitary, since 'a man who is guided by reason is more free in a state where he lives according to common decision than in solitude where he obeys himself alone' (Part 4, Proposition 73). This thought is one that Spinoza developed in more detail in his political writings. Although he had a sceptical view of the common people, and their ability to live by the dictates of reason, he nevertheless recognized the need for their company. It is true that 'a free man who lives among the ignorant strives, as far as he can, to avoid their favours' (Part 4, Proposition 70); but, as Spinoza adds, 'though men may be ignorant, they are still men, who in situations of need can bring human aid – and there is no better aid to be had' (ibid.). And although 'only free men are very grateful to one another' (Part 4, Proposition 71), free men are as much in need of political order as the ignorant, and must therefore live according to the law imposed upon them by the 'common decision'.

In his *Political Treatise*, Spinoza argues that 'the true aim of government is liberty'. By 'liberty' he means neither free will (which is metaphysically impossible) nor the kind of freedom discussed in Part 4 of the *Ethics*. He means the ability of people to pursue their projects in peace, and to entertain the opinions and ambitions that reason dictates to them, without interference from the state. His concern for political freedom arose from his suspicion of ordinary people, who are never pleased by beliefs, habits and ambitions other than their own. The art of good government is to enable such people to accept a regime in which the free man may live as his conscience directs. Spinoza is sometimes hailed as a defender of democracy. It would be better to see him as a defender of the liberal constitution, who sought to impart to the offices of government the wisdom that is usually absent from the heads of those who sit in them. Politics, for Spinoza, is the art of survival in the midst of ignorance.

Politics intrudes into the *Ethics* only glancingly. Nevertheless, it is very much in Spinoza's mind when, at the end of Part 4, he summarizes his moral conclusions in a long appendix. The following extracts will convey some of the flavour of this remarkable and uncompromising homily:

> In life . . . it is especially useful to perfect, in so far as we can, our intellect or reason, and this is man's highest happiness or blessedness – for blessedness is nothing but the contentment of mind that stems from the intuitive knowledge of God.

> No life . . . is rational without understanding, and things are good only in so far as they help man to enjoy the life of the mind . . . But those things which prevent man from perfecting his reason and enjoying a rational life – those only we call evil.

> It is, judged from the absolute perspective, permissible for everyone to do, by the highest right of nature, whatever he judges will be of advantage to him.

> Nothing is more useful to man in preserving his being and enjoying a rational life than a man who is guided by reason.

> Minds . . . are conquered not by arms, but by love and generosity.

It is especially useful to men to form associations, to bind themselves by those bonds most apt to make one people of them, and absolutely to do those things which serve to strengthen friendship.

But skill and vigilance are required for this. For men vary – there being few who live according to the rule of reason – and generally they are envious and more prone to vengeance than to compassion. So it requires a singular power of mind to deal with each according to his own understanding, and to contain oneself and refrain from imitating the emotions of those with whom one has to deal.

Although men are as a rule governed in everything by lust, yet from their common society many more advantages than disadvantages flow. Hence it is preferable to bear their wrongs with equanimity, and to be zealous for those things which produce harmony and friendship.

A purely sensual love . . . and absolutely all love that has a cause other than freedom of mind, easily passes into hate – unless (which is worse) it is a kind of madness.

In despondency there is a false appearance of morality and religion. And though despondency is the opposite of pride, yet the despondent man is very near to the proud man.

Because . . . shame is a species of sadness, it does not belong to the exercise of reason.

Apart from men we know no particular thing in nature whose mind we can enjoy, and which we can join to ourselves in friendship . . . And so whatever there is in nature apart from men, the principle of seeking our own advantage does not demand that we preserve it.

Since those things are good which assist the parts of the body to perform their function, and joy consists in the fact that man's power . . . is aided or increased, all things that bring joy are good.

Superstition, on the other hand, seems to maintain that the good is what brings sadness, and the evil what brings joy.

Human power is very limited, and infinitely surpassed by the power of external causes. So we do not have an absolute power to adapt things outside us to our use. Nevertheless, we shall bear with equanimity whatever happens to us contrary to our advantage, provided we are conscious that we have done what we ought, that the power we possess could not have been extended to avoid those things, and that we are part of the whole of nature, whose order we follow. If we understand this clearly and distinctly then that part of us which is defined by the understanding – the better part of us – will be entirely satisfied, and will strive to persevere in its satisfaction. For insofar as we understand, we can want nothing except what is necessary, nor absolutely be satisfied with anything except what is true. Hence, in so far as we understand these things rightly, the striving of the better part of us agrees with the order of the whole of nature.

THE HIGHER LIFE

The fifth part of the *Ethics*, subtitled 'On the Power of the Intellect, or on Human Freedom', is more or less entirely given over to a discussion of God, and the relation between God and man. Spinoza has already argued against the popular conception of freedom, according to which we choose always among open possibilities. The very idea of possibility stems from ignorance.

> I call . . . individual things possible in so far as, while we regard the causes by which they must be produced, we do not know whether they are determined to produce them.   (Part 4, Definition 4)

The more we know of the causality of our actions, the less room we have for ideas of possibility and contingency. However, the knowledge of causality does not cancel the belief in freedom, but vindicates it. It is the *illusory* idea of freedom, arising from imagination, that creates our bondage, for we believe in the contingency of things only in so far as our mind is passive. The more we see things as necessary (through the medium of adequate ideas), the more we increase our power over them, and so the more we are free (Part 5, Proposition 6). As we have seen, therefore, the free man is conscious of the necessities that compel him.

Such a person understands himself and his emotions, and also loves God, 'and the more so the more he understands himself and his emotions' (Part 5, Proposition 15). This love, which stems necessarily from the pursuit of knowledge, is an intellectual love (*amor intellectualis Dei*). That is to say, the mind is wholly active in loving God, and hence rejoices constantly, but without passion, in the object of its contemplation. God himself can experience neither passion, nor joy nor sorrow (Part 5, Proposition 17), and is therefore free from emotion, as we normally understand it. He neither loves the good nor hates the wicked: indeed he loves and hates no one (Part 5, Proposition 17, corollary). Hence, 'he who loves God cannot endeavour to bring it about that God should love him in return' (Part 5, Proposition 19). Love towards God is wholly disinterested, and 'cannot be polluted by an emotion either of envy or jealousy, but is cherished the more, the more we imagine men to be bound to God by this bond of love' (Part 5, Proposition 20). Indeed, man's intellectual love of God 'is the very love of God with which God loves himself' (Part 5, Proposition 36). In loving God we participate more fully in the divine intellect, and in the impersonal, universal love that reigns there, for although God cannot reciprocate our love, he nevertheless loves men, in so far as he loves himself in and through men. This eternal love constitutes our 'salvation, blessedness or liberty'.

During the course of his discussion of man's blessedness, Spinoza gives a singular proof of our immortality – or rather, of the proposition that 'the human mind cannot be absolutely destroyed with the human body, but something of it remains which is eternal' (Part 5, Proposition 23). The obscure proof of this depends upon Spinoza's view that, through adequate ideas, the mind comes to see the world *sub specie aeternitatis*, and therefore without reference to time. The essence of the mind consists in the capacity for adequate ideas. (Essence = *conatus* = activity = adequacy.) The instantiation of this essence in time (in the world of duration) cannot be explained by adequate ideas, since they contain no temporal reference. Such ideas are given 'duration' only through their attachment to the mortal body, and not intrinsically:

> Our mind therefore can be said to endure, and its existence can be defined by a certain time, only in so far as it involves the actual existence of the body, and thus far only does it have the power to determine the existence of things by time, and to conceive them under the aspect of duration.   (Part 5, Proposition 23, scholium)

We should not think of eternity as endless duration – since that is to confuse eternity with time. The eternity that we achieve through our thinking is like an escape from time to another dimension. The eternal part of us does not endure after death, but only because it does not endure in life. It comprises a vision, a point of view, a perspective outside time and change, in which we are one with God and redeemed by our knowledge of him. This blessed state is 'not the reward of virtue, but virtue itself; nor do we enjoy it because we restrain our lusts; on the contrary, because we enjoy it, we are able to restrain them' (Part 5, Proposition 42).

That – the last proposition of the *Ethics* – is Spinoza's answer to the religions of the ignorant, whose view of the after-life, as reward or punishment for behaviour here below, is an opinion 'so absurd as to be hardly worth mentioning' (Part 5, Proposition 41). Nevertheless the truth about our relation to God is both difficult and forbidding, and it is not surprising if ignorant people are unable to discover it. Hence, just as virtue is its own reward, so ignorance is its own punishment:

> not only is the ignorant man troubled in many ways by external causes, and unable ever to possess true peace of mind, but he also lives as if he knew neither himself, nor God, nor things; and as soon as he ceases to be acted upon, he ceases to be. On the other hand, the wise man, in so far as he is considered as such, is hardly troubled in spirit, but being, by a certain eternal necessity, conscious of himself, and of God, and of things, he never ceases to be, but always possesses true peace of mind.
>
> If the way I have shown to lead to these things now seems very hard, still it can be found. And of course, what is found so rarely must be hard. For if salvation were at hand, and could be found without great effort, how could nearly everyone neglect it? But all things excellent are as difficult as they are rare.

With those famous words Spinoza concludes his argument, bequeathing to posterity what is perhaps the most enigmatic book of philosophy that has ever been written.

CONCLUSION

In this brief summary, I have paid scant attention to the detail of Spinoza's proofs. Suffice it to say that their validity has ceaselessly been called in question by Spinoza's critics, who have accused him of bending the argument towards the conclusion desired. Still, how many philosophers are innocent of that failing? It would be more just to see Spinoza's quasi-geometrical proofs as bearing witness to his great elasticity and vigour of mind, and to his unparalleled gift for seeing far-reaching connections.

With the bare minimum of concepts, most of them taken or adapted from medieval and Cartesian philosophy, Spinoza undertook what has rarely been attempted, and never so boldly or arrogantly achieved: he gave a description in outline of all that there is, and a guide in detail as to how to live with it.

This is where we should take a step back from the *Ethics*, and ask ourselves what it means for *us* who think with other concepts, and in a more sceptical age. Here, I believe, is what Spinoza has to say to us:

The physical world is all that there is, and it is a system bound by laws that relate every part of it to every part. These laws can explain what we observe only if the system as a whole has an explanation – only if there is an answer to the question: why is there anything at all? But the cause of the world cannot exist outside it, for then the link between the world and its cause would be unintelligible. Nor can the cause be inside the world, for it is either a part of the world, and therefore unable to explain it, or the whole of the world, in which case the world is self-explanatory.

In other words, the world must be 'cause of itself': its existence must follow from its nature. But when we explain the world in this way, we are not engaged in ordinary science. The scientist explains one thing in terms of another, only by assuming a relation in time between them. When deducing the existence of the world, however, we are dealing with relations of logic, which are outside time and change.

We can easily see that this must be so. In the nature of the case, no scientific theory could explain why the Universe came into existence just when it did, for before that time there was nothing, and therefore nothing in terms of which this 'coming into existence' could be explained. Science, which links events in temporal chains, comes unstuck when there is no *previous* event to the one that needs explaining. Only if we step outside the temporal sphere, and see the world 'under a certain aspect of eternity' can we hope to solve the mystery of its origins.

There are cosmological theories that try to avoid this difficulty, by espousing the idea that there is no first moment – that time is a closed system, like a circle, which constantly returns to any given moment. If that is so, then no moment has any greater claim to be the beginning than any other. But even if we can make sense of this (and it is surely not obvious that we can), it leaves the crucial question unanswered: the question why such a temporal order should exist at all.

This mystery is solved only if the total system is such that it *must* exist, for only then could we have a logical argument for its existence, an argument that deduces the existence of the system without reference to time. It must exist, Spinoza argues, because there is nothing that could negate it. The total system of the world is self-dependent, and conceived through itself. Nothing that we encounter can take its existence away, since everything we encounter is a part of it, and explained through it.

The self-dependent cause of all things is what people have called God, and if this description applies to the total system of physical reality, then that is what God is. But it is not *all* that he is, for a crucial feature of our world is left out of physics: the feature of mind or consciousness. When the physicist lays down the laws of motion of the Universe, he deals in terms of space, time, matter and energy (or 'motion and rest', as Spinoza called it). And he reduces the world without remainder to those all-comprehending variables. Where you and I find thought and feeling, he finds only organisms with central nervous systems; where you and I find intention, desire and rational action, he finds only complex patterns of stimulus and response, mediated by some information-processing software. Yet we need only look into ourselves to discover that this is not all there is – that the crucial fact of consciousness, that strange transparency which veneers the world, has been left out of the physicist's account, for the simple reason that the account is, as it must be, complete without it. Everything physical has been included in his inventory, and nothing else remains.

But there is another aspect to things, and we know it from our own experience. All that the physicist describes as spatial and material can be redescribed as mental – not just you and me, but the entire world. If it were only you and I who could be described in mental terms, then mind would be a mystery, for there could be no *physical* explanation of what distinguishes us from the rest of nature (the mind being unmentionable in physics), and no *mental* explanation either. If the world contains anything mental at all, then it is mental through and through. And have we not felt from time to time that this might be so, felt, with Wordsworth,

> the sentiment of Being spread
> O'er all that moves and all that seemeth still;
> O'er all that, lost beyond the reach of thought
> And human knowledge, to the human eye
> Invisible, yet liveth to the heart;
> O'er all that leaps and runs, and shouts and sings,
> Or beats the gladsome air; o'er all that glides
> Beneath the wave, yea, in the wave itself,
> And mighty depth of waters . . . ?
> (*The Prelude*, Book 1, 401–9)

And when, a few lines later, Wordsworth describes himself as 'With God and Nature communing', we need only change 'and' to 'or' for the thought to be Spinoza's.

But if we see the world in this way – and there is no other vision that is both true to science, and true to our knowledge of ourselves – then we cannot hope to be released from natural laws, or to stand apart from the chain of causality. If we are free, then it must be in another and more elevated sense than that proclaimed in the old religions. Freedom can reside only in a *point of view*, a way of looking upon the system of necessity. And are we not all of us, in our thinking moments, familiar with what this means? Surely this is the one freedom that we may attain to: not to be released from physical reality, but to *understand* reality and ourselves as part of it, and so be reconciled to what we are. This work of reconciliation is the true religion, and it is what we owe to ourselves, and to the God from whom our being flows.

If this is so, however, Spinoza is right in thinking that we must strive to see the world under the aspect of eternity. There is no other release from the chain of causality than the kind of thinking that looks beyond causality, to the meaning and pattern of the whole. And when we discover this pattern, things change for us, as a landscape changes when the painter elicits its form, or sounds change when they are combined together as music. A kind of personality shines then through the scheme of things. We come face to face with God, in the very fact of his creation.

If religion is to be reconciled with science, it can be only in Spinoza's way. Spinoza is right in believing that God's majesty is diminished by the idea that things might have been otherwise. The belief in miracles does no credit to God, for what need has God to intervene in events that he originates? The laws of the Universe must be universally binding if we are to understand them, and the intelligibility of the Universe is the premise from which all science and all religion begin.

Nor should we disparage Spinoza's moral vision, remote though it may seem in our age of sensuous indulgence. Spinoza is right to believe that truth is our only standard, and that to live by any other is to surrender to circumstance. There is implanted in every rational being the capacity to distinguish the true from the false, to weigh evidence, and to confront our world without illusions. In this capacity our dignity resides, and in committing ourselves to truth we stand back from our immediate concerns and see the world as it should be seen – under the aspect of eternity. Truth cannot be fashionable, even if it so often offends. To take truth as our guide is to ponder time and all its minions with a sceptical disfavour.

Our age is more dominated by scientific theory than was Spinoza's; but only a fond illusion persuades us that it is more guided by the truth. We have seen superstition triumph on a scale that would have startled Spinoza, and which has been possible only because superstition has cloaked itself in the mantle of science. If the heresies of our day are, like Nazism and communism, the declared enemies of religion, this merely confirms, for the student of Spinoza, their superstitious character, and confirms, too, Spinoza's insight that scientific objectivity and divine worship are the forms of intellectual freedom. Spinoza, like Pascal, saw that the new science must inevitably 'disenchant' the world. By following truth as our standard, we chase from their ancient abodes the miraculous, the sacred and the saintly. The danger, however, is not that we follow this standard – for we have no other – but that we follow it only so far as to lose our faith, and not so far as to regain it. We rid the world of useful superstitions, without seeing it as a whole. Oppressed by its meaningless-ness, we succumb then to new and less useful illusions – superstitions born of disenchantment, which are all the more dangerous for taking man, rather than God, as their object.

The remedy, Spinoza reminds us, is not to retreat into the pre-scientific world-view, but to go further along the path of disenchantment; losing both the old superstitions and the new, we discover at last a meaning in truth itself. By the very thinking that disenchants the world we come to a new enchantment, recognizing God in everything, and loving his works in the very act of knowing them.

David Berman

BERKELEY

Experimental Philosophy

George Berkeley, it is generally agreed, was an empiricist philosopher; that is, he regarded experience as forming the basis of all human knowledge. As he classically put it in his *Principles of Human Knowledge* (1710) § 3: '*esse* is *percipi*', to be is to be perceived. My aim in this volume is to examine Berkeley's empiricism by looking closely at the specific experiences and experiments he used to understand the world and everything in it. Seeing Berkeley's work in this way has, I shall try to show, two advantages: it gives us an overview of his writings and philosophy; it also shows one way in which his philosophy may be relevant today.

Berkeley's birth (1685) and education (BA 1704) coincided with one of the radiant periods in modern experimental science, two of whose jewels were Newton's *Principia Mathematica* (1687) and *Opticks* (1704). Like many philosophers of the time, Berkeley himself was actively engaged in the new scientific developments. He was a precocious and accomplished mathematician, as can be seen from his two earliest publications, *Arithmetica* and *Miscellanea Mathematica* (1707). On the whole, however, he was critical of mathematics, which he regarded as a science of empty abstractions. And it was in his later tract, *The Analyst* (1734), that he gave eloquent expression to his criticism by pointing out a serious flaw in Newton's theory of fluxions as well as drawing theological consequences from it.

The key science for Berkeley was not mathematics – as it was for Descartes and Leibniz – but psychology, the science of experience. Indeed, Berkeley's first major work, an *Essay Towards a New Theory of Vision* (1709), is regarded as a landmark not only in philosophy but also in psychology – as 'psychology's first monograph', according to some historians.[1] However, to say that Berkeley was a pioneer psychologist is not to imply that he was the first great philosopher either to contribute to psychology or to use it for philosophical ends. Where Berkeley was exceptional was in showing how the two disciplines could be successfully brought together. It was his fruitful union of philosophy and psychology that exerted a considerable impact on nineteenth-century British philosophy, and particularly on J. S. Mill, the leading figure of the period, who regarded Berkeley as 'the one of greatest philosophical genius'.[2]

And yet this view of Berkeley as the psychological philosopher *par excellence* can be easily lost sight of, because Berkeley has also been a revered figure of the so-called revolution in twentieth-century philosophy that displaced Mill's psychological vision of philosophy, or mental science, as it was often called. This revolutionary movement went through a number of phases, including logical atomism, logical positivism and linguistic philosophy, until it finally settled into what is now called analytic philosophy, which, in common with its antecedents, is centrally concerned with language and logic, conceptual analysis and argument, and also with the negative recognition that philosophy is not mental science.[3]

Berkeley, the mental scientist, did not fit into this non-psychological, analytic picture of philosophy. Yet, fortunately for his reputation, there was that other side of his work where he shows himself to be a master of conceptual analysis and argument, as well as being sensitive to the complexity and pathology of philosophical language. The two sides of Berkeley's work can be seen in his general Introduction to the *Principles of Human Knowledge*, his *magnum opus*. As John Locke's main work, the *Essay Concerning Human Understanding* (1690), begins with a critique of innatism, so Berkeley began his with what he considers to be even more fundamental, a critique of language, especially of abstract and general words. Berkeley's main target here is Locke, who, while believing that only particular things exist in the objective world, also held that we human beings are able to form abstract and general ideas, and that these are essential for reasoning and demonstration. Berkeley quotes Locke in §12 of the Introduction to the *Principles*, but it is §13 where he offers his choicest quotation and conceptual criticism:

> To give the reader a yet clearer view of the nature of abstract ideas, and the uses they are thought necessary to, I shall add one more passage out of [Locke's] *Essay on Human Understanding*, which is as follows. '*Abstract Ideas* are not so obvious or easy to children or the yet unexercized mind as particular ones. If they seem so to grown men, it is only because by constant and familiar use they are made so. For when we nicely reflect upon them, we shall find that general ideas are fictions and contrivances of the mind, that carry difficulty with them . . . For example, does it not require some pains and skill to form the general idea of a triangle (which is yet none of the most abstract comprehensive and difficult) for it must be neither oblique nor rectangle, neither equilateral, equicrural, nor scalenon, but *all and none* of these at once. In effect, it is something imperfect that cannot exist, an idea wherein some parts of several different and *inconsistent* ideas are put together . . .' B.4. C.7. §9. [Now, comments Berkeley,] If any man has the

faculty of framing in his mind such an idea of a triangle as is here described, it is in vain to pretend to dispute him out of it, nor would I go about it. All I desire is, that the reader would fully and certainly inform himself whether he has such an idea or no. And this, methinks, can be no hard task for anyone to perform. What more easy than for anyone to look a little into his own thoughts, and there try whether he has, or can attain to have, an idea that shall correspond with the description that is here given of the general idea of a triangle, which is, *neither oblique, nor rectangle, equilateral, equicrural, nor scalenon, but all and none of these at once?*   (§13)

Berkeley's confidence that no one will be able to discover such an idea has two sources: (1) experience and (2) its flawed linguistic or conceptual character. It is the second of these which comes to the fore in §13, where Berkeley reveals the weakness in Locke's position, a weakness that we can easily see – once a Berkeley, like Sherlock Holmes, has pointed it out. When Dr Watson expresses astonishment at Sherlock Holmes's perspicacity, Holmes is famous for saying, 'Elementary, my dear Watson.' And Berkeley says something similar (in a somewhat different context) when he spoke of 'the obvious tho' Amazing truth . . . tis no Witchcraft to see.' (PC, no. 279). Berkeley calls our attention to the obvious flaw in Locke's description of abstract ideas by simply italicizing its key phrases, such as 'all and none' and 'inconsistent'. Earlier, in the *New Theory of Vision*, he had driven this conceptual point home less gently when he asserted that 'the above-mentioned idea of a triangle', as described by Locke, 'is made up of manifest, staring contradictions' (§125). Yet even here, Berkeley has not abandoned his psychological approach, since he says in §125 that he has made 'reiterated endeavours to apprehend the general idea'; and that the reader must 'look into his own thoughts' to see whether he can attain the idea described by Locke.

But there is a problem here: why should Berkeley repeatedly try to apprehend 'something' which he has shown to be self-contradictory? For surely that which is self-contradictory cannot exist. The answer, I think, is that Berkeley believes that language is so flawed that it cannot be relied upon, not even when it appears to be revealing a contradiction. What can be trusted is experience, whether inner or outer. So the only reliable test for determining whether an abstract idea of triangle, or any abstract idea, exists is to try to experience it by introspection.

That Berkeley's main argument against Locke is psychological or empirical, rather than linguistic or conceptual, can also be seen in §10 of the Introduction, where he writes:

Whether others have this wonderful faculty of abstracting their ideas, they best can tell: for myself I find indeed I have a faculty of imagining, or representing to myself the ideas of those particular things I have perceived and of variously compounding and dividing them. I can imagine a man with two heads or the upper parts of a man joined to the body of a horse. I can consider the hand, the eye, the nose, each by itself abstracted or separated from the rest of the body. But then whatever hand or eye I imagine, it must have some particular shape and colour. Likewise the idea of man that I frame to myself, must be either of a white, or a black, or a tawny, straight, or crooked, a tall, or a low, or a middle-sized man. I cannot by any effort of thought conceive the abstract idea above described. And it is equally impossible for me to form the abstract idea of motion distinct from the body moving, and which is neither swift nor slow, curvilinear nor rectilinear; and the like may be said of all the other abstract general ideas whatsoever. . . And there are grounds to think most men will acknowledge themselves to be in my case. The generality of men which are simple and illiterate never pretend to abstract notions   (§10)

Here we have Berkeley drawing mainly on his own experiences (or lack of them), but also on the (implicit) testimonies of most men. Further on, in §14, the empirical evidence Berkeley uses against the Lockean position is exclusively of the latter kind. Here his argument has two phases. In the first he draws attention to the fact that for most people talking is 'easy and familiar'. The second starts from the conscious awareness and memory of most adults and then moves to the observation of children:

Much is . . . said of the difficulty that abstract ideas carry with them, and the pains and skill requisite to the forming them. And it is on all hands agreed that there is need of great toil and labour of the mind, to emancipate our thoughts from particular objects, and raise them to those sublime speculations that are conversant about abstract ideas. From all which the natural consequence should seem to be, that so difficult a thing as the forming abstract ideas was not necessary for *communication* which is so easy and familiar to all sorts of men. But we are told, if they seem obvious and easy to grown men, *It is only because by constant and familiar use they are made so.* Now I would fain know at what time it is, men are employed in surmounting that difficulty, and furnishing themselves with necessary helps for discourse. It cannot be when they are grown up, for then it seems they are not conscious of any such pains-taking; it remains therefore to be the business of their childhood. And surely, the great and multiplied labour of framing abstract notions, will be found a hard task for that tender age. Is it not a hard thing to imagine that a couple of children cannot prate together, of their sugar plumbs and rattles and the rest of their little trinkets, till they have first tacked together numberless inconsistencies, and so framed in their minds *abstract general ideas*, and annexed them to every common name they make use of?   (§14)

However, the empirical data on which Berkeley mainly draws are his own subjective, first-person, introspective observations. As he bluntly puts it in a 1730 letter written in America: 'I cannot find I have any such [abstract] idea, and this is my reason against it.' (*Works* II, 293). For short, I call this Berkeley's subjective empiricism.

Subjective empiricism needs to be distinguished from objective empiricism, even though Berkeley makes abundant use of both in his work, and the difference for him is largely one of degree rather than kind. Thus for Berkeley, both what we perceive by our senses and what we perceive by looking inwards in our imagination and memory are all ideas; the former are simply more forceful, vivid, orderly and less subject to our wills, than the latter. Hence all experiences and experiments are essentially psychological: the former constitute the realm of objective empiricism, the latter that of subjective empiricism. However, objective empiricism does have another feature which is somewhat more problematic for Berkeley the idealist, but of which he nonetheless wishes to avail, namely, that it includes what other minds say they experience.

So while §10 is mainly in the realm of subjective empiricism, concerned with Berkeley's own introspective findings, §14 is almost exclusively objective, since it is based on the fact that most adults and children appear to use language in an easy way, and that adults do not report having gone through a painful period in their acquisition of abstract language and knowledge.

The empirical evidence that Berkeley assembles in §14 is not very specific. But this is not characteristic of his objective empiricism. Thus in *Alciphron, or the Minute Philosopher* (1732), his main defence of religion, Berkeley makes an appeal to experience that is both more specific and public. It is a counter-factual argument, aimed at defending the Mosaic or biblical chronology: that the world and human beings were created by God about 6,000 years ago. For, Berkeley argues, if people had been in the world for a significantly greater time – as some freethinkers claimed – then we should find durable objects, such as gems, utensils and medals, buried deep in the ground. But since no one, Berkeley maintains, has found such items, it follows that the world is most unlikely to be older than that calculated by Moses (Alc. VI. 23). Of course, Berkeley has been proved factually wrong, but not wrong in his empiricist method-ology. He was in this instance – and this is not untypical – wrong for the right reasons, which may well be better than being right for the wrong reasons.

Berkeley's objective empiricism comes out in a more positive manner in the *Theory of Vision Vindicated* (1733), where he quotes from William Cheselden's 1728 account of a boy who was blind from infancy, but was enabled to see by the surgical removal of cataracts. Thus

> Before I conclude, [Berkeley writes] it may not be amiss to add the following extract from the *Philosophical Transactions* [no. 402, 1728], relating to a person blind from his infancy, and long after made to see: 'When he [the boy] first saw, he was so far from making any judgement about distances that he thought all objects whatever touched his eyes (as he expressed it) as what he felt did his skin . . . He knew not the shape of any thing, nor any one thing from another, however different in shape or magnitude: but upon being told what things were, whose form he before knew from feeling, he would carefully observe that he might know them again: but having too many objects to learn at once, he forgot many of them: And (as he said) at first he learned to know, and again forgot, a thousand things in a day. Several weeks after he was couched, being deceived by pictures, he asked which was the lying sense, feeling or seeing? . . . The room he was in, he said, he knew to be but part of the house, yet he could not conceive that the whole house could look bigger. . .' Thus [Berkeley concludes], by fact and experiment, those points of the theory which seem the most remote from common apprehension were not a little confirmed, many years after I had been led into the discovery of them by reasoning.   (§71)

Berkeley takes this testimony as providing factual and experimental vindication of the main thesis of his *New Theory of Vision*, that what we see is entirely different from what we touch. So Berkeley is using publicly accessible material, the testimony of the boy as communicated by Cheselden; although it is based on the experiences of the boy. Berkeley first mentioned Cheselden's corroboration in the second edition of *Alciphron*, where he noted that the 'paradoxes' of his *New Theory of Vision* were 'first received with great ridicule', but were 'surprisingly confirmed by a case of a person made to see who had been blind from his birth. See "Philos. Transact." number 402' (*Works* III, 161). On a small but significant point of accuracy, it will be noticed that Berkeley made one change from *Alciphron* to the *Theory of Vision Vindicated* in his description of the case, that is, he changed 'blind from his birth' to 'blind from his infancy'. Here he was bringing himself into line with Cheselden, although possibly weakening the force of his claim.

The objective empiricism shown in the quotation from Cheselden is not in any way unusual for Berkeley. For although he is best known for his theoretical reasoning and thought experiments, contained in his three famous philosophical works of 1709–13, his lesser-known works are pervaded by physical observations. Thus his first extant composition, the essay on the Cave of Dunmore (*Works* IV, 257–64) was a detailed description of a large cave in the vicinity of Kilkenny, where he attended school. Berkeley explored the cave about 1699 while a schoolboy, but he did not write up his account until 1706, when at university in Dublin – which suggests, given the essay's accurate detail, that he had a considerable capacity for vivid visual recollection, perhaps even for eidetic imagery and memory.

Berkeley's interest in external empirical observation is shown, too, in his first-hand observations and description of an eruption of Mt Vesuvius, published in 1717 in the *Philosophical Transactions*, and his description of tarantulas in Italy, recorded in his 1717 travel notebooks. This aspect of Berkeley impressed some of his friends. Thus Thomas Blackwell, who knew Berkeley in Italy, wrote of him: 'He travelled through a great part of Sicily on foot, clambered over the mountains and crept into the caverns to investigate into its natural history, and discover the causes of its volcanoes; and I have known him sit for hours in forges and founderies to inspect their successive operations.'[4]

Berkeley's *Querist* (1735–7), his main work in economic theory, also contains considerable description of economic practices, particularly in Ireland. Yet here he goes further than natural history. In *Querist*, nos 46–7, he proposes the following thought experiment, with the aim of determining what basic economic forms of life will develop if sailors were marooned on an island:

46 Whether, in order to understand the true nature of wealth and commerce, it would not be right to consider a ship's crew cast upon a desert island, and by degrees forming themselves to business and civil life, while industry begot credit, and credit moved to industry?

47 Whether such men would not all set themselves to work? Whether they would not subsist by the mutual participation of each other's industry? Whether, when one man had in his way procured more than he could consume, he would not exchange his superfluities to supply his wants? Whether this must not produce credit? Whether, to facilitate these conveyances, to record, and circulate this credit, they would not soon agree on certain tallies, tokens, tickets, or counters?

(*Works* VI, 108–9)

But Berkeley's objective empiricism is most abundantly displayed in *Siris: A Chain of Philosophical Reflexions on Tar-Water* (1744), his last major work, written when he was Bishop of Cloyne in Ireland. Here, and in his subsequent writings on tar-water, he defends tar-water as a valuable, if not universal, medicine. To this end, he carefully describes tar in its various forms, the making of tar-water, his experiments with it and especially the physical effects that intensive drinking of tar-water had on himself, his family, neighbours, patients, and others who took tar-water at his recommendation.

In one of his later tar-water writings, the first *Letter to Thomas Prior on Tar-water* (1744), Berkeley also describes in some detail his empiricist methodology in his investigation of tar-water. In the beginning, he says, he started out with mere hearsay information about the medicinal value of tar (§14); from which he made some preliminary trials (§15), which, because they were successful, encouraged him to theorize about tar (§§15–17), which helped him to arrange more refined tests (§18). Now that he had a clear understanding of the medicine he believed was valuable, he 'tried many experiments' (§19), 'in many various and unlike cases' (§20). And it was on the basis of these experiments, rather than any theory, he says, that 'is founded my opinion of the salutary virtues of tar-water; which virtues are recommended from, and depend on, experiments and matters of fact, and neither stand nor fall with any theories or speculative principles whatsoever'. (§20)

Berkeley continued to be interested in the factual evidence for tar-water, as is shown in his last published essay, 'Farther Thoughts on Tar-water', which appeared in his *Miscellany* (1752), published a year before his death. Like his first extant essay of 1706, on the Dunmore cave, the 1752 essay is almost entirely given over to natural history description – in this case the successful cures brought about by tar-water. Berkeley also put forward here what may be one of the earliest proposals for a controlled medical experiment, to test tar-water's efficacy with smallpox:

The experiment may be easily made if an equal number of poor patients in the small-pox were put into two hospitals at the same time of the year, and provided with the same necessaries of diet and lodging; and, for further care, let the one have a tub of tar-water and an old woman, the other hospital, what attendance and drugs you please.

(*Works* V, 210)

The importance of physical experiment and observation is also evident in Berkeley's solution to the moon illusion in the *New Theory of Vision*.

Why, in short, does the moon always appear larger on the horizon than it does in the meridian? Here we move away from natural science and back closer to philosophy. In this case, too, it is not a matter of many observations, but of seeing the significance of one familiar but crucial one. For while many notable thinkers, beginning with Ptolemy and including Descartes, Gassendi and Hobbes, had tried to solve the illusion, none of them before Berkeley had seemed to notice that the moon seen on the horizon was not merely enlarged, but that it varied considerably in size, sometimes appearing as enormous. This observation proved, according to Berkeley, that most of the earlier solutions could not be correct or entirely correct, since they supposed a constant, invariable cause, as in the case of Ptolemy's solution, more recently restated in 1688 by John Wallis, that it was the intervening land or sea mass on the horizon that made the moon look large and hence produced the illusion. But if Ptolemy and Wallis were right, then 'the moon appearing in the very same situation' (NTV, §77) should always be the same size – but it isn't.

Berkeley's own solution was, in the first instance, that it was the presence of more atmosphere or vapours on the surface of the earth that explains the illusion and its fluctuations. By diffusing the light coming from the moon, the atmosphere or vapours makes the moon appear fainter which, as a cue for size, makes the moon seem large to an observer. Since the presence of vapours is something that is intermittent and varies in intensity, it is able to explain the variation in the illusion (§68). However, in the final analysis, Berkeley thought it was a contextual or gestaltist matter, comparing it with the way the meaning of a word is often determined by its context:

> Now, it is known a word pronounced with certain circumstances, or in a certain context with other words, hath not always the same import and signification that it hath when pronounced in some other circumstances or different context of words. [So] The very same visible appearance as to faintness and all other respects, if placed on high, shall not suggest the same magnitude that it would if it were seen at an equal distance on a level with the eye. (NTV, §73)

Berkeley also employs experiments to show that the previous solutions, such as those offered by Descartes and Ptolemy/Wallis, are incorrect. Thus if one blocks out surrounding objects, such as trees and chimneys (crucial in Descartes' solution), or the intervening land or sea mass (as in the Ptolemy/Wallis solution), by seeing the horizontal moon through a cylinder or over a wall, the illusion, Berkeley says, nonetheless persists.

Hence these factors cannot be responsible for the illusion. But there is a problem with these blocking out experiments, namely that according to recent psychological findings, the illusion does *not* persist. Berkeley himself seems to have recognized this, although reluctantly, since he tends to qualify the experiments and his conclusions in subsequent editions of the *New Theory of Vision*; indeed, he entirely omits the cylinder experiment in later editions, although unlike his correction in the *Theory of Vision Vindicated* (see above), he never fully withdrew his initial (probably mistaken) claim – a claim to which he was probably led by William Molyneux.[5]

Berkeley also uses some partly physical experiments in his *Principles* and *Three Dialogues between Hylas and Philonous* (1713) to support his idealism – that physical objects and their properties do not exist externally, but only in the mind. Thus he notes that if one puts one hand in a hot and the other in a cold place, then plunges both in luke warm water, the water will feel cold to one hand, hot to the other, which seems show that the water in itself is neither hot nor cold (*Works* II, 178–9). Yet in *Principles*, §§14 and 15, where Berkeley first mentions these relativity experiments, he makes it entirely clear that 'this method of arguing', which was used by Locke and other advanced thinkers to prove the mind-dependence of secondary qualities, such as warmth and coldness, odours and tastes, 'doth not so much prove that there is no extension or colour in an outward object, as that we do not know by sense which is the true extension or colour of the object' (§15).

However, in the *Three Dialogues* Berkeley introduces an experiment that is neither sceptical nor relativistic and does show, according to him, that heat (and also cold, tastes and odours) is mind-dependent, and not in the outward object. When you feel something very hot, for example a fire, it feels painful; both the extreme heat and the pain 'are immediately perceived at the same time, and the fire affects you only with one simple, or uncompounded idea'. Therefore, since you cannot separate the pain from the extreme heat, the heat must exist – as the pain does – in the mind (*Works* II, 176). And this, Berkeley shows, can be applied equally to all degrees of heat – since a moderate warmth feels pleasurable, which is a subjective state – and also to cold and, *mutatis mutandis*, to tastes and odours.

The form of this experimental argument – that x (extreme heat) cannot be divided or subtracted from y (pain) – is also used even more generally by Berkeley in his more ambitious thought experiment in *Principles*, §10: '. . . I desire anyone to reflect and try, whether he can by any abstraction of thought, conceive the extension and motion of a body, without all other sensible qualities. For my own part, I see evidently that it is not in my power to frame an idea of a body extended and moved, but I must withal give it some colour or other sensible quality which is acknowledged to exist only in the mind.' Because one cannot perceive or conceive a body without some sensible or secondary quality, such as colour, that body must exist in the mind, along with the secondary quality.

In the *New Theory of Vision*, §43, Berkeley shows in detail how it is impossible to separate colour from an extended object. 'I appeal', he says,

> to any man's experience, whether the visible extension of any object doth not appear as near to him as the colour of that object; nay, whether they do not both seem to be in the very same place. Is not the extension we see coloured, and is it possible for us, so much as in thought, to separate and abstract colour from extension? Now, where the extension is there surely is the figure, and there the motion too.

Against Berkeley, it is sometimes asserted that sighted persons can perceive an extended yet non-coloured thing, such as glass; although it is not clear how they would know the glass was there. It has also been suggested by Jonathan Bennett that Berkeley and Hume were wrong, that a blind person can perceive or conceive an extended object without colour.[6] But this criticism overlooks Berkeley's phrase 'or other sensible quality' (PHK, §10), which, although he does not elucidate, almost certainly means sensible qualities such as smooth, rough, heat, cold, and feelings of pressure and resistance. The question will then be: can a blind person frame an idea of extended tangible body without one of these mind-dependent qualities?

Whereas the two previous experiments are about the impossibility of subtracting x from y, the following from *New Theory of Vision*, §131, is about the impossibility of adding x and y:

> ... it is, I think, an axiom universally received that quantities of the same kind may be added together and make one entire sum. Mathematicians add lines together: but they do not add a line to a solid, or conceive it as making one sum with a surface: these three kinds of quantity being thought incapable of any such mutual addition, and consequently of being compared together in the several ways of proportion, as by them esteemed intirely disparate and heterogeneous. Now let any one try in his thoughts to add a visible line or surface to a tangible line or surface, so as to conceive them making one continued sum or whole. He that can do this may think them homogeneous: but he that cannot, must by the foregoing axiom think them heterogeneous: A blue and a red line I can conceive added together into one sum and

making one continued line: but to make in my thoughts one continued line of a visible and tangible line added together is, I find, a task far more difficult, and even insurmountable: and I leave it to the reflexion and experience of every particular person to determine for himself.

Here and in the previous experiment we are moving further from the objective to the subjective, that is, from physical to thought experiments.

Probably Berkeley's most famous (and contentious) thought experiment is summed up in the challenge: try to think of an object existing unperceived. This is sometimes called his master argument for his immaterialism, and is to be found in the *Principles*, §22–3:

... It is but looking into your own thoughts, and so, trying whether you can conceive it possible for a sound, or figure, or motion, or colour, to exist without the mind or unperceived. This easy trial may make you see, that what you contend for is downright contradiction. Insomuch that I am content to put the whole upon this issue; if you can but conceive it possible for one extended moveable substance, or in general, for any one idea or anything like an idea, to exist otherwise than in a mind perceiving it, I shall readily give up the cause ... I shall grant you its existence, though you cannot either give me any reason why you believe it exists, or assign any use to it when it is supposed to exist ...
23 But say you, surely there is nothing easier than to imagine trees, for instance, in a park or books existing in a closet, and nobody by to perceive them. I answer, you may so, there is no difficulty in it: but what is all this, I beseech you, more than framing in your mind certain ideas which you call books and trees, and at the same time omitting to frame the idea of anyone that may perceive them? But do not you yourself perceive or think of them all the while? This therefore is nothing to the purpose: it only shows you have the power of imagining or forming ideas in your mind; but it doth not shew that you can conceive it possible, the objects of your thought may exist without the mind: to make out this it is necessary that you conceive them existing unconceived or unthought of, which is a manifest repugnancy. When we do our utmost to conceive the existence of external bodies, we are all the while only contemplating our own ideas. But the mind taking no notice of itself, is deluded to think it can and doth conceive bodies existing unthought of or without the mind; though at the same time they are apprehended by or exist in itself.

This is Berkeley's more usual mode of experiment: division; try to divide your perception of a body (x) from that body itself (y). Berkeley sometimes states this as a conceptual point – a body unperceived or unthought of is contradictory – but more usually as an experimental one: *try* separating x and y. As he says in *Principles*, §6: 'To be convinced of which, the reader need only reflect and try to separate in his own thoughts the being of a sensible thing from its being perceived.' Here we are back to the 'obvious tho' amazing truth', for §6 begins:

Some truths there are so near and obvious to the mind, that a man need only open his eyes to see them. Such I take this important one to be, to wit ... that all the bodies which compose the mighty frame of the world, have not any subsistence without a mind, that their being is to be perceived or known ...

A version of the above (master) argument is used for a more limited purpose by Berkeley in *De Motu* (1721), his chief work in the philosophy of science. Here he says that the idea of one body moving in absolute, empty space is a fiction that is given illegitimate credence by the fact that we project our own body into such a scenario without recognizing it.

We are sometimes deceived by the fact that when we imagine the removal of all other bodies, yet we suppose our own body to remain. On this supposition we imagine the movement of our limbs fully free on every side ... no motion can be understood without some determination or direction, which in turn cannot be understood unless besides the body in motion our own body also, or some other body, be understood to exist at the same time ... So that if we suppose the other bodies were annihilated and, for example, a globe were to exist alone, no motion could be conceived in it ...   (§§55, 58)

So once again, x cannot be perceived or understood by itself (divided from y); hence it does not exist. Yet here Berkeley is also trying to help us appreciate why we are mistakenly inclined to believe that one body can move in absolute space, by providing a genetic explanation for our false belief: that we unknowingly smuggle in our own body.

In *Principles*, §§18 and 20, he offers another thought experiment, but unlike most of those we have considered, it is aimed not at proving that something does not exist; nor is it genetic or therapeutic as in the above statement from *De Motu*; rather it is designed to help us appreciate the feasibility of his immaterialism, by showing us how it might be possible.

For ... it is granted on all hands (and what happens in dreams, phrensies, and the like puts it beyond dispute) that it is possible we might be affected with all the ideas we have now, though no bodies existed without, resembling them ... In short, if there were external bodies, it is impossible we should ever come to know it; and if there were not, we might have the very same reasons to think there were that we have now. Suppose, what no one can deny possible, an intelligence, without the help of external bodies to be affected with the same train of sensations or ideas that you are, imprinted in the same order and with like vividness in his mind. I ask whether that intelligence hath not all the reason to believe the existence of corporeal substances, represented by his ideas, and exciting them in his mind, that you can possibly have for believing the same thing? ...   (PHK, §§18, 20)

Indeed, this thought experiment should probably have more impact at the present time, given developments in computer-generated experiences, than in Berkeley's day, since what he is suggesting is basically what is now called virtual reality. Thus anyone who wishes to see how flat patches or points of colour can appear to be three-dimensional, need only look at one of the ingenious, computer-generated stereograms.[7]

Another experiment used by Berkeley which goes further than that in *Principles*, §§18 and 20, but cannot be regarded as an experiment of proof or disproof (as are those in §§ 10 or 22–3), is the problem of the blind man made to see, the Molyneux problem. Although it was William Molyneux and not Berkeley who devised it, and although it was first printed by Locke in his *Essay* II.IX.8, it was Berkeley who uses it most effectively. (This may be said about most of his experiments, that although he did not devise them, he usually makes more interesting philosophical use of them than the devisers.) Indeed it is possible that it was the Molyneux problem that inspired Berkeley's interest in thought experiments. He touches on it again and again in his *New Theory of Vision* (and also in the PCs), but it is quoted and examined in detail in §§ 132–3, 135:

132 A farther confirmation of our tenet may be drawn from the solution of Mr Molyneux's problem, published by Mr Locke in his *Essay*: Which I shall set down as it there lies, together with Mr. Locke's opinion of it, ' "Suppose a man born blind, and now adult, and taught by his touch to distinguish between a cube and a sphere of the same metal, and nighly of the same bigness, so as to tell, when he felt one and t'other, which the cube and which the sphere. Suppose then the cube and sphere placed on a table, and the blind man to be made to see:

Quaere, Whether by his sight, before he touched them, he could now distinguish and tell which is the globe, which is the cube?" To which the acute and judicious proposer [Molyneux] answers: "Not. For though he has obtained the experience of how a globe, how a cube, affects his touch, yet he has not yet attained the experience that what affects his touch so or so must affect his sight so or so: Or that a protuberant angle in the cube that pressed his hand unequally shall appear to his eye as it doth in the cube." I agree with this thinking gentleman, whom I am proud to call my friend, in this answer to this his problem; and am of opinion that the blind man at first sight would not be able with certainty to say which was the globe which the cube, whilst he only saw them.' (*Essay* . . . B. ii. C. 9 §8).

133   Now, [comments Berkeley] if a square surface perceived by touch be of the same sort with a square surface perceived by sight, it is certain the blind man here mentioned might know a square surface as soon as he saw it: it is no more but introducing into his mind by a new inlet an idea he has been already well acquainted with. . . . We must therefore allow either that visible extension and figures are specifically distinct from tangible extension and figures, or else that the solution of this problem given by those two thoughtful and ingenious men [Locke and Molyneux] is wrong.

135   . . . In short, the ideas of sight are all new perceptions, to which there be no names annexed in his mind: he cannot therefore understand what is said to him concerning them: And to ask of the two bodies he saw placed on the table which was the sphere, which the cube? were to him a question downright bantering and unintelligible; nothing he sees being able to suggest to his thoughts the idea of body, distance, or in general of any thing he had already known.

So Berkeley takes his chief tenet to be confirmed, if the 'ingenious' Molyneux and Locke are right that the blind man made to see will not be able to identify the sphere and cube. Yet Berkeley also makes a conceptual point, that Locke's negative answer is inconsistent with his own theory that there are ideas (such as shape) common to what we see and touch.

As we have seen, Berkeley was delighted to be able to draw not merely testimonial but experimental confirmation of his tenet and his negative solution to Molyneux's problem from Cheselden's 1728 account of the boy couched for cataracts. And it was probably his wish to see Cheselden's case as corroborating his solution that initially made him misdescribe the boy as being blind from birth (in line with Molyneux's formulation) rather than infancy. Undoubtedly, Cheselden's patient supports a negative answer. He also probably supports Berkeley's more radical claim, or prediction, that not only will a newly sighted person be unable to distinguish by sight a cube from a sphere, but he will regard the question as unintelligible. For 'When he [the boy] first saw . . . he could *form no judgement* of their [visual objects'] shape . . .' (TVV, § 71, my italics).

Berkeley also uses Molyneux's problem more generally to make us appreciate the world from the perspective of the blind person made to see. And it may have been in this context that Berkeley was eventually able to make the *observation* that, although the question: 'Which is the sphere and which the cube?' will be 'unintelligible' to the newly sighted man, it may still be meaningful in a wider pragmatic sense. For in the *New Theory of Vision*, §148 Berkeley has this related thought experiment:

> Suppose one who had always continued blind be told by his guide that after he has advanced so many steps he shall come to the brink of a precipice, or be stopped by a wall; must not this to him seem very admirable and surprizing? He cannot conceive how it is possible for mortals to frame such predictions as these, which to him would seem as strange and unaccountable as prophesy doth to others. Even they who are blessed with the visive faculty may (though familiarity make it less observed) find therein sufficient cause of admiration. The wonderful art and contrivance wherewith it is adjusted to those ends and purposes for which it was apparently designed, . . . may, . . . give us some glimmering, analogous praenotion of things which are placed beyond the certain discovery and comprehension of our present state.

Here a blind person is told about visual things which he cannot conceive; therefore such words must be unintelligible or cognitively empty for him. And yet, by virtue of the experimental proof offered by his 'guide', he is able to accept that there are visual things and be full of admiration. Berkeley then suggests that this can help us to gain some notion of religious mysteries. Now consider an important entry from his notebooks, the *Philosophical Commentaries* (*c.* 1706–7), no. 720, where he speaks of a 'popish peasant' who can derive much edification from his Latin mass even though he does not understand it. For when it is a matter of words relating to Revelation and mystery, Berkeley says,

> an Humble Implicit faith becomes us just (where we cannot compre-hend & understand the proposition) such as a popish peasant gives to propositions he hears at Mass in Latin. This proud men call blind, popish, implicit, irrational. For my part I think it more irrational to

pretend to dispute at cavil & ridicule holy mysteries ... that are altogether ... above our knowedge out of our reach.

In short, Berkeley was, as I have elsewhere argued, on the verge here of his revolutionary non-cognitive, emotive theory of meaning: that words may be meaningful, even if they do not inform, provided they evoke appropriate emotions, attitudes or actions.[8]

In his use of the Molyneux problem and the thought experiment in §148 Berkeley is asking us to stretch our thinking. But it is at the end of the *New Theory of Vision* that he makes an even greater demand on our philosophical empathy. Here, conversely, we are asked to put ourselves in the position not of a blind person but of an unbodied mind that has *only* sight. As this is crucial for Berkeley's experimental approach, I quote it at length.

> ... consider the case of an intelligence, or unbodied spirit, which is supposed to see perfectly well, i.e. to have a clear perception of the proper and immediate objects of sight, but to have no sense of touch. Whether there be any such being in nature or no is beside my purpose to inquire. It sufficeth that the supposition contains no contradiction in it. Let us now examine what proficiency such a one may be able to make in geometry ...
>
> 154   First, then, it is certain the aforesaid intelligence could have no idea of a solid, or quantity of three dimensions, which followeth from its not having any idea of distance. We indeed are prone to think that we have by sight the ideas of space and solids, which ariseth from our imagining that we do, strictly speaking, see distance and some parts of an object at a greater distance than others; which have been demonstrated to be the effect of the experience we have had, what ideas of touch are connected with such and such ideas attending vision: but the intelligence here spoken of is supposed to have no experience of touch ... Whence it is plain he can have no notion of those parts of geometry which relate to the mensuration of solids ...
>
> 155   ... Nor it is an easier matter for him to conceive the placing of one plain or angle on another, in order to prove their equality: Since that supposeth some idea of distance or external space. All which makes it evident our pure intelligence could never attain to know so much as the first elements of plain geometry ...
>
> 156   All that is properly perceived by the visive faculty amounts to no more than colours, with their variations and different proportions of light and shade: But the perpetual mutability and fleetingness of those

immediate objects of sight render them incapable of being managed after the manner of geometrical figures . . .

157 I must confess men are tempted to think that flat or plain figures are immediate objects of sight, though they acknowledge solids are not. And this opinion is grounded on what is observed in painting, wherein (it seems) the ideas immediately imprinted on the mind are only of plains variously coloured, which by a sudden act of the judgement are turned into solids: But with a little attention we shall find the plains here mentioned as the immediate objects of sight are not visible but tangible plains. For when we say that pictures are plains, we mean thereby that they appear to the touch smooth and uniform. But then this smoothness and uniformity, or, in other words, this plainess of the picture, is not perceived immediately by vision: For it appeareth to the eye various and multiform.

159 . . . it is, indeed no easy matter for us to enter precisely into the thoughts of such an [unbodied sighted] intelligence, because we cannot without great pains cleverly separate and disentangle in our thoughts the proper objects of sight from those of touch which are connected with them. This, indeed, in a compleat degree seems scarce possible to be performed: Which will not seem strange to us if we consider how hard it is for anyone to hear the words of his native language pronounced in his ears without understanding them. Though he endeavour to disunite the meaning from the sound, it will nevertheless intrude into his thoughts, and he shall find it extreme difficult, if not impossible, to put himself exactly in the posture of a foreigner that never learned the language, so as to be affected barely with the sound themselves, and not perceive the signification annexed to them.

Berkeley's initial, specific use of this psychological experiment is to determine whether the object of geometry is visual or tangible, but he then employs it to determine what we immediately and directly see. The Molyneux problem is another, somewhat narrower way of attempting to understand this; trying to imagine what a newborn infant sees would be still another way. Berkeley's thesis is that what the disembodied sighted mind would see is a visual field of mutable coloured points. There is no visual object that undergoes alterations or changes in shape, size, colour, etc., hence the sighted mind could have no notion of visual shape or size. Put in another way: there would be no shape or size constants for such a perceiver. We think we have them when we see, because our visual experiences have been frequently associated and connected with tangible ones. As a consequence, when we see something we imagine it to be tangible. Really, what we immediately see is as sizeless and shapeless as what the sighted mind sees; it is only a flux of light or colour points.

Within Berkeley's metaphysics this insight can be expressed in this way: what the sighted mind sees (and what we *immediately* see) is non-representational, non-linguistic, because for Berkeley (normal) vision is a language whereby God tells us about the tangible world. But prior to having experience of the tangible world, the visual language would be as meaningless as an utterly alien language. It would convey no meaning to the sighted mind. It is hard for us to appreciate this, Berkeley observes, because having learned the visual language, a powerful synesthesia, as it has come to be called, develops between the visual and tangible such that the visible object seems, or is imagined, to be tangible. Hence we believe that there is a necessary connection between what we see and touch, or that we actually see a tangible object. Berkeley takes this to be deeply mistaken. Here, unusually, he argues that x *can* be psychologically divided from y, that the visual is entirely separable from the tangible, and that it is we who have mentally conflated or united them.

What underpins this claim is Berkeley's *observation* that it is very difficult to hear words spoken in a familiar language without understanding what they mean (see NTV, §159; see also §51); and that it would be even more difficult if the familiar language (like vision) was virtually universal. Similarly, it is very hard *not* to read meaning into what we see, that is, to see the visual as such. Locke had moved in the direction of this insight with his discussion of depth perception in *Essay* II. IX. 8, preceding the Molyneux problem; and Berkeley may well be alluding to him in the *New Theory of Vision*, §157, for Locke showed that what we immediately see was not solid or three-dimensional. But Berkeley believes that we need to go further, that what we immediately see is not even flat shapes. This, Berkeley recognizes, is more difficult to accept. Yet just as it is hard for me to see my computer keyboard as purely visual, as points of light and colour, rather than a flat surface with well-formed shapes that I recognize to be keys, so it is hard for me to hear my friend's words as just sounds. Yet, it is clear that I must first hear his pure sounds before I can understand his words (unless, perhaps, one wishes to posit some kind of telepathy).

So just because x (the visual keyboard, say) has been closely and frequently associated with y (the tangible keyboard), such that the two have become conflated, does not show that they are one. For someone might with practice be able to separate the two. As J. S. Mill pointed out in a similar context: 'a [psychological] difficulty is not an impossibility'.[9] (Of course this principle might be used against some of Berkeley's experiments, mentioned above, which try to show that x cannot be divided from y, for example extreme heat from pain.)

So it is essential for Berkeley to bring us as close as possible to the visual experience of the unbodied sighted mind, as it should help us to appreciate what we immediately see. To this end, I suggested above, a modern reader might be helped by looking at computer-generated stereograms, or at other forms of virtual reality. Another technique would be to suppose (as Roald Dahl does in his story called 'William and Mary') that in order to evade death, one has had one's brain put in a vat, and that the brain has one eye connected to it. Now suppose that someone moves your brain and eye about, and try to imagine the display of colours and light.

A warning, however, seems in order. Trying to put oneself in the position of the brain and eye, or Berkeley's more theological disembodied sighted mind, could be disorientating or even dangerous, since getting into that mode of perception might interfere with the normal one. It will be a very different world for such a perceiver, who will not have, as Berkeley believes, any notion of size or shape, since it has no grasp of position; indeed, it is unlikely that it will even have a notion of thingness. So although its grasp of the visual world may be truer, it will be virtually useless and hence probably indistinguishable from that of a blind person. In short, having deconstructed the visual world to its immediate sensations, a thought-experimenter might find it hard to return fully to our useful but fictitious (according to Berkeley) world of synthesized visual/tangible objects.

That Berkeley himself went very far in this experiment, despite its difficulties and dangers, seems evident from what he was able to bring back. There is also some evidence that he tried to do the above experiment not only for vision, but also for the senses individually. Thus his brief but confident description in *Principles*, §1, of the immediate data of the five senses, and especially that of touch, suggests first-hand experience: 'By touch [he says] I perceive, for example, hard and soft, heat and cold, motion and resistance, and of all these more and less either as to quantity or degree.' Moreover, in his essay no. 27 in the *Guardian* (1713), Berkeley considers the following:

Let us suppose a person blind and deaf from his birth, who, being grown to man's estate, is by the dead palsy or some other cause, deprived of his feeling, tasting, and smelling; and at the same time has the impediment of his hearing removed, and the film taken from his eyes. What the five senses are to us, that the touch, taste and smell were to him. And any other ways of perception of a more refined and extensive nature, were to him as inconceivable, as to us those are which will one day be adapted to perceive those things which *eye hath not seen, nor ear heard, neither hath it entred into the heart of man to conceive*. And it would be just as reasonable in him to conclude, that the loss of those three senses could not possibly be succeeded by any new inlets of perception; as in a modern free-thinker to imagine there can be no state of life and perception without the senses he enjoys at present. Let us further suppose the same person's eyes, at their first opening, to be struck with a great variety of the most gay and pleasing objects, and his ears with a melodious consort of vocal and instrumental music: Behold him amazed, ravished, transported; and you have some distant representation, some faint and glimmering idea of the exstatic state of the soul in that article in which she emerges from this sepulchre of flesh into Life and Immortalilty.

Here, as with the thought experiment in *New Theory of Vision*, §148 (quoted above), the aim is to give the reader some glimmering notion of the mysterious aspects of religion.

This thought experiment also helps to make sense of Berkeley's claim in his important letter of 1729 to his American friend, Samuel Johnson, that

I see no difficulty in conceiving a change of state, such as is vulgarly called Death, as well without as with material substance. It is sufficient for that purpose that we allow sensible bodies, i.e. such as are immediately perceived by sight and touch ... Now, it seems very easy to conceive the soul to exist in a separate state (i.e. divested from those limits and laws of motion and perception with which she is embarrassed here), and to exercize herself on *new ideas*, without the intervention of these tangible things we call bodies.

(*Works* II, 282, my italics)

Yet Berkeley went further in trying to understand the mystery of death. This is the most dramatic experiment he carried out, showing the deadly seriousness of his experimentalism. It is recorded in the earliest (1759) biographical essay on him, by Oliver Goldsmith, who describes how Berkeley had himself hung by a college friend 'to know what were the pains and symptoms ... felt upon such an occasion'. The arrangement was that

his companion [Goldsmith's uncle, would] take him down at a signal agreed upon ... Berkeley was therefore tied up to the ceiling, and the chair taken from under his feet, but soon losing the use of his senses, his companion it seems waited a little too long for the signal agreed upon, and our enquirer [Berkeley] had like to have been hanged in good earnest; for as soon as he was taken down he fell senseless and motionless upon the floor.[10]

It is not entirely clear what Berkeley hoped to gain from this nearly fatal Near Death Experience – or NDEs as they are now called. But it is likely that it was related to his suggestion (above) that death involves a total change in perceptions. Thus, in trying to experience the sensations immediately preceding death, Berkeley may have been testing to see whether he perceived totally new ideas, as he was emerging from the 'sepulchre of flesh'.

Apart from experimenting with a NDE, Berkeley also considered, more fancifully, the other main area of parapsychological investigation of death, that is OBEs, or Out of Body Experiences. For in another essay in the *Guardian*, no. 35, Berkeley tells of a philosopher who found a way 'for separating the soul for some time from the body, without any injury to the latter [thereby enabling the soul] to transport herself . . . wherever she pleases, [for example] into the pineal gland of the most learned philosopher . . .' By taking a philosophical snuff, Ulysses Cosmopolita, i.e. Berkeley, was able to enter into the minds of a freethinker and a critic in order to observe their ideas. It is, however, hard to know how seriously Berkeley thought about OBEs, even though it is certain he believed that the soul can exist in 'a separate state'.

Yet there can be no doubt about the seriousness of the next and final thought experiment I shall examine. It is probably Berkeley's most important and radical – that of the solitary man or philosopher, who thinks without language. In its own way, it is as daring as the unbodied sighted spirit and even his hanging experiment. Berkeley develops the experiment at length in the *Manuscript Introduction* (*c.* 1708) to the *Principles*, where it is presented as the guiding principle of his philosophical researches. In the published version it is much reduced, but the main point – that the philosopher should try to operate without language – remains. I quote from the more detailed *Manuscript* version:

Let us conceive a solitary man, one born and bred in such a place in the world, and in such circumstances, as he shall never have had occasion to make use of universal signs for his ideas. That man shall have a constant train of particular ideas passing in his mind. Whatever he sees, hears, imagines, or any wise conceives is on all hands, even by the patrons of abstract ideas, granted to be particular. Let us withall suppose him under no necessity of labouring to secure him self from hunger and cold: but at full ease, naturally of good faculties and contemplative. Such a one I should take to be nearer the discovery of certain great and excellent truths yet unknown, than he that has had the education of the schools, . . . and by much reading and conversation has attain'd to the knowledge of those arts and sciences, that make such a noise in the learned world. It is true, the knowledge of our solitary philosopher is not like to be so very wide and extended, it being confin'd to those few particulars that come within his own observation. But then, if he is like to have less knowledge, he is withall like to have fewer mistakes than other men . . .

I shall therefore endeavour as far as I am able, to take off the mask of words, and obtain a naked view of my own particular ideas, from which I may expect to derive the following advantages.

First, I shall be sure to get clear of all controversies purely verbal . . .

Secondly, 'tis reasonable to expect that hereby the trouble of sounding, or examining, or comprehending any notion may be very much abridg'd. For it oft happens that a notion, when it is cloathed with words, seems tedious and operose and hard to be conceiv'd, which yet being strip't of that garniture, the ideas shrink into a narrow compass, and are view'd almost by one glance of thought.

Thirdly, I shall have fewer objects to consider, than other men seem to have had . . .

Fourthly, having remov'd the veil of words, I may expect to have a clearer prospect of the ideas that remain in my understanding.

Fifthly, this seemeth to be a sure way to extricate myself out of that fine and subtile net of abstract ideas, which has so miserably perplex'd, and entangled the minds of men . . .

Sixthly, so long as I confine my thoughts to my own ideas divested of words, I do not see how I can easily be mistaken. The objects I consider I clearly and adequately know. I cannot be deceiv'd in thinking I have an idea which I have not. Nor, on the other hand, can I be ignorant of any idea that I have. . . .

But the attainment of all these advantages does presuppose an entire deliverance from the deception of words, which I dare scarce promise my self. So difficult a thing it is, to dissolve a union so early begun, and confirm'd by so long a habit as that betwixt words and ideas.

. . . I earnestly desire that every one would use his utmost endeavours to attain to a clear and naked view of the ideas he would consider, by separating them from all that varnish and mist of words, which so fatally blinds the judgement . . .

Unless we take care to clear the first principles of knowledge from the incumbrance & delusion of words, we may make infinite reasonings

upon them to no purpose. We may deduce consequences, and never be
the wiser . . .   (MI, pp. 115–25)

There are interesting connections between this non-linguistic experiment and that of the sighted, unbodied mind. Here the attempt is made to
perceive and think without words; in the former the aim was to see the
visual as mere (visual) words, without any ideas or meanings. So just as it
is hard for us to separate objects from words, so it is hard to perceive
(God's visual) words without ideas – that is, once one has learned the
relevant languages. Comparing the two thought experiments also reveals
a curious conflict. Berkeley suggests that the solitary man is without
language, but this cannot really be so if he is normally sighted, for then he
will at least have the visual language.

The thought experiment of the solitary philosopher returns us nearly
full circle to our starting point: Berkeley's critique of abstraction and
language in the Introduction to the *Principles*. For it was his recognition
of the perniciousness of language, of its fertile capacity to produce or reify
fictions, that determined him to embark on this attempt to do philosophy
without language. Berkeley's proposal is radical, yet it was by no means
sui generis. Rather, it represents a culmination of an anti-linguistic
tendency in philosophy that, although largely submerged, goes back at
least to Plato (Epistle VII), one of Berkeley's heroes. About this negative
view of language, Berkeley says in the *Manuscript Introduction*: 'Of late
many have been very sensible of the absurd opinions, and insignificant
disputes, that grow out of the abuse of words. . . . to redress these evils,
they advise well that we attend to the ideas that are signified and draw of
our attention from the words that signify them' (p. 123). For Berkeley,
however, it is not just that philosophical language can be pathological
and in need of therapy – as those in the more recent Wittgensteinian
tradition would hold – but that language is virtually always pathological;
hence the solution is to move as fast and far as possible from language to
experience, from linguistic to experimental or psychological philosophy.

In order to know that we are not in the linguistic maze, we need to
determine, according to Berkeley, whether the things we are talking about
exist; hence we need to look for the relevant perceptions. For him, this
usually means retiring into himself and trying to imagine whether x exists,
having formed the best definition possible of x. This is what he insists on
again and again. The philosopher must do armchair psychology. For
armchair psychology is hands-on philosophy. At one level, Berkeley's
method could hardly be simpler – the psychological philosopher need
only see if he can experience x, or experience x without y, or x with y. So
it is simply a matter of 'compounding and dividing' (PHK, Intro. 10), or

subtraction and addition. Yet Berkeley's results are anything but obvious, since on the basis of his experiments he maintains that abstract general entities, such as triangle, number and time, primary qualities such an extension and solidity, physical objects unperceived, tangible objects seen at a distance, are all fictions.

What Berkeley's experiments seem to show is that we live largely in a world of fictions created by language and imagination. Hence his stirring exclamation in his notebooks: 'Tis not to be imagined what a marvellous emptyness and scarcity of ideas that man shall descry who will lay aside all use of words in his meditations.' (PC, no. 600 and MI, p. 119). Yet Berkeley does not entirely condemn the fictions, for he believes that at least some of them are useful in ordinary life and even in science. In philosophy, however, he believes it is a different matter: *qua* philosophers, we ought to '*think with the learned, and speak with the vulgar*' (PHK, §51). But most speech is vulgar, generating fictions. Learned thinking is meditating, in the first instance, on particular perceptions, which for Berkeley are the things themselves.

Here we come to the chief difficulty in Berkeley's experimental method, which, at one level, appears so easy. For the Berkeleian philosopher, aiming to see the things themselves, has to see with his own external and internal eyes. He needs to be not only a careful observer, so that he can see, remember and imagine things accurately and in detail, but he needs to be sure of what he is perceiving. And this is harder than it sounds, for it is not at all easy to judge appearances and perceptions. After all, what nearly all adult people believe they perceive are solid, coloured objects at a distance. Berkeley would dispute this. But so, in an important sense, would most modern philosophers and scientists, since according to the scientific account accepted since the seventeenth century, what is really out there are clusters of particles or fields of energy, which, impinging on our sense organs, eventually produce in us or our brains the phenomena we experience. So what we perceive as the physical is structured by our modes of perceiving. Although this philosophical thesis is usually associated with Immanuel Kant, Berkeley agrees with it; although for him the structuring is more psychological than transcendental, more a matter of language and imagination than pure categories, and certainly not a matter of material brains and sense organs. What probably separates the Berkeleian most from either the Kantian or scientific account of perception is not that it is uncommonsensical – because they all are – but that Berkeley believes that individuals are able to unmask our ordinary, useful but fiction-laden judgements and experience things as they really are. Yet in order to do this, the philosopher needs to operate outside the normal socio-linguistic framework. Yet this, as I have noted, is not only difficult, but also potentially dangerous.

That Berkeley was aware of the dangers in moving outside the acceptable socio-linguistic matrix comes out in one of his sayings, recorded by his wife, Anne: 'His maxim [she writes] was that nothing very good or very bad could be done until a man entirely got the better of the fear of *que dira ton* [of what the fashionable world says] . . .'[11] So working outside the consensual can result in something 'very good or very bad'. Berkeley himself does not seem to have been daunted by this. As he once said to his friend John Percival: 'I know not what it is to fear, but I have a delicate sense of danger.' That he was a courageous, perhaps even a rash, experimenter and observer can be seen in his willingness to hang himself and also in his close-up description of an eruption of Mount Vesuvius.

Of course, Berkeley's experimentalism involves more than courage; it also required gifts such as accurate and conscientious observation and memory, which he displays in his natural history works, and which are ascribed to him by acquaintances such as Blackwell. Equally important, Berkeley was a strong observer, able to see things that were camouflaged by familiarity, e.g., that the horizontal moon varied greatly in size. He was also able to observe things which went against the ingrained philosophical prejudices of the time, notably that people could use and be meaningfully affected by words which they did not understand, e.g., the popish peasant at his Latin mass.

These, of course, are largely abilities in outward observation. It is the inner observations that are crucial for the experimental philosopher and for two reasons: (1) external observations, such as those relating to the moon illusion, have been largely taken over by empirical psychology; and (2) introspection or subjective inner observation is now generally viewed with extreme suspicion. Of course, (2) was not always so. Until a century ago, probably most philosophers and psychologists, from Descartes to Mill, would have regarded inner observation as most certain. Nor is Berkeley's approach that foreign even to elements in twentieth-century science. Thus he is very much in line with Ernst Mach – who coined the term thought experiment (*Gedankenexperimente*) – in his sensationalist view of science and experiments, according to which the difference between real experiments and thought experiments is a matter of degree not kind. On this view, the problem of inner, first-person observations loses its sting, since the inner laboratory, according to Mach, is not essentially different from the outer.[12] Hence if someone has shown himself good in the outer, it seems only fair to suppose him good in the inner. This, I have been suggesting above, was generally the case with Berkeley.

One way to underline this point is to look at whether the predictions he makes from thought experiments are then justified in the outward realm. Thus we can point to Berkeley's claim (in 1733) that his thought experiments of 1709 (about a blind man made to see) were publicly verified by Cheselden in 1728. It may also be relevant to mention in this respect that it has been claimed for Berkeley, by Karl Popper and others, that, particularly in *De Motu*, he strikingly anticipated developments in twentiety-century physics.[13]

Of course, for most present-day philosophers the problem of subjectivity, that is, the non-accessibility of first-person, subjective judgements, remains. Indeed for some philosophers, such as Gilbert Ryle and Daniel Dennett, the fact that only one person can fit into the subjective closet is evidence not only that such judgements are unreliable, but that they are spurious.[14] Nor was Berkeley unfamiliar with those who denied the existence of inner awareness and consciousness. In his *Guardian* essay, no. 130, he takes the following approach with such philosophers:

> The freethinkers have often declared to the world, that they are not actuated by any incorporeal being or spirit, but that all the operations they exert proceed from the collision of certain corpuscles, endued with proper figures and motions. It is now a considerable time that I have been their proselite in the point [namely that they are purely material] . . . it being plain that no one could mistake thought for motion, who knew what thought was. For these reasons . . . Christians [should] speak of [these] freethinkers in the neuter gender, using the term *it* for *him*. They are to be considered as *automata*, made up of bones and muscles, nerves, arteries and animal spirits . . . but as destitute of thought . . .[15]

What greater certainty could I have than that I am now thinking or having thoughts? For Berkeley, as for Descartes, there can be none. And I am inclined to agree. Similarly, can I seriously doubt that I am now hearing a hum (from my word processor)? Of course, under intense social, linguistic, or diabolical pressure, some people – including myself – might doubt their perceptions. Thus I might doubt – as Descartes did – that I am hearing, rather dreaming, a hum (although for Descartes and Berkeley I might still be sure that I was having an idea of humming). But I don't think I could doubt that I am now thinking. Yet I have heard students say that they were not certain that they existed at that moment.

One approach, following Berkeley, is not to dismiss the claims of Ryle, Dennett and these students. After all, how can I be certain that everyone is like me? Similarly it would be wrong of me to suppose that just because

I can form private mental images, that everyone can. As Francis Galton and William James long ago showed, a small proportion of adults – and some of these extremely intelligent – are unable to form such visual images.[16] Berkeley's point is that it would be equally arrogant for these non-thinkers or non-image formers to claim that everyone is like them in the relevant respect. The temptation to pontificate in that way reveals a narrowness and unwillingness to see the world from another perspective.

Berkeley's life and philosophy goes directly against such narrowness, as is shown in his attempts to see the world from different points of view. Not everyone can empathize with alien perpectives. But there is evidence that Berkeley was especially good at putting himself into the minds – or, as with the above materialistic freethinkers, the non-minds – of his philosophical opponents. This is clear especially from his *Three Dialogues* and *Alciphron*, but it also comes out in a rare autobiographical reflection, where he noted to himself:

> He that would win another over to his opinion must seem to harmonize with him at first and humour him in his own way of talking. From my childhood I had an unaccountable turn of thought that way.
>
> (*Works* IX, 153)

But Berkeley the experimental philosopher was endowed with more than merely a gift for good perceiving and imagining, more than courageous and strong observation and philosophical empathy. There is something, I suggest, which goes with and embraces these, namely, that the experimenter needs to understand himself. In one of his earliest extant letters, Berkeley describes this as 'a thing of the greatest advantage'. In this letter of 1709 to John Percival, he writes: 'There is a person whose acquaintance and conversation I do earnestly recommend unto you as a thing of the greatest advantage: you will be surprised when I tell you it is yourself.' Berkeley then suggests a simple regimen or exercise for moving towards self-knowledge, that is, 'to spend regularly and constantly two or three hours of the morning in study and retirement . . . I do not take upon me to prescribe what you shall employ yourself about. I only propose the passing two or three hours of the twenty-four in private . . .' (*Works* VIII, 20).

This encouragement to retirement and private meditation (and thereby self-understanding) would seem to be a modest form of Berkeley's chief methodological experiment, that of the solitary philosopher, who puts aside language for experience in the search for, and attainment of, truth. It is probably this proposal that would be greeted with the most horror and incredulity by present-day philosophers, who still largely believe that the revolution in philosophy, which I mentioned at the beginning of this volume, was a good thing, that it was right to oppose the psychological or mental science approach of J. S. Mill in favour of the conceptual and linguistic.

Now one curious feature of this opposition to the psychological approach was that it united a wide range of philosophical enemies. Thus it was attacked by Hegelians, such as F. H. Bradley, by phenomenologists or existentialists, such as Edmund Husserl and Martin Heidegger, as well as by analytic philosophers, such as Gottlob Frege and Ryle.[17] Yet why such philosophical unanimity? The underlying answer, I believe, was the fear that psychology was about to absorb or take over philosophy. What psychology was that? It was the empirical psychology of Wilhelm Wundt and E. B. Titchener, who in the late nineteenth century set up laboratories in which teams of introspectors were used to examine questions relating to perception, concept formation, etc. One irony is that, in the event, that form of introspectionist psychology really posed little threat to philosophy, since it was largely swept away later in the twentieth century by behaviourism.[18]

A second irony is that philosophy is once again being threatened with absorption by psychology, but this time by de-subjectivised psychology, or psychology from a third-person perspective – for example, the so-called neuro-philosophy of Paul and Patricia Churchland, but more importantly by the naturalized epistemology of W. V. Quine.

Richard Rorty has summed up admirably in his *Contingency, Irony and Solidarity* (Cambridge, 1989) one main reason why philosophy as traditionally understood must be considered untenable. Basically, it follows from the growing recognition that the old notion of objective truth is illusory. 'To say that truth is not out there [writes Rorty] is simply to say that where there are no sentences there is no truth, that sentences are elements of human languages, and that languages are human creations . . . The suggestion that truth . . . is out there is a legacy of an age in which the world was seen as the creation of a being who had a language of his own . . .' (p. 5; see also p. 21).

Berkeley's answer to Rorty would be disarmingly simple: give up the central dogma that it is only within language that human understanding is possible and traditional philosophy ceases to be untenable. Of course, just because Berkeley's psychological philosophy would fulfil our wishes does not mean that it is true or feasible. For the question will naturally arise: has it not been refuted long ago along with that of his admirer, J. S. Mill? Clearly this question is too large to be satisfactorily answered here. But it is possible to sketch some Berkeleian answers.

First, it is not at all clear that human understanding is impossible without language. Admittedly, this seems to be widely accepted, both in Analytic and Continental circles; but that may be, as Ray Monk remarked to me, the dogma of the twentieth century. Before our century, most philosophers, including rationalists and empiricists, believed that thinking without language was entirely possible. To be sure, Berkeley goes further than most philosophers in holding that 'We need only draw the curtain of words, to behold the fairest fruit of knowledge'. Now one twentieth-century response to Berkeley is bound to be: 'Then describe what you see!' But this challenge supposes that one can only understand what one can communicate in some form of language. What is the evidence for that? In favour of non-linguistic understanding, a Berkeleian could point to the behaviour of pre-linguistic infants, who – to tailor Berkeley's description in Introduction §14 – seem to be able to play intelligently and make mental judgements about their rattles and sugar plumbs without the use of language.

Second, it might be said that the reasons psychology abandoned introspectionism in the early part of this century were and are equally valid for philosophy. Yet it is far from evident that they do bear on Berkeley's use of introspection. Wundt used many introspectionists operating over many trials to determine inductively the nature of human perception, concept formation, etc. Berkeley, however, uses it to discover the truth: to determine if, for example, extreme heat is inseparable from pain and hence is mind-dependent; to see if he can separate the visual and the tangible. Berkeley, unlike Wundt, was not looking for the normal or a standard. However, this is not to say that some psychological philosophers in the late nineteenth century did not see philosophy in a Wundtian way. Thus, according to Frege, Benno Erdmann equated truth with 'general validity' and 'general agreement between subjects who judge'.[19] But Berkeley, being utterly opposed to sceptical relativism, would never accept such a consensus criterion of truth – a criterion that is more in accord with the views of Rorty and, it would seem, of Quine.

For Berkeley, the true psychological philosopher is like an Olympic athlete: he is not interested in a norm, but in trying to find out what can or cannot be done. For this reason, the chief objection to Wundt's use of introspection, that it did not reach generally agreed results, does not apply to Berkeley.[20] As he puts it in the *New Theory of Vision*, in relation to the Molyneux problem: it is not a matter of finding out 'the sentiments of the generality of men' on this question, but of getting the considered judgement of a single unprejudiced person who performs the experiment.[21] In this respect, Berkeley would agree with the French philosopher Denis Diderot, who in his discussion of the Molyneux problem said that to carry out the experiment effectively 'would be an occupation worthy of the combined talents of Newton, Descartes, Locke and Leibniz'.[22]

Of course, even such an experimental philosopher could get it wrong. But so, presumably, could the philosopher or scientist operating within the consensus, from a third-person perspective. Clearly there is something safe and sensible in the latter approach; but taken to an extreme there is also something absurd in it. For in some sense, at least some or one of us have to see things in a first-person way, or we would be in the position of the behaviourist (in the well-known joke), who after having sex says to his behaviourist partner: 'That was nice for you. How was it for me?' At the very least, Berkeley's approach should be an antidote to this form of absurdity.

Anthony Quinton

HUME

Hume is the greatest of British philosophers: the most profound, penetrating and comprehensive. His work is the high point of the predominant empiricist tradition in British philosophy that begins with William of Ockham in the fourteenth century and runs through Bacon and Hobbes, Locke and Berkeley, continues, after Hume, with Bentham and J. S. Mill and culminates in the analytic philosophy of the present century, which was inaugurated by Bertrand Russell and is still posthumously presided over by him.

He was neither as sensible nor, partly for that reason, as influential a philosopher as Locke. Where Locke recommended an attitude of caution or reserve in belief that was welcome to many after a century of horrible religious conflict, Hume seemed to deal in paradoxes, to end up in a total scepticism which could be relieved only by frivolity. Locke's political doctrines contributed to some extent, particularly through Voltaire's enthusiastic endorsement, to the thinking that inspired the French Revolution and played a much larger part in the design of the American Constitution. The utilitarians of the nineteenth century made a simplified version of Hume's moral and political theory effective, as the basis of a radical variety of liberalism of which he would hardly have approved. Until the twentieth century, the main effect of his theoretical philosophy was negative, provoking a number of philosophers to address themselves to the business of refuting him. Kant said that Hume had 'woken him from his dogmatic slumber'. Thomas Reid, the Scottish common-sense philosopher, saw Hume as having brilliantly demonstrated the implicit absurdity of the Lockian 'theory of ideas'. T. H. Green wrote an enormous introduction to an edition of Hume's works, pursuing his supposed mistakes with unwavering resolve. Only in the twentieth century has he been acknowledged as an important constructive philosopher.

Hume was profoundly Scottish, by birth, preferred residence, loyalty, accent and mannerisms. He was the most distinguished luminary of the Scottish Enlightenment of the eighteenth century, which also included Adam Smith, the great economist, Adam Ferguson, the founder of sociology, the historian William Robertson and many others. They made up a wonderfully lively and stimulating intellectual environment in which all the human sciences were pursued: philosophy, history, politics, economics, criticism and the non-dogmatic study of religion. The style of these eighteenth-century Scots compares very favourably, in its rigour and generality, with the more easy-going, literary mode of thought of their English contemporaries. (There is the exception of Samuel Johnson, but he might have benefited from a bit of system and from less watery people to dispute with.)

Hume shared with his associates, and, indeed, most philosophers of his epoch, two qualities that distinguish him and them from philosophers of the present day. In the first place, his scope of interests was extraordinarily wide. He did not just write about but made contributions of serious importance to theoretical and moral philosophy, political theory, economics and the study of religion, historical and doctrinal, writing memorably about miracles, the freedom of the will, the immortality of the soul and suicide, as well as devastating the kind of rational or natural religion, the deism, which was as far as most Enlightenment thinkers thought it practically or theoretically reasonable to go.

But he was far better known in his own time as a historian, and far better rewarded for it. His youthful philosophical masterpiece, the *Treatise on Human Nature*, if it did not, as he gloomily proclaimed, 'fall dead-born from the press', did not sell out its small first edition for several decades. His later six-volume *History of England* was a bestseller.

The other quality distinguishing Hume professionally from contemporary philosophers is the literary character of his ambitions. In his brief *Autobiography* he refers to 'my ruling passion, my love of literary fame'. He was a conscious, elegant writer of an Augustan type, producing courtly, balanced sentences, coloured by concrete analogies and examples. Samuel Johnson said, 'Why, Sir, his style is not English. The structure of his sentences is French.' That is not self-evidently a fault. Hume wrote the *Treatise* during a long stay in France and it may be that work which Johnson had in mind. Philosophy in the eighteenth century was part of polite literature; in the universities it was only a timid adjunct of theology and classical studies. Hume was addressing generally educated readers, not academics, who on the whole have never liked him. He is, indeed, a careless writer, too easy-going to bother about loose ends. More to the point stylistically, he was a good deal inferior to the more or less perfect Berkeley, but that is hardly a weakness and it is hard to think of any British philosopher after him who wrote as well as he did, with the possible exception of F. H. Bradley.

There is one important limitation to Hume's intellectual equipment. Marvellously knowledgeable about the humanities, he seems to have known next to nothing about, and to have had no interest in, mathematics and natural science. That did not do too much harm. He wrote perfectly good, more or less Leibnizian, sense about mathematics. If he wrongly supposed all natural science to be causal, at least its elementary parts are. Where his mathematical weakness let him down is in part 2 of the *Treatise*, in which some very weird things are said about space and time. He says, for example, that an extended whole must be composed of unextended parts, which are nevertheless finite in number and equipped with such perceptible qualities as colour. Commentators almost universally draw a veil over this part of Hume's work.

LIFE

Hume was born in Edinburgh in 1711. His family came from, and mainly lived in, the Borders, at their Ninewells estate, which lay between Berwick to the east and Duns (where Duns Scotus may have been born, but was probably not) to the west. His father died when he was two, so his devoted, intensely Calvinistic mother was the main early influence. The family's home and religion would have made them deeply unsympathetic to the Jacobite attempt in 1715 to install the legitimate, Catholic monarch, who should have been James III, on the throne.

Hume went to Edinburgh University at the early age of twelve, quite usual at the time, and left three years later. He then turned unwillingly to the study of law, but gave most of his attention to Cicero and other classical authors. After some sort of nervous breakdown and a brief spell in a Bristol merchant's office, he retired for three years to rural France, living frugally and writing his *Treatise*. He published its first two parts in 1739, two years after his return, and the third part in 1740. Two volumes of essays, published in 1741 and 1742, did a little better. He applied unsuccessfully for a philosophical chair at Edinburgh and, in need of an income, became tutor for a year to the insane marquess of Annandale. In 1746 he accompanied General St Clair on an invasion of Brittany that was called off, and a little later went with St Clair to Vienna and Turin. His *Enquiry concerning Human Understanding*, a somewhat mutilating revision of book I of the *Treatise*, came out at this time, in 1749, and he returned to Scotland to finish its companion-piece, *Enquiry concerning the Principles of Morals*, his own favourite amongst his works.

From 1751 to 1757 Hume served as Keeper of the Advocates' Library in Edinburgh, the best library in the country, and ideally convenient for the major historical project that he now began, his six-volume *History of England*. The volumes on the Stuarts came out, to some controversy for trying to do justice to that family, in 1754 and 1756; those on the Tudors in 1759; those on the dynasties back to Julius Caesar in 1772. He visited

London in 1758 and 1761, but his most satisfying foreign trip was his stay in Paris between 1763 and 1766 as secretary to the earl of Hertford. He was agreeably lionized by the *philosophes*, had a serious romance, of unknown intimacy, with the comtesse de Boufflers and saw a good deal of Rousseau, whom he brought back to refuge in England. Rousseau soon fled, spreading implausible paranoid fantasies about Hume.

His public career reached its high point with his appointment as under-secretary of state for the northern department between 1767 and 1769. This was the time of the last political gasp of the ageing, unhealthy and somewhat deranged William Pitt the elder. Hume seems to have given satisfaction. In 1769 he returned to Edinburgh and his circle of friends for eight happy final years. Before he died, of stomach cancer, in 1776 he had the pleasure of upsetting Boswell by his cheerful freedom from any fear of death.

Hume was a large man, gangling and bony in youth, but ever more corpulent and red in the face as the years went by. He was genial and kindly, good tempered and good company, an excellent friend and a placable enemy. He could see merit in an honest and serious opponent like Thomas Reid and mildly disposed of a fatuous one like James Beattie with the comment 'a silly, bigoted fellow'.

> I was born the 26th of April, old style, at Edinburgh. I was of a good family, both by father and mother: my father's family is a branch of the Earl of Home's, or Hume's; and my ancestors had been proprietors of the estate, which my brother possesses, for several generations . . . I passed through the ordinary course of education with success, and was seized very early with a passion for literature, which has been the ruling passion of my life, and the great source of my enjoyments. My studious disposition, my sobriety, and my industry, gave my family the notion that the law was a proper profession for me; but I found an unsurmountable aversion to everything but the pursuits of philosophy and general learning; and while they fancied I was poring upon Voet and Vinnius, Cicero and Virgil were the authors which I was secretly devouring.   (Ess 607–8)

Never literary attempt was more unfortunate than my *Treatise of Human Nature*. It fell *dead-born from the press*, without reaching such distinction, as even to excite a murmur among the zealots. But being naturally of a cheerful and sanguine temper, I very soon recovered the blow, and prosecuted with great ardour my studies in the country. In 1742 I printed at Edinburgh the first part of my *Essays*: the work was favourably received, and soon made me entirely forget my former disappointment. I continued with my mother and brother in the country, and in that time recovered the knowledge of the Greek language which I had too much neglected in my early youth.

(Ess 608–9)

But notwithstanding this variety of winds and seasons, to which my writings had been exposed, they had still been making such advances, that the copy-money given me by the booksellers, much exceeded any thing formerly known in England; I was become not only independent, but opulent. (Ess 613)

Those who have not seen the strange effects of modes, will never imagine the reception I met with at Paris, from men and women of all ranks and stations. The more I resiled from their excessive civilities, the more I was loaded with them. There is, however, a real satisfaction in living at Paris, from the great number of sensible, knowing and polite company with which that city abounds above all places in the universe. I thought once of settling there for life. (Ess 614)

To conclude historically with my own character. I am, or rather was (for that is the style I must now use in speaking of myself, which emboldens me the more to speak my sentiments); I was, I say, a man of mild dispositions, of command of temper, of an open, social and cheerful humour, capable of attachment, but little susceptible of enmity, and of great moderation in all my passions. Even my love of literary fame, my ruling passion, never soured my temper, notwithstanding my frequent disappointments. My company was not unacceptable to the young and careless, as well as to the studious and literary; and as I took a particular pleasure in the company of modest women, I had no reason to be displeased with the reception I met with from them. In a word, though most men anywise eminent, have found reason to complain of calumny, I never was touched, or even attacked by her baleful tooth; and though I wantonly exposed myself to the rage of both civil and religious factions, they seemed to be disarmed in my behalf of their wonted fury. My friends never had occasion to vindicate any one circumstance of my character and conduct; not but that the zealots, we may well suppose, would have been glad to invent and propagate any story to my disadvantage, but they could never find any which they thought would wear the face of probability. I cannot say there is no vanity in making this funeral oration of myself, but I hope it is not a misplaced one; and this is a matter of fact which is easily cleared and ascertained. (Ess 615–16)

PHILOSOPHICAL ASSUMPTIONS

Hume is doubly an empiricist. First, he regards philosophy as an empirical science. That position is announced in the subtitle of the *Treatise*: 'an attempt to introduce the experimental method of reasoning into moral subjects'. The experimental method is what Newton's sublime achievement is based on (but mathematics had a lot to do with it too), so Hume is reasonably credited with the ambition of being the Newton of the moral (i.e. human) sciences. To a considerable extent his procedure is in accord with this declaration of intent. He seeks to show how the complex detail of our intellectual life arises in accordance with the laws of association from its primary elements, the atoms of thought he calls impressions and ideas. But it is not for this general cognitive psychology on associationist principles that he is usually regarded as important.

Secondly, he is an empiricist in a more familiar sense. He maintains that all the raw material of our thoughts and beliefs comes from experience, sensory and introspective. He in fact applies this principle as a criterion of significance. Our thoughts are without content, and our words without meaning, unless they are connected to experience. He also holds that most of our knowledge rests on experience or, since the only certain knowledge we have is mathematical and concerned with the relations of ideas, that what we acceptably believe does. It might seem he was committed to his view that philosophy is an empirical science by his view that all factual belief is empirical. But that does not follow. Most modern sympathizers with Hume would say that philosophy, 'true' philosophy, is conceptual, not factual, as much a business of examining the relations of ideas as mathematics is.

He boldly asserts that philosophy is the first or master science. All sciences or bodies of professed knowledge are the work of the human understanding. Therefore the study of the human understanding is prior to all the others. Where Newton, in Hume's view, had explained the material universe by means of the law of gravitational attraction, his aim is to explain the workings of the mind by a parallel law of association.

The raw materials of thought, which is the work of the understanding, are impressions and their varyingly lively copies, ideas. Impressions are either of sensation, such as colours and sounds, or reflection, such as emotions and desires. They may also be simple – homogeneous and unanalysable – or complex. Every simple idea presupposes a corresponding simple impression. Complex ideas need not do so: we would all recognize a dragon if we came across one.

Ideas are distinguished from impressions by their lesser vivacity. If they are not at all lively, they are ideas of the imagination. If they are more lively, and retain their 'form and order', they are ideas of memory. Of the same degree of liveliness, it appears, are ideas of expectation, which are the elementary form of our causal beliefs. Belief is a feature of ideas of memory and expectation, as contrasted with mere imaginings. It is not a further idea, since, if so, it could be added to any other idea, however fantastic, and produce a belief in it. A related point, made at a later stage, is that there is no idea of existence. The idea of a thing is the same as the idea of that thing as existing. Presumably Hume would establish the empirical credentials of existence by saying that it is present in every impression, since impressions involve the infallible awareness of something (even if only a coloured patch in one's private field of vision).

Hume admits that his principle of the universal dependence of impressions on ideas is imperfect. One might recognize a shade of blue one had never met with, only its close neighbours on the spectrum. That is an unnecessary admission. The missing shade could be seen as a complex idea made of the blue next door to it and the idea, well exemplified empirically, of 'a little more blue than'.

There is much that is more seriously wrong with Hume's account of impressions and ideas than that. For him an idea is a mental picture or image. We do think in images to some extent, but we also think in words, and in diagrams and schemas, which are in a way image-like, although hardly copies. The crucial point is that all these items are the vehicles of concepts or meanings. It is easy to think of imaginings (hallucinations and dreams, for example) that are much more lively than most of what we perceive, let alone remember.

Hume's view that images are the primary vehicles of thought may have been assisted by his commitment to Berkeley's rejection of 'abstract ideas'. An impression is of one, particular, wholly determinate thing. How do we think of it as one of a kind, as having some general term truly applied to it? Locke thought we abstract the qualities common to all oranges and use the resulting abstract idea to recognize a particular orange as an orange. Berkeley rejected this, since different oranges have incompatible qualities. We use a particular image to 'represent' all the members of the kind. But in any one image a host of kinds will be representable: oranges, but also round things, orange-coloured things and so on. Hume coped with this by saying that when we allocate something to a kind because of its similarity to some standard image, we have a lot of other images at our disposal which we can bring to mind to guide our classification along the right path.

Finally, in this first part of the *Treatise*, Hume anticipates points he will develop more fully later in discussing material objects and persons, by a general dismissal of the legitimacy of the idea of substance. There is no impression from which it can be derived. All we perceive is collections of qualities, persistently associated with each other. If substance is defined as that which is capable of independent existence, then the only substances are impressions and ideas.

It is evident, that all the sciences have a relation, greater or less, to human nature; and that, however wide any of them may seem to run from it, they still return back by one passage or another. Even *Mathematics*, *Natural Philosophy* and *Natural Religion* are in some measure dependent on the science of MAN; since they lie under the cognisance of men, and are judged of by their powers and faculties . . . If, the sciences of Mathematics, Natural Philosophy, and Natural Religion, have such a dependence on the knowledge of man, what may be expected in the other sciences, whose connection with human nature is more close and intimate?   (T xix)

There is no question of importance, whose decision is not comprised in the science of man; and there is none, which can be decided with any certainty, before we become acquainted with that science. In pretending, therefore, to explain the principles of human nature, we in effect propose a complete system of the sciences, built on a foundation, and the only one upon which they can stand with any security. And as the science of man is the only solid foundation for the other sciences, so the only solid foundation we can give to this science itself must be laid on experience and observation.   (T xix-xx)

All the perceptions of the human mind resolve themselves into two distinct kinds, which I shall call *impressions* and *ideas*. The difference betwixt these consists in the degrees of force and liveliness, with which they strike upon the mind, and make their way into our thought and consciousness. Those perceptions which enter with most force and violence, we may name *impressions*; and under this name I comprehend all our sensations, passions and emotions, as they make their first appearance in the soul. By *ideas* I mean the faint images of these in thinking and reasoning; such as, for instance, are all the perceptions excited by the present discourse, excepting only those which arise from the sight and touch, and excepting the immediate pleasure or uneasiness it may occasion. I believe it will not be necessary to employ many words in explaining this distinction. Every one of himself will readily perceive the difference betwixt feeling and thinking. (T 1)

Every simple idea has a simple impression which resembles it, and every simple impression a correspondent idea. (T 3)

A very material question has been started concerning *abstract* or *general* ideas, *whether they be general or particular in the mind's conception of them*. A great Philosopher [Berkeley] has disputed the received opinion in this particular and has asserted, that all general ideas are nothing but particular ones annexed to a certain term, which gives them a more extensive signification, and makes them recall upon occasion other individuals, which are similar to them. As I look upon this to be one of the greatest and most valuable discoveries that has been made in late years in the republic of letters, I shall here endeavour to confirm it by some arguments, which I hope will put it beyond all doubt and controversy.

It is evident, that in forming most of our general ideas, if not all of them, we abstract from every particular degree of quality and quantity, and that an object ceases not to be of any particular species on account of every small alteration in its extension, duration and other properties. It may, therefore, be thought, that here is a plain dilemma, that decides concerning the nature of those abstract ideas, which have afforded so much speculation to philosophers. The abstract idea of a man represents men of all sizes and all qualities, which it is concluded it cannot do, but either by representing at once all possible sizes and all possible qualities, or by representing no particular one at all. Now it having been esteemed absurd to defend the former proposition, as implying an infinite capacity in the mind, it has been commonly inferred in favour of the latter; and our abstract ideas have been supposed to represent no particular degree either of quantity or quality. But that this inference is erroneous, I shall endeavour to make appear, *first*, by proving, that it is utterly impossible to conceive any quantity or quality, without forming a precise notion of its degrees; and, *secondly*, by showing, that though the capacity of the mind be not infinite, yet we can at once form a notion of all possible quantity and quality, in such a manner at least, as, however imperfect, may serve all the purposes of reflection and conversation.   (T 17–18)

All the objects of human reason or enquiry may naturally be divided into two kinds, to wit, *Relations of Ideas* and *Matters of Fact*. Of the first kind are the sciences of Geometry, Algebra and Arithmetic; in short every affirmation which is either intuitively or demonstratively certain. *That the square of the hypotenuse is equal to the square of the two sides*, is a proposition which expresses the relation between these figures, *That three times five is equal to the half of thirty*, expresses a relation between these numbers. Propositions of this kind are discoverable by the mere operation of thought, without dependence on what is anywhere existent in the universe. Though there never were a circle or triangle in nature, the truths demonstrated by Euclid would for ever retain their certainty and evidence.

Matters of fact, which are the second objects of human reason, are not ascertained in the same manner; nor is our evidence of their truth, however great, of a like nature with the foregoing. The contrary of every matter of fact is still possible; because it can never imply a contradiction, and is conceived by the mind, with the same facility and distinctness, as if ever so conformable to reality. *That the sun will not rise tomorrow* is no less intelligible a proposition and implies no more contradiction than the affirmation *that it will rise.*   (E 25–6)

CAUSATION

Hume's account of causation is, rightly, the best-known and the most influential part of his philosophy. Where others of his leading contentions are at best interestingly provocative, it remains a compelling object of concern for philosophers. He treats it as a relation between objects before he sets out his disconcertingly sceptical views about our knowledge of objects, but that is because he takes all our beliefs about matters of fact, in so far as they go beyond the impressions that are immediately present to the mind, as all but the most elementary do, to be the outcome of causal inference. That is not strictly correct. The sweet taste that I infer to be obtainable from the orange I see is neither the cause nor the effect of the seen orange. But it is still a 'distinct existence', which could have failed to occur even though the orange was present. Factual inference, of which causal inference is a primary example, is the universal link between the observed and the unobserved, between what we perceive to happen and what must have happened or must be going to happen.

Being a cause, or an effect, is not a quality of things, like being red or round. If it were, it would be a property of everything, like existence, and we should have no impression of it. It is, plainly enough, a relation: a complex, threefold one, composed of contiguity in space and time, succession and necessary connection. Neither contiguity nor succession is, in fact, essential to causation. There can be action at a distance and cause and effect can be simultaneous (Hume has an ingenious but invalid argument to prove that they cannot be). The matter is not important and most straightforward examples of causal relationship do have contiguous and successive terms, anyway. It is not important, since contiguity and succession are empirically unproblematic; we have impressions of both. Necessary connection is the indispensable but irksome ingredient. However closely we examine an alleged instance of causal relationship (the cue ball coming into contact with the red and the red shooting off to the pocket), we observe no necessary connection between them, although we believe there is one.

Hume poses two questions. Why do we think that every event must have a cause and why do we think that each particular cause must have the effect we take it to have? The general causal principle is neither self-evident nor provable. He disposes with typical neatness of some attempted proofs. Locke, for example, said that if the principle were false, something would have been caused by nothing; but nothing is far too weak to have caused anything. This anticipation of Lewis Carroll is easily shown to beg the question. Nor can it be proved that any particular event is the cause of what is taken to be its effect. Cause and effect are distinct existences; it is therefore never a contradiction to suppose that one occurred and the other did not.

Where we believe two kinds of event to be causally related, we believe them to be constantly conjoined at all times on the basis of our remembering them to have been constantly conjoined in our experience. The inference from the limited conjunction that we have observed to the universal conjunction that our causal belief embodies assumes that the unobserved resembles the observed or, more vaguely, that nature is uniform. But this, like the general principle, is neither self-evident nor provable. The unobserved is 'distinct' from the observed; its taking any form whatever is compatible with the observed being the way it is. Nor can it be established inductively on the evidence that hitherto, at any rate, the unobserved has largely resembled the observed. To do that would be to argue in a circle, to assume its validity in its own proof.

Tucked away in a discussion of probability is an interesting distinction between probable conclusions based on insufficient evidence (I have met five Dutchmen and they all like eels) and that based on contrary evidence (I have met a hundred Dutchmen and ninety-five of them like eels). In either case, coming across a new Dutchman, I shall conclude that he probably likes eels, but shall claim no more than that. In the second case I am relying on the general proposition that nineteen out of twenty Dutchmen like eels, which is the product of an inductive inference from the proportion of eel-fanciers I have observed. Hume's criticism, then, is not to be circumvented by arguing that nature is probably uniform or that the unobserved will probably resemble the observed, if it is the second kind of probability that is in question. For that can only be based on the constancy of observed frequencies or proportions. But the first kind of probability, which Hume brushes aside as figuring only in early life, which is surely incorrect, is not open to that objection. It has been argued that 'if all known As are Bs then it is probable that (i.e. there is some, if insufficient, evidence that) all As whatever are Bs' is demonstrable. It is because of the *meaning* of the word 'evidence' that the quoted statement about As and Bs is true; it states an 'abstract relation of ideas' not a matter of fact.

Hume, at any rate, convinced that the inductive inference which is embodied in our causal beliefs, and all other factual beliefs that go beyond present impressions, cannot be rationally justified, turns to explaining how it is that we inveterately have recourse to it. His answer is that our experience of constant conjunction, through the influence of association, leads us, as a matter of custom or habit, to have a lively expectation of a window's shattering when we observe a brick flying towards it. The impression from which our idea of necessary connection is derived is not of sensation, but of reflection, that of feeling compelled in expecting the broken window on perception of the brick flying towards it.

He concludes his main account of the subject by putting forward two definitions of 'cause' which are of two quite different, if not unrelated, things. The first is in terms of the constant conjunction of the two factors, the second is in terms of the impression of one factor determining the mind to form a lively idea of the other. The second of these seems to state what Hume thinks goes on in our minds when we form or have a causal belief; the first of them to state what we actually believe. They cannot both be correct. The first is what we believe; the second explains the belief and, perhaps, states all we are entitled to believe.

Until the twentieth century most commentators on Hume took him to be, whether seriously or frivolously, a complete sceptic about causal and inductive beliefs (and a good many other things). But he does set out 'rules for judging causes and effects', clearly takes it to be true that every event has a cause (for example, in insisting that chance events are really all the effects of unknown causes) and, of course, himself indulges in a great deal of inductive inference in his application of the 'experimental method' to the workings of the human mind.

> All reasonings concerning matter of fact seem to be founded on the relation of CAUSE AND EFFECT. By means of that relation alone we can go beyond the evidence of our memory and senses. If you were to ask a man, why he believes any matter of fact, which is absent; for instance, that his friend is in the country, or in France; he would give you a reason; and this reason would be some other fact; as a letter received from him, or the knowledge of his former resolutions and promises. A man finding a watch or any other machine in a desert island, would conclude that there had once been men in that island. All our reasonings concerning fact are of the same nature. And here it is

constantly supposed that there is a connexion between the present fact
and that which is inferred from it. Were there nothing to bind them
together, the inference would be entirely precarious.   (E 26–7)

If we would satisfy ourselves, therefore, concerning the nature of that
evidence, which assures us of matters of fact, we must enquire how we
arrive at the knowledge of cause and effect.

I shall venture to affirm, as a general proposition, which admits of no
exception, that the knowledge of this relation is not, in any instance,
attained by reasonings *a priori*; but arises entirely from experience,
when we find that any particular objects are constantly conjoined with
each other. Let an object be presented to a man of ever so strong
natural reason and abilities; if that object be entirely new to him, he
will not to able, by the most accurate examination of its sensible
qualities, to discover any of its causes or effects. Adam, though his
rational faculties be supposed, at the very first, entirely perfect, could
not have inferred from the fluency and transparency of water that it
would suffocate him, or from the light and warmth of fire that it would
consume him. No object ever discovers, by the qualities which appear
to the senses, either the causes which produced it, or the effects which
will arise from it; nor can our reason, unassisted by experience, ever
draw any inference concerning real existence and matter of fact.

                                                              (E 27)

Let us therefore cast our eye on any two objects, which we call cause
and effect, and turn them on all sides, in order to find that impression,
which produces an idea of such prodigious consequence. At first sight I
perceive, that I must not search for it in any of the particular *qualities*
of the objects; since, whichever of these qualities I pitch on, I find some
object that is not possessed of it, and yet falls under the denomination
of cause or effect. And indeed there is nothing existent, either externally
or internally, which is not to be considered either as a cause or an
effect; though it is plain that there is no one quality which universally
belongs to all beings, and gives them a title to that denomination.

The idea then of causation must be derived from some *relation*
among objects; and that relation we must now endeavour to discover. I
find in the first place, that whatever objects are considered as causes or
effects, are *contiguous*; and that nothing can operate in a time or place,
which is ever so little removed from those of its existence. Though
distant objects may sometimes seem productive of each other, that are
commonly found upon examination to be linked by a chain of causes,
which are contiguous among themselves, and to the distant objects; and
when in any particular instance we cannot discover this connection, we
still presume it to exist. We may therefore consider the relation of

contiguity as essential to that of causation; at least may suppose it such, according to the general opinion, till we can find a more proper occasion to clear up this matter, by examining what objects are or are not susceptible of juxtaposition and conjunction.

The second relation I shall observe as essential to causes and effects, is not so universally acknowledged, but is liable to some controversy. It is that of *priority* of time in the cause before the effect. Some pretend that it is not absolutely necessary a cause should precede its effect; but that any object or action, in the very first moment of its existence, may exert its productive quality, and give rise to another object or action, perfectly contemporary with itself. But beside that experience in most instances seems to contradict this opinion, we may establish the relation of priority by a kind of inference or reasoning. It is an established maxim, both in natural and moral philosophy, that an object, which exists for any time in its full perfection without producing another, is not its sole cause; but is assisted by some other principle which pushes it from its state of inactivity, and makes it exert that energy, of which it was secretly possessed. Now if any cause be perfectly contemporary with its effect, it is certain, according to this maxim, that they must all of them be so; since any one of them, which retards its operation for a single moment, exerts not itself at that very individual time, in which it might have operated; and therefore is no proper cause. The consequence of this would be no less than the destruction of that succession of causes, which we observe in the world; and indeed the utter annihilation of time. For if one cause were contemporary with its effect, and this effect with *its* effect and so on, it is plain there would be no such thing as succession, and all objects must be co-existent.

If this argument appear satisfactory, it is well. If not, I beg the reader to allow me the same liberty, which I have used in the preceding case, of supposing it such. For he shall find, that the affair is of no great importance.

Having thus discovered or supposed the two relations of *contiguity* and *succession* to be essential to causes and effects, I find I am stopped short, and can proceed no further in considering any single instance of cause and effect. Motion in one body is regarded upon impulse as cause of motion in another. When we consider these objects with the utmost attention, we find only that the one body approaches the other; and the motion of it precedes that of the other, but without any sensible interval. It is in vain to rack ourselves with *further* thought and reflection upon this subject. We can go no further in considering this particular instance.

We must therefore proceed like those who, being in search of anything that lies concealed from them, and not finding it in the place they expected, beat about all the neighbouring fields, without any certain view or design, in hopes their good fortune will at last guide them to what they search for. It is necessary for us to leave the direct survey of this question concerning the nature of that *necessary connection*, which enters into our idea of cause and effect; and endeavour to find some other questions, the examination of which will perhaps afford a hint, that may serve to clear up the present difficulty. Of these questions there occur two, which I shall proceed to examine, viz.

First, for what reason we pronounce it *necessary*, that everything whose existence has a beginning, should also have a cause?

Secondly, why we conclude, that such particular causes must *necessarily* have such particular effects; and what is the nature of that *inference* we draw from the one to the other, and of the belief we repose in it? (T 77–8)

We can never demonstrate the necessity of a cause to every new existence, or new modification of existence, without showing at the same time the impossibility there is, that anything can ever begin to exist without some productive principle; and where the latter proposition cannot be proved, we must despair of ever being able to prove the former. Now that the latter proposition is utterly incapable of a demonstrative proof, we may satisfy ourselves by considering, that as all distinct ideas are separable from each other, and as the ideas of cause and effect are evidently distinct, it will be easy for us to conceive any object to be non-existent this moment, and existent the next, without conjoining to it the distinct idea of a cause or productive principle. The separation therefore of the idea of a cause from that of a beginning of existence, is plainly possible for the imagination; and consequently the actual separation of these objects is so far possible, that it implies no contradiction nor absurdity; and is therefore incapable of being refuted by any reasoning from mere ideas, without which it is impossible to demonstrate the necessity of a cause.

(T 79–80)

It is therefore by experience only that we can infer the existence of one object from that of another. The nature of experience is this. We remember to have had frequent instances of the existence of one species of objects, and also remember, that the individuals of another species of objects have always attended them, and have existed in a regular order of contiguity and succession with regard to them. Thus we remember to have seen that species of object we call *flame*, and to have felt that species of sensation we call *heat*. We likewise call to mind their constant conjunction in all past instances. Without any further ceremony, we call the one *cause*, and the other *effect*, and infer the existence of the one from that of the other. In all those instances from which we learn the conjunction of particular causes and effects, both the causes and effects have been perceived by the senses, and are remembered, but in all cases, wherein we reason concerning them, there is only one perceived or remembered, and the other is supplied in conformity to our past experience.

Thus in advancing we have insensibly discovered a new relation betwixt cause and effect when we least expected it, and were entirely employed upon another subject. This relation is their *constant conjunction*. Contiguity and succession are not sufficient to make us pronounce any two objects to be cause and effect, unless we perceive that these two relations are preserved in several instances. We may now see the advantage of quitting the direct survey of this relation, in order to discover the nature of that *necessary connection* which makes so essential a part of it.   (T 86–7)

Having thus explained the manner *in which we reason beyond our immediate impressions, and conclude that such particular causes must have such particular effects*; we must now return upon our footsteps to examine that question which first occurred to us, and which we dropped in our way, viz. *What is our idea of necessity, when we say that two objects are necessarily connected together?* Upon this head I repeat, what I have often had occasion to observe, that as we have no idea that is not derived from an impression, we must find some impression that gives rise to this idea of necessity.   (T 155)

[We must] repeat to ourselves that the simple view of any two objects or actions, however related, can never give us any idea of power, or of a connection betwixt them; *that* this idea arises from the repetition of their union; *that* the repetition neither discovers nor causes anything in the objects, but has an influence only on the mind, by that customary transition it produces; *that* this customary transition is therefore the same with the power and necessity; which are consequently qualities of perceptions, not of objects, and are internally felt by the soul, and not perceived externally in bodies.   (T 166)

We may define a *cause* to be 'An object precedent and contiguous to another, and where all the objects resembling the former are placed in

like relations of precedency and contiguity to those objects that
resemble the latter'. If this definition be esteemed defective, because
drawn from objects foreign to the cause, we may substitute this other
definition in its place, viz. 'A cause is an object precedent and
contiguous to another, and so united with it, that the idea of the one
determines the mind to form the idea, and the impression of the one to
form a more lively idea of the other'.   (T 170)

MATERIAL THINGS

Having argued that all beliefs in matters of fact – apart from our
immediate awareness of our current impressions and, presumably,
memories of them – rests on causal belief, Hume has tried to show that
such beliefs are not justified. They are justified neither by experience,
since we have no impression of necessary connection, nor by reason, since
the contradictory either of any general causal or inductive principle or of
any particular causal belief is possible. All we can hope to do is to explain
how we come to have the causal beliefs we do, and make the predictions
to which they lead us, namely by experience of constant conjunction
which instils in us a habit of expectation.

Much the same strategy is employed in his accounts of our belief in an
external world of material things and our belief in ourselves as continuing
existences. He opens his discussion of material things by distinguishing
two questions. One of these, the question *whether there be body or not?*',
is, he says, 'vain to ask'. However, 'we may well ask *What causes induce
us to believe in the existence of body?*' To believe in the existence of body,
or material things, is to believe in something that has continued and
distinct existence, something that exists at times when we have no
impressions of it and which, therefore, exists independently of us. It is a
plain contradiction to suppose that the senses reveal to us the existence of
unperceived things (or unperceived tracts of their history). Nor can the
belief be based on causal inference from our impressions, which is what it
amounts to in these circumstances, as in the 'modern philosophy' of
Locke. We cannot experience a constant conjunction between the
perceived and the unperceived, let alone compare one with another to
discover the (partial) resemblance that Locke asserts to obtain between
them.

The question 'whether there be body or not' turns out to be 'vain' in
two ways. Since neither experience nor reason can answer it, we can give
no justified answer to the question. But he also says that 'nature has not

left this to [our] choice and has doubtless esteemed it an affair of too great importance to be trusted to our uncertain reasonings and specula- tions'. We cannot justify our belief in a world of continued and distinct material things, but we cannot help holding such a belief. What we can do is explain how it is forced upon us. The explanation lies in the constancy and coherence displayed by the impressions of the senses. We leave the dining-table to look out of the window and when we come back things just like the things that appeared on the dining-table appear there once more (constancy). The fire that was blazing in the hearth when we went out to make a long telephone call is now just smouldering in the way that continuously observed fires have been seen to die down steadily on other occasions (coherence).

The ordinary, 'vulgar', view of the matter 'feigns' or imagines unperceived perceptions to fill the steady or graduated gaps. That is a contradiction, but the unreflective mind passes over that. The 'system of the philosophers' (i.e. Locke) is even worse, since it supposes the existence of things that are neither causally related to nor like the impressions held to testify to their existence.

> We may well ask, *What causes induce us to believe in the existence of body?* but it is in vain to ask, *Whether there be body or not?* That is a point we must take for granted in all our reasonings.
>
> The subject, then, of our present inquiry, is concerning the *causes* which induce us to believe in the existence of body; and my reasonings on this head I shall begin with a distinction, which at first sight may seem superfluous, but which will contribute very much to the perfect understanding of what follows. We ought to examine apart those two questions, which are commonly confounded together, viz. Why we attribute a *continued* existence to objects, even when they are not present to the senses; and why we suppose them to have an existence distinct from the mind and perception? Under this last head I comprehend their situation as well as relations, their *external* position as well as the independence of their existence and operation. (T 186–7)

> That our senses offer not their impressions as the images of something *distinct*, or *independent*, and *external*, is evident; because they convey to us nothing but a single perception, and never give us the least intimation of anything beyond. A single perception can never produce the idea of a double existence, but by some influence of the reason or imagination. When the mind looks further than what immediately appears to it, its conclusions can never be put to the account of the senses; and it certainly looks further, when from a single perception it

infers a double existence, and supposes the relations of resemblance
and causation betwixt them.   (T 189)

We may observe, then, that it is neither upon account of the
involuntariness of certain impressions, as is commonly supposed, nor
of their superior force and violence, that we attribute to them a reality
and continued existence, which we refuse to others, that are voluntary
or feeble. For it is evident our pains and pleasures, our passions and
affections, which we never suppose to have any existence beyond our
perception, are equally involuntary, as the impressions of figure and
extension, colour and sound which we suppose to be permanent beings.
The heat of a fire, when moderate, is supposed to exist in the fire; but
the pain which it causes on a near approach is not taken to have any
being except in the perception.

These vulgar opinions, then, being rejected, we must search for some
other hypothesis, by which we may discover those peculiar qualities in
our impressions, which make us attribute to them a distinct and
continued existence.

After a little examination, we shall find that all those objects, to
which we attribute a continued existence, have a peculiar *constancy*,
which distinguishes them from the impressions whose existence
depends upon our perception. Those mountains, and houses, and trees,
which lie at present under my eye, have always appeared to me in the
same order; and when I lose sight of them by shutting my eyes or
turning my head, I soon after find them return upon me without the
least alteration. My bed and table, my books and papers, present
themselves in the same uniform manner, and change not upon account
of an interruption in my seeing or perceiving them. This is the case with
all the impressions whose objects are supposed to have an external
existence; and is the case with no other impressions, whether gentle or
violent, voluntary or involuntary.

This constancy, however, is not so perfect as not to admit of very
considerable exceptions. Bodies often change their position and
qualities, and, after a little absence or interruption, may become hardly
knowable. But here it is observable, that even in these changes they
preserve a *coherence*, and have a regular dependence on each other;
which is the foundation of a kind of reasoning from causation, and
produces the opinion of their continued existence. When I return to my
chamber after an hour's absence, I find not my fire in the same situation
in which I left it; but then I am accustomed, in other instances, to see a
like alteration produced in a like time, whether I am present or absent,
near or remote. This coherence, therefore, in their changes, is one of the
characteristics of external objects, as well as their constancy.

                                                            (T 194–5)

THE SELF

The self, conceived as something with a continuous identity through time, also falls victim to Hume's characteristic two-pronged style of attack. I know that I am now having certain experiences and I remember having had others. But I have no impression of an unchanging item to which all these things belong. Since it would have to be an unalterable, invariant content of my consciousness, it could not make itself felt. It would have the empirically elusive character of existence. In fact, Hume argues, whenever I look most closely into myself all I can find is a more or less chaotic sequence of particular perceptions, impressions and ideas of sensation and reflection, feelings and thoughts.

On the other hand, reason no more requires than experience does the supposition of a persisting bearer of my identity through time, a support for my varying experiences to inhere in. Each experience or 'perception' is a distinct existence from whose existence that of no other thing necessarily follows. That is, of all Hume's bold eliminations, the one that other philosophers have found it hardest to swallow. Does he not refute himself when he says 'for my part, when I enter most intimately into what I call *myself*, I always stumble on some particular perception or other'? What is this I that is doing the entering? J. S. Mill and others have thought it impossible that a mere series could be aware of itself as a series. Against that it could be argued that a present state of consciousness could contain or be a recollection of previous states of consciousness somehow related to it.

Indeed it has seemed to many, particularly Locke, that memory, in the sense of direct personal recollection, is the relation that connects a temporally spread-out bundle of experiences or mental states into a single, continuous self, mind or person. Hume rejected this theory, relying on Butler's argument that, as Hume puts it, memory does not constitute, but discovers, personal identity. I cannot judge that some idea is one of memory, rather than imagination, unless I have first found out that the experience supposedly remembered was an experience of *mine*.

Hume remained unsatisfied with the account of the relation which unites a series of experiences into a self that he gave in the *Treatise*, which was that it is a compound of resemblance and causation. Perhaps Butler's argument is a bit too swift. To decide that some past experience is one's own and that the idea one has of it is an idea of memory are not two things, of which the first has to precede the second; they seem much more like one and the same thing.

He has a long and entangled argument about the immateriality of the soul, a theologian's thesis which he mischievously assimilates to the monism of Spinoza. It turns on the view that the soul is an immaterial substance. But one can take the soul or self, even if conceived not as a substance but as a series, to be non-material, as Hume appears to do, and that leaves open the possibility of its survival of the death of the body. He takes up the problem in an attractive essay. If our minds are made of some spiritual stuff, why should that stuff not make up different minds in the way that matter enters into the composition of different bodies? Furthermore, 'the soul, if immortal, existed before our birth; and if the former existence noways concerned us, neither will the latter'.

There are some philosophers who imagine we are every moment intimately conscious of what we call our *self*; that we feel its existence and its continuance in existence; and are certain, beyond the evidence of a demonstration, both of its perfect identity and simplicity. The strongest sensation, the most violent passion, say they, instead of distracting us from this view, only fix it the more intensely and make us consider their influence on *self* either by their pain or pleasure. To attempt a further proof of this were to weaken its evidence; since no proof can be derived from any fact of which we are so intimately conscious; nor is there anything of which we can be certain if we doubt of this.

Unluckily all these positive assertions are contrary to that very experience which is pleaded for them; nor have we any idea of *self*, after the manner it is here explained. For from what impression could this idea be derived? This question is impossible to answer without a manifest contradiction and absurdity; and yet it is a question which must necessarily be answered, if we would have the idea of self pass for clear and intelligible. It must be some one impression that gives rise to every real idea. But self or person is not any one impression, but that to which our several impressions and ideas are supposed to have a reference. If any impression gives rise to the idea of self, that impression must continue invariably the same, through the whole course of our lives; since self is supposed to exist after that manner. But there is no impression constant and invariable. Pain and pleasure, grief and joy, passions and sensations succeed each other, and never all exist at the same time. It cannot therefore be from any of these impressions, or from any other, that the idea of self is derived; and consequently there is no such idea. (T 251–2)

I may venture to affirm of the rest of mankind that they are nothing but a bundle or collection of different perceptions, which succeed each other with an inconceivable rapidity, and are in a perpetual flux and movement. Our eyes cannot turn in their sockets without varying our perceptions. Our thought is still more variable than our sight; and all our other senses and faculties contribute to this change; nor is there any single power of the soul, which remains unalterably the same, perhaps for one moment. The mind is a kind of theatre, where several perceptions successively make their appearance; pass, repass, glide away, and mingle in an infinite variety of postures and situations. There is properly no *simplicity* in it at one time, nor *identity* in different, whatever natural propension we may have to imagine that simplicity and identity. The comparison of the theatre must not mislead us. They are the successive perceptions only, that constitute the mind; nor have we the most distant notion of the place where these scenes are represented, or of the materials of which it is composed. (T 252–3)

As memory alone acquaints us with the continuance and extent of this succession of perceptions, it is to be considered, upon that account chiefly, as the source of personal identity. Had we no memory, we never should have any notion of causation, nor consequently of that chain of causes and effects, which constitute our self or person. But having once acquired this notion of causation from the memory, we can extend the same chain of causes, and consequently the identity of our persons beyond our memory, and can comprehend times, and circumstances, and actions, which we have entirely forgot, but suppose in general to have existed. For how few of our past actions are there, of which we have any memory? Who can tell me, for instance, what were his thoughts and actions on the first of January 1715, the eleventh of March 1719, and the third of August 1733? Or will he affirm, because he has entirely forgot the incidents of these days, that the present self is not the same person with the self of that time; and by that means overturn all the most established notions of personal identity? In this view, therefore, memory does not so much *produce* as *discover* personal identity, by showing us the relation of cause and effect among our different perceptions. It will be incumbent on those who affirm that memory produces entirely our personal identity, to give a reason why we can thus extend our identity beyond our memory.   (T 261–2)

SCEPTICISM

The traditional view of Hume, as was mentioned earlier, takes him to be an extreme sceptic, to have undermined the claims to validity of the whole body of our beliefs in the external world, the self and causation. More recently, the idea has gained ground that he has sceptically established the limits of rational justification, turned reason on itself, in order to show that these beliefs are nevertheless natural, instinctive and inevitable. In explaining how we in fact come to have the beliefs that we do, he shows that we are so constituted that we cannot help having them. After all, unless there were something to be said for them, what does he think he is doing in explaining them, since explanation is a matter of bringing things under causal laws?

Interpretation of Hume is made difficult by a kind of oscillation between two moods in which he contemplates the results of his own investigations. In one of them he looks on them with depression and despair, not knowing which way to turn. In the other, more cheerfully, he observes that as soon as we reimmerse ourselves in everyday life, the injuries inflicted by reason on itself fade away and we comfortably fall back into our customary, natural habits of belief. We should not seek to find some external support for these habits, which is a quest doomed to depressing failure. We should carry on with them in a chastened way, realizing that there is no certainty outside the realm of the abstract relations of ideas and marginally regulating them by adhering to the 'settled principles of the understanding' and avoiding wild, superstitious, ways of believing.

Analytic philosophers in the twentieth century (anticipated by J. S. Mill) took the features of our experience, which Hume used to explain our beliefs in objects, selves and causes, rather as defining what those beliefs, despite first appearances, actually amount to. They have defined objects as systems of actual and possible impressions, whose structure is intimated by the constant and coherent bits that are actually experienced (phenomenalism), selves as related series of mental events (the bundle theory) and causality as regular succession (the regularity theory). That is less disconcertingly sceptical than Hume's position. But this strategy leaves us with what seems to be a seriously diminished residue of what we originally believed. What is more, in the case of objects and causes, since belief in them, even in its attenuated form, is an open, generalized inference from partial evidence, it remains exposed to doubt about induction.

It has been suggested that Hume was really interested more in the concrete, practical topics of the later books of the *Treatise* than in the theoretical philosophy of book I, in morals, politics and psychology rather than in the theory of knowledge. As a pyrotechnical display of the limits of our minds as sources of certain knowledge, its purpose was to incapacitate dogmatism in those regions of belief where the passions were strongly involved.

This sceptical doubt, both with respect to reason and the senses, is a malady which can never be radically cured, but must return upon us every moment, however we may chase it away, and sometimes seem entirely free from it. It is impossible, on any system, to defend either our understanding or senses; and we but expose them further when we endeavour to justify them in that manner. As the sceptical doubt arises naturally from a profound and intense reflection on those subjects, it always increases the further we carry our reflections, whether in opposition or conformity to it. Carelessness and inattention alone can afford us any remedy. For this reason I rely entirely upon them; and take it for granted, whatever may be the reader's opinion at this present moment, that an hour hence he will be persuaded there is both an external and internal world.   (T 218)

The *intense* view of these manifold contradictions and imperfections in human reason has so wrought upon me, and heated my brain, that I am ready to reject all belief and reasoning, and can look upon no opinion even as more probable or likely than another. Where am I, or what? From what causes do I derive my existence, and to what condition shall I return? Whose favour shall I court, and whose anger must I dread? What beings surround me? and on whom have I any influence, or who have any influence on me? I am confounded with all these questions, and begin to fancy myself in the most deplorable condition imaginable, environed with the deepest darkness, and utterly deprived of the use of every member and faculty.

Most fortunately it happens, that since reason is incapable of dispelling these clouds, Nature herself suffices to that purpose, and cures me of this philosophical melancholy and delirium, either by relaxing this bent of mind, or by some avocation, and lively impression of my senses, which obliterate all these chimeras. I dine, I play a game of backgammon, I converse, and am merry with my friends; and when, after three or four hours' amusement, I would return to these speculations, they appear so cold, and strained, and ridiculous, that I cannot find in my heart to enter into them any further.   (T 268–9)

SCEPTICISM

The traditional view of Hume, as was mentioned earlier, takes him to be an extreme sceptic, to have undermined the claims to validity of the whole body of our beliefs in the external world, the self and causation. More recently, the idea has gained ground that he has sceptically established the limits of rational justification, turned reason on itself, in order to show that these beliefs are nevertheless natural, instinctive and inevitable. In explaining how we in fact come to have the beliefs that we do, he shows that we are so constituted that we cannot help having them. After all, unless there were something to be said for them, what does he think he is doing in explaining them, since explanation is a matter of bringing things under causal laws?

Interpretation of Hume is made difficult by a kind of oscillation between two moods in which he contemplates the results of his own investigations. In one of them he looks on them with depression and despair, not knowing which way to turn. In the other, more cheerfully, he observes that as soon as we reimmerse ourselves in everyday life, the injuries inflicted by reason on itself fade away and we comfortably fall back into our customary, natural habits of belief. We should not seek to find some external support for these habits, which is a quest doomed to depressing failure. We should carry on with them in a chastened way, realizing that there is no certainty outside the realm of the abstract relations of ideas and marginally regulating them by adhering to the 'settled principles of the understanding' and avoiding wild, superstitious, ways of believing.

Analytic philosophers in the twentieth century (anticipated by J. S. Mill) took the features of our experience, which Hume used to explain our beliefs in objects, selves and causes, rather as defining what those beliefs, despite first appearances, actually amount to. They have defined objects as systems of actual and possible impressions, whose structure is intimated by the constant and coherent bits that are actually experienced (phenomenalism), selves as related series of mental events (the bundle theory) and causality as regular succession (the regularity theory). That is less disconcertingly sceptical than Hume's position. But this strategy leaves us with what seems to be a seriously diminished residue of what we originally believed. What is more, in the case of objects and causes, since belief in them, even in its attenuated form, is an open, generalized inference from partial evidence, it remains exposed to doubt about induction.

It has been suggested that Hume was really interested more in the concrete, practical topics of the later books of the *Treatise* than in the theoretical philosophy of book I, in morals, politics and psychology rather than in the theory of knowledge. As a pyrotechnical display of the limits of our minds as sources of certain knowledge, its purpose was to incapacitate dogmatism in those regions of belief where the passions were strongly involved.

This sceptical doubt, both with respect to reason and the senses, is a malady which can never be radically cured, but must return upon us every moment, however we may chase it away, and sometimes seem entirely free from it. It is impossible, on any system, to defend either our understanding or senses; and we but expose them further when we endeavour to justify them in that manner. As the sceptical doubt arises naturally from a profound and intense reflection on those subjects, it always increases the further we carry our reflections, whether in opposition or conformity to it. Carelessness and inattention alone can afford us any remedy. For this reason I rely entirely upon them; and take it for granted, whatever may be the reader's opinion at this present moment, that an hour hence he will be persuaded there is both an external and internal world. (T 218)

The *intense* view of these manifold contradictions and imperfections in human reason has so wrought upon me, and heated my brain, that I am ready to reject all belief and reasoning, and can look upon no opinion even as more probable or likely than another. Where am I, or what? From what causes do I derive my existence, and to what condition shall I return? Whose favour shall I court, and whose anger must I dread? What beings surround me? and on whom have I any influence, or who have any influence on me? I am confounded with all these questions, and begin to fancy myself in the most deplorable condition imaginable, environed with the deepest darkness, and utterly deprived of the use of every member and faculty.

Most fortunately it happens, that since reason is incapable of dispelling these clouds, Nature herself suffices to that purpose, and cures me of this philosophical melancholy and delirium, either by relaxing this bent of mind, or by some avocation, and lively impression of my senses, which obliterate all these chimeras. I dine, I play a game of backgammon, I converse, and am merry with my friends; and when, after three or four hours' amusement, I would return to these speculations, they appear so cold, and strained, and ridiculous, that I cannot find in my heart to enter into them any further. (T 268–9)

MORALITY AND THE PASSIONS

Hume devoted the second of the three books of the *Treatise* to the passions. In this he was following the example of his great systematic predecessors, Descartes, Hobbes and Spinoza. But where their procedure was analytic, almost algebraic, a matter of classifying feelings and emotions and then going on to define the bulk of them in terms of such elemental items as pleasure, pain and desire, his was more descriptive and psychologically explanatory. Although full of bright ideas, his discussion is, on the whole, tedious and meandering, a riot of associationist speculation, relieved here and there, nevertheless, with flashes of insight. It has never provoked the interest and discussion excited by his accounts of knowledge and morality.

But there are three important things in his exposition. The first is a set of large, general distinctions within the field it covers. Passions are distinguished as violent or calm (which shows that he does not mean what we do by 'passion', namely violent emotion), as direct (that is, natural or instinctive) or indirect, and as strong or weak. A calm passion (such as prudence) can overcome and so show itself to be stronger than a violent one (such as lust). Secondly, there is an interesting and influential treatment of the problem of the freedom of the will. Thirdly, and most important for the theory of morality that is to follow, he insists that reason is 'inert', that it can never, on its own, and without the support of passion, move us to action.

Hume's acceptance in practice, for all his theoretical doubts, of the law of universal causation, is shown by his contention that our actions are caused by our passions as much, and as comprehensively, as natural events are by natural causes. That rules out 'liberty of indifference'. But the non-existence of unmotivated action is hardly a cause of concern. We often feel free in action and that is because we sometimes act without coercion or constraint: that is to say, in accordance with our desires. That is the kind of freedom that should concern us, for we can only be sensibly held responsible for actions that we have caused. Only they are going to be amenable to the sanctions of praise and blame, reward and punishment.

Hume proclaims the inertness of reason in his notorious pronouncement 'reason is and ought only to be the slave of the passions'. 'Ought only to be' is an irrelevant rhetorical flourish. So is 'slave', which should be 'serves instrumentally for the satisfaction of' and so is 'passion' in the sense in which we understand the word now. Moral convictions move us to action; reason alone cannot do so; therefore, moral convictions are not the product of reason. He offers a number of other rather elaborate and not very persuasive arguments for the conclusion. But he has a significant argument to show that the morality of an action is not a matter of fact. Take any action agreed to be vicious; examine it as hard as you can. You will never find vice in it. Much the same point is made in his contention that the passage from *is* to *ought*, everywhere to be found in moral discourse, should be explained or justified.

The source of morality in the passions is sympathy, the natural inclination to be pleased by the happiness, pained by the suffering, of others. That explains, associatively, the natural impulse of benevolence.

Self-interest is natural or instinctive too, but it is not our exclusive form of motivation. Sympathy underlies the practice of disinterested contemplation of people's actions and characters. When the result of such contemplation is pleasant, it is moral approval; when unpleasant, disapproval. What is it about people's characters and actions that causes these emotional reactions (which, being emotions, are neither true nor false)? Hume's answer is that we react approvingly to what is useful or agreeable to the agent or others. But qualities useful or agreeable to the agent seem to be natural rather than moral virtues, gifts of character, like prudence or courage, rather than virtues strictly so called. Hume is not constrained by this over-inclusive formula. For the most part he explains the virtues by their contribution to the utility of society in general.

It is quite a short step from this position – but it is one that Hume does not take – to say that moral approval is not just *explained* by the utility of what it is bestowed on, but *implies* and is *justified* by the utility of what is approved. That would leave room – as Hume does not – for the correction of approvals as mistaken if they are based on false judgements of utility. He does not appear to doubt that utility, the 'good of society', is a straightforward matter of fact. That, of course, is the position of the utilitarians proper, Bentham above all, and, with qualifications, John Stuart Mill.

Hume recognizes that our natural instinct of benevolence, although an independent principle of action alongside self-interest, does not reach all that far and tends to prevail only in our dealings with those who are close to us. But, beside the natural virtue of benevolence, there is also the artificial virtue of justice. In human society we depend crucially on each other, much more than other, more self-reliant animals. But by co-operation we can increase our strength, by division of labour our skill and by mutual aid our security from misfortune. To establish these desirable arrangements we set up such institutions as promise-keeping, property and the state.

The duties of respect for property, fidelity and allegiance yield beneficial consequences only if they are generally adhered to. A single act of benevolence can do good on its own, but it is futile to respect property or obey a state that no one else respects or obeys. Hume on the whole identifies justice with respect for property. The scarcity of goods in relation to the strength of people's desire for them leads to conflict. Settled rules for the acquisition, possession and transfer of property are necessary for social peace. The rules of justice are useful only as a system, so the rules should be adhered to even where their application produces an exceptional bad result.

Justice and the other artificial virtues have no direct support from the passions. We all have a strong self-interested motive for general respect for them. That becomes moralized by the transfer of self-interested approval of them to a distinterested, moral approval of them as beneficial to society, an effect of sympathy.

Hume's treatment of allegiance, the duty to obey the state and abide by its laws, deserves separate consideration.

I shall first prove from experience, that our actions have a constant union with our motives, tempers, and circumstances, before I consider the inferences we draw from it.

To this end a very slight and general view of the common course of human affairs will be sufficient. There is no light, in which we can take them, that does not confirm this principle. Whether we consider mankind according to the difference of sexes, ages, governments, conditions, or methods of education; the same uniformity and regular operation of natural principles are discernible. Like causes still produce like effects; in the same manner as in the mutual action of the elements and powers of nature.   (T 401)

After we have performed any action; though we confess we were influenced by particular views and motives; it is difficult for us to persuade ourselves we were governed by necessity, and that it was utterly impossible for us to have acted otherwise; the idea of necessity seeming to imply something of force, and violence, and constraint, of which we are not sensible. Few are capable of distinguishing betwixt the liberty of *spontaneity*, as it is called in the schools, and the liberty of *indifference*; betwixt that which is opposed to violence, and that which means a negation of necessity and causes. The first is even the most common sense of the word; and as it is only that species of liberty, which it concerns us to preserve, our thoughts have been principally turned towards it, and have almost universally confounded it with the other.   (T 410)

Men are not blamed for such actions as they perform ignorantly and casually, whatever may be the consequences. Why? but because the principles of these actions are only momentary, and terminate in them alone. Men are less blamed for such actions as they perform hastily or unpremeditately than for such as proceed from deliberation. For what reason? but because a hasty temper, though a constant cause or principle in the mind, operates only by intervals and infects not the whole character. Again, repentance wipes off every crime, if attended with a reformation of life and manners. How is this to be accounted for? not by asserting that actions render a person criminal merely as they are proofs of criminal principles in the mind; and when, by an alteration of these principles, they cease to be just proofs, they likewise cease to be criminal. But, except upon the doctrine of necessity, they never were just proofs, and consequently never were criminal.

(E98–9)

Nothing is more usual in philosophy, and even in common life, than to talk of the combat of passion and reason, to give the preference to reason, and to assert that men are only so far virtuous as they conform themselves to its dictates. Every rational creature, it is said, is obliged to regulate his actions by reason; and if any other motive or principle challenge the direction of his conduct, he ought to oppose it, till it be entirely subdued, or at least brought to a conformity with that superior principle. On this method of thinking the greatest part of moral philosophy, ancient and modern, seems to be founded . . . In order to show the fallacy of all this philosophy, I shall endeavour to prove *first*, that reason alone can never be a motive to any action of the will; and *secondly*, that it can never oppose passion in the direction of the will.

(T 413)

It is obvious, that when we have the prospect of pain or pleasure from any object, we feel a consequent emotion of aversion or propensity, and are carried to avoid or embrace what will give us this uneasiness or satisfaction. It is also obvious, that this emotion rests not here, but making us cast our view on every side, comprehends whatever objects are connected with its original one by the relation of cause and effect. Here then reasoning takes place to discover this relation; and according as our reasoning varies, our actions receive a subsequent variation. But it is evident in this case, that the impulse arises not from reason, but is only directed by it. It is from the prospect of pain or pleasure that the aversion or propensity arises towards any object; and these emotions extend themselves to the causes and effects of that object, as they are pointed out to us by reason and experience. It can never in the least concern us to know, that such objects are causes, and such others effects, if both the causes and effects be indifferent to us. When the objects themselves do not affect us, their connection can never give them any influence; and it is plain, that as reason is nothing but the discovery of this connection, it cannot be by its means that the objects are able to affect us.

Since reason alone can never produce any action, or give rise to volition, I infer, that the same faculty is as incapable of preventing volition, or of disputing the preference with any passion or emotion . . . Thus it appears, that the principle, which opposes our passion, cannot be the same with reason, and is only called so in an improper sense. We speak not strictly and philosophically when we talk of the combat of passion and of reason. Reason is and ought only to be the slave of the passions, and can never pretend to any other office than to serve and obey them.   (T 414-15)

If morality had naturally no influence on human passions and actions, it were in vain to take such pains to inculcate it; and nothing would be more fruitless than that multitude of rules and precepts, with which all moralists abound. Philosophy is commonly divided into *speculative* and *practical*; and as morality is always comprehended under the latter division, it is supposed to influence our passions and actions, and to go beyond the calm and indolent judgements of the understanding. And this is confirmed by common experience, which informs us, that men are often governed by their duties, and are deterred from some actions by the opinion of injustice, and impelled to others by that of obligation.

Since morals, therefore, have an influence on the actions and affections, it follows, that they cannot be derived from reason; and that because reason alone, as we have already proved, can never have any such influence. Morals excite passions, and produce or prevent actions. Reason of itself is utterly impotent in this particular. The rules of morality, therefore, are not conclusions of our reason.   (T 457)

But can there be any difficulty in proving, that vice and virtue are matters of fact, whose existence we can infer by reason? Take any action allowed to be vicious; wilful murder, for instance. Examine it in all lights, and see if you can find that matter of fact, or real existence, which you call *vice*. In whichever way you take it, you find only certain passions, motives, volitions, and thoughts. There is no other matter of fact in the case. The vice entirely escapes you, as long as you consider the object. You never can find it till you turn your reflection into your own breast, and find a sentiment of disapprobation, which arises in you, towards this action. Here is a matter of fact; but it is the object of feeling, not of reason. It lies in yourself, not in the object. So that when you pronounce any action or character to be vicious, you mean nothing, but that from the constitution of your nature you have a feeling or sentiment of blame from the contemplation of it. Vice and virtue, therefore, may be compared to sounds, colours, heat and cold, which, according to modern philosophy, are not qualities in objects, but perceptions in the mind; and this discovery in morals, like that other in physics, is to be regarded as a considerable advancement of the speculative sciences; though, like that too, it has little or no influence on practice. Nothing can be more real, or concern us more, than our own sentiments of pleasure and uneasiness; and if these be favourable to virtue, and unfavourable to vice, no more can be requisite to the regulation of our conduct and behaviour.

I cannot forbear adding to these reasonings an observation, which may, perhaps, be found of some importance. In every system of morality, which I have hitherto met with, I have always remarked, that the author proceeds for some time in the ordinary way of reasoning, and establishes the being of a God, or makes observations concerning human affairs; when of a sudden I am surprised to find, that instead of the usual copulations of propositions, *is* and *is not*, I meet with no proposition that is not connected with an *ought*, or an *ought not*. The change is imperceptible; but is, however, of the last consequence. For as this ought, or ought not, expresses some new relation, or affirmation, it is necessary that it should be observed and explained; and at the same time that a reason should be given, for what seems altogether inconceivable, how this new relation can be a deduction from others, which are entirely different from it.   (T 468–9)

We may observe, that all the circumstances requisite for its [sympathy's] operation are found in most of the virtues; which have, for the most part, a tendency to the good of society, or to that of the person possessed of them. If we compare all these circumstances, we shall not doubt, that sympathy is the chief source of moral distinctions; especially when we reflect, that no objection can be raised against this hypothesis in one case, which will not extend to all cases. Justice is certainly approved of for no other reason, than because it has a tendency to the public good; and the public good is indifferent to us, except so far as sympathy interests us in it. We may presume the like with regard to all the other virtues, which have a like tendency to the public good. They must derive all their merit from our sympathy with those, who reap any advantage from them; as the virtues, which have a tendency to the good of the person possessed of them, derive their merit from our sympathy with him.   (T 618)

The only difference betwixt the natural virtues and justice lies in this, that the good, which results from the former, arises from every single act, and is the object of some natural passion; whereas a single act of justice, considered in itself, may often be contrary to the public good; and it is only the concurrence of mankind, in a general scheme or system of action, which is advantageous. When I relieve persons in distress, my natural humanity is my motive; and so far as my succour extends, so have I promoted the happiness of my fellow-creatures. But if we examine all the questions, that come before any tribunal of justice, we shall find, that, considering each case apart, it would as often be an instance of humanity to decide contrary to the laws of justice as conformable to them. Judges take from a poor man to give to a rich; they bestow on the dissolute the labour of the industrious; and put into the hands of the vicious the means of harming both themselves and others. The whole scheme, however, of law and justice is advantageous to the society; and it was with a view to this advantage, that men by their arbitrary conventions, established it. After it is once established by these conventions, it is *naturally* attended with a strong sentiment of morals; which can proceed from nothing but our sympathy with the interests of society. We need no other explication of that esteem, which attends such of the natural virtues as have a tendency to the public good. (T 579–80)

To avoid giving offence, I must here observe, that when I deny justice to be natural virtue, I make use of the word *natural*, only as opposed to *artificial*. In another sense of the word; as no principle of the human mind is more natural than a sense of virtue; so no virtue is more natural than justice. Mankind is an inventive species; and where an invention is obvious and absolutely necessary, it may as properly be said to be natural as anything that proceeds immediately from original principles, without the intervention of thought or reflection. Though the rules of justice be *artificial*, they are not *arbitrary*. Nor is the expression improper to call them *Laws of Nature*, if by natural we understand what is common to any species, or even if we confine it to mean what is inseparable from the species. (T 484)

Upon the whole, then, we are to consider this distinction betwixt justice and injustice, as having two different foundations, viz. that of *interest*, when men observe, that it is impossible to live in society without restraining themselves by certain rule, and that of *morality*, when this interest is once observed, and men receive a pleasure from the view of such actions as tend to the peace of society, and an uneasiness from such as are contrary to it. It is the voluntary convention and artifice of men, which makes the first interest take place; and therefore those laws of justice are so far to be considered as *artificial*. After that interest is once established and acknowledged, the sense of morality in the observance of these rules follows *naturally* and of itself; though it is certain, that it is augmented by a new *artifice*, and that the public instructions of politicians, and the private education of parents, contribute to the giving us a sense of honour and duty in the strict regulation of our actions with regard to the properties of others. (T 533–4)

RELIGION

Hume's writings on religion are as brilliant as anything he produced, and it seems reasonable to suppose that they are a large part of the practical point (which was never far from his thoughts) of his more theoretical inquiries. The least substantial, but by no means least entertaining, is *The Natural History of Religion*. Its main theme is the causes and consequences of the religious development of mankind from polytheism to monotheism. That there has been such a development is shown, he believes, by the polytheism of contemporary savages, whom our remote, primitive ancestors must have resembled. They were impelled into belief in gods by particular fearful or calamitous events, not by any sophisticated reflection on the origins of the universe as an ordered whole. A special concern to flatter and promote one god among the rest gave rise to monotheism. It is less tolerant than its savage predecessor. Another moral deficiency of monotheism is its preference for such 'monkish virtues' as humility as opposed to the courage and self-reliance of our ancestors. Belief in a god or gods is not natural like belief in an external world, since there are races in which it is not to be found.

The Dialogues on Natural Religion, which Hume prudently kept back from publication until after his death, is perhaps the most witty and scintillating of his works. It is certainly the most ironical, so that some readers have sought to identify the author, not with the most sceptical of the participants, Philo, but with the devout, but not fanatical, Cleanthes, who is the mouthpiece of Bishop Butler.

The principal target of the *Dialogues* is the argument from design, that well-loved intellectual device of the eighteenth century, which infers the existence of God from evidence of order and of the adaptation of means to ends in nature. Hume takes the argument to pieces with the utmost perseverance. The analogy between man and his productions on the one hand and God and nature on the other has a number of crippling defects. We have seen many men putting up buildings, but we have no direct access to gods putting up natures. It is wrong to ascribe perfections like unlimited power, wisdom and goodness to the hypothetical cause of something so suffused with imperfections as the natural world. Is it not, anyway, quite as much like a vegetable growth as it is like a mechanical contrivance? Perhaps, if of divine workmanship at all, it is the work of several gods, or of a young one or an old one. Whatever qualities his production justifies us in ascribing to the author of nature, they can have no bearing on our conduct. Never has such a large, widely believed and intellectually respectable doctrine been so devastatingly and so stylishly reduced to rubble.

Hume repels the claims of revelation, as contrasted with reason, in his essay on miracles in the first *Enquiry*. The central argument is concise but very hard to answer. Confronted by testimony to a supposed miracle, Hume says, we should ask whether it is even more of a miracle that the testimony should be false. Since the alleged miracles of the New Testament, observed by uneducated men with an emotional interest in their acceptance, have passed on to us through a long chain of limitedly reliable intermediaries, it is not in the least miraculous that the reports of them should be mistaken.

It appears to me, that, if we consider the improvement of human society, from rude beginnings to a state of greater perfection, polytheism or idolatry was, and necessarily must have been, the first and most ancient religion of mankind.

Polytheism or idolatrous worship, being founded entirely in vulgar traditions, is liable to this great inconvenience, that any practice or opinion, however barbarous or corrupted, may be authorized by it; and full scope is given, for knavery to impose on credulity, till morals and humanity be expelled from the religious systems of mankind. At the same time, idolatry is attended with this evident advantage, that, by limiting the powers and functions of its deities, it naturally admits the gods of other sects and nations to a share of divinity, and renders all the various deities, as well as rites, ceremonies, or traditions, compatible with each other. Theism is opposite in both its advantages and disadvantages. As that system supposes one sole deity, the perfection of reason and goodness, it should, if justly prosecuted, banish everything frivolous, unreasonable, or inhuman from religious worship, and set before men the most illustrious example, as well as the most commanding motives, of justice and benevolence. These mighty advantages are not indeed over-balanced (for that is not possible), but somewhat diminished, by inconveniences, which arise from the vices and prejudices of mankind. While one sole object of devotion is acknowledged, the worship of other deities is regarded as absurd and impious. Nay, this unity of object seems naturally to require the unity of faith and ceremonies, and furnishes designing men with a pretence for representing their adversaries as profane, and the objects of divine as well as human vengeance. For as each sect is positive that its own faith and worship are entirely acceptable to the deity, and as no one can conceive, that the same being should be pleased with different and opposite rites and principles; the several sects fall naturally into animosity, and mutually discharge on each other that sacred zeal and rancour, the most furious and implacable of all human passions. (N60)

There is an evident absurdity in pretending to demonstrate a matter of fact, or to prove it by any arguments *a priori*. Nothing is demonstrable, unless the contrary implies a contradiction. Whatever we conceive as existent, we can also conceive as non-existent. There is no being, therefore, whose non-existence implies a contradiction. Consequently, there is no being, whose existence is demonstrable. I propose this argument as entirely decisive, and am willing to rest the whole controversy on it.   (D 232–3)

You, then, who are my accusers, have acknowledged, that the chief or sole argument for a divine existence (which I never questioned) is derived from the order of nature; where there appear such marks of intelligence and design, that you think it extravagant to assign for its cause, either, chance, or the blind and unguided force of matter . . .

    When we infer any particular cause from an effect, we must proportion the one to the other, and can never be allowed to the cause any qualities, but what are exactly sufficient to produce the effect. A body of ten ounces raised in any scale may serve as a proof, that the counter-balancing weight exceeds ten ounces; but can never afford a reason that it exceeds a hundred. If the cause, assigned for any effect, be not sufficient to produce it, we must either reject that cause, or add to it such qualities as will give it a just proportion to the effect. But if we ascribe to it farther qualities, or affirm it capable of producing other effects, we can only indulge the licence of conjecture, and arbitrarily suppose the existence of qualities and energies, without reason or authority.   (E 135–6)

I much doubt whether it be possible for a cause to be known only by its effect (as you have all along supposed) or to be of so singular and particular a nature as to have no parallel and no similarity with any other cause or object, that has ever fallen under our observation. It is only when two *species* of objects are found to be constantly conjoined, that we can infer the one from the other; and were an effect presented, which was entirely singular, and could not be comprehended under any known *species*, I do not see, that we could form any conjecture or inference at all concerning its cause. If experience and observation and analogy be, indeed, the only guides which we can reasonably follow in inferences of this nature; both the effect and cause must bear a similarity and resemblance to other effects and causes, which we know, and which we have found, in many instances, to be conjoined with each other.   (E 148)

This contrariety of evidence, in the present case [miracles], may be derived from several different causes; from the opposition of contrary testimony; from the character or number of the witnesses; from the manner of their delivering their testimony; or from the union of all these circumstances. We entertain a suspicion concerning any matter of fact, when the witnesses contradict each other; when they are but few or of a doubtful character; when they have an interest in what they affirm; when they deliver their testimony with hesitation, or, on the contrary, with too violent asseverations. There are many other particulars of the same kind, which may diminish or destroy the force of any argument, derived from human testimony.   (Ess 522–3)

Let us suppose, that the fact which they affirm, instead of being only marvellous, is really miraculous; and suppose also, that the testimony considered apart and in itself, amounts to an entire proof; in that case, there is proof against proof, of which the strongest must prevail, but still with a diminution of its force, in proportion to that of its antagonist.

A miracle is a violation of the laws of nature; and as a firm and unalterable experience has established these laws, the proof against a miracle, from the very nature of the fact, is as entire as any argument from experience can possibly be imagined.   (Ess 524)

Nothing is esteemed a miracle if it ever happen in the common course of nature. It is no miracle that a man, seemingly in good health, should die on a sudden; because such a kind of death, though more unusual than any other, has yet been frequently observed to happen. But it is a miracle, that a dead man should come to life: because that has never been observed in any age or country. There must, therefore, be a uniform experience against every miraculous event, otherwise the event would not merit that appellation. And as a uniform experience amounts to a proof, there is here a direct and full *proof*, from the nature of the fact, against the existence of any miracle; nor can such a proof be destroyed, or the miracle rendered credible, but by an opposite proof which is superior.

The plain consequence is (and it is a general maxim worthy of our attention), 'That no testimony is sufficient to establish a miracle, unless the testimony be of such a kind, that its falsehood would be more miraculous, than the fact, which it endeavours to establish; and even in that case there is a mutual destruction of arguments, and the superior only gives us an assurance suitable to that degree of force, which remains, after deducting the inferior'. When anyone tells me, that he saw a dead man restored to life, I immediately consider with myself, whether it be more probable, that this person should either deceive or be deceived, or that the fact, which he relates, should really have happened. I weigh the one miracle against the other; and according to the superiority, which I discover, I pronounce my decision, and always reject the greater miracle. If the falsehood of his testimony would be more miraculous, than the event which he relates; then, and not till then, can he pretend to command my belief and opinion.

(Ess 525–6).

Upon the whole, we may conclude, that the *Christian Religion* not only was at first attended with miracles, but even at this day cannot be believed by any reasonable person without one.   (Ess 544)

EPILOGUE

In a short survey like this there is no room to do more than mention two more fields in which Hume was active: economics and aesthetics. Several of his essays are on economic subjects. In his powerful defence of free trade and in his refutation of mercantilist superstitions about retained gold and silver as a measure of a country's wealth, he anticipated, and perhaps influenced, his devoted friend Adam Smith, whose *Wealth of Nations* came out in the year of Hume's death, just in time for him to read it.

His views on 'taste' are what one might suspect from his account of morality. Beauty is not an intrinsic property of things, but is projected on to them by disinterested contemplators who find their 'form and disposition' pleasing. Association leads us from such direct responses to others, which take account of the utility of things. A tapered column pleases, since its broader base suggests greater strength and solidity. He tries with great ingenuity to answer the question: why does tragedy give us pleasure?

Hume was a wonderful man. He combined two pairs of qualities that have a certain affinity, but are quite often not found together. On the cognitive side, he was both supremely intelligent and extraordinarily clever, the exclusive gifts, one might suggest, of Aristotle and Jean Cocteau. In the domain of character and conduct, he was both morally virtuous (Adam Smith thought him the most perfectly virtuous man he had ever encountered) and inexhaustibly good-natured and sociable (the respective characteristics of Johnson and Boswell). He is at once the most admirable and the most lovable of philosophers, except in the judgement of pedants and prigs. He is also, for all his portly frame, red face and strong Scottish accent, the least ridiculous.

In his own time he was respected for his *History*, but his philosophy was ignored and his views about religion were regarded with horror. Kant claimed to have been woken from dogmatic slumber by reading him, but Hume would have acknowledged no responsibility for the result. Bentham was also dazzled, but more straightforwardly, even if he drew socially radical consequences from Hume's principles. Hume was not solemn enough to appeal to John Stuart Mill, whose theory of knowledge is, all the same, a kind of domestication of Hume. Russell, as mischievous and joke-loving as Hume, saw his own philosophy as a combination of Hume with modern logic. Wherever analytic philosophy is alive, as it still is in quite a number of places, Hume, more than any other great philosopher of the past, is still a force to reckon with.

Terry Eagleton

MARX

and Freedom

Hegel and Aristotle were certainly philosophers, but in what sense was Karl Marx? Marx wrote a good deal that has a philosophical look about it; but he was also brusquely scornful of the philosophic mind, and declared in his celebrated eleventh thesis on Feuerbach that 'the philosophers have only interpreted the world, in various ways; the point, however, is to change it'.[1] One might riposte that it would be hard to change a world which we did not understand, were it not for the fact that Marx himself would surely agree. He is not out to replace ideas with mindless action, but to fashion a kind of practical philosophy which will help to transform what it is seeking to comprehend. Social and intellectual change go together: 'Philosophy cannot realize itself without the transcendence of the proletariat', he writes, 'and the proletariat cannot realize itself without the realization of philosophy.'[2] His second thesis on Feuerbach runs:

> The question whether objective truth can be attributed to human thinking is not a question of theory, but a *practical* question. In practice man must prove the truth, that is, the reality and power, the this-sidedness of his thinking. The dispute over the reality or non-reality of thinking which is isolated from practice is a purely *scholastic* question.[3]

This special kind of action-orientated theory is sometimes known as 'emancipatory knowledge', and has a number of distinctive features. It is the kind of understanding of one's situation that a group or individual needs in order to change that situation; and it is thus among other things a new *self*-understanding. But to know yourself in a new way is to alter yourself in that very act; so we have here a peculiar form of cognition in which the act of knowing alters what it contemplates. In trying to understand myself and my condition, I can never remain quite identical with myself, since the self which is doing the understanding, as well as the self understood, are now different from what they were before. And if I wanted to understand all *this*, then just the same process would set in. It is rather like trying to jump on one's own shadow or yank oneself up by one's hair. And since such knowledge also moves people to change their condition in a practical way, it becomes itself a kind of social or political force, part of the material situation it examines rather than a mere 'reflection' of or upon it. It is knowledge as an historical event rather than as abstract speculation, in which knowing *that* is no longer clearly separable from knowing *how*. Moreover, to seek to emancipate yourself involves questions of value, while knowing about your situation is a matter of factual comprehension; so here the usual distinction philosophy acknowledges between facts and values becomes interestingly blurred. It is not just that this kind of knowledge can be put to valuable use, but that the motivation for understanding in the first place is bound up with a sense of value.

The eleventh thesis on Feuerbach, then, is not just some sort of philistine appeal to turn from abstract speculation to the 'real world', though there was a streak of this brisk anti-intellectualism in the early Marx. Such an appeal forgets that without abstract concepts there would be no real world for us in the first place. The irony of Marx's gesture is that he makes this demand as a philosopher, not just as a political activist. He can thus be said to join a distinguished lineage of 'anti-philosophers', one which includes Kierkegaard, Nietzsche, Heidegger, Adorno, Benjamin, Wittgenstein, and in our own time such thinkers as Jacques Derrida and Richard Rorty, for whom there is something fundamentally awry with the whole philosophical enterprise of their time. For these men, philosophy itself, not just this or that topic within it, has become a deeply problematic pursuit. They therefore want either to transcend the whole project for reasons which remain *philosophically* interesting, or to find some way of recasting it in a new key entirely, an aim which for many of these thinkers means forging a new style of theoretical writing. Most of them are out to deflate the metaphysical pretensions of philosophy, outflanking them with something apparently more fundamental: being, power, difference, practical forms of life, or in Marx's case 'historical conditions'. An anti-philosopher of this kind differs from a mere opponent of philosophy in much the same way that an 'anti-novel' like *Ulysses* differs from a non-novel like the telephone directory.

Why was Marx so sceptical of philosophy? For one thing, he saw it as starting from the wrong place. Philosophy did not begin far back enough. The fashionable German philosophy of his day – Idealism – began from ideas, seeing consciousness as the foundation of reality; but Marx was aware that just for us to have an idea, a good deal else must already have taken place. What must already have happened in order for us to begin to reflect? We must already be practically bound up with the world we are pondering, and so already inserted into a whole set of relations, material conditions, social institutions:

The production of ideas, of conceptions, of consciousness, is at first directly interwoven with the material activity and the material intercourse of men, the language of real life. Conceiving, thinking, the mental intercourse of men, appear at this stage as the direct efflux of their material behaviour. The same applies to mental production as expressed in the language of politics, laws, morality, religion, metaphysics, etc. of a people. Men are the producers of their conceptions, ideas, etc. – real, active men, as they are conditioned by a definite development of their productive forces and of the intercourse corresponding to these, up to its furthest forms. Consciousness can never be anything else than conscious existence, and the existence of men is their actual life-process.[4]

We should note here that while Marx wants, epistemologically speaking, to bind consciousness and the material world closely together, there is a *political* sense in which he wants to loosen up that relation. For him, as we shall see, we are most human and least like the other animals when we produce freely, gratuitously, independent of any immediate material need. Freedom for Marx is a kind of creative superabundance over what is materially essential, that which overflows the measure and becomes its own yardstick. It is just that, for all this to happen in society, certain material conditions are first required; so that the very 'excess' of consciousness over nature which Marx regards as a hallmark of our humanity is itself, ironically, a materially conditioned state of affairs. Where consciousness and social practice converge most obviously for Marx is in language itself:

Language is as old as consciousness, language *is* practical, real consciousness that exists for other men as well, and only therefore does it also exist for me; language, like consciousness, only arises from the need, the necessity, of intercourse with other men.   (GI 51)

But if language arises from need, as a necessary dimension of collective labour, it does not remain leashed to that necessity, as the phenomenon known as literature bears witness.

When it comes not just to 'consciousness', but to the systematic sort of reflection known as philosophy, then this clearly requires specialists, academies and a host of allied institutions, all of which can ultimately be funded only by the labour of others. This is one aspect of what Marx means by the division of mental and manual labour. Only when a society has achieved a certain economic surplus over material necessity, releasing a minority of its members from the demands of productive labour into the privilege of becoming full-time politicians, academics, cultural producers

and so on, can philosophy in its fullest sense flower into being. Now
thought can begin to fantasize that it is independent of material reality,
just because there is a material sense in which it actually is:

> Division of labour only becomes truly such from the moment when a
> division of mental and manual labour appears. (The first form of
> ideologists, *priests*, is concurrent.) From this moment onwards con-
> sciousness *can* really flatter itself that it is something other than
> consciousness of existing practice, that it *really* represents something
> without representing something real; from now on consciousness is in a
> position to emancipate itself from the world and to proceed to the
> formation of 'pure' theory, theology, philosophy, ethics, etc. (GI 51)

For Marx, culture really has only one parent, and that is labour – which
for him is equivalent to saying, exploitation. The culture of class society
tends to repress this unwelcome truth; it prefers to dream up for itself a
nobler progenitor, denying its lowly parenthood and imagining that it
sprang simply from previous culture, or from the unfettered individual
imagination. But Marx is out to remind us that our thought, like our very
physical senses, is itself a product of the history with which it engages.
History – the real world – always in some way outruns the thought which
seeks to enfold it, and Marx, who as a good dialectician emphasizes the
dynamic, open-ended, interactive nature of things, detested those over-
weening systems of thought which (like Hegelian Idealism) believed that
they could somehow stitch up the whole world within their concepts. It is
darkly ironic that his own work would, among other things, give birth in
time to just such sterile system-building.

The issue for Marx, then, is one of the material causes and conditions
of thought itself. We can inspect the causes of this or that, but can that
thought round upon itself, so to speak, to grasp something of the history
which produced it? Maybe for us moderns there are good reasons why
this can never be wholly attained, why there is always some kind of blind
spot, some necessary amnesia or self-opaqueness, which ensures that the
mind will always ultimately fail in this endeavour. Marx himself, as a
child of the Enlightenment, was perhaps rather more confident than we
are in the translucent power of reason; but as an historicist thinker – and
these twin currents, rationalist and historicist, are often in tension in his
work – he recognized that if all thought was historical, then this must
naturally be true of his own. There could not have been any Marxism in
the age of Charlemagne or Chaucer, since Marxism is more than just a set
of bright ideas which anyone, at any time, might have thought up. It is
rather a time- and place-bound phenomenon, which acknowledges that

the very categories in which it thinks – abstract labour, the commodity, the freely mobile individual and so on – could only have emerged from a heritage of capitalism and political liberalism. Marxism as a discourse emerges when it is both possible and necessary for it to do so, as the 'immanent critique' of capitalism, and so as a product of the very epoch it desires to move beyond. The *Communist Manifesto* is prodigal in its praise of the great revolutionary middle class, and of that mighty unshackling of human potential which we know as capitalism:

> The bourgeoisie, wherever it has got the upper hand, has put an end to all feudal, patriarchal, idyllic relations. It has pitilessly torn asunder the motley feudal ties that bound man to his 'natural superiors', and has left remaining no other nexus between man and man than naked self-interest, than callous 'cash payment'. It has drowned the most heavenly ecstasies of religious fervour, of chivalrous enthusiasm, of philistine sentimentalism, in the icy water of egotistical calculation . . . In one word, for exploitation, veiled by religious and political illusions, it has substituted naked, shameless, direct, brutal exploitation . . . [It] has torn away from the family its sentimental veil, and has reduced the family relation to a mere money relation . . . The bourgeoisie cannot exist without constantly revolutionizing the instruments of production, and thereby the relations of production, and with them the whole relations of society . . . Constant revolutionizing of production, uninterrupted disturbance of all social conditions, everlasting uncertainty and agitation distinguish the bourgeois epoch from all earlier ones. All fixed, fast-frozen relations, with their train of ancient and venerable prejudices and opinions, are swept away, all new-formed ones become antiquated before they can ossify. All that is solid melts into air, all that is holy is profaned, and man is at last compelled to face with sober senses, his real conditions of life, and his relations with his kind.[5]

It is these revolutionary energies, at once admirable and devastating, that on the one hand lay the material basis for socialism, and on the other hand frustrate that project at every turn. Capitalism sweeps aside all traditional forms of oppression, and in doing so brings humanity face to face with a brutal reality which socialism must then acknowledge and transform.

To grasp one's thought as rooted in the very material conditions it seeks to examine is to be a materialist philosopher, a phrase about which there is more than a hint of paradox. The task of a materialist thought is to calculate into itself that reality – the material world – which is external to thought itself, and which is in some sense more fundamental than it. This is what Marx means by claiming that, in the history of the human species, 'social being' determines consciousness, and not, as the Idealists would have it, vice versa:

> Morality, religion, metaphysics, all the rest of ideology and their corresponding forms of consciousness, thus no longer retain the semblance of independence. They have no history, no development; but men, developing their material production and their material intercourse, alter, along with this their real existence, their thinking and the products of their thinking. Life is not determined by consciousness, but consciousness by life.   (GI 47)

Here, then, is Marx's well-known inversion of Hegel, whose topsy-turvy dialectic, of ideas determining social existence, must be set firmly on its materialist feet. For Marx, what we say or think is ultimately determined by what we do. It is historical practices which lie at the bottom of our language games. But some caution is needed here. For what we do as historical beings is of course itself deeply bound up with thought and language; there is no human practice outside the realm of meaning, intention, imagination, as Marx himself insists:

> The animal is immediately at one with his life activity. It does not distinguish itself from it. It is *its life activity*. Man makes his life activity itself the object of his will and of his consciousness. He has conscious life activity. It is not a determination with which he directly merges. (EW 328) . . . A spider conducts operations that resemble those of a weaver, and a bee puts to shame many an architect in the construction of her cells. But what distinguishes the worst architect from the best of bees is that the architect raises his structure in imagination before he erects it in reality.[6]

Social being gives rise to thought, but is itself caught up in it. Even so, Marx wants to claim that the former is more fundamental – just as he wants to claim that the material 'base' of society gives rise to its cultural, legal, political and ideological 'superstructure':

> In the social production of their life, men enter into definite relations that are indispensable and independent of their will, *relations of production* which correspond to a definite stage of development of their material productive *forces*. The sum total of these relations of production constitutes the economic structure of society, the real

foundation, on which rises a legal and political superstructure and to which correspond definite forms of social consciousness. The mode of production of material life conditions the social, political and intellectual life process in general. It is not the consciousness of men that determines their being, but on the contrary, their social being that determines their consciousness. (Preface to *A Contribution to the Critique of Political Economy*, SW 182)

Here, then, is Marx's celebrated 'economic theory of history'. His claims about the priorities of social being and consciousness are ontological ones, concerned with the way he takes human beings to be. The base/superstructure doctrine may well be this too: it argues that all social and political forms, and all major historical change, are ultimately determined by conflicts within material production. But the doctrine can also be seen rather more historically, as describing the way in which politics, law, ideology and so on operate in class societies. Marx's point is that in such social orders, precisely because the 'base' of social relations is unjust and contradictory, these forms have the function of ratifying, promoting or concealing this injustice, and so can be said in this sense to be secondary or 'superstructural' to them. There may then be an implication that if the social relations were just, such a superstructure would be unnecessary. We are concerned here, in other words, with the *political* function of ideas in society, not just with their material origin. And this brings us to the Marxist concept of ideology.

The ideas of the ruling class are in every epoch the ruling ideas, i.e. the class which is the ruling *material* force of society, is at the same time its ruling *intellectual* force. The class which has the means of material production at its disposal, has control at the same time over the means of mental production, so that thereby, generally speaking, the ideas of those who lack the means of mental production are subject to it. The ruling ideas are nothing more than the ideal expression of the dominant material relationships, the dominant material relationships grasped as ideas . . . (GI 64)

When philosophy becomes ideology, it tends to distract men and women from historical conflicts by insisting on the primacy of the spiritual, or by offering to resolve these conflicts at a higher, imaginary level. It is for this that Marx upbraids the Hegelians. His own view of history, by contrast,

. . . depends upon our ability to expound the real process of production, starting out from the material production of life itself, and to comprehend the form of intercourse connected with this and created by this mode of production (i.e. civil society in its various stages), as the basis of all history; and to show it in its action as State, to explain all the different theoretical forms and products of consciousness, religion, philosophy, ethics, etc. etc. and trace their origin and growth from that basis; by which means, of course, the whole thing can be depicted in its totality (and therefore, too, the reciprocal action of these various sides on one another). (GI 58)

Unlike Idealist thought, such a materialist viewpoint 'remains constantly on the real *ground* of history':

[I]t does not explain practice from the idea but explains the formation of ideas from material practice; and accordingly it comes to the conclusion that all forms and products of consciousness cannot be dissolved by mental criticism, by resolution into 'self-consciousness' or transformation into 'apparitions', 'spectres', 'fancies', etc. but only by the practical overthrow of the actual social relations which gave rise to this idealistic humbug . . . (GI 58)

Marx's point is that if key theoretical problems have their anchorage in social contradictions, then they can only be *politically* rather than philosophically resolved. A certain style of philosophizing thus gives rise to a certain 'decentring' of philosophy itself. Like many an anti-philosopher, Marx is trying here to shift the whole terrain on which the discourse is pitched, grasping philosophical puzzles as both symptomatic of a real historical subtext, and as a way of thrusting that subtext out of sight. Much as philosophy would like to dream that it is self-begotten, it has to confront its dependency on that which transcends it. The materialist approach

. . . shows that history does not end by being resolved into 'self-consciousness' as 'spirit of the spirit', but that in it at each stage there is found a material result: a sum of productive forces, an historically created relation of individuals to nature and to one another, which is handed down to each generation from its predecessor; a mass of productive forces, capital funds and conditions, which, on the one hand, is indeed modified by the new generation, but also on the other prescribes for it its conditions of life and gives it a definite development, a special character. It shows that circumstances make men just as much as men make circumstances. (GI59)

Humanity, then, is not just the determined product of its material conditions; if it were, how could Marx hope that it might one day transform them? He is not a 'mechanical' materialist like, say, Thomas Hobbes, viewing consciousness as the mere reflex of circumstance, but an *historical* materialist in the sense that he wishes to explain the origin, character and function of ideas in terms of the historical conditions to which they belong.

He seems to have forgotten, however, that not all philosophy is necessarily Idealist. His own thought is not, and neither was that of the great bourgeois materialists of the French Enlightenment from whom he learnt. Nor, for that matter, is all ideology 'Idealist'. Even so, Marx's view of Idealist philosophy is an original one: he sees it as a form of fantasy, striving to attain in the mind what cannot yet be achieved in historical reality. And in this sense, the resolution of historical contradictions would spell the death of philosophical speculation. But this is true too of Marx's own thought. There would be no place for Marxist philosophy in a truly communist society, since such theory exists purely to help bring such a society into being. Indeed, in its anti-utopian way, Marx's work has strikingly little to say about what that future state of affairs would actually look like. His thought, like all radical political theory, is thus finally self-abolishing. And this is perhaps the most profound sense in which it is historical.

ANTHROPOLOGY

(Post) modern thought tends to be anti-foundationalist, suspecting any objective ground to our existence as some arbitrary fiction of our own. Marx, by contrast, is a more classical or traditional thinker, for whom the ground of our being is that shared form of material nature he names 'species-being'. Like the phrase 'human nature', this concept hovers ambiguously between description and prescription, fact and value, an account of how we are and how we ought to be. We are naturally social animals, dependent upon each other for our very survival, yet this must become a political value as well as an anthropological fact. As an historicist thinker, Marx is out to rescue human institutions from the false eternality with which metaphysical thought has endowed them; what was historically created can always be historically changed. But he is also, somewhat paradoxically, a sort of Aristotelian essentialist, who holds that there is a human nature or essence, and that the just society would be one in which this nature was allowed to come into its own. How, then, does he resolve this apparent discrepancy in his thought?

He does so, like Hegel before him, by seeing change, development, as of the essence of humanity. It is of our nature to realize our powers; but what kind of powers are in question, and under what conditions we actualize them, is an historically specific affair. For the young Marx of the *Economic and Philosophical Manuscripts*, we are human in so far as we share a specific kind of 'species-being' with our fellow human creatures:

> The *human* essence of nature exists only for *social* man; for only here does nature exist for him as a *bond* with other *men*, as his existence for others and their existence for him, as the vital element of human reality; only here does it exist as the *basis* of his own *human* existence. Only here has his *natural* existence become his *human* existence and nature become man for him. *Society* is therefore the perfected unity in essence of man with nature, the true resurrection of nature, the realized naturalism of man and the realized humanism of nature . . . It is above all necessary to avoid once more establishing 'society' as an abstraction over against the individual. The individual *is* the *social being*. His vital expression – even when it does not appear in the direct form of a *communal* expression, conceived in association with other men – is therefore an expression and confirmation of *social life*. Man's individual and species-life are not two *distinct things* . . .   (EW 350)

Does this species-being have an end or goal? Is Marx a teleological thinker? In one sense yes, in another sense no. For the end of our species-being, in a kind of creative tautology, consists just in realizing itself. For Marx, as for other Romantic radicals, there is or should be no ultimate point to human existence beyond its self-delighting development:

> When communist *workmen* gather together, their immediate aim is instruction, propaganda, etc. But at the same time they acquire a new need – the need for society – and what appears as a means has become an end. This practical development can be most strikingly observed in the gatherings of French socialist workers. Smoking, eating and drinking, etc., are no longer means of creating links between people. Company, association, conversation, which in its turn has society as its goal, is good enough for them. The brotherhood of man is not a hollow phrase, it is a reality, and the nobility of man shines forth upon us from their work-worn figures.   (EW 365)

This Romantic notion of a nature whose self-development is an end in itself stands opposed to two other powerful thought-forms of Marx's day. The first is that brand of metaphysical reasoning which would summon human activity to account before some higher tribunal: of duty, morality, religious sanctions, the Absolute Idea. Marx is profoundly hostile to such metaphysics, though he is a profound moralist in his own right. It is just that for him morality actually *consists* in this process of unfolding our creative powers and capacities, not in some law set above it or some august set of ends pitched beyond it. There is no need to *justify* this dynamic, any more than we need to justify a smile or a song; it just belongs to our common nature.

But this ethic also finds itself in conflict with that form of *instrumental* reason for which individuals exist for the sake of some greater goal: the political state, for example, or – as in the dominant Utilitarian thought of Marx's era – the promotion of universal happiness. This means/ends reasoning is the form of rationality which Marx believes to hold sway in class societies, in which the energies of the majority are made instrumental to the profit of the few. In capitalist society,

> labour, life activity, productive life itself appears to man only as a *means* for the satisfaction of a need, the need to preserve physical existence. But productive life is species-life. It is life-producing life. The whole character of a species, its species-character, resides in the nature of its life activity, and free conscious activity constitutes the species-character of man. [In capitalism], life itself appears only as a *means of life*.   (EW 328)

In class society, the individual is forced to convert what is least functional about herself – her self-realizing species-being – into a mere tool of material survival.

It is not, of course, that Marx disowns such instrumental reasoning altogether. Without it, there could be no rational action at all; and his own revolutionary politics necessarily involve the fitting of means to ends. But one of the many ironies of his thought is that this is in the service of constructing a society in which men and women would be allowed to flourish as radical ends in themselves. It is just because he values the individual so deeply that Marx rejects a social order which, while trumpeting the value of individualism in theory, in practice reduces men and women to anonymously interchangeable units.

If we were asked to characterize Marx's ethics, then, we might do worse than call them 'aesthetic'. For the aesthetic is traditionally that form of human practice which requires no utilitarian justification, but which furnishes its own goals, grounds and rationales. It is an exercise of self-fulfilling energy for the mere sake of it; and socialism for Marx is just the practical movement to bring about a state of affairs in which

something like this would be available to as many individuals as possible.
Where art was, there shall humanity be. This is why he wants a society in
which labour would be automated as far as possible, so that men and
women (capitalists as well as workers) would no longer be reduced to
mere tools of production, and would be free instead to develop their
personalities in more fully rounded ways. Socialism for him depends
crucially upon shortening the working-day, to allow this general
flourishing to become available:

> Freedom in this field [of labour] can only consist in socialized man, the
> associated producers, rationally regulating their interchange with
> Nature; and achieving this with the least expenditure of energy and
> under conditions most favourable to, and worthy of, their human
> nature. But it nonetheless remains a realm of necessity. Beyond it begins
> that development of human energy which is an end in itself, the true
> realm of freedom, which, however, can blossom forth only with this
> realm of necessity as its basis. The shortening of the working-day is its
> basic prerequisite.   (C Vol. 3 85)

Another way of putting the point is to claim that Marx wants to
liberate the 'use-value' of human beings from its enthralment to
'exchange-value'. An object for him is a sensuous thing which we should
use and enjoy with respect to its specific qualities; this is what he means
by its 'use-value'. Under capitalist conditions, however, objects are
reduced to commodities: they exist merely for the sake of their exchange-
value, of being bought and sold. And as far as that goes, any two
commodities of the same value are reduced to an abstract equality with
each other. Their specific sensuous features are thus damagingly ignored,
as difference is dominated by identity.

But this is equally true of human beings under the same social system.
Under market conditions, individuals confront each other as abstract,
interchangeable entities; working people become commodities, selling
their labour power to the highest bidder; and the capitalist does not care
what he produces as long as it makes a profit. What goes for the
economic realm is also true of the political arena: the bourgeois state
regards its citizens as abstractly equal when it comes, say, to the voting
booth, but only in a way which suppresses and conceals their specific
social inequalities. The aim of socialist democracy is to heal this fissure
between the political form and the social content, so that our presence
within the political state, as participating citizens, would be our presence
as actual individuals:

Only when real, individual man resumes the abstract citizen into himself and as an individual man has become a *species-being* in his empirical life, his individual work and his individual relationships, only when man has recognized and organized his *forces propres* as social forces so that social force is no longer separated from him in the form of political force, only then will human emancipation be completed.

(EW 234)

Just as Marx wants to abolish commodity exchange in the economic sphere, so that production becomes for use rather than for profit, so he wishes to 'de-commodify' the human personality, emancipating the wealth of sensuous individual development from the abstract, utilitarian logic in which it is currently imprisoned. Under capitalism, our very senses are turned into commodities, so that only with the abolition of private property would the human body be liberated and the human senses come into their own:

The supersession of private property is therefore the complete emancipation of all human senses and attributes; but it is this emancipation precisely because these senses and attributes have become *human*, subjectively as well as objectively. The eye has become a *human* eye, just as its object has become a social, human object, made by man for man. The senses have therefore become *theoreticians* in their immediate praxis. They relate to the thing for its own sake, but the thing itself is an *objective human* relation to itself and to man, and vice versa. Need or enjoyment have therefore lost their *egoistic* nature, and nature has lost its mere *utility* in the sense that its use has become *human* use.

(EW 352)

Marx's political anthropology is rooted in a very broad conception of labour, which is to say, in the notion of the human body as the source of social life.

As social life grows more complex, labour becomes inevitably more specialized, with different forms of it divided out between different producers; this is what Marx calls the division of labour. This is a necessary way of developing and refining the forces of production; but it also involves for Marx a kind of alienation, in which human powers are realized in cripplingly one-sided ways, as against his ideal of the 'all-round' individual who deploys a prodigal wealth of talent. The division of labour is thus another instance of the divorce in class society between the individual and the universal, as the full potential of our species-being dwindles to some single function such as the mechanical labour of the factory worker:

> . . . the division of labour offers us the first example of how, as long as man remains in natural society, that is, as long as a cleavage exists between the particular and the common interest, as long, therefore, as activity is not voluntary, but naturally, divided, man's own deed becomes an alien power opposed to him, which enslaves him instead of being controlled by him. For as soon as the distribution of labour comes into being, each man has a particular, exclusive sphere of activity, which is forced upon him and from which he cannot escape. He is a hunter, a fisherman, a herdsman, or a critical critic, and must remain so if he does not want to lose his means of livelihood; while in communist society, where nobody has one exclusive sphere of activity but each can become accomplished in any branch he wishes, society regulates the general production and thus makes it possible for me to do one thing today and another tomorrow, to hunt in the morning, fish in the afternoon, rear cattle in the evening, criticize after dinner, just as I have a mind, without ever becoming fisherman, herdsman or critic.
>
> (GI 54)

This, famously or notoriously, is one of Marx's few frankly utopian speculations.

There are, inevitably, many problems with Marx's political ethics, as there are with any other sort of ethics. Is this notion of a freely self-fashioning human subject perhaps just a more generous-spirited version of the bourgeois, patriarchal model of man as a strenuous self-producer? Is Marx's ideal human being a kind of proletarian Promethean? To what extent is this a left-wing version of the middle-class ideal of a limitless, Faustian realization of wealth, which treats the self as one's own possession? One might find a rather too relentless activism about the doctrine, which undervalues what Wordsworth called 'wise passiveness' or Keats named 'negative capability'. Are we to realize *all* of our powers and capacities? What about those which seem morbid or destructive? Perhaps Marx considers that our powers become destructive only by virtue of being constrained, in which case he is surely mistaken. And how are we to discriminate between our more positive and negative capacities, if we have no criteria beyond this historically relative process itself by which to do so? 'All-round' development may seem to some inferior to the cultivation of a single creative talent, just as self-denial may appear to some more commendable than self-expression.

Some of these critical points can be countered. Marx, good materialist that he was, plainly did not believe that human self-development could be unlimited; he was alert to the limitations of our estate as well as to its potentials:

> *Man* is directly a *natural being*. As a natural being and as a living natural being he is on the one hand equipped with *natural powers*, with *vital powers*, he is an *active* natural being . . . On the other hand, as a natural, corporeal, sensuous, objective being he is a *suffering*, conditioned and limited being, like animals and plants. That is to say, the *objects* of his drives exist outside him as *objects* independent of him; but these objects are objects of his *need*, essential objects, indispensable to the exercise and confirmation of his essential powers.   (EW 389)

Marx may have overrated production, but he certainly did not narrow the term to its economic sense. On the contrary, he thought it a spiritually impoverishing feature of capitalism that it did precisely that. 'Production' for him is a richly capacious concept, equivalent to 'self-actualization'; and to this extent savouring a peach or enjoying a string quartet are aspects of our self-actualization as much as building dams or churning out coat-hangers:

> . . . when the limited bourgeois form is stripped away, what is wealth other than the universality of individual needs, capacities, pleasures, productive forces etc. created through universal exchange? The full development of human mastery over the forces of nature, those of so-called nature as well as of humanity's own nature? The absolute working out of [the human being's] creative potentialities with no presupposition other than the previous historic development, which makes this totality of development, i.e. the development of all human powers as such the end in itself, not as measured on a *predetermined* yardstick? Where he does not reproduce himself in one specificity, but produces his totality? Strives not to remain something he has become, but is in the absolute movement of becoming?[7]

Our species-being, then, is naturally productive, concerned with unfolding its powers by transforming the world:

> The practical creation of an *objective* world, the *fashioning* of inorganic nature, is proof that man is a conscious species-being, i.e. a being which treats the species as its own essential being or itself as a species-being. It is true that animals also produce . . . But they produce only their own immediate needs or those of their young; they produce

one-sidedly, whereas man produces universally; they produce only when immediate physical need compels them to do so, while man produces even when he is free from physical need and truly produces only in freedom from such need.   (EW 329)

We are free when, like artists, we produce without the goad of physical necessity; and it is this nature which for Marx is the essence of all individuals. In developing my own individual personality through fashioning a world, I am also realizing what it is that I have most deeply in common with others, so that individual and species-being are ultimately one. My product is my existence for the other, and presupposes the other's existence for me. This for Marx is an ontological truth, which follows from the kind of creatures we are; but it is possible for certain forms of social life to drive a wedge between these two dimensions of the self, individual and communal, and this, in effect, is what the young Marx means by *alienation*. In one sense, such a fissure always exists, since it is of the essence of the human being that he can 'objectify' his own nature, stand off from it, and this is at the root of our freedom. But in class society, the objects produced by the majority of men and women are appropriated by the minority who own and control the means of production; and this means that they are now no longer able to recognize themselves in the world that they have created. Their self-realization is no longer an end in itself, but becomes purely instrumental to the self-development of others:

> This fact simply means that the object that labour produces, its product, stands opposed to it as *something alien*, as a power *independent* of the producer. The product of labour is labour embodied and made material in an object, it is the objectification of labour . . . In the sphere of political economy this realization of labour appears as a *loss of reality* for the worker, objectification *as loss of and bondage to the object*, and appropriation as *estrangement, as alienation* . . . Estranged labour not only (1) estranges nature from man and (2) estranges man from himself, from his own active function, from his vital activity; because of this it also estranges man from his *species*. It turns his *species-life* into a means for his individual life.
>
> (EW 324, 328)

The worker, as Marx comments, feels at home only when he is not working, and not at home when he is working. So alienation is a multiple process, divorcing the worker from nature, from her product and the labour process itself, from her own body, but also from that communal life-activity which makes of her a truly human being. 'In general,' Marx writes, 'the proposition that man is estranged from his species-being means that man is estranged from the others and that all are estranged from man's essence' (EW 330).

In suffering a 'loss of reality', the producers ironically strengthen by their labour the very regime which brings this about:

> . . . the more the worker exerts himself in his work, the more powerful the alien, objective world becomes which he brings into being over against himself, the poorer he and his inner world become, and the less they belong to him. It is the same in religion. The more man puts into God, the less he retains within himself. The worker places his life in the object; but now it no longer belongs to him, but to the object. The greater his activity, therefore, the fewer objects the worker possesses. What the product of his labour is, he is not. Therefore, the greater this product, the less he is himself. The alienation of the worker means not only that his labour becomes an object, an *external* existence, but that it exists *outside him*, independently of him and alien to him, and begins to confront him as an autonomous power; that the life which he has bestowed on the object confronts him as hostile and alien. (EW 324)

The labourer's products slip from his control, assume an autonomy of their own, and come to exert that quasi-magical power over him which Marx will later term 'the fetishism of commodities'. A commodity for Marx is a product which can exchange equally with another because it embodies the same amount of labour. As he explains in *Capital*,

> Let us take two commodities, e.g. iron and corn. The proportions in which they are exchangeable, whatever those proportions may be, can always be represented by an equation in which a given quantity of corn is equated to some quantity of iron . . What does this equation tell us? It tells us that in two different things – in 1 quarter of corn and x cwt of iron, there exists in equal quantities something common to both. The two things must therefore be equal to a third, which in itself is neither the one nor the other. Each of them, as far as it is exchange value, must be reducible to this third . . This common 'something' cannot be either a geometrical, a chemical, or any other natural property of commodities. Such properties claim our attention only in as far as they affect the utility of those commodities, make them use-values. But the exchange of commodities is evidently an act characterized by a total abstraction from use-value . . As use-values, commodities are, above all, of different qualities, but as exchange-values they are merely different quantities, and consequently do not contain an atom of use-value. If,

then, we leave out of consideration the use-value of commodities, they
have only one property left, that of being products of labour.

(C Vol. 1 37)

Commodities for Marx are thus duplicitous entities living a double life,
since what actually makes them commodities is curiously independent of
their material properties. They exist purely to be exchanged; and one
commodity, despite all sensuous appearances, is exactly equal to any
other commodity which embodies the same quantity of labour power. But
a commodity is therefore an entirely abstract phenomenon, which sets up
relations with other commodities in ways quite independent of the
concrete life of their producers:

> A commodity, therefore, is a mysterious thing, simply because in it the
> social character of men's labour appears to them as an objective
> character stamped upon the product of that labour; because the relation
> of the producers to the sum total of their own labour is presented to
> them as social relation, existing not between themselves but between
> the products of their labour .. [The] existence of things *qua*
> commodities, and the value-relation between the products of labour
> which stamps them as commodities, have absolutely no connection
> with their physical properties and with the material relations arising
> therefrom .. It is a definite social relation between men, that assumes,
> in their eyes, the fantastic form of a relation between things. In order
> .. to find an analogy, we must have recourse to the mist-enveloped
> regions of the religious world. In that world the productions of the
> human brain appear as independent beings endowed with life, and
> entering into relations both with one another and with the human race.
> So it is in the world of commodities with the products of men's hands.
> This I call Fetishism which attaches itself to the products of labour, so
> soon as they are produced as commodities, and which is therefore
> inseparable from the production of commodities.   (C Vol. 1 72)

Capitalism, in short, is a world in which subject and object are reversed –
a realm in which one is subjected to and determined by one's own
productions, which return in opaque, imperious form to hold sway over
one's existence. The human subject creates an object, which then becomes
a pseudo-subject able to reduce its own creator to a manipulated thing.
When capital employs labour rather than vice versa, the dead come to
assume a vampiric power over the living, since capital itself is simply
'dead' or stored labour:

The less you eat, drink, buy books, go to the theatre, go dancing, go drinking, think, love, theorize, sing, paint, fence, etc., the more you save and the greater will become the treasure which neither moths nor maggots can consume – your *capital*. The less you *are*, the less you give expression to your life, the more you *have*, the greater is your *alienated* life and the more you store up of your estranged life .. everything which you are unable to do, your money can do for you ..

(EW 361)

This process of reification, in which animate and inanimate are inverted and the dead tyrannize over the living, is particularly evident in the 'universal commodity', money:

The stronger the power of my money, the stronger am I. The properties of money are my, the possessor's, properties and essential powers. Therefore what I *am* and what I *can do* is by no means determined by my individuality. I *am* ugly, but I can buy the *most beautiful* woman. Which means to say that I am not *ugly*, for the effect of *ugliness*, its repelling power, is destroyed by money. As an individual, I am *lame*, but money procures me twenty-four legs. Consequently, I am not lame. I am a wicked, dishonest, unscrupulous and stupid individual, but money is respected, and so also is its owner. Money is the highest good, and consequently its owner is also *good*. (EW 377)

Money, Marx comments, is 'the universal whore, the universal pimp of men and peoples', a kind of garbled language in which all human and natural qualities are scrambled and inverted and anything can be magically transformed into anything else.

For men and women to have their world, their sensuous bodies, their life-activity and their being-in-common restored to them is what Marx means by communism. Communism is just the kind of political set-up which would allow us to reappropriate our confiscated being, those powers alienated from us under class society. If the means of production were to be commonly owned and democratically controlled, then the world we create together would belong to us in common, and the self-production of each could become part of the self-realization of all.

HISTORY

If Marx is a philosopher, what is he a philosopher of? Certainly nothing as grandiose as 'human existence', but also nothing as narrow as political economy. His thought is not intended as some kind of cosmic theory which like, say, religion is meant to account for all features of human life. It is true that his collaborator Frederick Engels evolved a vastly ambitious theory known as dialectical materialism, which seeks to weave together everything from physics and biology to history and society. But Marx's own writing represents a rather more modest, restricted enterprise, which aims to identify, and work to dismantle, the major social contradictions which at present prevent us from living what he would see as a truly human life, in all the wealth of our bodily and spiritual powers. He has very little to say of what would happen then, since for him this process would be the beginnings of human history proper, which lies beyond our present language. Everything that has happened to date is for him mere 'pre-history' – the succession of various forms of class society. And since Marx's own work belongs to this epoch, inevitably dependent on its thought forms and life models, it cannot, by its own historicist logic, seek to leap over it to imagine some sort of utopia. Marx is resolutely hostile to such utopianism, seeing his own task not as drawing up ideal blueprints for the future, but as analysing and unlocking the real contradictions of the present. He is not looking for a perfect state, a phrase which for him would be a contradiction in terms.

But that is not to say that Marx is just a political theorist of the present. The contradictions which he sees as preventing us from getting a true history off the ground, in all of its richness, enjoyment and individual variety, are for him part of a much more lengthy narrative. He is thus not primarily a political economist or sociologist, or – as we have seen – in the first place a philosopher. Rather, he is offering us a theory of history itself, or more precisely a theory of the dynamics of major historical change. It is this philosophy which has become known as historical materialism.

How, then, did Marx view history as developing? It is sometimes thought that what is central to his outlook here is the notion of social class. But Marx did not discover this idea, and it is not his most vital concept. It would be more accurate to claim that the idea of class *struggle* lies closer to the heart of his work: the doctrine that different social classes exist in a state of mutual antagonism on account of their conflicting material interests. As he writes in *Communist Manifesto*: 'The history of all hitherto existing society is the history of class struggles' (SW 35). But even this sweeping pronouncement does not quite lead us to the core of his thought. For we can always ask *why* social classes should live in this state of permanent warfare; and the answer for Marx has to do with the history of material production.

His key concept here is that of a 'mode of production', by which he means an historically specific combination of certain *forces* of production with certain social *relations* of production. By 'forces' he means the various means of production available to a society, along with human labour power. A power loom or a computer is a productive force, capable of producing value; but such material forces are only ever invented, developed and deployed within the framework of particular social relations of production, by which Marx refers mainly to the relations between those who own and control the means of production, and those non-owners whose labour power is placed at their disposal. On one reading of Marx, history progresses by the forces and relations of production entering into contradiction with each other:

> At a certain stage of their development, the material productive forces of society enter into contradiction with the existing relations of production, or – what is but a legal expression of the same thing – with the property relations within which they have been at work hitherto. From forms of development of the productive forces, these relations turn into their fetters. Then begins an epoch of social revolution.
> (Preface to *A Contribution to the Critique of Political Economy*,
> SW 182)

It is by this mechanism that one mode of production gives way to another. The first such mode for Marx is the 'tribal':

> It corresponds to the undeveloped stage of production, at which a people lives by hunting and fishing, by the rearing of beasts or, in the highest stage, agriculture. In the latter case it presupposes a great mass of uncultivated stretches of land. The division of labour is at this stage still very elementary and is confined to a further extension of the natural division of labour existing in the family. The social structure is, therefore, limited to an extension of the family: patriarchal family chieftains, below them the members of the tribe, finally slaves.(GI 44)

From this gradually evolves the 'ancient' mode of production,

> which proceeds especially from the union of several tribes into a *city* by agreement or by conquest, and which is still accompanied by slavery. Beside communal ownership we already find movable, and later also immovable, private property developing, but as an abnormal form subordinate to communal ownership. The citizens hold power over their labouring slaves only in their community, and on this account alone, therefore, they are bound to the form of communal ownership . . . the whole structure of society based on this communal ownership,

and with it the power of the people, decays in the same measure as, in particular, immovable private property evolves. (GI 44)

From this eventually follows the feudal mode of production:

> Like tribal and communal ownership, [feudal property] is based again on a community; but the directly producing class standing over against it is not, as in the case of the ancient community, the slaves, but the enserfed small peasantry. As soon as feudalism is fully developed, there also arises antagonism to the towns. The hierarchical structure of landownership, and the armed bodies of retainers associated with it, gave the nobility power over the serfs. This feudal organization was, just as much as the ancient communal ownership, an association against a subjected producing class; but the form of association and the relation to the direct producers were different because of the different conditions of production. (GI 45)

Along with the feudal landed estates grew up mercantile guilds in the towns, with small-scale production and scant division of labour. But the social relations of feudalism, with its restricted guild system, end up holding back the development of the emerging middle classes of the towns, who finally break through these constrictions in a political revolution and release the forces of production on an epic scale. Later however, as a fully fledged industrial capitalist class, this same bourgeoisie finds itself unable to continue to develop those forces without generating extreme inequalities, economic slumps, unemployment, artificial scarcity and the destruction of capital. It will thus lay the ground for its own supersession by the working class, whose task is to seize control of the means of production and operate them in the interests of all:

> As soon as this process [of the rise of capitalism] has sufficiently decomposed the old society from top to bottom, as soon as the labourers are turned into proletarians, their means of labour into capital, as soon as the capitalist mode of production stands on its own feet, then the further socialization of labour and further transformation of the land and other means of production into socially exploited, and, therefore, common means of production, as well as the further expropriation of private property, takes a new form. That which is now to be expropriated is no longer the labourer working for himself, but the capitalist exploiting many labourers. This expropriation is accomplished by the action of the immanent laws of capitalistic production itself, by the centralization of capital. One capitalist always kills many.
> ('Historical Tendency of Capitalist Accumulation', SW 236)

Capitalism, in other words, prepares the way for its own negation, by socializing labour and centralizing capital:

> Hand in hand with this centralization, or this expropriation of many capitalists by few, develop, on an ever-extending scale, the cooperative form of the labour-process, the conscious technical application of science, the methodical cultivation of the soil, the transformation of the instruments of labour into instruments of labour only usable in common, the economizing of all means of production by their use as the means of production of combined, socialized labour, the entanglement of all peoples in the net of the world market, and with this, the international character of the capitalistic regime.   (Ibid., SW 236)

It is capitalism, then, which brings its own collective antagonist – the workers – into being, giving birth in a wry irony to its own gravediggers:

> Along with the constantly diminishing number of the magnates of capital, who usurp and monopolize all advantages of this process of transformation, grows the mass of misery, oppression, slavery, degradation, exploitation; but with this too grows the revolt of the working class, a class always increasing in numbers, and disciplined, united, organized by the very mechanism of the process of capitalist production itself. The monopoly of capital becomes a fetter upon the mode of production, which has flourished and sprung up along with, and under it. Centralization of the means of production and socialization of labour at last reach a point where they become incompatible with their capitalist integument. This integument is burst asunder. The knell of capitalist private property sounds. The expropriators are expropriated.
> (Ibid., SW 237)

Stated as such, the whole process of proletarian revolution sounds implausibly automatic. On this version of Marx's thought, ruling classes rise and fall according to their capacity to develop the forces of production, and one mode of production – primitive communism, slavery, feudalism, capitalism – thus mutates by its own immanent logic into another. We have here a kind of historicized verison of Marx's anthropology: what is positive is human development, and what is negative is whatever impedes that process. But it is not quite clear how to square this model with those parts of Marx's work which suggest that what is central is not the forces but the *relations* of production, as ruling

classes develop the forces of production in their own interests and for
their own exploitative purposes. Since this leads to the deprivation of the
subordinate classes, political revolution on this model comes about
directly through class struggle, not because of some general trans-
historical impulse to free the productive forces of their social constraints.
It is class conflict which is the dynamic of history, but one rooted in the
business of material production.

Marx's particular attention, not least in his major work *Capital*, is
naturally to the mode of production of his own day. Under this system,
the worker, who owns nothing but his or her capacity to labour (or
labour power), is compelled to sell that capacity to an owner of capital,
who then puts it to work for his own profit. Human beings themselves are
turned into replaceable commodities in the marketplace. The capitalist
pays for the hire of the worker's labour power in that exchange of
commodities we know as wages – wages being the cost of what the
worker needs to 'reproduce' her labour power, i.e. the goods necessary for
her to stay alive and keep working. But labour power, since it is never a
fixed object but a matter of human energy and potential, is a peculiarly
open-ended, indeterminate sort of commodity; and in putting it to work,
the capitalist is able to reap from it more value, in the form of goods
produced and sold, than it is necessary to pay to the worker. This process,
which Marx calls the extraction of 'surplus value' from the working class,
is the key to the exploitative nature of capitalist social relations; but
because the exchange of wages for labour appears an equitable one, this
exploitation is necessarily concealed by the very routine workings of the
system itself.

The capitalist system, however, is a competitive one, in which each
manufacturer must strive to expand his capital or go under. One result of
this in Marx's view is a tendency for the rate of profit to fall, leading to
the notorious recessions which have characterized the system to date. The
system's contradictions thus sharpen, and along with them the class
struggle itself, since it is in the interests of capital to appropriate as much
as possible of the fruits of its workers' labour in the shape of profit, and in
the interests of the workers to claw back as much of the proceeds of their
own labour as they can. For Marx, the only final resolution of this
deadlock is socialist revolution, as the working class expropriates capital
itself, asserts its collective control over it, and places it in the service of the
needs of all rather than the benefit of a few.

Marxism is not some form of moralism, which denounces the
capitalists as villains and idealizes the workers. It aims rather for a
'scientific' theory of historical change, in which no ruling class can be said
to be unequivocally positive or negative. On one reading, a class is

'progressive' if it is still able to develop the forces of production – which may be taken to mean that slavery was in its day a progressive mode. This clearly offends our sense of justice; but Marx himself would sometimes seem to have regarded concepts like justice as mere bourgeois ideology masking exploitation, even if his own work is ironically fuelled by a passionate desire for a just society. The bourgeoisie may be an obstacle to freedom, justice and universal wellbeing today; but in its heyday it was a revolutionary force which overthrew its own feudal antagonists, which bequeathed the very ideas of justice and liberty to its socialist successors, and which developed the forces of production to the point where socialism itself might become a feasible project. For without the material and spiritual wealth which capitalism has developed, socialism itself would not be possible. A socialism which needs to develop the forces of production from the ground up, without the benefit of a capitalist class which has accomplished this task for it, will tend to end up as that authoritarian form of state power we know as Stalinism. And a socialism which fails to inherit from the middle class a rich legacy of liberal freedoms and civic institutions will simply reinforce that autocracy. The bourgeoisie may have done what they did from the least creditable of motives, that of individual profit; but taken collectively this proved a remarkably efficient way of bringing the forces of production to the point where, given a socialist reorganization of them, they could provide the resources to wipe out poverty and deprivation throughout the world.

But the achievement of the revolutionary middle class was not just material. In bringing the individual to new heights of complex development, it also unfolded a human wealth to which socialism would be enduringly indebted. Marxism is not a question of thinking up some fine new social ideals, but rather of asking why it is that the fine ideals we already have, have proved structurally incapable of being realized for everyone. It is out to create the material conditions in which this might become possible; and one such condition is the fact that the bourgeoisie is the first genuinely *universal* social class, which breaks down all parochial barriers and breeds the kind of truly global communication which might form the basis of an international socialist community.

A truly dialectical theory of class history, then, strives to grasp its emancipatory and oppressive aspects together, as elements of a single logic. Marx summarizes this view in a typically eloquent passage:

In our days, everything seems pregnant with its contrary. Machinery gifted with the wonderful power of shortening and fructifying human labour, we behold starving and overworking it. The new-fangled sources of wealth, by some strange weird spell, are turned into sources of want. The victories of art seem bought by the loss of character. At the same pace that mankind masters nature, man seems to become enslaved to other men or to his own infamy. Even the pure light of science seems unable to shine but on the dark background of ignorance. All our invention and progress seem to result in endowing material forces with intellectual life, and stultifying human life into a material force. This antagonism between modern industry and science on the one hand, between misery and dissolution on the other hand; this antagonism between the productive forces and the social relations of our epoch is a fact, palpable, overwhelming, and not to be controverted.   (*The People's Paper*, 1856)

Irony, inversion, chiasmus, contradiction lie at the heart of Marx's conception of things. In accumulating the greatest wealth that history has ever witnessed, the capitalist class has done so within the context of social relations which have left most of its subordinates hungry, wretched and oppressed. It has also brought to birth a social order in which, in the antagonisms of the marketplace, each individual is set against the other – in which aggression, domination, rivalry, warfare and imperialist exploitation are the order of the day, rather than cooperation and comradeship. The history of capitalism is the history of possessive individualism, in which each self-owning human being is locked off from others in his solipsistic space, seeing his fellows only as tools to be used to promote his appetitive interests. But it is not that Marx is opposed to individualism, wishing to sink it in some faceless collectivity. On the contrary, his aim is to re-establish communal bonds between men and women *at the level of their fully developed individual powers*. As he puts it in the *Communist Manifesto*, the free development of each must become the condition for the free development of all. And this can be achieved only through the abolition of private property.

There are, inevitably, a number of problems with this audacious, imaginative theory. For one thing, it is not exactly clear what Marx means by social class. It is a wry joke among his commentators that just as he is about to examine the concept fully, his work breaks off. But it is clear that he sees class primarily as an economic category: it denotes, roughly speaking, those who stand in the same relation as each other to the mode of production, so that, for example, small independent producers such as peasants and artisans can be classified together as 'petty bourgeois', whereas those who must sell their labour power to another are proletarians. Does this, then, make a millionaire film star and a garbage collector both part of the working class? Or should political, cultural and ideological factors be allowed to enter into what we mean by the category? What are the relations or non-relations between social class and other human groupings, national, ethnic or sexual, to which Marx himself gives much less attention? Must a class be conscious of itself as such to be, properly speaking, a class? It is a question which Marx considers in his discussion of the French peasantry in *The Eighteenth Brumaire of Louis Bonaparte*:

> The small-holding peasants form a vast mass, the members of which live in similar conditions but without entering into manifold relations with one another. Their mode of production isolates them from one another instead of bringing them into mutual intercourse . . . In so far as millions of families live under economic conditions of existence that separate their mode of life, their interests and their culture from those of other classes, and put them in hostile opposition to the latter, they form a class. In so far as there is merely a local interconnection among these small-holding peasants, and the identity of their interests begets no community, no national bond and no political organization among them, they do not form a class.   (SW 172)

As for the theory of historical change: if Marx really does hold that the point is always and everywhere to *develop* the productive forces, then he is vulnerable to an ecological critique. We may ask, too, whether he regards this historical dialectic as inevitable. In the *Communist Manifesto* he declares that the downfall of the bourgeoisie and the victory of the proletariat 'are alike inevitable'; and in *Capital* he writes of the laws of capitalism as 'working with iron necessity towards inevitable results' (C Vol. 1 9). Elsewhere, however, Marx pours scorn on the idea that there is an entity called History which operates in deterministic style through human beings:

> . . . *History* does *nothing*, it 'possesses no immense wealth', it 'wages no battles'. It is *man*, real living man, that does all that, that possesses and fights; 'history' is not a person apart, using man as a means for *its own* particular ends; history is *nothing but* the activity of man pursuing his aim . . .[8]

He also rejects the idea that the various historical modes of production must follow upon one another in some rigidly determined way. Nor does he seem to think that the productive forces are always inexorably expanding. Anyway, if the overthrow of capitalism is inevitable, why should the working class not just sit back and wait for it to happen rather than organizing to bring it politically about? One might claim, as Marx seems to, that it is inevitable that the working class will grow to consciousness of its plight and act to change it, so that its 'free' action is somehow calculated into the broader deterministic narrative. Some Christians have tried in similar ways to resolve the apparent discrepancy between free will and divine providence. But in practice, when he is analysing particular political situations, Marx would seem to believe that political revolution depends on the struggle of contending social forces, and the outcome of this is in no sense historically guaranteed. There are, to be sure, historical laws; but these are the results of concerted human action, not of some destiny grandly independent of it. As Marx famously puts it in *The Eighteenth Brumaire*:

> Men make their own history, but they do not make it just as they please; they do not make it under circumstances chosen by themselves, but under circumstances directly encountered, given and transmitted from the past. The tradition of all the dead generations weighs like a nightmare on the brains of the living . . . The social revolution of the nineteenth century cannot draw its poetry from the past, but only from the future. It cannot begin with itself before it has stripped off all superstitions in regard to the past. Earlier revolutions required recollections of past world history in order to drug themselves concerning their own content. In order to arrive at its own content, the revolution of the nineteenth century must let the dead bury their dead.
>
> (SW 97)

POLITICS

If Marx is indeed some sort of philosopher, he differs from most such thinkers in regarding his reflections, however abstruse, as being ultimately practical – as being wholly at the service of actual political forces, and indeed as a kind of political force in themselves. This is the celebrated Marxist thesis of the unity of theory and practice – though one might add that one aim of Marx's theory is to arrive at a social condition in which thought would no longer need to be simply instrumental, geared to some practical end, and could be enjoyed instead as a pleasure in itself.

Marx's political doctrine is a revolutionary one – 'revolution' for him being defined less by the speed, suddenness or violence of a process of social change (though he does seem to consider that insurrectionary force will be involved in constructing socialism), than by the fact that it involves the ousting of one possessing class and its replacement by another. And this is a process which might clearly take a good deal of time to accomplish. We can note here the peculiar feature of socialism: that it involves the working class coming to power, but in doing so creating the conditions in which all classes may be abolished. Once the means of production are communally owned and controlled, classes themselves will finally disappear:

> All the preceding classes that got the upper hand, sought to fortify their already acquired status by subjecting society at large to their conditions of appropriation. The proletarians cannot become masters of the productive forces of society, except by abolishing their own previous mode of appropriation, and thereby also every other previous mode of appropriation. They have nothing of their own to secure and fortify; their mission is to destroy all previous securities for, and insurances of, individual property.   (*Communist Manifesto*, SW 45)

Or as Marx puts it in the idiom of his earlier writings:

> A class must be formed which has *radical chains*, a class in civil society which is not a class of civil society, a class which is the dissolution of all classes, a sphere of society which has a universal character because its sufferings are universal, and which does not claim a *particular redress* because the wrong which is done to it is not a *particular wrong* but *wrong in general*. There must be formed a sphere of society which claims no traditional status but only a human status ... This dissolution of society, as a particular class, is the *proletariat*.[9]

If the proletariat is the last historical class, it is because its coming to power in what Marx calls the 'dictatorship of the proletariat' is the prelude to the building of a society in which all will stand in the same relation to the means of production, as their collective owners. 'Worker' now no longer designates a particular class membership, but simply all men and women who contribute to producing and sustaining social life. This first phase of the anti-capitalist revolution is known to Marx as socialism, and it is not one which will involve complete equality. Indeed, Marx sees the whole notion of 'equal rights' as itself inherited from the bourgeois epoch, as a kind of spiritual reflection of the exchange of abstractly equal commodities. This is not to say that for him the concept lacks value, but that it inevitably represses the particularity of men and women, their uniquely different endowments. It thus acts among other things as a form of mystification, concealing the true content of social inequalities behind a mere legal form. In the end, Marx himself is concerned more with difference than with equality. Under socialism, it remains the case that

> ... one man is superior to another physically or mentally and so supplies more labour in the same time, or can labour for a longer time; and labour, to serve as a measure, must be defined by its duration or intensity, otherwise it ceases to be a standard of measurement. This *equal* right is an unequal right for unequal labour. It recognizes no class differences, because everyone is only a worker like everyone else; but it tacitly recognizes unequal privileges. *It is, therefore, a right of inequality, in its content, like every right.* Right by its very nature can consist only in the application of an equal standard; but unequal individuals (and they would not be individuals if they were not unequal) are measurable only by an equal standard in so far as they are brought under an equal point of view, are taken from one *definite* side only, for instance, in the present case, are regarded *only as workers* and nothing more is seen in them, everything else being ignored. Further, one worker is married, another not; one has more children than another, and so on and so forth. Thus, with an equal performance of labour, and hence an equal share in the social consumption fund, one will in fact receive more than another, one will be richer than another, and so on. To avoid all these defects, right instead of being equal would have to be unequal.   ('Critique of the Gotha Programme', SW 324)

Socialism, then, is not about some dead-levelling of individuals, but involves a respect for their specific differences, and allows these differences for the first time to come into their own. It is in this way that Marx resolves the paradox of the individual and the universal: for him, the latter term means not some supra-individual state of being, but simply the imperative that everyone should be in on the process of freely evolving their personal identities. But as long as men and women still need to be rewarded according to their labour, inequalities will inevitably persist.

The most developed stage of society, however, which Marx dubs communism, will develop the productive forces to a point of such abundance that neither equality nor inequality will be in question. Instead, men and women will simply draw from the common fund of resources whatever meets their needs:

> In a higher phase of communist society, after the enslaving subordination of the individual to the division of labour, and therewith also the antithesis between mental and physical labour, has vanished; after labour has become not only a means of life but life's prime want; after

the productive forces have also increased with the all-round development of the individual, and all the springs of cooperative wealth flow
more abundantly – only then can the narrow horizon of bourgeois right
be crossed in its entirety and society inscribe on its banners: 'From each
according to his ability, to each according to his needs!' (Ibid. 325)

In communist society we would be free of the importunity of social class,
and have the leisure and energy instead to cultivate our personalities in
whatever way we chose, provided that this respected the injunction that
everyone else should be allowed to do so too. What distinguishes this
political goal most sharply from liberalism is the fact that, since for Marx
an expression of our individual being is also a realization of our species-
being, this process of exploring and evolving individual life would be
carried out reciprocally, through mutual bonds, rather than in splendid
isolation. The other is seen by Marx as the means to my own self-
fulfilment, rather than as at best a mere co-entrepreneur in the project or
at worst as an active obstacle to my own self-realization. Communist
society would also turn the productive forces bequeathed to it by
capitalism to the end of abolishing as far as possible all degrading labour,
thus releasing men and women from the tyranny of toil and enabling
them to engage in the democratic control of social life as 'united
individuals' newly in charge of their own destinies. Under communism,
men and women can recuperate their alienated powers and recognize the
world they create as their own, purged of its spurious immutability.

But socialist revolution requires an agent, and this Marx discovers in
the proletariat. Why the proletariat? Not because they are spiritually
superior to other classes, and not necessarily because they are the most
downtrodden of social groups. As far as that goes, vagrants, outcasts, the
destitute – what Marx rather witheringly calls the 'lumpenproletariat' –
would serve a good deal better. One might claim that it is capitalism
itself, not socialism, which 'selects' the working class as the agent of
revolutionary change. It is the class which stands to gain most by the
abolition of capitalism, and which is sufficiently skilled, organized and
centrally located to carry out that task. But the task of the working class
is to carry out a specific revolution – that against capitalism; and it is thus
in no sense necessarily in competition with other radical groups – say,
feminists or nationalists or ethnic activists – who must carry through their
own particular transformations, ideally in alliance with those most
exploited by capitalism.

What form would this society take? Certainly not that of a state-run
social order. The political state for Marx belongs to the regulatory
'superstructure' of society: it is itself a product of class struggle rather

than sublimely beyond that conflict, or some ideal resolution of it. The state is ultimately an instrument of the governing class, a way of securing its hegemony over other classes; and the bourgeois state in particular grows out of an alienation between individual and universal life:

> . . . out of this very contradiction between the interest of the individual and that of the community the latter takes an independent form as the *State*, divorced from the real interests of individual and community, and at the same time as an illusory communal life, always based, however, on the real ties existing in every family and tribal conglomeration – such as flesh and blood, language, division of labour on a larger scale, and other interests – and especially, as we shall enlarge upon later, on the classes, already determined by the division of labour, which in every such mass of men separate out, and of which one dominates all the others. It follows from this that all struggles within the State, the struggle between democracy, aristocracy, and monarchy, the struggle for the franchise, etc. etc., are merely the illusory forms in which the real struggle of the different classes are fought out among one another.   (GI 53)

Marx did not always take such a briskly instrumentalist view of the state in his detailed analyses of class conflicts; but he is convinced that its truth, so to speak, lies outside itself, and sees it moreover as a form of alienation all in itself. Each individual citizen has alienated to the state part of his or her individual powers, which then assume a determining force over the everyday social and economic existence which Marx calls 'civil society'. Genuine socialist democracy, by contrast, would rejoin these general and individual parts of ourselves, by allowing us to participate in general political processes as concretely particular individuals – in the workplace or local community, for example, rather than as the purely abstract citizens of liberal representative democracy. Marx's final vision would thus seem somewhat anarchistic: that of a cooperative commonwealth made up of what he calls 'free associations' of workers, who would extend democracy to the economic sphere while making a reality of it in the political one. It was to this end – not one, after all, very sinister or alarming – that he dedicated, not simply his writings, but much of his active life.

Ray Monk

RUSSELL

Mathematics: Dreams and Nightmares

THE PYTHAGOREAN DREAM

The first thing that led me to philosophy', Bertrand Russell wrote late in life, 'occurred at the age of eleven.' It was then that his older brother, Frank, taught him Euclid's system of geometry. As he describes it in his *Autobiography*

> This was one of the great events of my life, as dazzling as first love. I had not imagined that there was anything so delicious in the world. After I had learned the fifth proposition, my brother told me that it was generally considered difficult, but I had found no difficulty whatever. This was the first time it had dawned upon me that I might have some intelligence. From that moment until Whitehead and I finished *Principia Mathematica*, when I was thirty-eight, mathematics was my chief interest, and my chief source of happiness. Like all happiness, however, it was not unalloyed. I had been told that Euclid proved things, and was much disappointed that he started with axioms. At first I refused to accept them unless my brother could offer me some reason for doing so, but he said: 'If you don't accept them we cannot go on', and as I wished to go on, I reluctantly accepted them *pro tem*. The doubt as to the premises of mathematics which I felt at that moment remained with me, and determined the course of my subsequent work.
>
> (*Auto I*, 36)

'Dazzling' and 'delicious' are not words that one would normally associate with learning geometry, and yet Russell's rapturous reaction has an intriguing precedent. According to Aubrey's *Brief Lives*, when the seventeenth-century British philosopher Thomas Hobbes was forty years old, he happened to glance at a copy of Euclid's *Elements* that was lying open on a desk in a library he visited. It was open at the proof of the famous Pythagorean Theorem. 'By God, this is impossible!' Hobbes exclaimed:

> So he reads the Demonstration of it, which referred him back to such a Proposition; which proposition he read. That referred him back to another, which he also read. *Et sic deinceps* [and so on] that at last he was demonstratively convinced of that truth. This made him in love with Geometry.

For both Hobbes and Russell, the almost erotic delight they took in learning Euclid's geometry ('as dazzling as first love') was aroused by the feeling of finally coming to know something with complete certainty. The beauty of Euclid's system is that it is axiomatic. Everything that it teaches about circles, triangles, squares, etc. is not just stated but *proved*; complicated and surprising things about the relations between angles and lengths and so on are shown to be merely logical consequences of a few, simple axioms. It's as if a whole, vast body of knowledge has been spun out of virtually nothing, but, more than that, this body of knowledge is not tenative or provisional, it does not depend upon the contingencies of the world, but rather can be established once and for all. If one accepts the axioms, one *has* to accept the rest; no further doubt is possible. To someone who wishes, as Russell passionately wished, to find *reasons* for their beliefs, the exhilarating possibility this opens up is that some beliefs at least can be provided with absolutely cast-iron foundations.

Bertrand Russell had special reason to find the experience of certain knowledge intoxicating, for, up until his introduction to Euclidean geometry, his world had been alarmingly changeable and shrouded in mystery. He was born in 1872 into one of the very grandest Whig families. His ancestor, John Russell, the first Earl of Bedford, was one of the richest and most powerful members of the new aristocracy created by Henry VIII, and his grandfather, Lord John Russell, had twice served as Prime Minister during Queen Victoria's reign. Russell was brought up fully conscious of the proud tradition into which he had been born – he once said that he was raised to live his life in such a way that after his death an equestrian statue would be built in his honour – but he was also brought up in almost complete ignorance of his parents. His mother and his sister died when he was two, and his father a year later, leaving him in the care of his grandparents. When he was six, his grandfather died, leaving him in the sole care of his grandmother, Countess Russell. After this, he later said, he used to lie awake at night wondering when she too would die and leave him.

This series of bereavements was dreadful enough, but what made the situation much worse was that his grandmother learned that Russell's mother had had an affair with Douglas Spalding, a tutor the Russells had hired to teach their children. Lady Russell's shock at this was such that she hardly mentioned Russell's parents to him and when she did, it was to hint that he had had a lucky escape not to have been brought up by such wicked people. As a result, Russell 'vaguely sensed a dark mystery' about his parents and, as a child, spent much time alone in his garden wondering what sort of people they had been and why his grandmother maintained a disapproving silence about them.

Against the background of such awful loss, uncertainty and the frustrated yearning to know something about his parents, the experience of discovering a realm of truth free from the vicissitudes of human existence was ecstatic to Russell, and it inspired in him a desire to found *all* knowledge upon the kind of rock-solid foundations provided by Euclid's system of geometry.

> I found great delight in mathematics – much more delight, in fact, than in any other study. I liked to think of the applications of mathematics to the physical world, and I hoped that in time there would be a mathematics of human behaviour as precise as the mathematics of machines. I hoped this because I liked demonstrations, and at most times this motive outweighed the desire, which I also felt, to believe in free will.   (*PFM*, 20)

But, apart from the hope it aroused of applying mathematics to the physical world and to human behaviour, there was another aspect to the delight that the young Russell found in Euclidean geometry that was to influence his philosophical development enormously, and that was the introduction it provided him to what philosophers often call 'Plato's World of Ideas'. As he was later to put it in *History of Western Philosophy*:

> Mathematics is, I believe, the chief source of the belief in eternal and exact truth, as well as in a super-sensible intelligible world. Geometry deals with exact circles, but no sensible object is *exactly* circular; however carefully we may use our compasses, there will be some imperfections and irregularities. This suggests the view that all exact reasoning applies to ideal as opposed to sensible objects; it is natural to go further, and to argue that thought is nobler than sense, and the objects of thought more real than those of sense-perception.
> (*HWP*, 55–6)

In his essay, 'Why I took to Philosophy', Russell made clear the importance this form of mysticism had for his own philosophical motivations:

> For a time I found satisfaction in a doctrine derived, with modification, from Plato. According to Plato's doctrine, which I accepted only in a watered-down form, there is an unchanging timeless world of ideas of which the world presented to our senses is an imperfect copy. Mathematics, according to this doctrine, deals with the world of ideas

and has in consequence an exactness and perfection which is absent from the everyday world. This kind of mathematical mysticism, which Plato derived from Pythagoras, appealed to me.   (*PFM*, 22)

In *My Philosophical Development*, he was blunter: 'I disliked the real world and sought refuge in a timeless world, without change or decay or the will-o'-the-wisp of progress' (*MPD*, 210).

Though the notion of a world of ideas, in which truths are timeless and discoverable by reason alone, is more commonly associated with Plato, Russell always insisted on attributing it to Pythagoras, who thus became for him a figure of emblematic importance, 'intellectually one of the most important men that ever lived', as Russell describes him in *History of Western Philosophy*. Pythagoras is an elusive figure in the history of philosophy; no text of his has survived and little is known of his life. It is generally agreed that he lived from about 550 to 500 BC, but that is almost where the agreement stops, and most of what Russell says about Pythagoras's philosophy has been disputed by other scholars. Nevertheless, what Russell believed about Pythagoras was of great importance to him, because it fixed Pythagoras as the type of philosopher Russell aspired to be and gave shape to the dream which Russell pursued in his philosophy of mathematics.

As Russell presents him, Pythagoras was both a religious prophet and a pure mathematician: 'In both respects he was immeasurably influential, and the two were not so separate as they seem to a modern mind.' Pythagoras's religion, according to Russell, was a reformed version of Orphism, which was, in turn, a reformed version of the worship of Dionysus. Central to all three was the exaltation of ecstasy, but in the cult of Pythagoras, this ecstasy is to be achieved not by drinking wine or indulging in sexual activity, but rather by the exercise of the intellect. The highest life, on this view, is that devoted to 'passionate sympathetic contemplation', which Russell (following F. M. Cornford) says was the original meaning of the word 'theory'.

For Pythagoras, the 'passionate contemplation' was intellectual, and issued in mathematical knowledge. In this way, through Pythagoreanism, 'theory' gradually acquired its modern meaning; but for all who were inspired by Pythagoras it retained an element of ecstatic revelation. To those who have reluctantly learnt a little mathematics in school this may seem strange; but to those who have experienced the intoxicating delight of sudden understanding that mathematics gives, from time to time, to those who love it, the Pythagoras view will seem completely natural, even if untrue. It might seem that the empirical philosopher is the slave of his material, but the pure mathematician, like the musician, is a free creator of his world of ordered beauty.

(*HWP*, 52–3)

Pythagoras ('as everyone knows', according to Russell) believed that 'all things are numbers'. Everything in the world, whether it be the building of pyramids, the things of nature, the harmonies of music, or whatever, expresses a series of numerical relations, and can be described by those relations. The tragedy for the Pythagoreans (and, as we shall see, a similar tragedy was played out in Russell's own philosophical development) was that their greatest, most well-known discovery was the one that undermined this point of view: namely the famous Pythagorean Theorem concerning right-angled triangles, which led immediately to the discovery of incommensurables.

According to the Pythagorean Theorem, the length of the hypotenuse of a right-angled triangle in which the other two sides are one unit long will be equal to the square root of 2. The trouble is that the square root of 2 is incommensurable; that is, it cannot be expressed as the relation between two numbers, or, to put it another way, it is 'irrational'. It follows that there is at least one thing in the world which is *not* the expression of a numerical relation. Others, of course, followed; the best known of which is *pi*, the relation between the circumference and the diameter of a circle. To the ancient Greeks, this suggested that geometry, not arithmetic, was the surest source of exact knowledge, which is one reason for the pre-eminence given to Euclid's *Elements*.

The Pythagorean Dream of showing everything to be reducible to arithmetic was, it seemed, over. New mathematical techniques, however, developed during the Scientific Revolution of the seventeenth and eighteenth centuries, served to revive the dream, at least to the extent of re-establishing arithmetic as the supreme form of mathematics. Chief among these were the co-ordinate geometry introduced by Descartes, which allowed geometrical theorems to be expressed and proved arithmetically, and the differential calculus, developed (independently) by Newton and Leibniz, which enabled mathematics, for the first time, to represent *motion* arithmetically, thus providing the sciences of mechanics, dynamics and physics with an immensely powerful new tool. The problem of incommensurables, however, continued to haunt those who looked to mathematics for perfect rigour and exactitude. Quantities like $\sqrt{2}$ and *pi* were included in the domain of 'real' numbers, though no satisfactory definition of them – or, therefore, of the notion of a 'real number' in general – was yet available. And, indeed, the new techniques brought with them further problems in trying to make sense of the world of numbers, problems which opened up the science of mathematics to the charge of being riddled with inconsistencies.

Three fundamental notions in mathematics – infinity, the infinitesimal, and continuity – seemed inherently paradoxical. The paradoxes of infinity and continuity had been known since ancient times, but they acquired a new importance as the power of mathematics to represent continuous and infinite sequences grew. Both take many forms. The form of the paradox of infinity that especially worried Leibniz was this: even numbers are only a part, a half, of the whole realm of whole numbers (which, of course, includes both odd and even numbers), and yet, to every whole number we can assign a corresponding even number:

$$
\begin{array}{cccccccccc}
1 & 2 & 3 & 4 & 5 & 6 & . & . & . \\
2 & 4 & 6 & 8 & 10 & 12 & . & . & . \\
\end{array}
$$

The two sets, in other words, can be put into a *one-to-one correspondence*. But, surely, two sets can only be paired off in this way if they have the *same* number of members (in a monogamous society, for example, we know that the number of wives is equal to the number of husbands, since to each member of one set there corresponds a member of the other). How can the set of even numbers be, at one and the same time, both *smaller than* and *the same size as* the set of natural numbers? The problem arises, of course, from the fact that both sets are infinite (even though one is a proper sub-set of the other), which led many philosophers to conclude that the notion of infinity is inherently contradictory.

The paradoxes of continuity had been known since antiquity and were associated with a disciple of Paramenides called Zeno, who had used them to argue that there was no such thing as motion. They arise from considering a continuous line as a sequence of discrete points. The problem is that this sequence must be infinitely divisible. Take, for example, the flight of an arrow. Before it reaches its target, Zeno argued, it must reach a point halfway towards its target; but, before it can reach *that* point, it must reach a point halfway to it, and so on *ad infinitum*. As the chain of presuppositions involved in the claim that the arrow moves never comes to an end, its supposed motion can never begin and thus, Zeno urges, must be regarded as illusory. Despite what we appear to see with our own eyes, reason will tell us that the arrow never moves! Few have been prepared to accept this conclusion, but the mathematical difficulty it raises of how a continuous quantity can be understood as a sequence of discrete points remained unsolved until the nineteenth century.

Related to the problems of continuity were those surrounding the notion of an infinitesimal, a notion that plays a central role in the differential calculus, as originally devised. An infinitesimal is supposed to be an infinitely small quantity, smaller than any quantity one could think of and yet not nothing. It cannot be nothing, since continuous lines are regarded as being made up of them. And yet, in the calculation of a derivative – in, for example, the calculation of the velocity of a moving object at a certain point in time – an infinitesimal quantity is treated as no quantity at all. This process, though it works in practice, is quite manifestly inconsistent, and was famously ridiculed by Bishop Berkeley in his attack on Newton's calculus, *The Analyst*. What are these 'evanescent Increments' used in the calculus? Berkeley sneered. 'They are neither finite Quantities, nor Quantities infinitely small nor yet not nothing. May we not call them the Ghosts of departed Quantities?' Anyone who could accept such a notion, Berkeley suggested, ought to have no qualms in accepting the mysteries of Christianity, for do not mathematicians have their own mysteries, 'and what is more, their repugnancies and contradictions?'

By the middle of the nineteenth century, these embarrassing logical problems at the heart of mathematics had inspired a movement, led by German mathematicians, to provide mathematics, and particularly the calculus, with more rigorous foundations. Despite his passion for mathematics, however, Russell did not learn of the work of these mathematicians until after he had finished his mathematics studies at Cambridge. When he did learn of it, it changed his philosophical outlook fundmentally. Much to Russell's disgust, the mathematics that he was taught, both prior to and during his time as an undergraduate, treated the subject, not in the Pythagorean spirit as the establishment of exact truths concerning the abstract world of ideas, but rather in a more pragmatic spirit as a series of useful techniques.

> Those who taught me the infinitesimal Calculus did not know the valid proofs of its fundamental theorems and tried to persuade me to accept the official sophistries as an act of faith. I realized that the calculus works in practice, but I was at a loss to understand why it should do so. However, I found so much pleasure in the acquisition of technical skill that at most times I forgot my doubts. (*MPD*, 35–6)

> ... The mathematical teaching at Cambridge when I was an undergraduate was definitely bad. Its badness was partly due to the order of merit in the Tripos, which was abolished not long afterwards. The necessity for nice discrimination between the abilities of different examinees led to an emphasis on 'problems' as opposed to 'bookwork'.

The 'proofs' that were offered of mathematical theorems were an insult to the logical intelligence. Indeed, the whole subject of mathematics was taught as a set of clever tricks by which to pile up marks in the Tripos. The effect of all this upon me was to make me think mathematics disgusting. When I had finished my Tripos, I sold all my mathematical books and made a vow that I would never look at a mathematical book again. And so, in my fourth year, I plunged with whole-hearted delight into the fantastic world of philosophy.

(*MPD*, 37–8)

Despairing of mathematics as it was then taught, Russell looked to metaphysics to satisfy the Pythagorean yearnings that his intoxication with Euclidean geometry had aroused in him. He began philosophy in 1893 and within a year had chosen to concentrate on the subject that had first inspired his hopes of finding exact and certain knowledge: the foundations of geometry. Now, however, he sought those foundations not in mathematics, but in philosophy, and in particular in a form of Kantian transcendental idealism. In *Critique of Pure Reason*, Kant had raised the following problem: how can the theorems of Euclidean geometry be established on the basis of reason alone and yet hold true for the physical world? Most of the things we know about the physical world have to be arrived at by observation and experiment; how is it that such truths as, for example, the Pythagorean Theorem can be known *a priori*, without reference to our experience of the world? Kant concluded that Euclidean geometry describes not the world as it is in itself, but the world as it appears to us. The world does not *have* to be as Euclid describes it, but we *have* to see and imagine it as such. We look at the world, so to speak, through Euclidean spectacles. Or, to put it into Kantian jargon, what Euclidean geometry describes is our 'form of intuition' with regard to space. That is why the theorems of Euclidean geometry look to us as if they were *necessarily* true, as if, like the principles of logic, their truth was guaranteed by the nature of reason itself.

Some doubt was thrown on this view after Kant's death by the creation of alternative systems of geometry, so-called *non-Euclidean* geometries. Of these, the two most famous were those created by the German mathematician, Georg Riemann, and the Russian, Nikolai Lobachevsky. Both these systems dropped Euclid's fifth postulate (the one that ensures that parallel lines never meet) and produced in consequence descriptions of 'curved' space. In this kind of space, everything is different; the angles of a triangle, for example, do not add up to 180 degrees, but either slightly more (in the case of Riemannian geometry) or slightly less (in Lobachevskyan). Given that these systems are internally consistent (which they are) and that we can imagine the spaces they describe (which is often disputed), it looks as though Kant was wrong: we do not *have* to perceive the world as Euclidean. Why should we not see it as Riemannian or Lobachevskyan? This also threatens the thought that had excited the eleven-year-old Bertrand Russell, the thought that we can know, *a priori* and with complete certainty and exactitude, the spatial relations that exist in the physical world.

In his first philosophical book, *The Foundations of Geometry*, Russell responded to this dilemma in a quasi-Kantian manner. What Kant had claimed for Euclidean geometry, Russell argued, is in fact true of the relatively recent subject of projective geometry, which studies geometrical figures not in regard to their size but only with respect to their shape, their 'congruence' with each other. The axioms of projective geometry would be true whether space was curved or not, so long as its curvature was constant. Whether Euclid, Riemann or Lobachevsky has given us a correct description of physical space is, Russell thus claimed, an empirical matter, but what we *can* know with certainty is that *if* space is curved, its curvature is constant. To understand the issue involved here, think of the difference between the surface of a football and the surface of an egg. If you drew a triangle on a football, you could imagine sliding that triangle around the surface of the ball without having to distort its shape; a triangle in one part of the football would, that is, be *congruent* with a triangle in another. But now imagine drawing a triangle on the fat end of an egg and trying to slide it towards the thin end: the triangle would have to change its shape. This is because the space on the surface of an egg, though curved, does not curve constantly. Whatever real physical space is like, Russell maintained, it *cannot* be like the surface of an egg. Unfortunately for this view, the space of relativity theory *is* like the surface of an egg, its curvature varying with respect to varying degrees of mass gravitational force. Russell's earliest published philosophical theory, therefore, is now regarded as one of the few philosophical theories capable of conclusive scientific refutation.

In later life, Russell was dismissive of his earlier work on geometry and pronounced it 'somewhat foolish', but at the time of its publication he considered himself to be on the brink of realising through philosophical Idealism something like the Pythagorean Dream of revealing a rational reality of eternal truths behind the messy appearance of contingent facts. This reality, however, was to be apprehended not through geometry or through arithmetic, but rather through logic and, in particular, through the dialectical kind of logic introduced into philosophy by the German Absolute Idealist, Friedrich Hegel. This kind of logic arrives at conclusions not by ordinary inference, but by a process of *synthesis* that seeks to overcome contradictions by bringing opposites together to form new 'transcendent' unities. Eventually, in Hegel's philosophy, this process reaches the conclusion that Reality as a whole is one Absolute Idea.

Russell's conversion to neo-Hegelianism came about through his contact with J. M. E. McTaggart, whose *Studies in the Hegelian Dialectic* was widely influential among Cambridge philosophers of the 1890s. McTaggart's emphasis was on the interconnectedness of everything in the world as perceived by Hegel's philosophy. Separateness, according to this doctrine, is an illusion, and is shown to be such by a dialectic that proceeds from the lower categories of understanding – things like space, time and matter – to the highest, the Absolute. Only this latter is independent and real, and only this is rational; all the lower categories are enmeshed in contradictions that are resolved by successive synthesis until one reaches the Absolute. In this vision (analogous, in this respect, to the Pythagorean Dream), logic and religion meet, for the logic of this dialectic shows us that, in McTaggart's words, 'all reality is rational and righteous . . . the highest object of philosophy is to indicate to us the general nature of an ultimate harmony, the full content of which it has not yet entered into our hearts to conceive'. 'All true philosophy', McTaggart declares, 'must be mystical, not indeed in its methods, but in its final conclusions.'

For a short period, Russell was inspired by this peculiar form of mysticism to embrace an ambitious scheme of writing a 'dialectic of the sciences' that would, by successively exposing the contradiction inherent in mathematics, physics and the other sciences, demonstrate the superiority of Hegelian philosophy over all over attempts to make sense of the world. His work during this period (most of which remained unpublished) contains repeated admonitions to mathematicians for refusing to acknowledge the logical contradictions that beset their subject. For example, in a paper he wrote in 1896 called 'On Some Difficulties of Continuous Quantity', he begins:

> From Zeno onwards, the difficulties of continua have been felt by philosophers, and evaded, with ever subtler analysis, by mathematicians . . . it seemed worth while to collect and define, as briefly as possible, some contradictions in the relation of continuous quantity to number, and also to show, what mathematicians are in danger of forgetting, that philosophical antinomies, in this sphere, find their counterpart in mathematical fallacies. These fallacies seem, to me at least, to pervade the Calculus.   (CPBR 2, 46)

In other words, bad philosophy – or worse, indifference to philosophy – produces bad mathematics (the 'official sophistries' and 'clever tricks' of which he had complained earlier). If mathematicians genuinely wanted to understand mathematical truth, they would do well to turn their attention to the contradictions of continuity, infinity and the infinitesimal and rethink the logical and philosophical foundations of their subject.

As Russell belatedly began to discover in the last few years of the nineteenth century, mathematicians, particularly German mathematicians, had been doing just that for some time. As a result of the work of Weierstrass, Dedekind and Cantor, pure mathematics had been provided with much more sophisticated foundations. The notion of an infinitesimal had been banished, 'real' numbers had been provided with a logically consistent definition, continuity had been redefined and, more controversially, a whole new branch of arithmetic had been invented ('transfinite arithmetic') which addressed itself to the paradoxes of infinity. Many philosophers have regarded the picture of the mathematical realm that results from all this work as even more bewildering than that that emerges from the mathematics of Newton and Leibniz. Wittgenstein, for example, has described the entire body of work of these German mathematicians as a 'cancerous growth'. And, it is true, it offends common sense at almost every point. It requires, for example, one to believe that there exist *different* infinities so that, for example, the number of points in a continuum is greater than the number of natural numbers, though both are infinite. It also requires one to embrace precisely the conclusions that had previously been thought paradoxical: for example, that in a continuous series of points there is no such thing as 'the next' point, so that, as Russell once put it, Zeno's arrow 'at every moment of its flight, is truly at rest'.

For Russell, however, the abandonment of common sense was a small price to pay for a logically consistent theory of mathematics. He never much cared for common sense anyway, declaring it to be the 'metaphysics of savages'. His joy at discovering *mathematical* solutions to the logical problems of mathematics was almost unconfined and within a couple years of first being acquainted with the work of Weierstrass, Cantor and Dedekind, he abandoned altogether the neo-Hegelianism of his 'dialectic of the sciences'. 'Mathematics', he now believed, 'could be *quite* true, and not merely a stage in dialectic', and he had no further use for 'the Absolute'. This produced a fundamental change in his philosophical outlook, what he would later call the 'one major division' in his thinking. There were, Russell was fond of saying, just two types of philosopher: those who think of the world as a bowl of jelly and those who think of it as a bucket of shot. Having, through the work of modern mathematicians, rediscovered his faith in *analysis*, Russell could give up the jelly and embrace the shot. The task of philosophy, then, was no longer to demonstrate the interconnectedness of everything, to prove that Reality was an indivisible whole; rather the task was to identify, through analysis, the discrete atoms – material, psychological and logical – of which the world is constructed.

With regard to mathematics, this enabled Russell to adopt a very robust form of Pythagoreanism: there really is a mathematical realm, and its truths are indeed discoverable through reason alone. All the old barriers to believing this – problems of incommensurables, the paradoxes of continuity, infinity and the infinitesimal – had been overcome, and there was no longer any need to resort to Idealism, whether Kantian or Hegelian, to make sense of mathematics: ordinary (not dialectical) logic was enough. Russell's delight in this aroused in him an unrestrained triumphalism:

> One of the chief triumphs of modern mathematics consists in having discovered what mathematics really is ... All pure mathematics – Arithmetic, Analysis, and Geometry – is built up by combinations of the primitive ideas of logic, and its propositions are deduced from the general axioms of logic, such as the syllogism and the other rules of inference. And this is no longer a dream or an aspiration. On the contrary, over the greater and more difficult part of the domain of mathematics, it has already been accomplished; in the remaining cases, there is no special difficulty, and it is now being rapidly achieved. Philosophers have disputed for ages whether such deduction was possible; mathematicians have sat down and made the deduction. For the philosophers there is now nothing left but graceful acknowledgements.
>
> ... Zeno was concerned ... with three problems, each presented by motion, but each more abstract than motion, and capable of a purely arithmetical treatment. There are the problems of the infinitesimal, the infinite, and continuity. To state clearly the difficulties involved was to accomplish perhaps the hardest part of the philosopher's task. This was done by Zeno. From him to our own day, the finest intellects of each generation in turn attacked the problems, but achieved, broadly speaking, nothing. In our own time, however, three men – Weierstrass, Dedekind, and Cantor – have not merely advanced the three problems, but have completely solved them. The solutions, for those acquainted with mathematics, are so clear as to leave no longer the slightest doubt or difficulty. This achievement is probably the greatest of which our age has to boast; and I know of no age (except perhaps the golden age of Greece) which has a more convincing proof to offer of the transcendent genius of its great men.   (*ML*, 76–82)

Russell's conversion from synthesis to analysis, and from Idealism to Realism, is more frequently credited to the influence of G. E. Moore, but the impact of the work of Weierstrass, Cantor and Dedekind was, in fact, far greater. In the final chapter of his *History of Western Philosophy*, Russell extols the achievements of analytic philosophy (or 'the philosophy of logical analysis', as he calls it) and though he does not mention Moore at all, he emphasizes the importance of the work of these German mathematicians. 'The origin of this philosophy', he writes, 'is in the achievements of mathematicians who set to work to purge their subject of fallacies and slipshod reasoning.'

Russell's greatest work in philosophy was inspired by the example of these mathematicians. They had shown that mathematics was logically consistent – or, in any case, they had removed what were, historically, the most important reasons for thinking that it was not – what Russell now dreamed of was a demonstration that mathematics *was* logic. The vision that opened up to him was of an axiomatic system, more rigorous even than Euclid's, in which the *whole* of mathematics could be spun out of a few trivial axioms. These axioms would not be specifically mathematical, they would not mention points, straight lines, or even numbers; they would be simple truths of logic, things like: if p implies q, and q implies r, then p implies r. In this way, mathematics would be shown not only to be free from contradiction, but also to be absolutely and irrefragably *true*. A vast realm of knowledge would have been shown to be immune to any sceptical doubt whatsoever.

Russell's immediate starting point in this quest was the mathematical logic of the Italian mathematician Giuseppe Peano, whom Russell met at an academic congress in Paris in 1900. 'I was impressed', Russell later said, 'by the fact that, in every discussion, he [Peano] showed more precision and more logical rigour than was shown by anybody else. I went to him and said, "I wish to read all your works. Have you got copies with you?" He had, and I immediately read them all.' By using a specially invented logical notation (the basic elements of which are still in use today and familiar to all undergraduate students of formal logic), Peano was able to show that the whole of arithmetic could be founded upon a system that used only three basic notions and five initial axioms. His three basic notions were: zero, number, and 'successor of', and his five axioms were:

1. 0 is a number
2. If x is a number, the successor of x is a number
3. If two numbers have the same successor, the two numbers are identical

4. 0 is not the successor of any number
5. If S is a class containing 0 and the successor of every number belonging to S, then S contains all numbers

To reduce the whole of arithmetic to such a small handful of initial assumptions was a tremendous achievement and Russell was fulsome in his praise of it. Peano, he wrote, is 'the great master of the art of formal reasoning, among the men of our own day'. But, Russell thought, Peano had not *quite* reached logical rock-bottom; Peano's basic notions, he was convinced, could be reduced yet further by defining them in terms of the logically still more primitive notion of *class*. If an axiomatic theory of classes could be constructed in which Peano's basic notions were definable and his five axioms demonstrable, then, Russell reasoned, arithmetic could be shown to be nothing more than a branch of logic. This is the central idea of Russell's great work, *The Principles of Mathematics*, the first draft of which he finished at the end of 1900, just months after his meeting with Peano, but which was not finally published until 1903, by which time Russell's Pythagorean visions had received a mortal blow.

Unlike the mathematician who inspired him, Russell was motivated by primarily philosophical considerations. For him, a large part of the purpose of deriving mathematics from logic was to show that the Kantian philosophy of mathematics – and still more, of course, the Hegelian philosophy – was false. If mathematics is a branch of logic, Russell believed, then Kant's appeal to subjective, psychological notions like 'forms of intuition' was unnecessary. *The Principles of Mathematics* thus begins with a trenchant and self-confident dismissal of Kant's philosophy of mathematics, and a bold statement of both the definitive correctness and the philosophical importance of the thesis that mathematics is logic:

The Philosophy of Mathematics has been hitherto as controversial and unprogressive as the other branches of philosophy. Although it was generally agreed that mathematics is in some sense true, philosophers disputed as to what mathematical propositions really meant; although something was true, no two people were agreed as to what it was that was true, and if something was known, no two people were agreed as to what it was that was known. So long, however, as this was doubtful, it could hardly be said that any certain and exact knowledge was to be had in mathematics. We find, accordingly, that idealists have tended more and more to regard all mathematics as dealing with mere appearance, while empiricists have held everything mathematical to be approximation to some exact truth about which they had nothing to tell us. This state of things, it must be confessed, was thoroughly unsatisfactory. Philosophy asks of Mathematics: What does it mean? Mathematics in the past was unable to answer, and Philosophy answered by introducing the totally irrelevant notion of mind. But now Mathematics is able to answer, so far at least as to reduce the whole of its propositions to certain fundamental notions of logic. At this point, the discussion must be resumed by Philosophy. I shall endeavour to indicate what are the fundamental notions involved, to prove at length that no others occur in mathematics, and to point out briefly the philosophical difficulties involved in the analysis of these notions. A complete treatment of these difficulties would involve a treatise on Logic, which will not be found in the following pages.

There was, until very lately, a special difficulty in the principles of mathematics. It seemed plain that mathematics consisted of deductions, and yet the orthodox accounts of deduction were largely or wholly inapplicable to existing mathematics. Not only the Aristotelian syllogistic theory, but also the modern doctrines of Symbolic Logic, were either theoretically inadequate to mathematical reasoning, or at any rate required such artificial forms of statement that they could not be practically applied. In this fact lay the strength of the Kantian view, which asserted that mathematical reasoning is not strictly formal, but always uses intuitions, *i.e.*, the *a priori* knowledge of space and time. Thanks to the progress of Symbolic Logic, especially as treated by Professor Peano, this part of the Kantian philosophy is now capable of a final and irrevocable refutation. By the help of ten principles of deduction and ten other premises of a general logical nature (*e.g.*, 'implication is a relation'), all mathematics can be strictly and formally deduced; and all the entities that occur in the mathematics can be defined in terms of those that occur in the above twenty premises. In this statement, Mathematics includes not only Arithmetic and Analysis, but also Geometry, Euclidean and non-Euclidean, rational Dynamics, and an indefinite number of other studies still unborn or in their infancy. The fact that all Mathematics is Symbolic Logic is one of the greatest discoveries of our age; and when this fact has been established, the remainder of the principles of mathematics consists in the analysis of Symbolic Logic itself.   (*POM*, 4–5)

The Principles of Mathematics is a difficult book, full of abstruse and sophisticated reasoning, and written in a more technical and formal style than had been, up until then, customary in philosophical literature. However, it is not a work either of formal logic or of mathematics, and Russell does not actually construct the system of logic to which he claims mathematics to be reducible, nor does he attempt to carry out the reduction. His aim is rather to argue that such a reduction is possible. He does, however, specify the basic notions and the axioms that his preferred system of logic would contain. Of central importance to Russell is the notion of a *class*, which, it is important to realize, is rather different from the notion of a set, as that appears in mathematics. Set Theory had been a branch of mathematics for some time before *The Principles of Mathematics* was written and if all Russell was proposing was that mathematics be reduced to Set Theory, that would not have had the momentous philosophical importance that Russell claimed for his work; it would simply be to reduce the whole of mathematics to one particular branch of it. What Russell was proposing was a demonstration that mathematics could be reduced to *logic*, and it was thus vital to him that he should begin with a purely *logical* notion.

What, then, is the difference between a set and a class? A set, typically, is defined by enumeration: {2,4,6}, for example, is a set containing three members. Russell, originally, had difficulty in accepting Cantor's transfinite set theory, because he could not see how an infinite *set* could be well defined, for clearly we cannot enumerate the members of an infinite collection. One of the things he got from Peano, however, which helped him overcome these doubts, was the rather different notion of *class*, which is defined, not in terms of its members, but rather in terms of what is called a *propositional function*. Broadly speaking, a propositional function is a proposition with a variable. 'Plato is a man' and 'Socrates is a man' are propositions, but 'x is a man' is a propositional function. The class of men is then defined as the things of which 'x is a man' is true, *whatever they may be*. To grasp the notion of 'the class of men', we do not need to know how many members the class has, nor whether the number of members is infinite, nor even if it has any members at all; we only need to know what the propositional function 'x is a man' *means*. Thus 'class' is a purely logical notion, derived not only from a branch of mathematics, but from quite general considerations about propositions: every meaningful proposition has a form that can be expressed by a propositional function, and to every propositional function there corresponds a class.

Essentially, Russell's task in reducing Peano's system of arithmetic to a system of logic was to show how Peano's three basic notions and five basic axioms could be recast in terms of classes. In other words, he had to demonstrate that numbers could be defined as classes. He did this by taking as fundamental the notion of a *one-to-one correspondence* between classes, and adopting Cantor's idea that two classes were *equinumerous* (or 'similar' as Russell puts it) if they could be put into such a correspondence. A number is then defined as a class of 'similar' classes: the number 3, for example, would be the class of classes having three members. 0 is the class of empty classes, and 1 is the class of classes containing only a single member. Having defined 0 and 1, Russell is able to define the notion '+1' (Peano's notion of 'successor') and thus all five of Peano's axioms.

From this basis, Russell goes on to define rational numbers, irrational numbers, real numbers, complex numbers, transfinite numbers and continuity. He also gives a sketch of how ordinary geometry, projective geometry, the differential calculus, Newton's Laws of Motion and Heinrich Hertz's Theory of Dynamics would appear within his theory. The scope of the book, and of his ambition, was breathtakingly large. As he put it in a letter to a friend: 'I invented a new subject, which turned out to be all mathematics, for the first time treated in its essence.' He had, he believed, shown what mathematics really was and in doing so, he had realized his and Pythagoras's dream of revealing it to be a body of abstract yet objective truth, our knowledge of which was perfectly and apodictically demonstrable. Intellectually, he later said, the writing of the first draft of *The Principles of Mathematics* was 'the highest point of my life', an 'intellectual honeymoon such as I have never experienced before or since':

> Every day I found myself understanding something that I had not understood on the previous day. I thought all difficulties were solved and all problems were at an end. (*MPD*, 73)

But, he adds, 'the honeymoon could not last, and early in the following year intellectual sorrow descended upon me in full measure.'

THE MATHEMATICIAN'S NIGHTMARE

Russell's 'intellectual honeymoon' came to an end with his nightmarish discovery that the notion of a class, to which he had wanted to reduce the whole of mathematics, was itself contradictory. To understand the impact this discovery had on him, one has to retrace his thoughts concerning classes. According to Russell's version of Pythagoras's mathematical mysticism, classes were a kind of object. They were not, to be sure, the kind of object that can be seen or touched, but nevertheless they had for him a real, objective existence. They did not exist 'in the mind', but in, so to speak, the 'world of forms'. They had, that is, the kind of existence that Pythagoras and Plato had claimed for numbers; indeed, *exactly* the same kind of existence, since for Russell, numbers *were* classes. Numbers, on Russell's theory, were classes *of classes*, and this, for Russell, meant that classes had to be some kind of object, for otherwise how could one form classes *of* them?

That there was something wrong with this conception of class was suggested to Russell by his reflections upon Cantor's theory of infinite sets. Cantor had a famous proof that there is no such thing as the highest cardinal number. A *cardinal* number is a number that is used to answer the question: how many? For example, if you count the number of people in a room and come to, say, 4, then the number 4 is being used as a cardinal. If, on the other hand, you were to put the people in a queue, and say: 'You're first, you're second, you're third, and you're fourth', then you would be using 1, 2, 3 and 4 as *ordinal* numbers. In Cantor's theory, cardinal numbers belong to sets, and there are infinite as well as finite cardinals. The set of natural numbers, for example, has an infinite cardinal – to which Cantor assigned the symbol $\aleph_0$ – and so does the set of real numbers. But Cantor had a proof – eventually accepted by Russell – that the set of real numbers has *more* members than the set of natural numbers. This proof works by demonstrating first that the natural numbers are a proper sub-set of the reals, and second that the reals *cannot* be put into a one-to-one correspondence with the naturals. It follows, Cantor argues, that the set of reals is *bigger than* the set of naturals.

Cantor also had a proof that, in general, a set has fewer members than its *power set* (that is, its set of subjects). If a set has n members, then there will be 2^n subsets of it, and 2^n is always greater than n. Putting these two together, Cantor concluded that the set of real numbers has the cardinal number $2^{\aleph_0}$. From here, Cantor constructed an entire hierarchy of different infinite numbers that can be continued indefinitely. There cannot be a greatest infinite cardinal number, Cantor reasoned, because *whatever* cardinal number one may take, one can always construct a larger one by forming its power set.

In the first flush of his enthusiasm for the work of Weierstrass, Dedekind and Cantor, Russell was convinced that there must be some mistake in this reasoning. Surely, he argued, if numbers are classes and classes are 'things', there *must* be a greater number, the number, that is, of total number of 'things' that exist (not in the physical world – for presumably that number is finite – but in the world of forms in which classes have their existence). As he put it in 1900:

> There is a greatest of all infinite numbers, which is the number of things altogether, of every sort and kind. It is obvious that there cannot be a

greater number than this, because, if everything has been taken, there is nothing left to add. Cantor has a proof that there is no greatest number, and if this proof were valid, the contradictions of infinity would reappear in a sublimated form. But in this one point, the master has been guilty of a very subtle fallacy, which I hope to explain in some future work.   (*ML*, 88)

Russell could, not, at first, accept Cantor's proof, because to do so would be to admit that the theory of classes contains a contradiction. The contradiction arises from considering the class of *all* classes. Surely this class has the highest cardinal number there could be, since numbers are classes and this class contains every class – and therefore every number – there could possibly be. But if Cantor is right, there is a simple method of constructing a larger class; namely by collecting together all of its sub-sets. But, if this *is* a larger class, then it could not be contained in the 'class of all classes', and how could the class of all classes *not* contain all classes?

After Russell had tried and failed to find a flaw in Cantor's argument, he reluctantly accepted its paradoxical consequence, and indeed, in his *Lectures on Logical Atomism*, made it the basis for what is surely one of the cleverest (though, admittedly, not one of the funniest) jokes in the literature of philosophy:

> Every class of things that you can choose to mention has some cardinal number. That follows very easily from the definition of cardinal numbers as classes of similar classes, and you would be inclined to suppose that the class of all the things there are in the world would have about as many members as a class could be reasonably expected to have. The plain man would suppose you could not get a larger class than the class of all the things there are in the world. On the other hand, it is very easy to prove that if you take selections of some of the members of a class, making those selections in every conceivable way that you can, the number of different selections that you can make is greater than the original number of terms ... Generally speaking, if you have n terms, you can make 2^n selections. It is very easy to prove that 2^n is always greater than n, whether n happens to be finite or not. So you find that the total number of things in the world is not so great as the number of classes that can be made up out of those things. I am asking you to take all these propositions for granted, because there is not time to go into the proofs, but they are all in Cantor's work. Therefore you will find that the total number of things in the world is by no means the greatest number. On the contrary, there is a hierarchy

of numbers greater than that. That, on the face of it, seems to land you in a contradiction. You have, in fact, a perfectly precise arithmetical proof that there are *fewer* things in heaven or earth than are dreamt of in *our* philosophy. That shows you how philosophy advances.

(*LA*, 129–30)

Actually, Russell's own philosophy advanced by ridding itself of this luxuriant ontology. If Cantor's proof is valid, he reasoned, then classes could not be objects; they were not, after all, among the 'things in the world'. Classes were, he now declared, 'logical fictions', and so were numbers: the Pythagorean world was, at least in part, an illusion.

He was strengthened in this view by his discovery of a contradiction in the notion of class that seemed more fundamental even than the paradox of the largest cardinal. This contradiction is now known as 'Russell's Paradox', and has become Russell's best known contribution to mathematical logic. It arises from the following considerations. The 'class of all classes' that Russell had been led to think about in his reflections on Cantor would be unusual among classes in having *itself* as a member. Most classes, clearly, are *not* members of themselves: the class of men, for example, is not a man. Now, suppose we construct the 'class of all classes that do not contain themselves' (that is, so to speak, the class of all *normal* classes), and ask: is that class a member of itself or not? We arrive at a logical impasse: if it is a member of itself, then it is not, and if it is not, then it is.

If Russell's delight in contemplating the world of mathematics could be regarded – as he himself was inclined to regard it – as a kind of religon, then these paradoxes brought him to the brink of atheism. He felt about them, he later said, 'much as an earnest Catholic must feel about wicked Popes'. From 1901 to 1906 he laboured hard on trying to find a way round them. Many times he thought he had found a solution, only to find that the contradiction, lke a cancerous growth, reappeared when he thought he had cut it out. He was helped in this work by his old tutor in mathematics, Alfred North Whitehead, with whom he had agreed to produce a joint work that would fulfil the promise of *The Principles of Mathematics* by actually carrying out, theorem by theorem, the reduction of mathematics to logic. Eventually, this collaboration produced the massive – and almost completely unreadable – classic three-volumed work *Principia Mathematica*, which was published from 1909 to 1913.

The system of logic contained in *Principia Mathematica* is a far cry indeed from the one envisaged by Russell in *The Principles of Mathematics*. In place of the beautifully clear and simple theory of classes that Russell had considered to be the essence of mathematics, Russell and

Whitehead created a system of quite monstrous complexity. Many of the complications introduced to the theory were forced upon them by the need to avoid paradoxes, but others were motivated by Russell's rapidly changing philosophical views. Broadly speaking, the change in Russell's philosophical outlook between *Principles* and *Principia* might be characterized as a shift from ontology to semantics, from questions about what does and does not exist to questions about what it does and does not make sense to say. In the process, he was forced to embark on what he later described as 'the retreat from Pythagoras'.

The retreat was gradual and, as we shall see, traces of Platonism (or Pythagoreanism) survive even in *Principia*. How reluctant he was to give up the Pythagorean mysticism that had inspired his work on mathematics is shown clearly in an article he wrote a year after his discovery of the paradox called 'The Study of Mathematics', in which he speaks of the objective truths of mathematics still in the exalted tones of a devout believer:

> Mathematics, perhaps more even than the study of Greece and Rome, has suffered from oblivion of its due place in civilization. Although tradition has decreed that the great bulk of educated men shall know at least the elements of the subject, the reasons for which the tradition arose are forgotten, buried beneath a great rubbish heap of pedantries and trivialities. To those who inquire as to the purpose of mathematics, the usual answer will be that it facilitates the making of machines, the travelling from place to place, and the victory over foreign nations, whether in war or commerce ... yet it is none of these that entitles mathematics to a place in every liberal education. Plato, we know, regarded the contemplation of mathematical truths as worthy of the Deity; and Plato realized, more perhaps than any other single man, what those elements are in human life which merit a place in heaven.
> ... Mathematics, rightly viewed, possesses not only truth, but supreme beauty – a beauty cold and austere, like that of sculpture, without appeal to any part of our weaker nature, without the gorgeous trappings of painting or music, yet sublimely pure, and capable of stern perfection such as only the greatest art can show. The true spirit of delight, the exaltation, the sense of being more than man, which is the touchstone of the highest excellence, is to be found in mathematics as surely as poetry ... Real life is, to most men, a long second-best, a perpetual compromise between the ideal and the possible; but the world of pure reason knows no compromise, no practical limitations, no barrier to the creative activity embodying in splendid edifices the

passionate aspiration after the perfect from which all great work springs.

. . . Of the austerer virtues the love of truth is the chief, and in mathematics, more than elsewhere, the love of truth may find encouragement for waning faith.   (*ML*, 62–74)

Russell's determination to hold onto this exalted view faced two considerable problems: 1, he had to show that the 'splendid edifices' of mathematics were soundly built, even after the foundations he had intended to give them had developed major cracks; and 2, he had to answer the question of what, if classes and numbers were 'fictions', Plato's Deity was thinking about when He contemplated the 'truths of mathematics'.

As Russell wrestled with these questions, he embarked on a programme of savagely pruning his ontology, concluding time and time again that what he had thought were 'things' were in fact just words or symbols, signifying nothing. First classes (and therefore numbers), then definite descriptions, and then propositions themselves were declared by him to be 'incomplete symbols'. The assumption guiding this pruning was that, if a symbol were 'complete' – i.e., meaningful – there would be an object corresponding to it. The cornerstone of his thinking about classes, it will be remembered, was that to every meaningful propositional function there corresponded a class. Russell now subjected this assumption to rigorous examination, putting stricter and stricter limits on what counted as meaningful in the light of his increasingly *un*-Pythagorean conception of what kinds of things exist. The first to go were classes. There are no such things and therefore the question as to whether a class does or does not belong to itself does not arise: the question is nonsense. But, if classes do not exist, upon what do the foundations of mathematics now stand? Russell's provisional answer was: propositional functions. Just as every statement about numbers can be analysed as being about classes, every statement about classes can be analysed as being about propositional functions. As Russell put it in *Lectures on Logical Atomism*:

I have been talking, for brevity's sake, as if there really were all these different sorts of things [numbers, classes, classes of classes, etc.]. Of course, that is nonsense. There are particulars, but when one comes on to classes, and classes of classes, and classes of classes of classes, one is talking of logical fictions . . . what are the sort of things you would like to say about classes? They are just the same as the sort of things you want to say about propositional functions. You want to say of a propositional function that is is sometimes true. That is the same thing as saying of a class that it has members. You want to say that it is true for exactly 100 values of the variables. That is the same as saying of a class that it has a hundred members. All the things you want to say about classes are the same as the things you want to say about propositional functions excepting for accidental and irrelevant linguistic forms ... In that way you find that all the formal properties that you desire of classes, all their formal uses in mathematics, can be obtained without supposing for a moment that there are such things as classes, without supposing, that is to say, that a proposition in which symbolically a class occurs, does in fact contain a constituent corresponding to that symbol, and when rightly analysed that symbol will disappear.   (*LA*, 136–8)

In the light of such considerations, Russell made central to his philosophy a kind of analysis that sought to reveal the *real* logical form that lies hidden behind 'accidental and irrelevant linguistic forms'. 'The problem that there is arises from our inveterate habit of trying to name what cannot be named', he said. 'If we had a proper logical language, we should not be tempted to do that.' His and Whitehead's task, then, was to construct such a 'proper logical language', a language in which there would be no symbols for numbers or classes, but only for particulars and propositional functions. As a matter of convenience, symbols for numbers and classes would be introduced, but a systematic and rigorous technique would be provided for translating them back into a more 'logically proper' form, and cautions would be issued that the things these symbols *appear* to name do not actually exist.

The most celebrated example of this kind of analysis in Russell's work is his Theory of Descriptions, first published in an article called 'On Denoting' in 1905. Russell's purpose in developing this theory was closely tied to his efforts to repair the damage done to his philosophy of mathematics by the Paradox – and in particular to his efforts to remove classes from his ontology – but this aspect of the theory tends now to be forgotten. 'Denoting' is the word that Russell gave in *The Principles of Mathematics* to the logical relation between a concept and an object, class, or number (these, of course, not being distinct categories in *Principles*, for at that stage in Russell's thought a number was a class and a class was an object). Thus, the concept 'the first woman Prime Minister of Great Britain' denotes Margaret Thatcher; 'the next prime after 7' denotes the number 11; 'all even numbers' denotes the infinite class of even numbers, etc. Denotation is rather different from the notion of *reference* with which it is often confused; reference is a linguistic relation between a word or string of words and an object, for example between a name and a person. On Russell's theory, names do not denote; what denotes is a *concept* and in language denotation is achieved by means, not of a name, but of a *description*. More especially, in *Principles of Mathematics*, denotation is achieved by a description that begins with one of the following six words: *all*, *every*, *any*, *a*, *some* and *the*.

The importance of denotation for Russell is that denoting phrases are central to mathematics (*the* square root of 2', '*all* even numbers are the sum of 2 primes', etc.) and also that denotation and propositional functions go hand in hand with each other. As he put it in *Lectures on Logical Atomism*: 'Whenever you get such words as "a", "some", "all", "every", it is always a mark of the presence of a propositional function.' So, for example, for Russell the statement 'All dogs are dirty' would be understood as asserting that the propositional function, 'if x is a dog, x is dirty' is always true, 'I met a man' as asserting that the propositional function 'I met x and x is human' is not always false, and so on. Just as, at the time of writing *Principles*, Russell held that every meaningful propositional function defined a class (even if the class was empty), so he believed that every meaningful denoting phrase denoted *something*, even some 'thing' that did not exist. Now, taking a sterner line on existence, Russell held that things that did not exist were nothing at all, and that denoting phrases that *appeared* to denote non-existent things were, in fact, meaningless.

In 'On Denoting' Russell undertook to analyse statements containing denoting phrases in such a way as to remove altogether the appearance of denoting things that did not exist. The theory he advanced is that *all* denoting phrases are, in themselves, meaningless. They are 'incomplete symbols' that only acquire a meaning in the context of a proposition. Take, for example, definite descriptions (phrases beginning with the word 'the'): 'the present King of France', 'the next prime after 7', etc. These phrases, Russell now held, do not mean anything. However, statements containing them *do* mean something, but *what* they mean can only properly be understood when they are translated in such a way that the definite description does not occur. Take, for example, the statement, 'The present King of France is bald.' This appears to assume, falsely, that there *is*, at present, a King of France and, moreover, it appears to denote this non-existent entity and to predicate baldness of it. Russell's proposed translation transforms this assumption into an explicit statement. According to his Theory of Descriptions, 'The Present King of France is bald' is *really* a conjunction of three assertions:

1. The propositional function, 'x is at present King of France' is not always false.
2. If the propositional *function* 'y is at present King of France' is true for

any y, then y is identical to x [i.e., there is only *one* present King of France]

3. x is bald.

The first assertion amounts to an explicit statement that the present King of France exists and as this is false, the entire conjunction is false. So, by means of this rather convoluted analysis, 'The present King of France is bald' is shown to be a meaningful, but false, proposition.

In Russell's 'logically proper language', then, denoting phrases do not occur. There is, contrary to what he had said in *Principles*, no such thing as denotation (in a way, this follows immediately from the denial of the existence of classes, for in most cases the 'denoted object' was a class). Instead of denotation, what we have are statements to the effect that a given propositional function ('x is F') is always true, always false, or sometimes true ('not always false'). This last becomes, in effect, a statement of existence. To say that angels exist, for example, is to say that the propositional function 'x is an angel' is sometimes true.

Russell's determination to do away with classes and rest his entire theory on propositional functions is, in some ways, rather odd. For, as he realized at a fairly early stage, the paradox of classes that do or do not belong to themselves has its analogue in the realm of propositional functions, where the problem is caused by propositions which are, or are not, *true* of themselves. He seemed to think that propositional functions were somehow more manageable than classes. In any case, he was by now convinced on quite general philosophical grounds – independently, that is, of the formal problem of constructing a consistent theory of logic and mathematics – that classes do not exist. A further step in his ontological pruning was taken soon after writing 'On Denoting', when he became convinced on similar grounds that there were no such 'things' as propositions.

Until 1907, Russell conceived of propositions as being, in some sense, abstract objects. Propositions, for him, were not sentences; they were not, that is, units of language, they were the objects of thoughts. Thus, if I think that 2 plus 2 is 4, and so do you, then '2 + 2 = 4' is the proposition to which both our thoughts refer. This proposition has some kind of objective status; it has its being, that is, not in my mind or yours, but in, so to speak, the realm of truth. For a short while, after he had eliminated numbers and classes, Russell made this notion the basis of a vestigial Platonism about mathematics, which he described in a letter to his friend Margaret Llewelyn Davies on 26 March 1906:

I did not mean [in his article, 'The Study of Mathematics'] that the objects of mathematics or other abstract thoughts *exist* outside us, still less that there is any universal or divine mind whose ideas we are reproducing when we think. What I meant to say was that the object of any abstract thought is not a thought, either of the thinker or of any one else, and does not *exist* at all, though it *is* something. Thus in mathematics a new theorem is a *discovery* in the sense that the discoverer for the first time apprehends the fact discovered, which fact has a timeless *being*, not *existence*.

This distinction between 'being' and 'existence', however, sat uncomfortably with Russell's new-found ontological austerity, and the same force that impelled him to abandon the non-existent 'things' denoted by definite descriptions impelled him also to get rid of propositions. If something does not exist, then it cannot *be* anything. This was brought home to Russell by reflecting upon *false* propositions. The idea that '2 + 2 = 4' *is* something, that it has 'a timeless being', has some plausibility, especially to someone with vestiges of a Pythagorean belief in the timeless world of arithmetical truth. But, what if you and I both thought that 2 plus 2 was 5? Would the object of that thought too have a timeless being? With a ruthlessness typical of the way he treated his earlier opinions, Russell came to ridicule the view:

> Time was when I thought there were propositions, but it does not seem to me very plausible to say that in addition to facts there are also these curious shadowy things going about such as 'That today is Wednesday' when it is in fact Tuesday. I cannot believe they go about in the real world. It is more than one can manage to believe, and I do think no person with a vivid sense of reality can imagine it.   (*LA*, 87)

Propositions, then, do not exist and therefore sentences expressing propositions have to be regarded, like definite descriptions, as 'incomplete symbols', only now the context that is required to make them significant is a person's mind. Propositions do not mean anything until they are *judged* true or false by someone. The judgement is true if it corresponds with the facts and false otherwise. Thus, facts exist 'in the world' and thoughts exist 'in the head', but propositions, 'these curious shadowy things' that were alleged to be somewhere between the two, have no existence whatever. In the Introduction to *Principia Mathematica*, Russell expresses the point like this:

> What we call a 'proposition' (in the sense in which this is distinguished from the phrase expressing it) is not a single entity at all. That is to say,

the phrase which expresses a proposition is what we call an 'incomplete' symbol; it does not have meaning in itself, but requires some supplementation in order to acquire a complete meaning . . . Thus 'the proposition "Socrates is human"' uses 'Socrates is human' in a way which requires a supplement of some kind before it acquires a complete meaning; but when I judge 'Socrates is human' the meaning is completed by the act of judging, and we no longer have an incomplete symbol. The fact that propositions are 'incomplete symbols' is important philosophically, and is relevant at certain points in symbolic logic.   (PM, 44)

What, then *is* a judgement? Clearly not a relation between a mind and a proposition, for if propositions do not exist, they cannot stand in any kind of relation with anything. In the face of this, Russell developed what he called the 'multiple relation theory of judgement', according to which a judgement is a series of relations between a mind and the *constituents* of a proposition. Thus, the judgement 'Socrates is mortal' is a series of relations between three things: the individual, Socrates, the predicate 'mortality', and the mind that brings them together to judge that Socrates is mortal.

Having eliminated numbers, classes, denoting phrases and propositions, Russell was left with a horribly complicated 'logically proper language', in which even the simplest mathematical formula would be expressed in an almost incomprehensibly convoluted manner. But worse was to come, for he had still not solved the paradox, which, he now came to think, had its roots in the possibility of *self-reference*. Cantor's Paradox of the largest cardinal and his own paradox of the class of classes which do not contain themselves were, he believed, variants of the old paradox of the Cretan who says 'All Cretans are liars': if he is telling the truth, then he is lying and if he is lying, then he is telling the truth. The problem, of course, is generated by the fact that his sentence includes itself. In a logically perfect language, therefore, it should be impossible for a judgement to include itself. This is the basic idea behind the Theory of Types that Russell built into the logical system of *Principia Mathematica*.

Expressed, for a moment, in terms of logical fictions, the Theory of Types says that there is a hierarchy of objects: first particulars, then classes, then classes of classes, and so on. A class can only be constructed of the objects on one particular level of the hierarchy, namely, the level immediately below itself, so a class cannot include itself. It follows immediately, of course, that there is no such thing as the class of all classes and that therefore neither Cantor's paradox, nor Russell's, applies to the system. But, of course, classes do not exist, so the Theory of Types has to be expressed instead in terms of propositional functions, and now it says that a propositional function is *meaningless* if it takes itself as a value of its variable (i.e., a proposition cannot meaningfully refer to itself). The hierarchy now becomes one of propositions and propositional functions: at the bottom level are elementary propositions containing no variables; at the next level are propositional functions whose variables range only over particulars; then propositional functions that can take other, lower-level propositional functions as their values, etc. At this point, the Theory of Types becomes what Russell always claimed it was, namely a 'theory of symbolism'. Of course, to be philosophically scrupulous, propositions do not exist either, so ultimately the Theory of Types has to be regarded as establishing different levels of judgements.

From a formal point of view, the system of logic outlined in *Principia Mathematica* is one of quite dizzying complexity. It has been said that it is probably the most complicated structure ever invented by a single human mind (for, though Whitehead collaborated with Russell on the mathematical parts of the enterprise, the Theory of Types was Russell's own). Statements about number are reduced to statements about classes, which are, in turn, reduced to the theory of propositional functions, which is, ultimately grounded in the Theory of Types. So many definitions and preliminary theorems are needed before arithmetic can get started that, for example, the proposition '1 plus 1 is 2' is arrived at only halfway through Volume II.

But philosophically, the picture is, if anything, still more murky. When Russell believed in classes, it was fairly clear what the point was of reducing mathematics to logic: it was to show that the truths of mathematics were a part of the larger realm of objective logical truth. This still, of course, is the purpose of *Principia Mathematica*, but it is now much less clear what the 'objects' are that inhabit the realm of logical truth. It is easy to say what they are not. They are not numbers, classes, or propositions. Can one say, perhaps, that they are *forms*? In an unfinished paper called 'What is Logic?' that he wrote soon after the completion of *Principia*, Russell struggled to make this idea plausible. 'A *form* is something', he wrote, and yet the paper shows him at a loss to explain what kind of 'thing' it is.

By 1913, Russell became persuaded by his brilliant young student, Ludwig Wittgenstein, that there were no such things as logical objects, and yet he still insisted that there *was* such a thing as logical knowledge. This, according to Russell's epistemology at the time, required there to be such a thing as *acquaintance* in logic, acquaintance being, in other contexts, a direct relation between ourselves and the objects of our knowledge. Again, Russell struggled with the obvious inconsistency.

'Logical objects cannot be regarded as "entities"', he wrote, and yet there *must* be 'something which seems fitly described as "acquaintance with logical objects".'

Between 1914 and 1917, Russell abandoned philosophy in favour of campaigning against the First World War, but in the summer of 1917 he returned once more to the question of what, if anything, the objects of logic are. In this, he was inspired to some extent by the encouragement of his friend, the mathematician Philip Jourdain, who urged him to write a series of articles under the title, 'What is Logic?' 'I want to know badly what logic is', Jourdain wrote. In *Introduction to Mathematical Logic*, written the following year, Russell took up the question and answered that logic was 'concerned with the real world just as truly as zoology, though with its more abstract and general features'. What he meant is explained to some extent in *Lectures on Logical Atomism*, written the same year. Logic, he says there, is 'concerned with the forms of facts, with getting hold of the different sorts of facts, different *logical* sorts of facts, that there are in the world'. But are these forms 'objects' in any sense? Well, in any case, Russell seems to suggest that they can – with great difficulty – be made the objects of our thoughts, and that they are distinct from the symbols we use to represent them. Logic *does* have its own subject-matter, only it is a very rarefied and elusive one:

> [In philosophical logic] the subject-matter that you are supposed to be thinking of is so exceedingly difficult and elusive that any person who has ever tried to think about it knows that you do not think about it except perhaps once in six months for half a minute. The rest of the time you think about the symbols, because they are tangible, but the thing you are supposed to be thinking about is fearfully difficult and one does not often manage to think about it. The really good philosopher is the one who does once in six months think about it for a minute. Bad philosophers never do.   (*LA*, 44)

Within a year, having in the meantime read Wittgenstein's *Tractatus Logico-Philosophicus*, Russell abandoned this view. The reason it is so difficult to distinguish the symbols of logic from what they represent, he now came to think, is because there is no difference. 'Logic and the so-called "Laws of Thought"', he now roundly declared 'are concerned with symbols; they give different ways of saying the same thing . . . only an understanding of language is necessary in order to know a proposition of logic.' A logical principle, he wrote, asserts nothing but 'that this symbol and that have the same meaning', adding: 'I have adopted this view from Mr Wittgenstein.'

The 'retreat from Pythagoras' was now complete: logical forms, like numbers, classes and propositions, were consigned to the wastepaper basket of metaphysical illusions. Russell still believed that mathematics was reducible to logic, but what this showed, he now believed, is that it is concerned only with 'different ways of saying the same thing':

> Mathematics has ceased to seem to me non-human in its subject-matter. I have come to believe, though very reluctantly, that it consists of tautologies. I fear that, to a mind of sufficient intellectual power, the whole of mathematics would appear trivial, as trivial as the statement that a four-footed animal is an animal . . . I cannot any longer find any mystical satisfaction in the contemplation of mathematical truth . . . I have no longer the feeling that intellect is superior to sense, and that only Plato's world of ideas gives access to the 'real' world.
>
> (*MPD*, 211–12)

Indeed, it now became important to Russell *not* to believe in the world of ideas, a belief he now began to ridicule as a morbid dislike of the real world.

Ironically, shortly after Russell abandoned the last traces of his Pythagoreanism on the grounds that mathematics had been shown to be nothing more than logic and, therefore, linguistic, a proof was published that threw serious doubt upon the supposed reduction of mathematics to logic. This was the famous Gödel Incompleteness Proof, first published in January 1931 in a paper called 'On Formally Undecidable Propositions of *Principia Mathematica* and Related Systems'. In it, Gödel provided a strict formal proof that what Russell and Whitehead had tried to achieve in *Principia Mathematica* could never be fully realized: there cannot, in principle, be a single system of logic in which the whole of mathematics can be derived. Gödel himself was a Platonist, and he and others regarded his proof as providing some support for the Platonist view.

Russell was surprisingly slow to react to Gödel's proof. When, in 1937, he produced a new edition of *The Principles of Mathematics*, he wrote a new Introduction that discussed some of the work done in the area since 1903, but he conspicuously failed to mention Gödel. In 1942, however, Gödel was commissioned to write an article for the volume on Russell in Paul Schilpp's series *The Library of Living Philosophers*, and took the opportunity to combat what he considered to be the baleful influence of Wittgenstein on Russell's philosophy of mathematics. His article, 'Russell's Mathematical Logic', criticizes Russell for his abandonment of classes in *Principia Mathematica* and argues for the kind of Platonic conception of mathematics with which Russell had begun. Classes, says

Gödel, may indeed be regarded as real objects: 'It seems to me that the assumption of such objects is quite as legitimate as the assumption of physical bodies and there is quite as much reason to believe in their existence.'

Russell, however, was not to be drawn into the debate that Gödel had hoped to provoke. He replied to all the essays published in the Schilpp volume *except* Gödel's, to which he responded only with the lame remark: 'His [Gödel's] great ability, as shown in his previous work, makes me think it highly probable that many of his criticisms of me are justified.' Soon afterwards, however, he met Gödel himself at Princeton, and seemed surprised to find that Gödel 'turned out to be an unadulterated Platonist, and apparently believed that an eternal "not" was laid up in heaven where virtuous logicians might hope to meet it hereafter'. To this, Gödel responded that his own Platonism was no more 'unadulterated' than Russell's had been when he talked, for example, of logic being concerned with the real world just as truly as zoology: 'At that time evidently Russell had met the "not" even in this world, but later on under the influence of Wittgenstein he chose to ignore it.'

Russell never did respond in detail to Gödel's arguments for Platonism. Perhaps they came too late for him; he was nearly sixty when the Incompleteness Theorem was published and over seventy when asked to reply to Gödel's essay for Schilpp. In any case, his mind was made up: the Platonic world of objective mathematical truth was an illusion. In one of his very last philosophical essays, written in 1951 and called 'Is Mathematics Purely Linguistic?', he, as it were, laid a wreath on the tomb of his early hopes for mathematics:

> Pythagoras, and Plato after him, had a theory of mathematics as charming as it was simple . . . Pythagoras thought that mathematics is the study of numbers, and that each number is a separate eternal entity dwelling in a super-sensible heaven. When I was young I believed something like this . . . But study gradually dispelled this belief . . . it turns out that numbers are nothing but a verbal convenience, and disappear when the propositions that seem to contain them are fully written out. To look for numbers in heaven is therefore as futile as to look for (say) 'etc'.
>
>   . . . All the propositions of mathematics and logic are assertions as to the correct use of a small number of words.
>
>   This conclusion, if valid, may be regarded as an epitaph on Pythagoras.   (*EA*, 300–6)

At about the same time, Russell wrote a short story which dramatized the intellectual road he had travelled in his thinking about mathematics. It is called 'The Mathematician's Nightmare', and tells the story of 'Professor Squarepunt', who 'worn out by a long day's study of the old theories of Pythagoras' falls asleep in his chair, 'where a strange drama visited his sleeping thoughts':

> The numbers, in this drama, were not the bloodless categories that he had previously supposed them: They were living breathing beings endowed with all the passions which he was accustomed to find in his fellow mathematicians. In his dream he stood at the centre of endless concentric circles. The first circle contained the numbers from 1 to 10; the second, those from 11 to 100; the third, those from 101 to 1,000; and so on, illimitably, over the infinite surface of a boundless plain. The odd numbers were male; the evens, female. Beside him in the centre stood Pi, the Master of Ceremonies. Pi's face was masked, and it was understood that none could behold it and live. But piercing eyes looked out from the mask, inexorable, cold, and enigmatic. Each number had its name clearly marked upon its uniform. Different kinds of numbers had different uniforms and different shapes: the squares were tiles, the cubes were dice, round numbers were balls, prime numbers were indivisible cylinders, perfect numbers had crowns.
>
> ... The numbers danced round Professor Squarepunt and Pi in a vast and intricate ballet ... At a sign from Pi the ballet ceased, and the numbers one by one were introduced to Professor Squarepunt. Each number made a little speech explaining its peculiar merits.
>
> ... [After a while] the mathematician got bored and turned to Pi, saying: 'Don't you think the rest of the introductions could be taken for granted?' At this there was a general outcry.
>
> ... There was such a din that the mathematician covered his ears with his hands and turned an imploring gaze upon Pi. Pi waved his conductor's baton and proclaimed in a voice of thunder: 'Silence! Or you shall all become incommensurable'. All turned pale and submitted.
>
> Throughout the ballet the Professor had noticed one number among the primes, 137, which seemed unruly and unwilling to accept its place in the series ... At length 137 exclaimed: 'There's a damned sight too much bureaucracy here! What I want is liberty for the individual.' Pi's mask frowned. But the Professor interceded, saying, 'Do not be too hard on him ... I should like to hear what 137 has to say.'
>
> Somewhat reluctantly, Pi consented. Professor Squarepunt said: 'Tell me, 137, what is the basis of your revolt?' ... At this, 137 burst into excited speech: 'It is their metaphysic that I cannot bear. They still

pretend that they are eternal, though long ago their conduct showed that they think no such thing. We all found Plato's heaven dull and decided that it would be more fun to govern the sensible world. Since we descended from the Empyrean we have had emotions not unlike yours: each Odd loves its attendant Even; and the Evens feel kindly towards the Odds, in spite of finding them very odd. Our empire now is of this world, and when the world goes pop, we shall pop too.'

Professor Squarepunt found himself in agreement with 137. But all the others, including Pi, considered him a blasphemer, and turned upon both him and the Professor. The infinite host, extending in all directions farther than the eye could reach, hurled themselves upon the poor Professor in an angry buzz. For a moment he was terrified. Then he pulled himself together and, suddenly recollecting his waking wisdom, he called out in stentorian tones: 'Avaunt! You are only Symbolic Conveniences!'

With a banshee wail, the whole vast array dissolved in mist. And, as he woke, the Professor heard himself saying, 'So much for Plato!'

(*NEP*, 48–53)

The 'Pythagorean Dream', Russell came finally to think, had been nothing but a nightmare all along.

Jonathan Rée

HEIDEGGER

History and Truth in Being and Time

Universities often seem more like asylums for the protection of deluded academics than workshops producing real knowledge. Take a glance, for example, at this heavy bible-black volume issued in Halle in 1927: *Jahrbuch für Phänomenologie und phänomenologische Forschung*, Vol. 8. It is 800 pages long, and contains just two philosophical treatises, divided into numbered sections like insurance regulations. Unreadable, you will conclude: just another meaningless monument to academic pride and grandiosity.

Back in 1927, however, the German philosophical public leapt on the *Jahrbuch*. It was not Oskar Becker's meticulous discussion of 'Mathematical Existence' that attracted them, but the other article, even longer and more forbidding. The author was only an assistant professor at Marburg in Hessen at the time, but he already enjoyed a strange notoriety. It was said that he was not just a philosopher, but – on the contrary – a *thinker*, and that he cared nothing for the cosmopolitan elegance of the German intellectual aristocracy, preferring the gruff peasant manners he had been born to 37 years before, in the Catholic village of Messkirch, down in Baden. Instead of frequenting professorial dinner tables, he liked to stay with his wife and two young sons in the mountain hut he had built above Todtnauberg in the Black Forest a few years before. There he could ski across country, chop wood, gaze into the distance, and think. But he needed a better-paid job – ideally, a Chair at his old university in Freiburg-im-Breisgau, an easy car-journey from his hut – and he could not get promotion unless he published a substantial article. He sent off some manuscripts to the *Jahrbuch*, and so it was that *Being and Time: First Half* by Martin Heidegger made its entrance into the world.

The philosophical issue of the day was the relation between truth and history. Enlightenment faith in science and progress had been devastated by the war of 1914–18, leaving the field open to corrosive 'relativism'. Beliefs, it seemed, depended on the fickleness of history, not on some transcendently trustworthy absolute truth.

Heidegger's big argument would be that, if the concepts of historical particularity and scientific truth are clearly thought through, then the apparent conflict between them disappears: that our individual peculiarities are not a chrysalis that we leave behind in order to rise to an exalted realm of truth, but the origin and anchor of all our knowledge. It was going to be a hard lesson, however, since it ran counter to our most immediate sense of ourselves – to the dichotomy between mind and world or subjectivity and objectivity which, as well as being built into the brickwork of western philosophy, is woven into the fabric of our everyday self-understandings. The necessary task of clarification would require not only intellectual virtuosity, but a labour of self-transformation as well.

AN ONTOLOGY OF OURSELVES

At first it is a disappointment to move from these tantalizing expectations to the treatise Heidegger actually wrote. For a start, what title could be more outdated than *Being and Time*? Was Heidegger unaware that the philosophical study of being – 'ontology', in the jargon of the academy – had been definitively discredited by Kant at the end of the eighteenth century, and replaced by empirical natural science? And had no one told him that, following Einstein's special theory of relativity of 1905, the concept of time now belonged to physics rather than philosophy?

But we should take care. Philosophers often write with a canny sense of paradox, and eventually make fools of those with too little wariness about their own unclarified and unironic certitudes. Heidegger may not be about to bore us with some foolhardy new solutions to the problems or pseudo-problems of traditional ontology – philosophical equivalents to perpetual motion or squaring the circle. He may have something rather subtler up his sleeve.

Still, our hearts will sink again when we turn the page and discover a quotation in Greek – a remark addressed by the mysterious Eleatic stranger to the radiant youth Theaetetus in Plato's dialogue *The Sophist*: 'for manifestly you have long been aware of what you mean when you use the expression "being" '.[1] So it will be just another debate over the meanings of words, we sigh. Heidegger pursues the quotation: 'we, however, who used to think we understood it, have now become perplexed'.[2] Here is a twofold surprise. 'We *used to* think we understood it': but surely our certainties are meant to grow with age, not diminish? And '*now* we are perplexed': but is it not perpetual truth, rather than mounting perplexity, that is supposed to be the daughter of time?

At least we can be reassured that Heidegger is not going to lay down the law about the nature of being as such. His theme is less portentous – the 'meaning of being' – and this 'meaning', as he explains later, is not some mystery that 'stands behind being', but simply whatever sense the term may happen to have within our ordinary languages and understandings: the investigation, he says, will be anything but 'deep'.[3] And even if we end up discovering nothing positive, we can at least hope to clarify our understanding of the question we are asking, the '*question of the meaning of being*'.[4]

When we turn another page and start reading the Introduction ('Exposition of the question of the meaning of being'), we find Heidegger taking yet another step backwards. 'This question has today been forgotten', he writes. The question of being may have had some urgency when Plato and Aristotle wrestled it into submission in Athens long ago; but ever since that time it has been ignored or languidly dismissed as 'superfluous'.[5]

If the question has been forgotten, however, it is not because it has been censored and suppressed, but because it has been paraded in public so shamelessly that it has lost its original pungency. Like a poem or prayer that we learned by rote in childhood, the question of the meaning of being feels so dull and familiar that we never notice that we are ignorant of what it means: 'that which the ancient philosophers found continually disturbing as something obscure and hidden', Heidegger says, has declined into 'clarity and self-evidence'.[6]

It is precisely because of this distracting banality that Heidegger refuses to tell us directly what we no doubt want to know: what exactly does he mean by 'being'? How would he define it? He reminds us that it has always been one of the grand themes of western philosophy, but beyond that he offers only broad hints: being is a crucial question, perhaps the mother and father of all questions; it is an issue that belongs to all of us, whether we know it or not; it is what we are ultimately talking about, whenever we talk at all; and it has been disgracefully trivialized by the very philosophical tradition that is supposed to celebrate it. This explanation of 'being' may seem exceedingly enigmatic, but Heidegger promises that if we follow him we will eventually be able to discover within ourselves not only some glimmer of its meaning, but also some understanding of why we are all inclined to dismiss the entire issue as trivial and vexatious.

Our predictable weariness about ontology rests on some quite intriguing prejudices. First, as Heidegger points out, it presumes that being must be the most universal of concepts, since it designates what all things have in common. Secondly, it assumes that being is vague and indefinable: for how could something so general have any distinctive characteristics? The third presumption is that all of us already understand being without even having to think about it: after all, any child can use the verb 'to be', and what more could we mean by an understanding of the meaning of being?

Yet these three prejudices against ontology are themselves assumptions about being. They are ontological judgements and, as Heidegger points out, they are 'rooted in ancient ontology itself'. If we examine them closely, therefore, they may disclose something about the meaning of being, and illuminate the play of recognition and forgetting that constitutes the history of ontology. If being is indeed the most universal of concepts, then 'this cannot mean that it is the one which is clearest or that it needs no further discussion'; it suggests, on the contrary, that 'it is rather the darkest of all'. And secondly, if being is truly 'indefinable', it follows that it is categorially different from the kinds of entity we interact with in everyday life; and this seems to show that ontological issues (questions about being as such) cannot be approached in the same way as *ontical* ones (questions about particular entities). Thirdly, if we possess an adequate understanding of being anyway, then we must recognize that this untutored 'average kind of intelligibility' is itself a significant fact, which deserves patient and attentive analysis.[7]

Of course, we may always be mistaken about ontological issues, whether our attitude be credulous or hostile or somewhere in between. In particular, we will be constantly tempted to treat them as if they were 'ontical' – as if they concerned one entity amongst others, and could be sufficiently explained by 'telling a story' (as in a 'history of philosophy') and tracing them 'back in their origin to some other entities, as if being had the character of some possible entity'.[8] But if we are perpetually misconstruing ontological questions by offering ontical answers to them, this only confirms that they remain an issue for us. After all, we could not exist at all without some understanding of the nature of the world around us and our place in it. This understanding need not take the form of explicit ontological opinions, of course; rather it will find expression in the way we lead our lives. From the first dawning of our existence, as Heidegger puts it, we 'already live in an understanding of being'.[9] Even if we despise the whole idea of ontology, our attempts to avoid it will still bear the imprint of what repels us. And if our ways of avoiding ontology are themselves interpretations of ontology, then we must all already be our own ontologists – amateur ontologists of our own existence.

The Question and the Questioner
But what are we doing when we inquire into the question of the meaning of being? Indeed, what does it mean to ask questions at all? Heidegger offers the following brisk analysis.

Every inquiry is a seeking. Every seeking gets guided beforehand by what is sought ... Any inquiry, as an inquiry about something, has *that which is asked about*. But all inquiry about something is somehow a questioning of something. So in addition to what is asked about, an inquiry has *that which is interrogated* ... Furthermore, in what is asked about there lies also *that which is to be found out by the asking*.[10]

These words may well strike us as ungainly and defiantly obscure – especially in English. Macquarrie and Robinson's translation is a classic, but it is not perfect. Indeed, no translation could possibly do justice to the sinewy style of *Being and Time*, which constantly draws on procedures of word-formation peculiar to the German language. In this instance, Heidegger is spelling out how every *Fragen*, or asking, comprises not only (a) a preliminary notion of 'what is sought', but also (b) a *Gefragte*, which is 'asked about', (c) a *Befragte*, which is 'interrogated', and (d) an *Erfragte*, which is 'to be found out'. Part of the poetry of Heidegger's analysis might be reproduced by saying that every *asking* compromises (a) its initial orientation, (b) its *asked-about*, (c) its *asked-after* and (d) its *asked-for* – except that this sounds ridiculous in English, whereas in German the effect is simple, even beautiful.

Heidegger then applies this general analysis to the question of the meaning of being. Our preliminary orientation, he says, is provided by the 'vague average understanding of being' in terms of which we 'always conduct our activities'. This initial understanding may 'fluctuate and grow dim, and border on mere acquaintance with a word', though 'its very indefiniteness is itself a positive phenomenon which needs to be clarified'. What is *asked about* is 'being', of which we know very little except that it is utterly unlike the particular entities we encounter in everyday life. What is *asked after* or 'interrogated', on the other hand, must be 'entities' of specific kinds, 'questioned as regards their being'. And finally, what is *asked for*, or 'to be found out', is the 'meaning of being' itself.[11]

But this fourfold analysis is not complete. In order to understand a question, you also need to take account of a fifth factor – *where* it is coming from, or *who* the questioner (or 'asker' – *Frager*) is. A question about the weather obviously calls for a different response when asked by a sailor, a farmer or a back-packer. So what of the question of the meaning of being in general – the vague, obscure, charming and alarming question that we all like to think we can easily answer or as easily dismiss? Who are we when we ask it? What is the essence of its *asker*?

The peculiarity of this question is that we are engaged with it all the time. Whenever we orientate ourselves in the world and make some sense of it, or fail to do so, we stand in some relation to the question of the meaning of being: our asking of it is coextensive with our existence. One might almost say that our capacity for asking it corresponds to what is usually referred to by such terms as 'human nature' or 'mind' or 'soul', except that this vocabulary is so stuffed with strange residues of mysticism and metaphysics that it might constrain or misdirect our inquiries.

The entity we are when confronted by ontological questions is simply us, as ordinary and familiar as can be. Heidegger therefore chooses the most ordinary of German words to describe it: *Dasein*. *Dasein* can often be translated as 'existence', but in *Being and Time* that term is needed to express the concept of *Existenz*, so the only feasible solution has been to create a new English word to serve as its equivalent: 'Dasein' (written without italics; plural: 'Daseins'). In practice we can often paraphrase it by using 'we' in its place, but not always. If the foreignism still makes us stumble, we should simply remind ourselves that the German word *Dasein* is as colloquial as can be. It is not a technical term, and as Daseins, we are simply entities with ontological attitude.

If our understanding of questions always presupposes some knowledge of who is asking them, it follows, as Heidegger says, that our understanding of ontological questions will require a 'proper explication' of Dasein. The explication of Dasein will not be a logical or natural-scientific analysis, however. As human beings, we can be analysed either as logical reasoners or as physical bundles of meat and bone; but as Daseins we are nothing but our understandings and misunderstandings of the world and our place in it, and our more or less clear understandings and misunderstandings of these understandings, and so on for ever and ever without end. The connotations of the word 'analysis' may seem too hard-edged, therefore, and we may well prefer 'hermeneutic of Dasein', which is Heidegger's alternative phrase for the infinitely prolific art of interpreting our interpretations of being.[12]

There would appear to be two ways of approaching the hermeneutic of Dasein: one ontological, the other ontical. The first would seek to enter into Dasein's understanding of the meaning of being and clarify it from within, whilst the second would offer an external description of the characteristics that distinguish us, as Daseins, from other kinds of entity. But as Heidegger points out, ontical description and ontological interpretation are bound to get tangled up with each other.

Dasein is an entity which does not just occur amongst other entities. Rather it is ontically distinguished by the fact that, in its very being, that being is an *issue* for it. But in that case, this is a constitutive state of Dasein's being, and this implies that Dasein, in its being, has a relationship towards that being . . . And this means further that there is some way in which Dasein understands itself in its being, and that to some degree it does so explicitly. It is peculiar to this entity that with and through its being, this being is disclosed to it. *Understanding of being is itself a definitive characteristic of Dasein's being*. Dasein is ontically distinctive in that it *is* ontological.[13]

Dasein's ontical speciality, one might say, is universal ontology. For Dasein, to exist is to ontologize. We all have 'an understanding of being', Heidegger says, even if we are not conscious of it, and even if we have never heard of ontology and are happy to stay that way. If our existence is not always explicitly ontological, it is at least 'pre-ontological'.[14]

The purpose of deliberate ontological inquiry, then, will be a 'clarification' and 'radicalization' of our 'pre-ontological understanding of being'.[15] Through clarification and radicalization our pre-ontologies will be transformed into what Heidegger called 'fundamental ontology'. The phrase has proved an unlucky one, however: it sounds like 'fundamental physics' and evokes an image of specialized professional ontologists formulating universal principles by which to judge the fumbling efforts of us ordinary amateurs. But the journey we have already made – through the analysis of questioning to the identification of Dasein as the asker of ontological questions – should have taught us that there will be no principles of ontology outside the intersecting spirals of our own understandings of the meaning of being. Fundamental ontology will be essentially reflexive, and the 'of' of the 'hermeneutic of Dasein' will have to be understood in two different directions. The hermeneutic of Dasein is also Dasein's hermeneutic: interpretation of Dasein, by Dasein, for Dasein.

Ontological analysis of Dasein – that is, our own analysis of ourselves in our existence – can also be described as 'existential'. But existential analysis comprises nothing except our interpretations of ourselves as entities that interpret and misinterpret being. If we succeed in replacing our unconsidered pre-ontologies with more fundamental ones, it will not be by uncovering structures that are already buried there, like solid rock beneath the quaking sands of our existence, but by releasing ourselves from the illusion that our existence has any foundations at all, apart from our interpretations of it. '*Fundamental ontology*', as Heidegger puts it, 'must be sought in the *existential analytic of Dasein*.'[16] Fundamental ontology will dissolve ontological foundations and reveal that our existence has no basis but itself.

These arguments are one of the main sources of the concept of 'existentialism', which became modish in the 1950s and deeply unfashionable thereafter. But it is a term that Heidegger always shunned. Like all the 'isms' used by historians of philosophy, it presumes that the classification of ontological attitudes can have the same kind of detached objectivity as the classification of botanical specimens. It overlooks the fact that, if the history of philosophy is to be reduced to a story of philosophers making choices between various 'positions', then the historian must choose some particular position in order to make a map of the others. It forgets that there can be no position about philosophy which is not also a position within it. The self-forgetful self-certainties that underpin the concept of 'existentialism', it seems, are precisely what existential analysis is meant to save us from.

Presence and the Deconstruction of Tradition

It would be easy to interpret Heidegger's shift from the ontology of being to a hermeneutic of ourselves as reproducing the traditional philosophical turn from external observation to inner intuition, from reality to ideality, from empiricism to speculation, or from classical objectivity to romantic subjectivity. But that, Heidegger argues, would be to misconstrue our existence as Dasein, and to think of ourselves ontically rather than ontologically.

> Ontically, of course, Dasein is not only close to us – even that which is closest: we *are* it, each of us, we ourselves. In spite of this, or rather for just this reason, it is ontologically that which is farthest.[17]

Ontically, our existence can perhaps be understood as an 'inner', 'ideal' and 'subjective' process; but ontologically it occurs at a distance from ourselves, strange to us even in its familiarity. (The reader may well think of Freud at this point, though Heidegger probably did not. Like ships in the night, Freud and Heidegger were converging on the same paradox: that the vivid certainties that make up our conscious sense of who we are may always – perhaps of necessity – be self-deceptions and mistakes.) It is characteristic of Dasein, Heidegger says, that 'its own specific state of being . . . remains concealed from it'.[18]

For Heidegger the fundamental mechanism of self-misrecognition is our sense of 'historicality'. Perhaps we can all accept that each of us is defined, at least in part, by our place in history. Very few of us are born, as the saying goes, with a silver spoon in our mouth; but nearly all of us come into possession of an infinitely richer oral inheritance a few months later, when we learn our first language – the language that gives us names and forms for articulating the significant structures of our world. But a language is self-evidently a historical entity – an ever-changing and many-layered cultural heirloom of baffling intricacy, the product of the poetic, grammatical and philosophical labours of countless previous generations. As language-users we cannot help being part of a history that always exceeds us.

But our historicality can itself be interpreted either ontically or ontologically. Ontically, we will treat it as the passive outcome of tradition, a conglomeration of ancient cultural treasures that happen to have been handed over to us from the past. For example, we may consider western philosophy as a practice that began when Parmenides first had the idea of conceptualizing the meaning of being and making it fully 'present' to consciousness. Then we can observe how the project was passed down through Plato and Aristotle to the Latin philosophy of the Roman empire and medieval Christianity, and thence to Descartes, Kant and ourselves. Within philosophy understood in this way, as Heidegger puts it, entities have always been 'grasped in their being as "presence"', and 'this means that they are understood with regard to a definite mode of time – the "*present*"'.[19]

Ontologically, however, presence is the poisoned chalice of western philosophy as well as its Holy Grail. For the traditional understanding of presence may itself be an obstacle to our understanding of the presence of tradition. We become so keen on commemorating the tradition as a monumental intellectual heritage that we actively forget the question that set it in motion: the question of the meaning of being. Inheriting a tradition is not the same as commemorating it; indeed, it is rather the opposite. You come into possession of an inheritance by taking it over and giving it a new opening on to the future, not by tagging along behind it and taking your orientation from its past.

> When tradition thus becomes master, it does so in such a way that what it 'transmits' is made so inaccessible . . . that it rather becomes concealed. Tradition takes what has come down to us and delivers it over to self-evidence; it blocks our access to those primordial 'sources' from which the categories and concepts handed down to us have been in part quite genuinely drawn. Indeed it makes us forget that they have had such an origin, and makes us suppose that the necessity of going back to these sources is something which we need not even understand . . . Dasein no longer understands the most elementary conditions which would alone enable it to go back to the past in a positive manner and make it productively its own.[20]

If, as the traditional metaphor suggests, our traditions are our roots, then the traditional idea of tradition uproots us from it. If we want our existence to root itself genuinely in tradition, we must look ahead, not behind:

> Any Dasein . . . *is* its past, whether explicitly or not. And this is so not only in that its past is, as it were, pushing itself along 'behind' it, and that Dasein possesses what is past as a property which . . . sometimes has after-effects upon it: Dasein 'is' its past in the way of *its* own being, which, to put it roughly, 'historizes' out of its future on each occasion . . . Its own past – and this always means the past of its 'generation' – is not something which *follows along after* Dasein, but something which already goes ahead of it.[21]

Within the western philosophical tradition, ontology has been boxed in by the notion of presence, and as a result the very notion of tradition has been deformed. We cannot do justice to the tradition without doing violence to the past-oriented view of history that it has bequeathed to us. We must therefore attempt what Heidegger calls a *Destruktion der Geschichte der Ontologie*: 'destroying the history of ontology' in the classic translation, though we might prefer to say 'de-structuring' or – to borrow Jacques Derrida's coinage – *deconstruction*. Destroying or deconstructing the history of ontology is not a matter of annihilating the philosophy of the past, but of retrieving it as a philosophy to come – a future philosophy that will look forward to its past and revel in its endless novelty.

At the end of the Introduction to *Being and Time*, Heidegger explains that he has set himself a twofold task, which will demand a treatise divided into two parts. Part One will pursue the analysis of Dasein in the light of the paradox that what is ontically most familiar to us is ontologically most strange. (Specifically, it will show, in three systematic divisions, that whenever we try to understand ourselves, we automatically reach for categories that are not really applicable to us as questioners, but only to ordinary 'worldless' items that we encounter in our world.)[22] And Part Two will plot the ins and outs of traditional ontology by means of a kind of inverted history of philosophy. (There will be one division each on Aristotle, Descartes and Kant, but in reverse chronological order, so as to show how – by giving a false value to 'presence' – the traditional understanding of the Great Philosophers, including their own self-understanding, perpetuates a misunderstanding of the tradition to which they belong.)[23] We should be prepared, therefore, for an uncomfortable journey – a disconcerting voyage through paradox and inversion, in which we shall always be trying to understand ourselves in our own self-understanding, despite its inherent tendency to misunderstand us.

EVERYDAYNESS, UNDERSTANDING AND THE HISTORY OF TRUTH

We are ourselves the entities to be analysed.'[24] That is how *Being and Time* opens, when at last it gets under way; and for a while we will be engaged in an unexpectedly pleasant and relaxing cruise around the familiar structures of our 'being-in-the-world' in its 'average everydayness'.[25] We all know, as Heidegger points out, that we need some general sense of our environment and where we are in it before we can understand anything else. As infants clinging to our mothers, or drivers planning a cross-country route, or scientists conducting an experiment, we are always 'already in a world'.[26] The 'spatiality' of Dasein, as Heidegger calls it, is a finite human situation comprising qualitatively differentiated places, rather than a homogeneous geometrical space pervading an infinite cosmos. Places lie above or below us, to our left or right, on our path or off it, and they are defined by the various activities or amenities – cooking or sleeping, toothbrush or telephone – that are 'ready-to-hand' (*zuhanden*) within them. 'What we encounter as closest to us', Heidegger says, 'is the room; and we encounter it not as something "between four walls" in a geometrical spatial sense, but as equipment for residing.'[27] Even the sun functions for us as a piece of ready-to-hand 'equipment':

> The sun, whose light and warmth are in everyday use, has its own places – sunrise, midday, sunset, midnight . . . Here we have something which is ready-to-hand with uniform constancy, although it keeps changing . . . The house has its sunny side and its shady side; the way it is divided up into 'rooms' is orientated towards these, and so is the 'arrangement' within them, according to their character as equipment. Churches and graves, for instance, are laid out according to the rising and the setting of the sun – the regions of life and death.[28]

The system of equipment with which we surround ourselves may be rough and ready, but in its own terms it is, as Heidegger observes, perfectly clear and precise. When we say that it is 'half an hour to the house', or 'a stone's throw' or 'as long as it takes to smoke a pipe', we are not attempting to 'measure off a stretch of space' for the benefit of some 'eternal observer exempt from Dasein'. Our descriptions may be 'imprecise and variable if we try to compute them', but 'in the everydayness of Dasein they have their own definiteness which is thoroughly intelligible'.[29]

The familiar human world is as close to us as could be, but also curiously inconspicuous. There is nothing harder than 'just looking' at the geometry of a room in which you live, for instance, or inspecting your hands as if they were hunks of meat on a butcher's bench. Rooms, hands, toothbrushes and telephones show their readiness-to-hand precisely by *not* attracting our attention. It is only when they break or stop working that we notice them as physical objects in their own right, characterized no longer by 'readiness' but by what Heidegger calls 'presence-at-hand' (*Vorhandenheit*) – that is to say, the kind of unbiddable neutral objectivity sought after by the natural sciences.[30]

The suggestion that everyday practical readiness-to-hand has priority over scientific and theoretical presence-at-hand has proved congenial to 'pragmatist' followers of William James or the later Wittgenstein, and it accords well with humanist, feminist and deep-ecological criticism of 'scientism'. But the resemblances, though real, are also misleading. In expounding the distinction between readiness and presence-at-hand, Heidegger was trying to explicate Dasein's own understanding of its everyday being-in-the-world, rather than proposing a fresh theory of his own. Moreover, having shown how Dasein accords a certain priority to readiness, Heidegger immediately identified an equal and opposite force impelling it to give precedence to presence-at-hand – a kind of destiny that turns us against the human world and towards abstract knowledge, against the warm and many-coloured 'entities which we proximally encounter' in favour of the chilly grey-on-grey of impersonal theory. Heidegger was not taking sides, but merely showing how the supposed conflict between practical readiness and theoretical presence takes shape within our ontologizing, and how – whether well founded or not – it is certainly 'not accidental'.[31]

According to Heidegger, the effects of the dispute between practice and theory can be discovered writ large throughout the traditions of western philosophy. The ancient Greeks, for instance, had an excellent word for items of everyday equipment: they called them *pragmata*, meaning 'that which one has to do with in one's concernful dealings or *praxis*'.[32] But when they came to philosophize, they attributed supreme reality not to *pragmata* but to other-worldly objects beyond our reach. Their theoreticist interpretation of being was subsequently translated into Latin and became, first, the scholastic 'onto-theology' of the middle ages, and then the science-oriented 'metaphysics' of Descartes, which 'narrowed down the question of the world to that of things of nature', in particular to those aspects of reality that can be represented by 'clear and distinct' ideas: in other words, the concepts and metrics of mathematical physics.[33] The essential tendency of Cartesianism was to downgrade the practical human world by treating it as an obscure confusion due to the projection of 'subjective values' on to an indifferent world of 'objective facts'.[34]

> The kind of being which belongs to entities within-the-world is something which they themselves might have been permitted to present; but Descartes does not let them do so. Instead he prescribes for the world its 'real' being, as it were, on the basis of . . . an idea in which being is equated with constant presence-at-hand.[35]

Despite its violence, however, Cartesianism is hard to resist. It is 'not an oversight which it would be simple to correct', as Heidegger puts it. It is more than the musing of a lonely French meditator, and it is not mere error, if indeed it is error at all. And it is also more than just the court philosophy of modernity, or a culmination of the ontological tradition of ancient Greece; for it is rooted in our existence, and 'grounded in a kind of being which belongs essentially to Dasein itself'.[36]

Once we have grasped how our understanding and misunderstanding of the world are structured by the distinction between readiness and presence-at-hand, we may recall that the world also contains entities of a third kind, namely ourselves. And we do not need to be very experienced in philosophical rumination to realize that when we pursue the question of our own nature we are liable to end up on rather marshy ground. 'I am myself', we may say, half-consciously imagining that the world contains entities called 'selves' (or 'personalities' or 'identities'), one of which happens to be our own. In that case, however, we will be taking ourselves to be distinct from our selves, which is paradoxical, to say the least.

We may never have heard of Descartes, but we seem to fall very easily into the habits of ontologizing associated with his name – 'reifying' ourselves, or treating the 'I' as if it were a 'thing' at large in the world, though a thing of a rather peculiar kind: soul, perhaps, or spirit, consciousness, person, subject, or mind – in short, a ghost somehow imprisoned in the machine of our body.[37] We keep returning to the idea that the foundation of our knowledge is 'the givenness of the "I"'.[38] We construe our perceptions of the world as if they were a matter of 'returning with one's booty to the "cabinet" of consciousness after one has gone out and grasped it'.[39] Similarly, we assume that our knowledge of others depends on jumping, by means of 'empathy' or 'projection', out of our own self-enclosed subjectivity and hoping to land in that of someone else.[40]

But we will not be able to sustain this proto-Cartesian egocentrism for ever. We need only glance at 'the stock of phenomena belonging to everyday Dasein' to become uneasy about treating selfhood as if it were an isolated private inner space. We know perfectly well that consciousness does not start with self-consciousness: we perceive things out in the world, not inside our heads, and when we relate to other people we encounter them directly, without first having to 'project' a 'self' into them. Indeed, it is common knowledge that self-consciousness takes us away from ourselves: we cannot even speak normally or walk naturally across a room when we are self-conscious about it.

> Perhaps when Dasein addresses itself in the way which is closest to itself, it always says 'I am this entity', and in the long run says this loudest when it is 'not' this entity. Dasein is in each case mine, and this is its constitution; but what if this should be the very reason why, proximally and for the most part, Dasein *is not itself*. What if the aforementioned approach, starting with the givenness of the 'I' to Dasein itself, and with a rather patent self-interpretation of Dasein, should lead the existential analytic, as it were, into a pitfall?[41]

It is clear, for instance, that our existence in the everyday world of ready-to-hand equipment is always social. It occurs essentially 'with others', rather than in the 'isolated "I"' of our Cartesian imaginations.[42]

> When, for example, we walk along the edge of a field but 'outside it', the field shows itself as belonging to such and such a person, and decently kept up by him; the book we have used was bought at so-and-so's shop and given by such-and-such a person, and so forth.[43]

Everyday existence always takes place in a world shared with others – not others as opposed to us, but others like us and with us. We are never Dasein on our own, but always 'Dasein-with' (*Mitdasein*); our being is 'being-with' (*Mitsein*), and, despite the gravitational pull of our spontaneous Cartesianism, even self-knowledge is 'grounded in being-with'.[44] Thus those who work together in a common cause do not obstruct each other's existence but enhance it:

> When they devote themselves to the same affair in common . . . they thus become *authentically* bound together, and this makes possible the

right kind of objectivity (*Sachlichkeit*), which frees the other in his freedom for himself.

In the same way, we may cherish someone 'not in order to take away his "care" but rather to give it back to him authentically as such for the first time' – and that, presumably, is the essence of genuine teaching and true friendship.[45] 'The world of Dasein', as Heidegger puts it, 'is a with-world (*Mitwelt*).'[46]

Inauthenticity and the They-self

It may be one of the best-known phrases in English poetry, but 'I wandered lonely as a cloud' is also one of the strangest. No one can really be as lonely as a cloud – not even Descartes, try as he might to reify his meditative soul. Indeed, the cloud itself cannot be that lonely: loneliness can only afflict an entity whose being is essentially being-with. In the same way, treating others 'as if they did not exist' is an insult only if they have first been recognized as 'existing'. Loneliness and rudeness, in short, are not negations of being-with, but perverse or distressed forms of it.[47]

Heidegger will now dwell at some length on how authentic being-with-others degenerates into mere 'being-among-one-another', and thus into inauthenticity (*Uneigentlichkeit*). Inauthenticity is what happens when we do not 'own' ourselves – when we overlook the peculiarity of our existence as interpreters of the world, that is to say as Daseins, and treat ourselves as if we were just another of the ready-to-hand or present-at-hand entities that we have come across in the course of our experience. Inauthenticity arises, in particular, when we understand ourselves as Cartesian selves, and live our lives in terms of what Jean-Jacques Rousseau would call *amour propre*, constantly looking over our shoulders and comparing our 'selves' with those of others. We become obsessed with being ahead or behind, or grander or pettier, with whether we are as stylish as others, or as clever and experienced, or as pretty and young. In our anxiety to differentiate ourselves from others, however, we become dependent on them – not on anyone in particular, but on the other in general, or what Heidegger called *das Man*, or the 'they'. (The German word *Man* corresponds to the pronoun 'one' – as in 'a room of one's own' – but the phrase *the 'one'* sounds so strange in English that we have to make do with *the 'they'*.) Under the sway of the 'they', we descend from 'being-with' into 'being-among-one-another'.

We take pleasure as *they* take pleasure; we read, see, and judge about literature and art as *they* see and judge; likewise we shrink back from the 'great mass' as *they* shrink back . . . Everyone is the other, and no one is himself. The '*they*', which supplies the answer to the '*who*' of everyday Dasein, is the '*nobody*' to whom every Dasein has already surrendered itself in being-among-one-another.[48]

The 'they', Heidegger explains, teaches us to pass everything off as 'familiar and accessible to everyone', thereby making sure that 'everything gets obscured'.[49]

The fifteen pages that Heidegger devoted to the flourishing of 'inauthenticity' under the 'dictatorship of the "they"'[50] are probably the best known in the whole of *Being and Time*, but perhaps the least understood as well. As usual, the language of Heidegger's analysis is drawn from ordinary life; but on this occasion it has a shrill tone of moralistic indignation. The 'they-self' (*das Man-selbst*) is described in terms of its threefold 'falling' (*Verfallen*) into inauthenticity. As the they-self, we have always fallen into 'idle talk': we 'scribble' and 'gossip', and 'pass the word along', not in order to say things about the world, but merely to fend off silence and maintain 'communication' for communication's sake. In idle talk, we

> do not so much understand the entities which are talked about; we already are listening only to what is said-in-the-talk as such. What is said-in-the-talk gets understood; but what the talk is about is understood only approximately and superficially.[51]

The corruption of discourse means that genuine questioning gets overwhelmed by our nervous desire to be well informed and up-to-date about what is generally believed to be going on – in other words, it declines into 'curiosity', the second form of inauthenticity.

> Curiosity is characterised by a specific way of *not tarrying* alongside what is closest . . . In not tarrying, curiosity is concerned with the constant possibility of *distraction* . . . It concerns itself with a kind of knowing, but just in order to have known.[52]

Thanks to idle talk and curiosity, we learn to occupy ourselves with issues about which 'anyone can say anything'. We inoculate ourselves against surprises, grow indifferent to the distinctions between proof and suspicion or truth and belief, and descend into the third form of inauthenticity, which Heidegger calls 'ambiguity'.

> Everything looks as if it were genuinely understood, genuinely taken hold of, genuinely spoken, though at bottom it is not; or else it does not

look so, and yet at bottom it is . . . Idle talk and curiosity take care in
their ambiguity to ensure that what is genuinely and newly created is
out of date as soon as it emerges before the public . . . Talking about
things ahead of the game and making surmises about them curiously,
gets passed off as what is really happening.[53]

To make matters still worse, we embrace our they-self existence with
enthusiasm, congratulating ourselves on the maturity of our self-knowledge, the fullness of our lives, and the richness of our culture. Our
'downward plunge' is concealed from us, as Heidegger says, and even
'gets interpreted as a way of "ascending" and "living concretely"'.[54]

These bilious evocations of the pompous triviality of everydayness have
obvious affinities with the celebrated denunciations of industrialism to be
found in Ruskin, D. H. Lawrence and F. R. Leavis, with the romantic
anti-capitalism of Thoreau or William Morris, with Marx's critique of the
'fetishism of commodities', or with conservative laments about the
erosion of true community in 'modernity'. Heidegger, however, protested
that his analyses were 'far removed from any moralizing critique' – they
did not, he claimed, 'express any negative evaluation' or imply 'a "fall"
from a purer and higher "primal status"'.[55] Indeed, he pointed out that
generalized denunciations of the 'great mass' of humanity are themselves
the work of the they-self.[56] Falling into idle talk, curiosity and ambiguity
was a feature of 'primitive societies' and of ancient Greece, as much as of
modern Europe. Inauthenticity was not an ethical defect of the weak-
willed, but a necessary structure of our existence as self-interpreting
entities who cannot help interpreting ourselves inappropriately: that is to
say, in terms of the world.

Our inherent 'capacity for delusion', Heidegger says, has an 'existentially
positive character'. We are constantly in a state of 'falling' because as
long as we live we can never achieve stable equilibrium, let alone a state
of rest.[57] At best, we are held in suspense between opposed but
incommensurable movements. The first movement is simply 'how we are'
at any moment. Whether serene or indignant, elated or sad, we are always
'thrown' into some mood or other.[58] And any mood is bound to be
delusive in some connections but revealing in others. If we are tormented
by jealousy or immobilized by grief, then the 'abundance of things which
can be discovered by simply characterizing them' will become inaccessible
to us, and we will be incapacitated for purely factual scientific inquiry.
On the other hand, there are some matters that we cannot understand
unless we are upset: 'it is precisely when we see the "world" unsteadily

and fitfully', Heidegger says, 'that the ready-to-hand shows itself in its specific worldhood, which is never the same from day to day'.[59]

But our 'thrownness' – the movement that has always landed us, willy nilly, in some mood that we cannot fully comprehend – is countered by a movement in which we 'throw' ourselves outwards, becoming 'more' than we already are as we attempt to understand the world.[60] Every understanding is projected from a mood we have been thrown into, and every mood throws out an understanding that it projects into the world: we exist, essentially, as 'thrown projection'.[61]

The two movements of our existence – 'thrown' mood and 'projective' understanding – can never be synthesized or harmonized or mutually calibrated. In our attempts at self-understanding, we will always be neglecting one or other of them. Projecting out of thrownness and thrown into projection, 'Dasein has in every case already gone astray and failed to recognise itself.'[62]

This does not mean that self-knowledge cannot hope to become rigorous and even scientific; only that it can 'never be as independent of the standpoint of the observer as our knowledge of nature is supposed to be'. Self-understanding never starts work on a new canvas: it is always in progress, and never reaches completion. We cannot understand ourselves, or see through our own self-misunderstandings and correct them, except in terms of our own understanding. We have no choice but to argue in a circle. 'What is decisive', Heidegger says, 'is not to come out of the circle but to come into it in the right way.'[63]

Anxiety and Truth in the Clearing of Care

When we think of 'authentic existence', the picture that at first suggests itself is of a rugged and defiant individual who refuses to be smoothed out by convention or swept along by the crowd. But it should not take us long to see that this image has that peculiar combination of 'sham clarity' and profound muddle typical of the they-self: it represents, in fact, an inauthentic interpretation of authenticity.[64] It draws on the myth of a prelapsarian 'self-point', or 'isolated "I"', or 'idealised absolute subject' – so many 'residues of Christian theology', as Heidegger says, 'which have not as yet been radically extruded'.[65] Deep down, however, we know that we do not exist in the same thing-like way as clouds or clocks. We are not 'worldless' items within the world, but sites at which the world is revealed – disclosed to each of us according to our idiosyncratic spins and angles of interpretation. We are essentially 'worlded': in the world rather than of it. '*Dasein is its disclosedness*', as Heidegger puts it. '*As* being-in-the-world it is cleared in itself . . . in such a way that it *is* itself the clearing (*die Lichtung*).'[66] We are not like a sturdy oak in the great forest of being, but an aimless winding path or an open glade.

The peculiarities of existence as the clearing of being can all be captured, Heidegger suggests, by a single word: 'care' (*Sorge*). The world can be defined as what we care for, and we can be defined as what cares for the world. But as care we are riven in two, in a way that recalls the unsynthesizable movements of 'thrown projection': we are divided, one might say, between *having care* (bearing down on us as a burden from the past) and *taking care* (over possibilities that we project into the future). As care, we are not a steady object within the world, but an extended network of attentiveness to it. Contrary to what the they-self would imagine, we cannot approach authenticity by trying to absent ourselves from the world, but only by identifying ourselves scrupulously with the threads of care that bind it together. Care reveals our existence as always '*ahead-of-itself-in-already-being-in-a-world*'.[67]

'This above all: to thine own self be true', says Polonius to Laertes. It may seem an uncharacteristically authentic remark to emerge from the lips of Hamlet's 'foolish prating knave', but in fact it is a typical counsel of the they-self. For Polonius is advising his son to cleave to a 'self' that supposedly lurks within him like a magic jewel: he wants him to be *sincere* rather than authentic. Authenticity, threading its way through the world with lucid care, would destroy the Polonian illusion of an 'own self'. The emblem of authenticity is not a clenched fist but an open hand.

Your existence as an individual is not a given fact of nature; rather you are 'individualized' in your existence, either authentically or inauthentically. In your average everydayness, you will have identified with the listless isolation of the they-self; but you can always be brought round to yourself again, not as a mythical concentrated 'self-point', but as the dispersed clearing and disclosedness that you authentically are. For example, you may be taken aback by a work of art: and instead of being carried away from the world, as classical aesthetics might lead you to expect, you find yourself attached to it more decisively then ever. The same may happen if you are dumbfounded by the beauty of a landscape or a human body. Within *Being and Time*, however, it is anxiety (*Angst*) that provides the royal road to authenticity. Anxiety, Heidegger argues, is a kind of ontological queasiness that creeps up on you whenever you come close to understanding the inherent instability of your existence. It is like fear, only worse: a bottomless apprehensiveness that you can never comprehend.

That in the face of which one has anxiety is characterised by the fact that what threatens is *nowhere*. Anxiety 'does not know' what that in the face of which it is anxious is. . . . That which threatens cannot bring itself close from a definite direction within what is close by; it is already 'there', and yet nowhere; it is so close that it is oppressive and stifles one's breath, and yet it is nowhere.[68]

The indefiniteness of anxiety is not due to imperceptiveness, however: it gives perfect expression to the quality of authentic existence, with its strangely familiar combination of the utterly familiar with the totally strange – in short, its uncanniness (*Unheimlichkeit*).

In anxiety one feels '*uncanny*'. Here the peculiar indefiniteness of that which Dasein finds itself alongside in anxiety, comes proximally to expression ... As Dasein falls, anxiety brings it back from its absorption in the 'world'. Everyday familiarity collapses. Dasein has been individualized, but individualized *as* being-in-the-world.[69]

Yet your individuality as being-in-the-world has nothing in common with the individualism of the they-self:

Anxiety individualizes Dasein and thus discloses it as '*solus ipse*' [itself alone]. But this existential 'solipsism' is so far from the displacement of putting an isolated subject-thing into the innocuous emptiness of a worldless occurring, that in an extreme sense what it does is precisely to bring Dasein face to face with its world as world, and thus bring it face to face with itself as being-in-the-world.[70]

Existential solipsism is the exact opposite of solipsism in the classical sense: not a timid retreat from the world, but a bold discovery and reappropriation of it.

On the other hand, Heidegger's account of anxiety and authenticity seems to lend itself to formulation as an old-fashioned moral fable: a story of how Dasein when young was nothing but natural disclosedness in the with-world; how it was then seduced and corrupted by the blandishments of inauthenticity; and how it at last succumbed to anxiety, repented, and came back home to authentic selfhood. But this kind of narrativization destroys Heidegger's argument, since disclosedness, the they-self and authentic individualization are not alternative ways of life, like that of the fool, the sinner and the saint, but mutually dependent forms of self-interpretation, as inseparable and indistinguishable as the opposite sides of a Möbius strip.

Different forms of self-understanding, moreover, correspond to different interpretations of philosophical tradition. The conventional view of it,
codified in textbooks since the middle of the nineteenth century, is centred
on the 'problem of knowledge'. The issue is supposed to have come to
light when Descartes refuted 'naive realism' by showing that our
perceptions often mislead us, which suggested that we might never know
anything except the interior fixtures and furnishings of our own minds.[71]
This, so the story goes, left philosophy with the task of 'refuting the
sceptic', which divided philosophers into 'realists' (like Descartes), who
believed they could prove the existence of an 'external world', and
'idealists' (like Berkeley) who did not.[72] At the end of the eighteenth
century, however, Kant denounced this dispute as 'a scandal of philosophy and of human reason in general' and brokered a kind of compromise
between the two sects.[73]

Heidegger has no difficulty in showing that this interpretation of the
history of philosophy is itself founded on a philosophical prejudice – the
view that knowledge must start from the 'inner experience' of an 'isolated
subject'.[74]

> If one were to see the whole distinction between the 'inside' and the
> 'outside' and the whole connection between them which Kant's proof
> presupposes, and if one were to have an ontological conception of what
> has been presupposed in this presupposition, then the possibility of
> holding that a proof of the 'existence of things outside me' is a
> necessary one which has yet to be given, would collapse.
>
> The 'scandal of philosophy' is not that this proof has yet to be given,
> but that *such proofs are expected and attempted again and again.*[75]

The 'scandal', in other words, is that philosophy is expected to bend its
efforts to 'refuting the sceptic' – a task which is not only intellectually
boring but existentially incoherent. Who, after all, is this 'sceptic'
supposed to be? 'The question of whether there is a world at all and
whether its being can be proved, makes no sense if it is raised by *Dasein*
as being-in-the-world; and who else would raise it?'[76] The problem can be
taken seriously only as long as 'the kind of being of the entity which does
the proving and makes requests for proofs has *not been made definite
enough*'. It assumes, in other words, that Dasein is 'a subject which is
proximally *worldless* or unsure of its world, and which must, at bottom,
first assure itself of a world'.[77] We cannot even say that Dasein
'presupposes' the existence of the world, since 'with such presuppositions,
Dasein always comes "too late"; . . . it is, *as an entity*, already in a
world'.[78] And if a real sceptic does exist, then 'he does *not* even *need* to be

refuted', since 'in so far as he *is*, and has understood himself in this being, he has obliterated Dasein in the desperation of suicide; and in doing so, he has also obliterated truth'.[79]

The histories of philosophy inform us that the 'problem of truth' goes back to Aristotle, who defined truth as a 'correspondence' between two kinds of entity: judgements on the one hand and objects on the other.[80] But this problem too is existentially incoherent. We could not grasp the idea of a correspondence between judgements and objects unless we already had some more fundamental understanding of truth, and a rudimentary appreciation of its intrinsic superiority to falsehood. As beings-in-the-world, we must always already exist 'both in the truth and in untruth'.[81] Yet our precious original understanding of truth, instead of being treasured and lovingly nurtured by the philosophical tradition, seems to have been brutally ignored ever since the time of 'the Greeks', and 'the concealment implicit in their ontology'.

> Truth as disclosedness and as being-towards uncovered entities – a being which itself uncovers – has become truth as agreement between things which are present-at-hand within-the-world.

The 'traditional conception of truth', Heidegger concludes, is 'ontologically derivative'. It goes back to the moment when Greek philosophers tried to remove truth and falsehood from the world and 'switched' them for inert logical properties of abstract intellectual conjectures.[82]

But Heidegger does not recommend that we scrap the dogged ratiocinations of 'the "good" old tradition' and return to a kind of sentimental subjectivistic irrationalism. That, as he remarks, would be a 'dubious gain'.[83] But it is not the choice we face. Everything can be interpreted either authentically or inauthentically, and that includes not only Dasein but also the philosophical tradition. As traditionally understood, the classics of philosophy are guided by existentially incoherent questions that reduce words like 'world' and 'truth' to mere shadows of themselves, 'levelling them off to that unintelligibility which functions in turn as a source of pseudo-problems'. If we reinterpret them in the light of authentic problems, however, they will come back into their own, and we will discover that 'the *force of the most elemental words* in which Dasein expresses itself' is 'simultaneously alive' within them.[84]

The existential analysis of truth will reveal that traditional philosophy is rather more intelligent than philosophical tradition makes it out to be.

If the analysis has any novelty, it will not be because it is unprecedented, but because it reaches authentically to the past, responding freshly to 'what was primordially surmised in the *oldest* tradition of ancient philosophy'. Authentic philosophizing does not require us to have *'shaken off* the tradition', but rather to have made it authentically our own, and *'appropriated* it primordially'.[85]

The classics of philosophy all bear witness to a certain affinity between being and truth. 'In ontological problematics,' as Heidegger says, '*being* and *truth* have, from time immemorial, been brought together if not entirely identified.'[86] But whilst the association is familiar, it is also surprising, since 'truth' is clearly a property of our judgements, and therefore dependent on the historical conventions that give our words their meanings, whereas 'being' has traditionally been exalted above contingency, and accorded an objective existence quite independent of us. By associating being with truth, therefore, philosophy seems to have been whispering seditiously against its own official doctrine of absolute objectivity.

But maybe being has nothing to fear from its relationship with truth. The achievements of science need not be endangered when objectivity is interpreted in terms of Dasein's existence as disclosedness; indeed, if Heidegger is right, they will be 'rescued' by such an interpretation.[87]

Dasein, as constituted by disclosedness, is essentially in the truth. Disclosedness is a kind of being which is essential to Dasein. *'There is'* *truth only in so far as Dasein is and so long as Dasein is*. Entities are uncovered only *when* Dasein *is*; and only as long as Dasein *is*, are they disclosed. Newton's laws, the principles of contradiction, any truth whatever – these are true only as long as Dasein *is*. Before there was any Dasein, there was no truth; nor will there be any after Dasein is no more. For in such a case truth as disclosedness, uncovering, and uncoveredness, *cannot* be. Before Newton's laws were discovered, they were not 'true'; it does not follow that they were false, or even that they would become false if ontically no discoveredness were any longer possible. Just as little does this 'restriction' imply that the being-true of 'truths' has in any way been diminished.

To say that before Newton his laws were neither true nor false, cannot signify that before him there were no such entities as have been uncovered and pointed out by those laws. Through Newton the laws became true; and with them, entities became accessible in themselves to Dasein. Once entities have been uncovered, they show themselves

precisely as entities which beforehand already were. Such uncovering is
the kind of being which belongs to 'truth'.[88]

It is only because Newton's laws are projections of Dasein's historically
situated existence that they can reveal to us a permanent aspect of nature
as it really is. '*All truth is relative to Dasein's being*', Heidegger says:
otherwise science would be beyond us. Science is undoubtedly historical;
but history is no enemy to truth.

CONSCIENCE, TIME AND THE
TRUTH OF HISTORY

If Division One of *Being and Time* has been successful, it will have
persuaded us that our existence is nothing but our being-in-the-world,
whether in falsehood or in truth. We will have accepted that within this
world there are items of everyday 'equipment' which we relate to in a
practical human way, as well as present-at-hand 'things of nature' which
we can treat as objects of impersonal theory. We will also have
acknowledged our inherent tendency to interpret ourselves 'in terms of
the world', and thus to falsify our existence and entangle ourselves in the
inauthenticity of the they-self. Furthermore, we will have noticed that
traditional philosophy as a whole can be seen as conspiring to underwrite
our inauthenticity.

But we have also been shown some paths that lead away from
inauthenticity, demonstrating that we are not in fact self-enclosed and
self-centered Cartesian selves, but receptive openings on to the world. We
have been reminded of 'a potentiality-for-hearing which is genuine, and a
being-with-one-another which is transparent', and thus granted a certain
intimation of authentic selfhood.[89]

Authenticity can never be a comfortable condition, however. It means
understanding ourselves existentially, and making this understanding our
own; but that entails accepting that we are no more than shifting
networks of interpretations, without any internal 'essence' to hold our
existence together, and this prospect may not please us. We would prefer
to be something rather more substantial, so we flee from our authentic
self again and construe ourselves as items of equipment or things of
nature rather than mere beings-in-the-world.[90]

At the same time, our tendency to avoid the truth about ourselves and
take refuge in inauthenticity is more than just a mistake – a foolish error
that we might hope to correct and grow out of; indeed it is a genuine part
of authentic existence. Inauthentic and authentic selfhood are not like a

forged banknote as opposed to a genuine one, or ersatz coffee compared to the real thing. Inauthenticity is nothing but authenticity misunderstood, and authenticity is the understanding of inauthenticity. Authenticity is 'not something which floats above falling everydayness', Heidegger says, but simply 'a modified way in which such everydayness is seized upon'.[91] It haunts us as we surrender ourselves to the protection of the they, like a difficult truth that we always ignore but can never quite forget. 'Common sense misunderstands understanding', as Heidegger puts it.[92] It does so of necessity, but with an always uneasy conscience.

Conscience is itself a prime example of a form of understanding that common sense misunderstands. We imagine it as a kind of voice that murmurs to us with uncannily accurate reproaches about our most secret faults. Then, with the encouragement of traditional philosophy and Christian theology, we go on to interpret it as a call from a transcendent power that has unlimited access to our secrets, and we envisage some terrible checklist in which all our faults, however slight, will be mercilessly and irrevocably ticked off. But even as we articulate this image, something – our conscience, perhaps – will tell us that our interpretation has gone astray. We know that the voice in which our conscience calls to us is not that of an outside agency, noisy and importunate. The voice of conscience is our own voice, a still and patient potentiality whose very silence, as Heidegger puts it, can remind us of 'the possibility of another kind of hearing'.[93] Conscience is our own authentic self summoning itself from out of the they-self:

> When the they-self is appealed to, it gets called to the self. But it does not get called to that self which can become for itself an 'object' on which to pass judgment, nor to that self which inertly dissects its 'inner life' with fussy curiosity, nor to that self which one has in mind when one gazes 'analytically' at psychical conditions and what lies behind them. The appeal to the self in the they-self does not force it inwards upon itself, so that it can close itself off from the 'external world'. The call passes over everything like this and disperses it, so as to appeal solely to that self which, notwithstanding, is in no other way than being-in-the-world.[94]

Conscience is not a spiritual hygienist, instructing us to wash off the grime of the world and hold ourselves aloof from it; it is, on the contrary, a reminder of the fact that we are inextricably tied to the world by threads of care. It recalls us to our existence as thrown projection, and renews our recognition that it is impossible to have 'power over one's

ownmost being from the ground up'.⁹⁵ That is why an authentic
conscience is always a 'guilty' one: to have a 'good conscience' is to have
no conscience at all. Moreover, conscience is ontological before it is
ethical: it is 'the call of care', revealing to us the chronic raggedness,
disunity and incompletion of our being-in-the-world.⁹⁶

Death and the Time of Existence

There is an obvious sense, however, in which each of us will eventually
reach completion, whether we like it or not. We do not live for ever, after
all; and the sum total of our existence could be defined as what will be
subtracted from the world by our death. But that only intensifies the
problem, for how could we ever be in a position to conceptualize this
totality? As long as we live, we anticipate the future: we are essentially
inhabited by what Heidegger calls 'a constant "lack of totality"', a
perpetual overhang of unfinished business. It is not only our present
existence but also this reaching forwards that eventually 'finds an end
with death'.⁹⁷ It will always be both too early and too late to grasp our
existence as a whole.

You might imagine that you could totalize your existence analogically,
by observing the deaths of others and applying what you learn to your
own case. But the analogy will always let you down at the crucial point.
The death of someone else is the end of their world, not yours; it occurs in
the midst of your world, not theirs; and it will be remembered by you, not
by them. When we mourn, as Heidegger points out, it is because 'the
deceased has abandoned our "*world*" and left it behind'. It is always '*in
terms of that world*' that we grieve.⁹⁸

Alternatively, you might try to think of a life as reaching 'fulfilment',
rather like a fruit that swells to mellow perfection and then falls plumply
to the ground. But that comparison will not help you either.

> With ripeness, the fruit *fulfils* itself. But is the death at which Dasein
> arrives, a fulfilment in this sense? With its death, Dasein has 'fulfilled its
> course'. But in doing so, has it necessarily exhausted its specific
> possibilities? Rather, are not these precisely what gets away from
> Dasein? Even 'unfulfilled' Dasein ends. On the other hand, so little is it
> the case that Dasein comes to its ripeness only with death, that Dasein
> may well have passed its ripeness before the end. For the most part,
> Dasein ends in unfulfilment, or else by having disintegrated and been
> used up.⁹⁹

You will always be too young or too old to die.

The only way you can ever understand the significance of the entirety of your existence, Heidegger suggests, is by regarding your death not as some distant but well-defined contingency, like being struck by lighting, but as an indefinite but impending certainty that is *'possible at any moment'*.[100] You do not live your life for a number of years and then stop, like an engine that keeps turning over till eventually it runs out of fuel. Every moment of your existence is affected by your death, or rather your 'being towards death'. You are essentially finite: your days are numbered. (People are sometimes praised for being 'generous with their time'; and perhaps there is no other kind of generosity: the idea of generosity would not make much sense if we were never going to die.) You may strive to forget it, but your life is always informed by your sense of its ending.

It is a commonplace that death is the great leveller; but in another way, as Heidegger points out, it is what 'individualizes' us most absolutely. Death does not endow us with 'individuality' in the sense of a distinctive inner personality, but it establishes the bare differences that separate one existence from another: the tombstone facts of life. Despite the thorough-going sociality of the 'with-world', every existence is, in the end, radically 'non-relational'. Your death concerns you uniquely, because when you die, your being-in-the-world-with-others comes to an end, but theirs, though it may be affected in one way or another, continues. The only sense in which you can grasp your existence as a whole is by confronting the 'possibility of no-longer-being-able-to-be-there' as your 'ownmost possibility', and thus seeing your life as a permanent incompleteness that will nevertheless come to an end.[101]

Of course, the common sense of our they-self will find all this philosophizing about death rather morbid and irritating. It will acknowledge the fact of death with a wave of the hand and 'an air of superiority', but it will avoid thinking about its implications.[102]

> 'Dying' is levelled off to an occurrence which reaches Dasein, to be sure, but belongs to no one in particular. Dying, which is essentially mine in such a way that no one can be my representative, is perverted into an event of public occurrence which the 'they' encounters ... This evasive concealment in the face of death dominates everydayness so stubbornly that, in being with one another, the 'neighbours' often still keep talking the 'dying person' into the belief that he will escape death and soon return to the tranquillized everydayness of the world of his concern. Such 'solicitude' is meant to 'console' him ... At bottom, however, this is a tranquillization not only for him who is 'dying' but just as much for those who 'console' him ... Indeed the dying of others

is seen often enough as a social inconvenience, if not even a downright tactlessness, against which the public is to be guarded.[103]

'Everyone's got to die', we will say with a shrug and a comic-glum expression. But it is only the chatter of the they-self, trying as usual to distract us from the fact that we all have to die our own deaths, alone in our non-relational contingency.

No doubt common sense will suspect a conflict between the open involvement with the world to which we are summoned by our conscience, and the non-relational isolation that comes to light in our being-towards-death. But common sense misinterprets death and conscience just as it misinterprets everything else. Moreover – or so Heidegger will try to persuade us – all its misinterpretations, and hence all our inauthenticity, can be traced back to a single source: our common-sense understanding of time.

In the first place, time can be understood as 'world-time', the practical time of ready-to-hand equipment – of harvests and meals, trysts and tasks, of getting up and going to bed.[104] World-time is quite literally the time of 'everydayness', because, like everyday spatiality, it is defined for us by the rising and setting of the sun.

> In its thrownness Dasein has been surrendered to the changes of day and night . . . The 'then' with which Dasein concerns itself gets dated in terms of something which is connected with getting bright . . . – the rising of the sun . . . Concern makes use of the 'being-ready-to-hand' of the sun, which sheds forth light and warmth . . . In terms of this dating arises the 'most natural' measure of time – the day.[105]

Under the guidance of common sense, however, we contrive to misunderstand world-time. We uncouple it from the web of its involvements with the world, and link it to a 'now' conceived of as a fleeting instant that is momentarily present to us. We forget about the temporality of anticipation and memory, and reduce futurity to the 'not yet now – but later', and pastness to the 'no longer now – but earlier'.[106] We picture ourselves as leaning over the parapet of a bridge, staring down at a mighty river. Shrouded in mist, it sweeps towards us from its inscrutable sources in time future; we catch a glimpse of it for the brief instant when it passes beneath us as time present; and then it hurries out behind us into the unfathomable oceans of time past.

Taking our clue from this image of time 'as a succession, as a "flowing stream" of nows, as the "course of time"', we go on to treat it as if it were present-at-hand to us within-the-world – in short, as what Heidegger calls *now-time* – the objective, infinite, homogeneous time of the natural sciences.[107] We then project this conception of time back on to ourselves, and start to think of our lives as made up of self-sufficient 'now-points' (rather like the 'I-points' of the ordinary conception of selfhood). We come to regard a lifetime as a series of 'experiences', as separate from each other as the frames of a film-strip, each one 'present' to us for only a fleeting instant.

> The remarkable upshot is that, in this sequence of experiences, what is 'really' 'actual' is, in each case, just that experience which is present-at-hand 'in the current 'now' '', while those experiences which have passed away or are only coming along, either are no longer or are not yet 'actual'. Dasein traverses the span of time granted to it between the two boundaries, and it does so in such a way that, in each case, it is 'actual' only in the 'now', and hops, as it were, through the sequence of 'nows' of its own 'time'. Thus it is said that Dasein is 'temporal'. In spite of the constant changing of these experiences, the self maintains itself throughout with a certain selfsameness.[108]

We may, of course, find some comfort in this conception of temporality: if our lives are strings of separate experiences then we can imagine them continuing for ever. But we must also be aware, if only obscurely, that it is inauthentic: ontologically, we know that to live our lives in terms of now-time is to be 'in flight' from finitude or 'looking away' from it. Living in the 'now', we transform ourselves into they-selves.

> The inauthentic temporality of inauthentic Dasein as it falls, must, as such a looking-away from finitude, fail to recognise authentic ... temporality in general. And if indeed the way in which Dasein is ordinarily understood is guided by the 'they', only so can the self-forgetful 'representation' of the 'infinity' of public time be strengthened. The 'they' never dies because it *can*not die ... To the very end 'it always has more time.'[109]

But we all have an ontological conscience, and we can never delude ourselves entirely. Even in the dazzling noon of sunlit everydayness, our being-towards-death casts its shadow.

Common sense has made us think of time as an infinite river, and often we will wistfully implore it to slow down, or indignantly rebuke it for the ruthlessness with which it snatches away our brief moments of happiness and hurries them off to oblivion. If we were more consistent, however, we would be equally inclined to praise the rapidity with which the river of time is carrying our future joys towards us, and to thank the providence which constantly replenishes it and ensures that it never runs dry.

> Why do we say that time *passes away*, when we do not say with *just as much* emphasis that it arises? Yet with regard to the pure sequence of nows we have as much right to say one as the other. When Dasein talks of time's *passing away*, it understands, in the end, more of time than it wants to admit.[110]

Understanding more than we admit, we begin to be seized by an authentic understanding of time's finitude. Our ontological conscience warns us that the temporality of our existence cannot be authentically understood in terms of now-time. We do not 'exist as the sum of the momentary actualities of experiences which come along successively and disappear', but as entities whose every moment is already structured in terms of existing between birth and death.

> Dasein does not fill up a track or stretch 'of life' – one which is somehow present-at-hand – with the phases of its momentary actualities. It stretches *itself* along in such a way that its own being is constituted in advance as a stretching-along. The 'between' which relates to birth and death already lies *in the being* of Dasein . . . It is by no means the case that Dasein 'is' actual in a point of time, and that, apart from this, it is 'surrounded' by the non-actuality of its birth and death. Understood existentially, birth is not . . . something past in the sense of something no longer present-at-hand; and death is just as far from having the kind of being of something . . . not yet present-at-hand but coming along . . . Factical Dasein exists as born; and, as born, it is already dying, in the sense of being-towards-death. As long as Dasein factically exists, both the 'ends' and their 'between' *are*, and they *are* in the only way possible on the basis of Dasein's being as *care* . . . As care, Dasein *is* the 'between'.[111]

Authentic temporality belongs to us as much as we belong to it; it is not a force of nature so much as the way our existence 'temporalizes' itself and its world. It is not an infinite sequence of uniform self-contained now-points, but a finite structure of differentiated 'moments'.

The moments of authentic temporality are 'ecstatic' in the sense that they 'stand outside of themselves'. They are linked to each other by countless pathways of memory and anticipation: they are not positions fixed on a bridge over time, but indefinite fields that reach out into both past and future.[112] Moments are 'futural', but not in the sense of being oriented towards infinite times to come. Each moment is magnetized by finitude, anticipating death like a compass needle pointing to the North pole.

> By the term 'futural', we do not here have in view a now which has *not yet* become 'actual' . . . [but] the coming in which Dasein, in its own most potentiality-for-being, comes towards itself . . . Only so far as it is futural can Dasein *be* authentically as having been. The character of 'having been' arises, in a certain way, from the future . . . and in such a way that the future which 'has been' (or better, which 'is in the process of having been') releases from itself the present. This phenomenon has the unity of a future which makes present in the process of having been; we designate it as *temporality*.[113]

Common sense and natural science may try to persuade us that this finite, qualitative temporality is merely an arbitrary, human-centred interpretation of the objective flow of infinite time, rather like the grid of colour-distinctions that we lay over the continuum of different wavelengths of light. But we know in our ontological conscience that the analogy is false. Light is a natural phenomenon within the world, and we may or may not understand it. Time is different: like truth, we need to have some grasp of it if we are to understand anything else at all. And if we did not already understand time authentically, in terms of the ecstatic moments of our finite existence, then we would never be able to construe 'the "time" which is accessible to the ordinary understanding' – the world-time of everyday common sense and the now-time of natural science.[114] World-time and now-time arise when 'the ecstatical character of primordial temporality has been levelled off', and the moments of our existence have been 'shorn' of their relations to birth and death so that they can 'range themselves along one after the other' and thus 'make up the succession'.[115] Ordinary knowledge, in short, depends on a misconstrual of authentic temporality; and we have no understanding of the world that is not attended by misunderstanding.

Science and History

If Heidegger is right, then our attempts to radicalize our pre-ontological interpretations will have led us to a fairly clear result: that (though he never expresses it so baldly) our existence as Dasein consists in the ecstatic temporalization of our finite temporality. Equipped with this conclusion, we can now revisit the phenomena explored in Division One, and instead of groping our way from the everyday world towards an

authentic selfhood that remains a foggy mystery to us, we can start from
an ontological concept of authentic temporality and work our way back
to the everyday phenomena that both express and conceal it. The
unsynthesizable movements of thrown projection, for instance, or the
totalizing ambitions of discourse and care, will now be defined as various
general forms of temporalization, while understanding is specifically
aligned with futurity, mood with the past, and falling with the present.[116]
Finally we can begin to understand why authentic temporality had to be
'levelled off' into world-time and now-time in order for the world and
the items that are ready-to-hand and present-at-hand within it to become
accessible to us in everydayness and in science.[117]

At first sight, there appears to be a trade-off between scientific
enlightenment and existential authenticity: in winning the world for
science, it would seem, we lose our selves to the world. The world of
objective nature may have been brought within the scope of our
understandings; but our understandings have been abandoned to the
world, and they wander through it in such aimless bemusement that we
can scarcely recognize them as our own.

But perhaps the dilemma is unreal. Maybe we can, as Heidegger
suggests, develop an 'existential conception of science' that will enable us
to recognize the sciences as Dasein's handiwork without diminishing their
claim to objectivity. He begins with natural science, considered as 'the
theoretical discovery of the present-at-hand'. It cannot, he points out, be
defined in terms of theory as opposed to practice, since every theoretical
inquiry involves 'a praxis of its own', from the construction of
experimental apparatuses in physics, to the preparation of samples in
biology, and techniques of writing and notation in more formal
disciplines.[118] But what makes a theoretical practice scientific?

Heidegger's paradigm of a scientific theoretical practice was the kind of
mathematical physics associated with Newton: for him it remained an
unrivalled example of successful science, even though it had been thrown
into crisis by Einstein.[119] Traditionally, there were two antithetical
explanations for its success, one stressing Newton's attentiveness to the
messy empirical facts of experience, the other emphasizing his determination to apply pure mathematical reasoning to them. Heidegger advises us
to be suspicious of both interpretations:

> What is decisive for its development does not lie in its rather high
> esteem for the observation of 'facts', nor in its 'application' of
> mathematics in determining the character of natural processes; it lies
> rather in *the way in which nature herself is mathematically projected*
> . . . by looking at those constitutive items in it which are quantitatively

determinable (motion, force, location, and time). Only 'in the light' of a nature which has been projected in this fashion can anything like a 'fact' be found and set up for an experiment regulated and delimited in terms of this projection. The 'grounding' of 'factual science' was possible only because the researchers understood that in principle there are no 'bare facts'.[120]

The truths discovered by Newtonianism depend, in other words, not only on nature's regular habits, but also on the conjectures of those seventeenth-century investigators who chose to 'project' it in a way that brought themes like motion, force, time and location into focus and made them available for objective knowledge. The 'thematization' performed by scientific inquirers is not so much the effect of objectivity as its precondition:

> Its aim is to free the entities we encounter within-the-world, and to free them in such a way that they can 'throw themselves against' a pure discovering – that is, that they can become 'objects'. Thematizing objectifies.[121]

Different thematizations (Newtonian and Einsteinian for example) deliver different aspects of nature to scientific knowledge, and the choice of thematization depends on scientists rather than on nature itself. Scientific progress does not follow a path predetermined by nature itself: like all our activities, science always has an open future.

But what if the object of inquiry is ourselves, as entities whose existence consists in our temporalization of temporality and hence in our interpretations and misinterpretations of ourselves and our world? The clue, according to Heidegger, lies in the 'fundamental existential ontological assertion' that 'Dasein is historical'. If we are essentially temporalization, then we are essentially 'historicality' too. Only by understanding our historicality existentially, and making it our own, can we ever hope to construct a 'science' of history.[122]

On first hearing, this suggestion sounds similar to the traditional doctrine of 'historicism', according to which human affairs are 'essentially historical' and therefore not representable with that peculiar combination of universality and precision that characterizes the natural sciences. Historicism can be divided into two diametrically opposed forms. The first is associated with the historian Leopold von Ranke, and states that human events can be understood only in terms of their own specific place and time; the other, associated with the philosopher G. W. F. Hegel,

insists that they cannot be grasped in their full significance unless they are
set in the context of the overall progressive sweep of history as it moves
towards its final goal. But the two kinds of historicism have a great deal
in common, and both of them are very congenial to common sense. For
we are all everyday historians in our own case, rather as we are all our
own ontologists. We can scarcely exist without having some sense of
history and our place in it – of the oddity of 'the past', the historically
distinctive features of 'the present', and the dangers and opportunities of
the 'coming age'.

But even if historicism in its various forms joins with existential
analysis in trumpeting the theme of historicality, their interpretations of it
are fundamentally opposed. From the existential point of view, historicism attributes a false objectivity to history: it not only forgets that the
historian's existence is itself historical, but also insists on slicing the
historical record into separate 'epochs', thus locking past existences inside
closed temporal cells as if their significance were a matter for their age
only. Just as scientism reduces temporality to the self-enclosed instants of
'now-time', so historicism reduces historicality to the sealed epochs of
'world-history'.[123]

Historicism adapts history to the tastes of our they-self, which is not
only anxious to keep up to date and conform with the norms of its epoch,
but also susceptible to the charms of anything quaint and old-fashioned.
The they-self finds in historicism a mechanism for evading authentic
historicality.

> It cannot repeat what has been, but only retains and receives the
> 'actual' that is left over, the world-historical that has been, the leavings,
> and the information about them that is present-at-hand . . . Lost in the
> making present of the today, it understands the 'past' in terms of the
> 'present' . . . When . . . one's existence is inauthentically historical, it is
> loaded down with the legacy of a past which has become unrecogniz-
> able, and it seeks the modern.[124]

If Descartes offered the supreme philosophical expression of inauthentic
spatiality, then Hegel performed the same service for inauthentic
temporality. He interpreted history as the work of 'the negative', which
required us to pass wearily from error to error, negating each one on our
way, until eventually we would arrive at the single great truth that had
always been awaiting us at the end. Hegelian progress, as Heidegger
comments, occurs 'knowingly and knows itself in its goal'.[125] For Hegel,
history would end in the fullness of time, when we finally achieved

complete self-understanding through 'the tremendous power of the negative'.[126]

But our conscience ought to grow restive at this point, for we know very well that history is not a gale that blows us where it wishes, any more than temporality is a river that flows inexorably on. Time and history are not forces that act on our existence from outside, but its very substance: we exist in-the-world by temporalizing our ecstatic temporality and by 'historizing' our ecstatic historicality. Historizing always takes place in the midst of an endlessly irreconcilable strife between 'destiny' and 'fate' – between the unchosen circumstances into which our 'community' and 'generation' have been 'thrown', and the 'essentially futural' resoluteness with which we project our inheritance and make it, for the moment, our own.[127]

Historicism tries to extinguish the essential conflict between destiny and fate by reducing history to a mere chronicle of an inert past – an unfolding sequence of unambiguous realities that are now over and done with. Authentic history, in contrast, is a constant struggle to keep past existences open to the future.[128] The motor of history, for Heidegger, is not the 'tremendous power of the negative' but the 'quiet force of the possible'.[129]

We must hope that this quiet force will be strong enough to sustain us through the tasks that Heidegger has planned for the remainder of *Being and Time*. We need to be prepared not only for the third division of Part One (which will 'seek a *way* of casting light on the fundamental question of ontology'), but also for the whole of Part Two (devoted to 'destroying [or 'deconstructing'] the history of philosophy' in three backward historical steps).[130] But perhaps we can already make out the path that Heidegger will want us to take: a path that keeps us away from both absolutism and relativism, and repeatedly brings us back, surprised, to our own finite existence as interpreters and misinterpreters of the world, as askers of the question of the meaning of being, and as ontologists who can at last see why history is truth's best friend.

CONCLUSION

But that is all. Part One lacks its third division, and the three divisions of Part Two are missing as well. Perhaps fittingly, Heidegger never completed his treatise on the impossibility of completion.

In one sense the purpose of the work was fully achieved, for in 1928 Heidegger secured the professorship at Freiburg that was to satisfy his

academic ambitions for the rest of his life. Meanwhile *Being and Time:
First Half* had become a vast public success, indeed a classic, and
Heidegger soon gave up the dream of publishing a complete version. He
went on writing for another 50 years – till his death in 1976 at the age of
86 – but his favoured forms, brilliantly used, would now be the essay and
the lecture rather than the systematic treatise. There have been several
attempts to 'reconstruct' the missing divisions from this later material,
but Heidegger's frequent remarks about his enigmatic 'turn' from the
problematics of *Being and Time* throw grave doubt on them all. The
title's implicit promise of a second 'half' was dropped in 1953.

The easiest way of conferring a retrospective completion on *Being and
Time* is by connecting its idea of the historicality of truth with the fact
that from 1933 to 1945 Heidegger was a member of the Nazi party in
Baden, and that he was then suspended from teaching for a period of
'denazification' which lasted six years. In 1948 he told Herbert Marcuse
that he had originally expected Nazism to bring about 'a spiritual renewal
of life in its entirety, a reconciliation of social antagonisms, and a
deliverance of western existence from the dangers of Communism', but
that it had not worked out as he hoped. He also quoted Jaspers: 'that we
remain alive is our guilt'.

Alternatively, one might see *Being and Time* as seeking completion in
the work of others, including many who would be affronted by any
association with 'Heideggerianism'. For instance, there are Levinas's
invocations of the unassimilable 'other', Simone de Beauvoir's critiques of
'feminine' inauthenticity, Sartre's criticisms of traditional psychology and
ethics, and Althusser's and Foucault's revolts against 'historicism' and
'humanism', not to mention Derrida's unmistakable Heideggerian programme of 'deconstruction'. Or there are the attempts by theologians
such as Bonhoeffer, Buber, Bultmann and Tillich to 'demythologize'
religious belief, Lacan's revolt against 'ego-psychology', or the 'humanis-
tic' psychologies of Binswanger, Rogers and R. D. Laing. Then there is
the vast tradition of 'western' or 'cultural' Marxism, carried forward by
Lukács, Marcuse and Adorno; the various strands of 'interpretative'
sociology from Schütz to Bourdieu; and the 'history from below' initiated
by E. P. Thompson and Emmanuel Leroi Ladurie. Or there is Anglo-
American 'philosophy of mind', rooted in the anti-Cartesianism of
Gilbert Ryle, and the anti-positivistic theory of science pioneered by
Alexandre Koyré and Thomas Kuhn. The greatest adventures of twentieth-century thought, in other words, may be little more than an
incomplete series of footnotes to Heidegger's *Being and Time*.

P. M. S. Hacker

WITTGENSTEIN

on Human Nature

INTRODUCTION

Ludwig Wittgenstein was born in Vienna in 1889. He came to Britain to study aeronautical engineering at Manchester University in 1908. A growing interest in the foundations of mathematics and logic took him to Cambridge in 1911 to work with Bertrand Russell. There he began work on what was to become his first great masterpiece. With the outbreak of war, he returned home to enlist in the army. Despite his involvement in heavy fighting on the Russian and Italian fronts, by 1918 he had completed his book: the *Tractatus Logico-philosophicus*, which was published in 1921. Its primary themes were the general nature of representation, the limits of thought and language, and the character of logical necessity and of the propositions of logic. Its greatest achievement was its elucidation of the truths of logic, not as the most general laws of thought (as they were commonly conceived to be) or as the most general truths about the universe (as Russell held), but rather as tautologies which are true come what may and say nothing at all, but which constitute forms of proof. The book was the primary inspiration for the Vienna Circle, the fountainhead of the movement known as 'logical positivism' which flourished in the inter-war years. It was also the major influence on the Cambridge school of analysis in the 1920s and 1930s. The *Tractatus* engendered the 'linguistic turn' characteristic of twentieth-century analytic philosophy, directing philosophical investigation and methodology towards the study of the logic of our language and its use.

After completing the *Tractatus*, Wittgenstein abandoned philosophy for a decade. In 1929 he returned to Cambridge and resumed work. The first years were spent dismantling the philosophy of the *Tractatus*, in which he now saw grave flaws, and replacing it with a diametrically opposed viewpoint. Over the next sixteen years he worked on what was to become his second, posthumous masterpiece: the *Philosophical Investigations* (1953). In it he presented a revolutionary conception of philosophy, a completely new approach to the philosophy of language and a highly original philosophy of mind. Side by side with this, he worked extensively on the philosophy of mathematics, in which his results were no less radical than in the other parts of philosophy on which he wrote. Although he published nothing, through his teaching and his pupils he exerted great influence upon the development of analytical philosophy in Britain in the post-war years. After his death in 1951, the

flood of his posthumous books ensured that his thought dominated
Anglophone philosophy for the next quarter of a century.

Wittgenstein's philosophical psychology undermined the Cartesian,
empiricist and behaviourist traditions. In place of the Cartesian *res
cogitans* – a spiritual substance which is the bearer of psychological
properties, Wittgenstein put the human being – a psychophysical unity,
not an embodied *anima* – a living creature in the stream of life. For it is
human beings, not minds, who perceive and think, have desires and act,
feel joy and sorrow. By contrast with the Cartesian and empiricist
conception of the mental as an inner realm of subjective experience
contingently connected with bodily behaviour, Wittgenstein conceived of
the mental as *essentially manifest* in the forms of human behaviour which
give *expression* to 'the inner'. While the Cartesians and empiricists alike
thought of the inner as 'private' and truly known only to its introspecting
subject, Wittgenstein denied that introspection is a faculty of 'inner sense'
or a source of knowledge of private experience at all. On the other hand,
he insisted that others could often know perfectly well about what is thus
'private' to oneself. While Cartesians and behaviourists represented
behaviour as bare bodily movement, Wittgenstein emphasized that
human behaviour is, and is experienced as being, suffused with meaning,
thought, passion and will.

The very conception of the nature of a human being that had
dominated the philosophical tradition was distorted. It had been distorted
not through folly or blindness, but by the pressure of philosophical
questions concerning the essence of the self, the nature of the mind, the
possibility of self-knowledge, the relation of mind and body, and the
possibility of knowledge of other minds. It was in the struggle to answer
such questions, which seemed to *demand* certain kinds of answer, that the
Cartesians and empiricists subtly and progressively twisted our concepts
of person, human being, mind, thought, body, behaviour, action and will
out of all recognition. Hence it is these puzzles that must first be solved or
dissolved before we can hope to attain a correct human point of view and
to see ourselves aright.

In this book, I shall sketch some of Wittgenstein's reflections on these
great themes. It will be fruitful to do so against a backcloth of his radical
conception of philosophy, for the movement on centre-stage will be
highlighted by the setting.

WITTGENSTEIN'S CONCEPTION OF PHILOSOPHY

Throughout its history, philosophy has always been thought to be part of
the general quest for truth. The physical sciences aim at knowledge of the

laws of nature; the a priori mathematical sciences were conceived to give us knowledge of the laws of number and space. Since philosophy was likewise thought to aim at knowledge, it too must have a subject matter of its own. This was variously conceived. According to Platonists, the aim of philosophy is the investigation of abstract objects – Platonic Ideas or Forms – which will disclose the essential natures of all things. Aristotelians thought of philosophy as continuous with the sciences, distinct from the special sciences primarily in its generality. Its role is to investigate the fundamental principles of each science and of reasoning in general. Cartesians held philosophy to be foundational. Its task is to lay the foundations of all knowledge on secure and indubitable grounds. The British empiricists, by contrast, thought of philosophy as an investigation into the origins of our ideas, the extent and nature of human knowledge. The Kantian revolution shifted ground: the task of philosophy is to uncover the preconditions for the *possibility* of knowledge in any given domain, the upshot of which should be an array of propositions which are both necessary truths about the realm of experience and nevertheless known independently of experience. Common to this long tradition was the conviction that philosophy is a cognitive discipline: that is, that it aims at truth, and strives to add to human knowledge.

Despite two and a half millenniums of endeavour, there is no agreed canon of philosophical knowledge. There are no well-established philosophical laws or theories on the model of the empirical sciences, nor are there proven philosophical theorems on the model of the a priori theorems of mathematics. It is tempting to explain this fact by reference to the intrinsic difficulty of the subject, but to argue that philosophy is now on the brink of delivering its long-awaited results. Such promises ring hollow, for they have been made with tiresome regularity over many centuries by successive philosophers. The failure of philosophy to establish a body of certified knowledge needs a more convincing explanation.

It was characteristic of Wittgenstein not to take sides in pre-existing philosophical debates, weighing up the pros and cons of the arguments and siding with the most persuasive. Rather, he strove to uncover the points of agreement between the disputing parties, the shared presuppositions which were taken for granted by all, and to challenge these. 'One keeps forgetting to go right down to the foundations,' he wrote. 'One doesn't put the question marks *deep* enough down' (CV 62). In the debate about the nature of philosophy, he questioned the assumption that philosophy is a cognitive discipline in which new knowledge is discovered, theories are constructed, and progress is marked by the growth of knowledge and well-confirmed theory. He wrote ironically:

> I read 'Philosophers are no nearer to the meaning of "Reality" than
> Plato got . . .' What an extraordinary thing. How remarkable that Plato
> could get so far! Or that we have not been able to get any further. Was
> it because Plato was *so* clever? . . .
>
> You always hear people say that philosophy makes no progress and
> that the same philosophical problems which were already preoccupying
> the Greeks are still troubling us today. But people who say that do not
> understand the reason why it has to be so. The reason is that our
> language has remained the same and always introduces us to the same
> questions. As long as there is a verb 'to be' which seems to work like 'to
> eat' and 'to drink'; as long as there are adjectives like 'identical', 'true',
> 'false', 'possible'; as long as people speak of the passage of time and of
> the extent of space, and so on; as long as all this happens people will
> always run up against the same teasing difficulties and will stare at
> something which no explanation seems able to remove.   (BT 424)

Philosophical problems arise primarily out of misleading features of our
language, for our language presents very different concepts in similar
guise. The verb 'to exist' looks no different from such verbs as 'to eat' or
'to drink', but while it makes sense to ask how many people in College
don't eat meat or drink wine, it makes no sense to ask how many people
in College don't exist. To be red is a property some things have and other
things lack, but is existence a property some things have and others lack?
Things may come into existence and later cease to be – but does that
mean that they acquire a property they initially lacked and later lose it? It
makes sense to investigate the nature of various things that exist, but it
makes little sense to investigate the nature of existence or 'Being', let
alone of non-existence or 'Nothing' (as Heidegger tried to). In philosophy
we are constantly misled by grammatical similarities which mask
profound logical differences. So we ask questions which are intelligible
when asked of certain categories of things, but which make no sense or a
very different sense when asked of things that belong to a different
category. Philosophical questions are frequently not so much questions in
search of an answer as questions in search of a sense. 'Philosophy is a
struggle against the bewitchment of our understanding by means of
language' (PI §109).

Philosophy is categorically different from science. Science constructs
theories, which enable us to predict and explain events. They are testable
in experience, and may only approximate the truth. But in this sense of
'theory', there can be none in philosophy. The task of philosophy is to

resolve or dissolve philosophical problems by clarification of what makes sense. But any determination of sense antecedes experience, and is presupposed by true or false judgements. There can be nothing hypothetical in philosophy, for it cannot be a *hypothesis* that a proposition one understands makes sense. In the sense in which science explains phenomena – that is, by causal hypotheses and hypothetico-deductive inference from a statement of laws and initial conditions – there are no explanations in philosophy. The only kinds of explanation in philosophy are explanations by *description* – description of the use of words. This Wittgenstein does, *inter alia*, by describing 'language-games': the practices, activities, actions and reactions in characteristic contexts in which the rule-governed use of a word is integrated. These descriptions and associated explanations of meaning are not a philosophy, but a methodology. According to Wittgenstein what is distinctively philosophical is the purpose which they serve. Describing the use of words is a method for disentangling conceptual confusions – confusions that arise, *inter alia*, through the unnoticed misuse of words. It serves to resolve or dissolve philosophical problems. An approximation to sense, unlike an approximation to truth such as occurs in science, is one form or another of nonsense. In so far as philosophical difficulties are produced by our unwitting abuse of our existing concepts, they cannot be resolved by replacing these with different concepts, since all that does is to sweep the difficulties under the carpet. It is the business of philosophy not to resolve a contradiction or paradox by means of a conceptual innovation, but rather to attain a clear view of the conceptual structure that troubles us: the state of affairs *before* the contradiction is resolved. We get entangled in the rules for the use of our expressions, and the task of philosophy is to get a clear view of this entanglement, not to mask it. There can be no discoveries in philosophy, for everything that is relevant to a philosophical problem lies open to view in our rule-governed use of words. All the information we need lies in our knowledge of how to use the words we use, and of this we need only to be reminded. 'The work of the philosopher consists in assembling reminders for a particular purpose' (PI §127): namely, for the purpose of resolving philosophical, conceptual, problems.

Philosophy has a double aspect. Negatively, it is a cure for the diseases of the intellect. Philosophical problems are symptoms of conceptual entanglement in the web of language. Success lies in disentangling the knots, making the problem disappear, just as success in treating a disease lies in making it disappear and restoring the patient to good health. In this respect,

Philosophy results in the disclosing of one or another piece of plain
nonsense and in the bumps that the understanding has got by running
its head up against the limits of language. These bumps make us see the
value of that disclosure.   (PI §119)

To be sure, this negative aspect may well seem destructive,

since it seems to destroy everything interesting, that is, all that is great
and important.[1] (As it were all the buildings, leaving behind only bits of
stone and rubble.) What we are destroying is nothing but houses of
cards and we are clearing up the ground of language on which they
stand.   (PI §118)

More positively, philosophy is a quest for a perspicuous representation of
segments of our language which are a source of conceptual confusion.
Our grammar, the rules for the use of our words (syntax *and* lexicon), is
lacking in surveyability – it cannot be taken in at a glance. And some
segments of language – psychological terms such as 'mind', 'thought',
'experience', etc. – present greater barriers to attaining an overview than
others, such as terms in engineering. For the surface grammar of
expressions – that part that can be taken in at a glance, such as the
distinctions between nouns, verbs and adjectives – is often misleading.
The verb 'to mean' in sentences such as 'I meant him' looks as if it
describes an act, but it does not; the substantive 'the mind' looks as if it is
the name of a substance or thing, like 'the brain', but it is not; the
possessive 'have' in the sentence 'I have a pain' looks as if it signifies
possession, as in the sentence 'I have a penny', but it does not. Hence 'The
concept of a perspicuous representation is of fundamental significance for
us. It earmarks our form of representation, the way we look at things' (PI
§122). A perspicuous representation provides us with a map of the
conceptual terrain.

The aim is a surveyable comparative representation of all the
applications, illustrations, conceptions [of the relevant part of the
grammar of a philosophically problematic array of expressions] ...
The complete survey of everything that may produce unclarity. And
this survey must extend over a wide domain, for the roots of our ideas
reach a long way.   (Z §273)

Such an overview produces just that understanding which consists in
seeing conceptual connections which we commonly overlook, and which,

if overlooked, generate confusion. A perspicuous representation is a rearrangement of the rules for the use of words which lie open to view, with which we are indeed perfectly familiar, but which are not readily taken in as a whole. They *become surveyable* by such a rearrangement which makes clear the *logical* character of the words that baffle us in philosophical reflection. Hence, 'The problems are solved, not by giving new information, but by arranging what we have always known' (PI §109).

This may appear to trivialize a profound subject, reducing philosophy to a matter of mere words. But this is deceptive. There is nothing trivial about language. We are *essentially* language-using creatures. Our language, and the forms of our language, mould our nature, inform our thought, and infuse our lives.

> The problems arising through a misinterpretation of the forms of our language have the character of *depth*. They are deep disquietudes; their roots are as deep in us as the forms of our language and their significance is as great as the importance of our language. (PI §111)

This may appear to render philosophy easy – merely a matter of clarifying the use of words, so that the solution of its problems is readily obtained. But this too is mistaken:

> How is it that philosophy is such a complicated structure? After all, it should be completely simple if it is that ultimate thing, independent of all experience, that it claims to be. – Philosophy unravels the knots in our thinking; hence its results must be simple, but its activity is as complicated as the knots it unravels . . .
>
> Why are grammatical problems so tough and seemingly ineradicable? – Because they are connected with the oldest thought habits, i.e. with the oldest images that are engraved into our language itself.
>
> (BT 423)

Nowhere are the ancient images more pervasive, powerful and misleading than in our discourse about the mental. We speak of ideas being *in* the mind, as if the mind were a kind of space; of *introspecting* what is in the mind, as if introspection were a kind of seeing; of *having* a mind and a body, as if mind and body were kinds of possession; of having mental images 'before the mind's eye', as if mental images were non-physical pictures which a mental organ of sight can inspect; and so on. This ancient verbal iconography is not *false* – we do have ideas in mind, thoughts do flash across our minds, we often engage in reflective introspection, people do have minds of their own and to be sure they have a body. But it *is* a kind of iconography. And we are misled by the imagery embedded in our language, no less than someone from a primitive culture might be misled by the literal iconography of Love (as a putto) or Death (as an aged man with a scythe) in western art. We misconstrue the meanings of these well-worn phrases, and construct houses of cards in our reflections on the nature of the human mind. It is far from easy to dislodge these picturesque but misleading images.

> Teaching philosophy involves the same immense difficulty as instructions in geography would have if the pupil brought with him a mass of false and falsely simplified ideas about the course and connections of rivers and mountains.
>
> People are deeply embedded in philosophical, i.e. grammatical confusions. And to free them from these presupposes pulling them out of the immensely manifold connections they are caught up in. One must, so to speak, regroup their entire language . . .
>
> Language contains the same traps for everyone; the immense network of well-kept false paths. And thus we see one person after another walking the same paths and we know already where he will make a turn, where he will keep on going straight ahead without noticing the turn, etc., etc. Therefore wherever false paths branch off I should put up signs which help one get by the dangerous places.
>
> (BT 423)

Wittgenstein's radical conception of philosophy is exemplified in his treatment of the salient questions in the philosophy of mind – questions about the nature of the mental, about the 'inner' and the 'outer', about our knowledge of ourselves and of others. It is vindicated by the extent to which he sheds light upon what puzzles us, and thereby dissolves or resolves our problems.

MIND, BODY AND BEHAVIOUR: THE POWER OF A PHILOSOPHICAL ILLUSION

The thought that a human being is a composite creature consisting of body and soul (or mind, or spirit) is an ancient one. It is bound up with our fear of death, with the craving for an afterlife in a happier world, with our grief at the death of our loved ones and our longing to be reunited with them. It is associated with common phenomena of human lives which mystify us, such as dreaming, in which we seem to inhabit a different world, unconnected with our sleeping body, or in which we seem to have commerce with the dead. It is connected with more recherché phenomena, such as visionary experiences and 'out of the body' experiences. And it is deeply rooted in the grammar of our languages.

This conception, in different forms, was articulated in the religious and philosophical thought of antiquity and the Middle Ages. It was given its most powerful philosophical expression in our era by Descartes. According to Descartes, a human being is composed of two distinct substances, the mind and the body. A person's innermost self, that in which his essential identity consists, and that to which he refers when he uses the first-person pronoun 'I', is his mind or soul, the *res cogitans*. The essence of the mind is thought, the essence of the body extension. A person is an embodied anima, for while the body is destructible, the mind or soul is not. Interaction between the two is causal, being mediated by the pineal gland in the brain. In perception, stimulations of the nerve endings in the body affect the mind, giving it ideas of the environment. In volition, the will brings about motions of the limbs. What passes in one's own mind is immediately accessible to oneself by consciousness – one is invariably conscious of, and knows indubitably, what one is thinking, feeling or wanting. The minds of others are only indirectly knowable, by inference from what they do and say.

Cartesian dualism provided the agenda for philosophers for the next three centuries. They found much to disagree with. The idea of an immaterial soul-substance was found wanting. If the mind is immaterial and non-spatial, what would differentiate two or two dozen minds all enjoying the same experiences? In other words, what is the principle of individuation for immaterial substances? Even if experiences require a substance in which to inhere (since experiences must surely be the experiences *of something*), the persistence of the same substance seems, as Locke argued, irrelevant to the self-identity of a person through time, for that requires only psychological, mnemonic, continuity. Moreover, what grounds in experience do we have for supposing there to be any soul-*substance* constituting the self at all? As Hume famously remarked, 'when I enter most intimately into what I call *myself*, I always stumble on some particular perception or other, of heat or cold, light or shade, love or hatred, pain or pleasure. I never can catch *myself* at any time without a perception, and never observe anything but the perception.'[2] The self or *Ego*, that immaterial thing to which Descartes thought the first-person pronoun refers, is not itself an object of experience. Is it not a mere fiction? Had Descartes not confused the unity of one's own subjective experience with the experience of a unity – of a soul-substance or ego, as Kant argued? And how can an immaterial, non-spatial substance interact causally with a physical body in space? Is it not absurd to suppose that all statements about voluntary human action, such as promising, paying a bill, speaking or writing, are analysable into descriptions of mental acts of volition and of consequent bodily movements?

The Cartesian myth, like all great myths, is insidious. It can assume many guises, and even those who think of themselves as liberated from Cartesianism adopt crucial elements of the tale. A striking feature of contemporary philosophers, psychologists and neurophysiologists is that, while rejecting mind/body dualism, they accept the fundamental conceptual structure of the Cartesian picture. While rejecting the idea of an immaterial substance, they are prone to *identify* the mind with the brain (sometimes speaking of 'the mind/brain'), or the mental with the neural – arguing that mental states just *are* states of the brain. Alternatively, it is argued that the mind stands to the brain as the software of a computer stands to its hardware – that the brain is, as it were, a biological computer, and man a machine. There is no difficulty in envisaging causal interaction between the brain and the body; hence Descartes' difficulties regarding interaction are apparently readily resolved. The brain is conceived to be an information-processing device. The afferent nerves from the sense organs transmit information to the brain, which the brain processes to yield perception. Perceiving something is thought to be identical with a brain state produced by the informational input. Wanting and believing are conceived to be identical with brain states which are the cause of the bodily movements that we make when we act voluntarily. Consciousness is compared with a self-scanning mechanism in the brain; hence the knowledge which we allegedly have of our current experience is explained by reference to consciousness thus conceived. In short, mind/body dualism has been replaced by brain/body dualism, immaterial substance by grey glutinous matter, and the large part of the general structure of the Cartesian picture survives intact.

Wittgenstein was little concerned with the details of the philosophical systems of his predecessors. His preoccupation was with the roots of philosophical error, in particular with its *grammatical* roots – and by 'grammar' he meant not merely syntax, but *all* the rules for the use of words, including those that fix their meaning. Hence I shall first sketch a composite picture of the philosophical conception of human beings which he was concerned to expose as illusion. It is, at first blush, a natural and tempting picture. But we should be forewarned – what is most natural in philosophy is to err. And:

What we 'are tempted to say' in such a case, is, of course, not philosophy – but its raw material. Thus, for example, what a mathematician is inclined to say about the objectivity and reality of mathematical facts, is not a philosophy of mathematics, but something for philosophical *treatment*. (PI §254)

We speak of the 'external world' of physical objects, states, events and processes in space. But, as Frege put it, 'even an unphilosophical man soon finds it necessary to recognize an inner world distinct from the outer world, a world of sense impressions, of creatures of his imagination, of sensations, of feelings and moods, a world of inclinations, wishes and decisions'.[3] The physical world is public, accessible to all by perception. The mental world is the world of subjective experience. It too consists of objects (pains, mental images, sense-impressions), states (of joy or sorrow), events (the occurrence of a thought, a pain, a sudden recollection) and processes (thinking, calculating) – although these are mental and mysterious, curiously aethereal, intangible. To have an experience, such as a pain, is to stand in a relation to such a mental object. The proposition 'A has a penny' describes a situation in the physical world, whereas the proposition 'A has a pain' describes a situation in the inner world. One can *have* a penny, and one can *have* an idea – possess a coin or possess a thought. While objects in the physical world may be owned or ownerless, objects in the inner world must be owned by a subject. 'It seems absurd to us that a pain, a mood, a wish should go around the world without an owner independently. A sensation is impossible without a sentient being. The inner world presupposes someone whose inner world it is.'[4] Moreover, the items in the inner world are *essentially private*: 'Nobody else has my pain. Someone may have sympathy with me, but still my pain belongs to me and his sympathy to him. He has not got my pain, and I have not got his feeling of sympathy.'[5] I cannot have the same pain as you, but only a similar one. Experiences are inalienable 'private property'.

When the owner of an inner realm has an experience, he cannot doubt it. I cannot have a pain and doubt or wonder whether I do, cannot think I have a pain and be wrong. I *know indubitably* that I do – and if someone were to challenge me, I should reply, 'Surely I must know whether I have a pain or not.' In short, 'we find certainty in the inner world, while doubt never leaves us in our excursions into the external world'.[6] What perception is for the external world, introspection, consciousness or awareness is to the inner world. What the subject observes introspectively he reports for others in such sentences as 'I have a pain', 'I want such and such', 'I intend to do so and so', which *describe* how things are with him. Such descriptions of private, subjective experience are given independently of one's behaviour – I do not look to see whether I am groaning before I can report that I have a pain, nor do I wait to see what I say before I know what I think. So the 'inner' – the subjective – is epistemically independent of the 'outer' – of bodily behaviour.

Clearly, one cannot know of the inner world of others as one knows one's own. One can introspect only one's own mind. Rather, one observes the behaviour of others, and infers from this what experiences are causally responsible for their behaviour. The mental states of others are *hidden*, inaccessible to direct observation by outsiders. Even if they tell us how things are with them, what is given in such communication is merely words, and, to be sure, these may be lies. However another behaves, it may always be dissimulation. The behaviour of others is the outer husk behind which lies private experience. The body that behaves is just a physical organism, subject to the causal laws that govern all physical bodies. Behaviour is mere physical movement and emission of sounds. Since a person may have an experience or be in a certain mental state without showing it, and since pretence is possible, the connection between behaviour and the mental is non-logical. Hence the inference from the behaviour of others (e.g. their cries when they injure themselves) to their mental states or experiences (e.g. their being in pain) cannot be logical. But it cannot be inductive either, since inductive correlation presupposes non-inductive identification, and I cannot directly identify, be acquainted with, the experiences of others. So the inference must be by analogy with my own case: when I am injured, I have a pain and cry out; I observe others injuring themselves and then crying out, and infer that they too feel pain. Alternatively, it must be a hypothetical inference to the best explanation: that is, from the observation of certain effects to the existence of unperceived entities which are hypothesized as their causes) on the model of scientific inferences to unobservables: that is, the best explanation of the behaviour of others is that it is caused by hidden and unobservable experiences. So one cannot have genuine *knowledge* of the inner life of others, as one does of one's own. One can at best *surmise* or *believe* that things are thus-and-so with them.

This picture of human nature is widely held. It is, Wittgenstein argued, misguided in every respect, even though it contains kernels of truth 'seen through a glass darkly'. For it is indeed based on features of our language, but it distorts and misrepresents them. His criticisms demolish the Cartesian picture and undermine contemporary brain/body dualism equally effectively.

PRIVATE OWNERSHIP OF EXPERIENCE

The temptation to conceive of experiences as privately owned and inalienable is great. 'If we are angry with someone for going out on a cold day with a cold in his head, we sometimes say: "I won't feel your cold". And this can mean: "I won't suffer when you catch a cold". This is a proposition taught by experience' (BB 54). But we also 'say "I *cannot* feel your toothache"; when we say this, do we only mean that so far we have never as a matter of fact felt someone else's toothache? Isn't it rather, that it's logically impossible?' (PR 90). But there is a confusion lurking here:

> For we could imagine a, so to speak, wireless connection between the two bodies which made the one person feel pain in his head when the other had exposed his to the cold air. One might in this case argue that the pains are mine because they are felt in my head; but suppose I and someone else had a part of our body in common, say a hand. Imagine the nerves and tendons of my arm and A's connected to this hand by an operation. Now imagine the hand stung by a wasp. Both of us cry, contort our faces, give the same description of the pain, etc. Now are we to say we have the same pain or different ones? If in such a case you say: 'We feel pain in the same place, in the same body, our descriptions tally, but still my pains can't be his', I suppose as a reason you will be inclined to say: 'because my pain is my pain and his pain is his pain'. And here you are making a grammatical statement about the use of such a phrase as 'the same pain'. You say that you don't wish to apply the phrase, 'he has got my pain' or 'we both have the same pain', and instead, perhaps you will apply such a phrase as 'his pain is exactly like mine'.   (BB 54)

But this is confused on three counts. First,

> If the word 'toothache' means the same in 'I have toothache' and 'He has toothache', what does it then mean to say he can't have the same toothache as I do? How are toothaches to be distinguished from one another? By intensity and similar characteristics, and by location. But suppose these are the same in both cases? But if it is objected that the distinction is simply that in the one case *I* have it, in the other *he*; then the owner is a defining mark of the toothache itself. (PR 90)

But the 'owner' of pain is not a property of the pain. Rather, *having a pain* is a property of the suffering person. Two distinct substances are distinguishable by the different properties they severally have, but the pain I have is not differentiated from the pain you have by belonging to me rather than to you. That would be like arguing that two books cannot have the same colour, since *this* red colour belongs to *this* book and *that* red colour belongs to *that* book.

Second, this amounts to claiming that two people cannot have the numerically same pain, but only a qualitatively identical one. But 'Consider what makes it possible in the case of physical objects to speak of "two exactly the same", for example, to say "This chair is not one you saw here yesterday, but is exactly the same as it"' (PI §253). The distinction between numerical and qualitative identity is a distinction which applies to physical objects, space-occupying particulars, but not to *qualities* – or to pains. If two people both have a sharp throbbing pain in their left eye, then they have the same pain – neither qualitatively *nor* numerically the same, just the same – and may well be suffering from the same disease.

Third, to have a pain is not to own anything. One might object:

> States or experiences, one might say, owe their identity as particulars to the identity of the person whose states or experiences they are. From this it follows immediately that if they can be identified as particular states or experiences at all, they must be possessed or ascribable . . . in such a way that it is logically impossible that a particular state or experience in fact possessed by someone should have been possessed by anyone else. The requirements of identity rule out logical transferability of ownership.[7]

To such an objection Wittgenstein replies: '"Another person can't have my pains." – *My* pains, what are they supposed to be? What counts as a criterion of identity here?' (PI §253). In other words, the phrase '*my* pains' does not specify *what* pains I have, does *not* identify my pains at all. It merely specifies *whose* pains I am speaking of. The criteria of identity of pain – that is, the criteria by which we determine *what* pain we are speaking of – are given by specifying its intensity, phenomenal characteristics and location (a dull, throbbing pain in the left temple). But the question 'What pain?' is distinct from the question 'Whose pain?' Two people can and often do have the same pain. To *have* a pain is no more to own anything, logically or otherwise, than is to have a bus to catch. *My* pain is not the pain that *belongs* to me, but simply the pain I have – but to say that I have a pain is not to say *what* pain I have. It is misleading to conceive of pains as particulars. To have a pain (or a mental image, or an idea) is not to own a kind of mental *object*. Though we speak of things (although not pains) as being *in* the mind, the mind is not an inner stage and what is in the mind is not a protagonist in a private play.

The first-person pronoun 'I', *pace* Descartes, does not refer to my mind (that I have a toothache does not mean that my mind has a toothache). One reason why we are deluded here is that, when we say such things as 'I have a pain',

> we don't use ['I'] because we recognize a particular person by his bodily characteristics; and this creates the illusion that we use this word to refer to something bodiless, which, however, has its seat in our body. In fact *this* seems to be the real ego, the one of which it was said, 'Cogito, ergo sum'. – 'Is there then no mind but only a body?' Answer: The word 'mind' has meaning, i.e. it has a use in our language; but saying this doesn't yet say what kind of use we make of it.   (BB 69f.)

'I' no more refers to an immaterial entity than do 'you', 'he' and 'she'. Nor does it refer to the body: 'I am thinking' does not mean that my body is thinking. Is the mind then just an aspect of the body? 'No', Wittgenstein replied, 'I am not that hard up for categories' (RPP II §690). Build, height and weight are aspects of the body. To have a mind of one's own is to be independent in thought, decision and action. To make up one's mind is to decide, and to be in two minds whether to do something is to be undecided. To have an idea cross one's mind is suddenly to think of something; to have an idea at the back of one's mind is to have an incipient thought; to keep something in mind is not to forget it; to call something to mind is to recollect it; something out of mind is forgotten or not thought about: and so on.

EPISTEMIC PRIVACY

We construe the mind as an inner world to which only it's 'owner' has access. If only the 'owner' can *have* a given experience, then it seems plausible to hold that only he can know what experience he has – for someone else *logically* cannot have the same experience, and cannot 'peer into the mind' of another person. But private ownership of experience is an illusion. Epistemic privacy is also illusory, but more than one prop holds it in place, and each misleading support needs to be removed.

We are inclined to think that we have privileged access to our own mind by introspection. 'The word introspection need hardly be defined – it means, of course, the looking into one's own mind and reporting what we there discover. Everyone agrees that we there discover states of consciousness.'[8] Surely we are *aware* of our inner states, are *conscious* of them. This faculty of 'inner sense' is the source of our knowledge of the inner. That knowledge seems *certain* and *indubitable*: 'when a man is conscious of pain, he is certain of its existence; when he is conscious that he doubts or believes, he is certain of the existence of these operations'.[9] Indeed, some philosophers have held the mind to be *transparent* to the subject, and the deliverances of consciousness to be incorrigible. Hume argued that

> Since all actions and sensations of the mind are known to us by consciousness, they must necessarily appear in every particular what they are, and be what they appear. Everything that enters the mind, being in reality a perception, 'tis impossible anything should to *feeling* appear different. This were to suppose that even where we are most intimately conscious, we might be mistaken.[10]

Others disagreed, holding error to be possible, but they did not doubt that knowledge of the inner is obtained by inner sense. Their point was rather that 'introspection is difficult and fallible; and that difficulty is simply that of all observation of whatever kind'.[11]

Our talk of introspection is metaphorical. I may see that another sees something, but not that I do; hear what he is listening to, but not perceive that I am hearing something. I can no more *look into* my mind than I can look into the mind of another. There is such a thing as introspection, but it is not a form of inner perception. Rather, it is a form of self-reflection in which one engages when trying to determine, for example, the nature of one's feelings (e.g. whether one loves someone); it is 'the calling up of memories; of imagined possible situations, and of the feelings that one would have if . . .' (PI §587). Such soul-searching requires imagination and judgement, but no 'inner eye', for there is nothing to *perceive* – only to reflect on.

When one has a pain or thought, sees or hears, believes or remembers something, one can *say so*. But the ability to say so does not rest on observing objects, states or events in one's mind. There is no such thing as an inner sense, there are no inner conditions of observation which might be poor or optimal (no 'More light!' or 'Louder please!'), nor can one move closer to any observed mental 'object' and have another look. There is such a thing as observing the course of one's pains or the fluctuation of one's emotions, but this is a matter of registering how one feels, not of *perceptually* observing anything. One may be conscious or aware of a pain, but there is no difference between having a pain and being conscious or aware of it – one cannot say, 'He is in severe pain, but fortunately he is not aware of it' or 'I have a pain, but since I am not conscious of it, it is really quite pleasant'. To be aware or conscious of a pain, of a mood, or of thinking does not belong to the category of *perceptual* awareness. Of course, unlike other sentient creatures, we can *say* that we have pain when we do. But we must not confuse the ability to say how things are with us with the ability to *see* (with the 'mind's eye', by introspection) – and thence think that *that* is why we can say what is 'within' us. To be able to say that one has a headache, that one believes such-and-such, that one intends to do so-and-so, is not to have access, let alone privileged access, to anything perceptible, for one does not *perceive* one's headache, belief or intention.

Nevertheless, do we not *know* how things are with us? Can I be in pain and *not* know it? And when I thus know that I am in pain, am I not *certain*? Can I be in pain and nevertheless *doubt* or *wonder* whether I am? Wittgenstein's response was dramatic and original: 'It can't be said of me at all (except perhaps as a joke) that I *know* that I am in pain. What is it supposed to mean – except perhaps that I *am* in pain?' (PI §246).

> 'I know what I want, wish, believe, feel . . .' (and so on through all the psychological verbs) is either philosophers' nonsense, or at any rate not a judgement *a priori*.
>   'I know . . .' may mean 'I do not doubt . . .' but does not mean that the words 'I doubt . . .' are *senseless*, that doubt is logically excluded.
>   One says 'I know' where one can also say 'I believe' or 'I suspect'; where one can find out. (PI p. 221)

> I can know what someone else is thinking, not what I am thinking.
>   It is correct to say 'I know what you are thinking', and wrong to say 'I know what I am thinking'.
>   (A whole cloud of philosophy condensed into a drop of grammar.)
>   (PI p. 222)

The compression is excessive and Wittgenstein's drop of grammar must be evaporated if we are to see the cloud of philosophy it condenses.

In repudiating the idea of privileged, direct access to our own mental states, Wittgenstein was not affirming the idea that we have unprivileged, indirect access. In denying that we always *know* what mental states we are in, he was not claiming that we are sometimes *ignorant* that we are, for example, in pain. He did not reject the putative certainty of the inner in order to affirm its dubitability. Rather, he rejected the received picture not because it is *false* and its negation true, but because it and its negation alike are nonsense or, at least, do not mean what philosophical reflection takes them to mean. He turns our attention to our use of words, to what he called 'grammatical rules', with which we are familiar, in order to show how we go wrong. We mistakenly construe a grammatical connection or exclusion of words for an empirical or metaphysical connection or exclusion determining the essential nature of the mind.

Seeing and hearing are ways of acquiring information about our surroundings. Having a toothache, feeling depressed and expecting something are not ways of acquiring knowledge about our pains, moods and expectations. It makes sense to say that a person knows that p only if it also makes sense to deny that he does – for an ascription of knowledge is supposed to be an empirical proposition which is informative in so far as it *excludes* an alternative. But we have no use for the form of words 'I was in terrible pain but I didn't know this' or 'He was in agony but he didn't know it'. If 'A was in pain but didn't know it' is excluded, then so too is 'A was in pain and knew it'. 'I know I am in pain' can be a claim to *know* something only if 'I do not know whether I am in pain' is intelligible. But there is no such thing as being ignorant of whether one is in pain – if A said, 'Perhaps I am in agony, but I don't know whether I am', we would not understand him. There is room for indeterminacy (is it just an ache or a pain?) and for indecision ('I am not sure what I think about that'), but not for ignorance. It makes sense to talk of knowing where it also makes sense to talk of finding out, coming to know, or learning. But when one has a pain, one does not *find out* that one has. One does not come to know or learn of one's pains, one *has* them. If one knows that p, one can answer the question 'How do you know?' by adducing evidence or citing a perceptual faculty used in the acquisition of the knowledge. But one cannot say, 'I know that I have a pain because I feel it', for to feel a pain (unlike to feel a pin) just *is* to have a pain; and the question 'How do you know that you are in pain?' has no sense. Where we speak of knowing that p, we can also speak of guessing, surmising and conjecturing that p. But it makes no sense to guess that one is in pain. In short, our conception of epistemic privacy of experience confuses the *grammatical* exclusion of ignorance (the *senselessness* of 'Perhaps I am in pain, but I don't know whether I am', the fact that we have given *no use* to this form of words) with the presence of knowledge.

One might think that there is nevertheless a difference between being in pain and knowing that one is. For one must be conscious of the pain, be aware of it, which is something only *self-conscious* creatures can do. But to be aware of or conscious of a pain just is to have a pain – this is a distinction without a difference. It is striking that we do not say of our sick pets that they know that they are in pain – or that they do not know. When our cat is suffering, we do not console ourselves with the thought that, although the poor thing is in pain, luckily it does not know it because it is not a self-conscious creature. Animals do not *say* that they are in pain, whereas human beings do. That they do not say so does not show that they are ignorant, and the fact that we do does not show that we are better informed. It shows that we have learnt to manifest pain in ways unavailable to animals who cannot speak. A self-conscious being is not a creature who is conscious of his aches and pains, but rather one who is aware of his motives, knows what moves him and why, who reflects on his emotions and attitudes. That, indeed, is a capacity which only language-users have, and here error, doubt and self-deception are possible. Such self-knowledge, genuine self-knowledge, is hard won – it is not given by any supposed transparency of the mental. Others often know us better than we do ourselves.

Indeed, the very idea of the transparency of the mental is confused. It is intelligible to say that something is as it appears only if it also makes sense to say that it is other than it appears. But 'It seems to me that I have a pain, although in fact I don't' and 'You think you are in pain, but actually you are not' are senseless. So one cannot go along with Hume in arguing that it is a distinctive feature of the mental that things are exactly as they appear and that therefore we know how things are in our private inner world. Similar confusion of grammatical exclusion with empirical absence characterizes the thought that subjective experience is indubitable or even incorrigible. To be sure, I cannot doubt whether I am in pain, but not because I am certain that I am. Rather, nothing counts as doubting whether one is in pain. Doubt is not refuted by available grounds for certainty, but excluded by grammar. It is senseless to say, 'I may be in pain, but I am not sure'. 'I thought I was in pain, but I was mistaken' is nonsense. Reid was right to say 'I cannot be deceived by consciousness' with regard to my sensations, but not because I am so perceptive or because consciousness is so reliable – rather because *there is no such thing as deception* in this domain (although, of course, there is such a thing as self-deception in the domain of feelings and beliefs – which is another tale). 'I cannot make a mistake here' is not like 'I cannot make a mistake in counting from 1 to 10', but like 'I cannot be beaten at solitaire'.

Does this mean that there is no use for the form of words 'I know that I have . . .' in the domain of the mental? No – only that they do not have an *epistemic* use.

If you bring up against me the case of people's saying 'But I must know if I am in pain!', 'Only you can know what you feel', and similar things, you should consider the occasion and purpose of these phrases. 'War is war' is not an example of the law of identity either.   (PI p. 221)

'I know I am in pain' may be just an emphatic assertion that one is in pain; or it may be an exasperated concession ('I am indeed in pain, you needn't keep on reminding me'). And 'Surely I must know if I am in pain' can be used to emphasize the exclusion of ignorance and doubt, and so as a way of specifying a grammatical rule – that it makes no *sense* not to know or to doubt that one is in pain. Wittgenstein was not legislating about usage, but describing it. He was pointing out that certain forms of words do not have the use they appear to have and cannot be used to support the philosophical theories which invoke them.

> If I say 'This statement has no sense', I could just point out statements with which we are inclined to mix it up, and point out the difference. This is all that is meant. – If I say 'It seems to convey something and doesn't', this comes to 'it seems to be of this kind and isn't'. This statement is senseless only if you try to compare it with what you can't compare it with. What is wrong is to overlook the difference.
>
> (LSD 359)

I can say how things are with me, and typically *my word* has privileged *status*. This is not because I have access to a private peep-show and describe what I see in it, which others cannot see. Rather, what I say is an *expression* of the inner. 'I have toothache' is often an *expression* of pain, comparable to a moan. 'I want to win' is not a *description* of my state of mind but a *manifestation* of it. 'I think (or believe) such-and-such' is an *expression* of opinion. This must be clarified.

DESCRIPTIONS AND EXPRESSIONS

Perception is a primary source of knowledge of the world. We perceive the facts, as it were, and read off their description from what we perceive, depicting what we thus apprehend in words. If we think of the inner as a private world to which the subject has privileged access, then we will be prone to think that here too we read off a description, such as 'I have a pain', 'I believe he is out' and 'I intend to go', from the facts accessible to us alone. Other features encourage this misguided thought. (1) Propositions such as 'A is angry' describe a person, characterizing his mental state. But if 'A is angry (wants X, intends to V)' is a description, then so too surely is 'I am angry (want X, intend to V)'. For does not the first-person utterance say of the speaker precisely what the corresponding third-person statement says of him? Indeed, is not the first-person utterance grounds for the third-person one precisely because it describes how things are with the speaker and *therefore* provides the evidence for the third-person description? (2) Not only is there this apparent logical symmetry between first- and third-person sentences, there seems a further tense symmetry. 'I had toothache yesterday' describes how things were with me. But does it not say of me precisely what 'I have toothache' said yesterday of me? (3) A true proposition describes things as they are. The assertion that A has toothache is true if and only if A has toothache. But A's utterance 'I have toothache' may be true (if he is sincere) or false (if he is lying). It is true if and only if he has toothache. So one and the same fact makes the two assertions true. So surely, they express the very same proposition, describe the same state of affairs and are true in virtue of what they thus describe.

These apparent logical symmetries generate the very epistemological picture that we have now begun to challenge. If 'I have a pain' is no less a description than 'He has a pain', then it seems it is one that is *justified* by the facts. So I am justified in asserting it only in so far as I know it to be true. But to know it to be true, I must verify it – by introspection, by comparing it with the facts to which only I have direct access. And if introspection is the method of verification of first-person present-tense statements about the inner, then third-person statements cannot be directly verified at all, but must be analogical inferences, or inferences to the best explanation. We have gone wrong somewhere. But, as Wittgenstein remarked, 'To smell a rat is ever so much easier than to trap it' (MS 165 152).

A fundamental reorientation of our thought is necessary. We must 'make a radical break with the idea that language always functions in one way, always serves the same purpose: to convey thoughts – which may be about houses, pains, good and evil, or anything you please' (PI §304), 'As if the purpose of the proposition were to convey to one person how it is with another: only, so to speak, in his thinking part and not in his stomach' (PI §317). For on the *cognitivist* account, the function of 'I have a pain' or 'I intend to V', etc. is to convey something I *know* to others, something which I apprehend by introspection and then describe in words for the benefit of others.

> We are so much accustomed to communication through speech, in conversation, that it looks to us as if the whole point of communication lay in this: someone else grasps the sense of my words – which is something mental: he as it were takes it into his own mind. If he then does something further with it as well, that is no part of the immediate purpose of language.
>
> One would like to say 'Telling brings it about that he *knows* that I

am in pain; it produces this mental phenomenon; everything else is inessential to the telling.' As for what this queer phenomenon of knowledge is – there is time enough for that. Mental processes just are queer. (It is as if one said: 'The clock shows us the time. *What* time is, is not yet settled. And as for what one tells the time *for* – that doesn't come in here.')　　　　　　　　　　　　　　　　　　　　　(PI §363)

We must get away from the preconception that the fundamental role of the first-person psychological utterance is to *describe* how things are with us, to impart a piece of privileged information to others. When the child hurts himself and screams, he is not imparting to his mother a piece of information which he has attained by introspection, and the response 'How interesting' is out of place. Rather, the child manifests pain and his mother consoles him. And when the adult groans, 'I have a terrible pain', he is not conveying an item of knowledge to his hearer. If one is asked, 'Where is N.N.?' and one replies, 'I believe he is in London', the response 'What an interesting piece of autobiography; now tell me where N.N. is' would be a joke. If one says to the bar-tender, 'I want a scotch', he does not reply, 'Really; what else have you to tell me?' These utterances are *expressions* of pain, belief and desire respectively, not *descriptions* of objects and events on a private stage.

We must beware of too facile a use of the word 'description': 'Perhaps the word "describe" tricks us here. I say "I describe my state of mind" and "I describe my room". You need to call to mind the differences between the language-games' (PI §290). The concepts and activities that belong with describing one's room are observing, scrutinizing, examining, descrying. Here questions of perceptual competence (good or poor eyesight) and observational conditions (day or dusk) can be raised. The upshot may be identifying or misidentifying, recognizing or failing to recognize what is visible. One may be trained to observe better, and there are more or less skilful observers. One may make mistakes and correct them on closer inspection. It makes sense here to ask, 'How do you know?' or 'Why do you think so?', for in many cases one has evidence for one's identifications and characterizations. One may be certain (and yet wrong) or unsure of one's description. Not so in the case of many typical first-person present-tense psychological utterances such as 'I have a pain', 'I intend to be there', 'I believe he is in London', 'I am so pleased' and 'I'm afraid'. Used spontaneously in appropriate circumstances, they diverge markedly from the above paradigm of description (and from other members of the family, which we shall not examine). First, they are not grounded in perception. Hence, second, there are no observational conditions, no organs of perception, no perceptual faculty of 'inner sense', and no skills in apprehending one's pains, fears, intentions or beliefs. Third, one does not recognize or fail to recognize, identify or misidentify how things are with one (although there is room for realization, for example, that one's pain is a symptom of angina pectoris or that one's intentions are disreputable). 'I thought I had a pain but I was wrong' makes no sense. Fourth, there is no such thing as checking what one has said by looking more closely (but only, in certain cases, by reflecting further), no comparison of what one has (a pain, a thought, an emotion) with paradigms for correctness or accuracy of description. Fifth, as noted, there is here no knowledge or ignorance, certainty or doubt, but only indecision ('I'm not sure what I'll do' does not mean that I intend something but have to find out what it is; rather it means that I haven't yet made up my mind). Finally, one's utterance does not rest on evidence, and it makes no sense to ask, for example, 'How do you know that you are in pain?' or 'Why do you believe that you intend to go?'

None of this implies that there is no such thing as describing one's state of mind; but it is a rather more specialized language-game than one might think. It is something at which a highly self-conscious person, such as a Proust, excels. Whether a use of a form of words counts as a description of a state of mind depends upon the context and manner of utterance, upon the antecedent discourse, the tone of the speaker and his purposes. The concept of a state of mind is more restrictive than one assumes. Intending, believing and thinking are not states of mind, and to say what one intends, believes or thinks is never to describe one's state of mind. States of mind are states of consciousness (e.g. moods, emotional states) which have genuine duration: that is, they lapse during sleep and can be interrupted and later resumed. They are typically described in the imperfect or progressive tense, interwoven with descriptions of one's actions and reactions. And such spontaneous utterances as 'I'm going', 'I think he's in London' and 'I don't believe you' are not such descriptions. The classical picture nevertheless exerts a compelling force:

> There seems to be a *description* of my behaviour, and also, in the same sense, a description of my pain! The one, so to speak, the description of an external, the other of an internal fact. This corresponds to the idea that in the sense in which I can give a part of my body a name, I can give a name to a private experience (only indirectly).
>
> And I am drawing your attention to this: that the language-games are very much more different than you think.
>
> You couldn't call moaning a description! But this shows you how far the proposition 'I have toothache' is from a description . . .

> In 'I have toothache' the expression of pain is brought to the same form as a description 'I have five shillings'.   (LPE 262f.)

In place of the descriptivist, cognitivist, conception, Wittgenstein proposes a completely different picture – an *expressivist, naturalist* one. The verbal expression of pain is grafted on to the *natural* expressive behaviour in circumstances of injury, for 'The origin and the primitive form of the language-game is a reaction; only from this can the more complicated forms develop. Language – I want to say – is a refinement, "in the beginning was the deed"' (CV 31).[12]

> How do words *refer* to sensations? – There doesn't seem to be a problem here; don't we talk about sensations every day, and name them? But how is the connection between the name and the thing named set up? This question is the same as: how does a human being learn the meaning of the names of sensations? – of the word 'pain' for example? Here is one possibility: words are connected with the primitive, the natural, expressions of the sensation and used in their place. A child has hurt himself and he cries; and then adults talk to him and teach him exclamations and, later, sentences. They teach the child new pain-behaviour.
>
> 'So are you saying that the word "pain" really means crying?' – On the contrary: the verbal expression of pain replaces crying and does not describe it.
>   (PI §244)

A child cries out when he injures himself, grimaces, screams or groans, and assuages the injured limb. Here lie the roots of the language-game, not in observations of a private peep-show. There is no room here for asking the child how he knows that he has hurt himself, and we do not ask him whether he is sure that it hurts – we comfort him.

Something similar holds of other psychological terms – though not for all, and not for the more developed forms of psychological states and conditions. A child who wants his teddy reaches for it and cries out in frustration – we teach him the use of 'I want'. In reaching for his teddy, he does not first introspectively identify his inner state as volitional, and he no more does so when he says, 'I want Teddy.' A child is frightened by a barking dog, he blanches with fear and shrinks back; he does not recognize his feeling as fear before he responds to the dog, and no more does he do so when he has learnt to say 'I am frightened'. A child shrieks with delight at a Christmas present; later he learns to exclaim 'Oh, I like that' – his primitive behaviour is no description, and nor is his later exclamation. These primitive forms of natural behaviour are antecedent to our learnt language-games. They provide the behavioural bedrock for them, the stock upon which verbal *manifestations* and *expressions* of the mental are grafted.

Avowals of pain are learnt *extensions* of natural expressive behaviour, and are themselves forms of behaviour. Rudimentary expressions of wanting are partial *replacements* of natural conative behaviour. Spontaneous expressions of emotion, 'I like . . .', 'I love . . .', 'I hate . . .', are *manifestations* of affective attitudes. And like the natural forms of behaviour which these learnt utterances replace, such verbal forms of behaviour are *logical criteria* for corresponding third-person ascriptions of sensation, desire and emotion. It is not an empirical discovery based on inductive correlation that human beings cry out, moan, assuage their injury when they hurt themselves, try to get what they want, or fear what they take to be dangerous. There is no such thing as a non-inductive identification of pain in one's own case, which can then be inductively correlated with pain-behaviour. 'We must not look for "toothache" as something independent of behaviour. We cannot say: "Here is toothache, and here is behaviour – and we can put them together in any way we please"' (LSD 298). For in one's own case, one does not *identify* one's toothache, one *manifests* it. It is part of what we mean by 'toothache' that it is exhibited in these forms of pain-behaviour. We learn to say, 'He is in pain' when he behaves thus, and his utterance 'It hurts' is no less a criterion for being in pain than the groan. Of course, pretence and dissimulation are sometimes possible (though not with the neonate – for pretence too has to be learnt); and the criteria for being in pain do not *entail* that the person is in pain. They are logically good evidence, which is, in certain circumstances, *defeasible*. But if not defeated, the criteria confer certainty.

Not all the psychological terms are thus connected with natural manifestations of the inner. There is such a thing as primitive intending behaviour: 'Look at a cat when it stalks a bird; or a beast when it wants to escape' (PI §647). But 'I'm going to V' or 'I intend' are not partial substitutes for this behaviour as an avowal of pain is a partial substitute for a groan. Rather, we are taught that when one says, 'I'm going to V', one must then go on to V – but one is not taught first to identify an inner state of intending, which one then describes with the words 'I intend'. Dreaming is different again. The child wakes up screaming, 'Mummy, a tiger is chasing me' and its mother replies, 'No dear, you had a dream – look, you are in your own room and there is no tiger here'; gradually the child will learn to say, 'I dreamt . . .' on awaking. 'I think . . .' and 'I believe . . .' are not learnt or used to describe an inner state which we observe within ourselves and then describe for the benefit of others. Rather, they are used to qualify a claim about how things are – to signify that we are not in a position to guarantee the sequel (that we are not in a position to vouch for it or to claim knowledge of it), to signify that we are unsure or that, even if sure, we acknowledge that doubting is not irrational. The pegs upon which different psychological terms hang are various, but the differences do not reinstate the classical picture of the inner.

THE INNER AND THE OUTER: KNOWLEDGE OF OTHERS

The complement of the misconception of privileged access is that we can know how things are with others only indirectly, that the 'inner' is *hidden* behind the 'outer' (i.e. mere behavioural externalities – bodily movements and the sounds of speech). This too, Wittgenstein argued, is a misconception – but not because the inner is, as the behaviourists argued, a fiction. Far from it: pleasure and pain, joy and grief are not mere behaviour. But contrary to the Cartesian and empiricist traditions, mental objects, events, states and processes are not just like physical ones save for being immaterial; and *pace* Hume, the mind is *not* 'a kind of theatre, where several perceptions successively make their appearance; pass, re-pass, glide away, and mingle in an infinite variety of postures and situations'.[13] It is such a *philosophical conception* of the inner that is a *grammatical fiction* which Wittgenstein aimed to extirpate. The inner is much more *unlike* the outer than such philosophical construals of it suggest.

Our talk of 'inner' and 'outer' is metaphorical. One does not normally say that toothache is something 'inner' or that pain is 'mental'. On the contrary, we speak of *physical* pain and contrast it with mental suffering such as grief. Toothache is in teeth, not in the mind (although it is not in a tooth in the sense in which a cavity is). But we compare toothache and its expression with 'internal' and 'external', for I do not say I have toothache on the grounds of observation, but I say that he has toothache on the grounds of his behaviour. So 'We must get clear about how the metaphor of revealing (outside and inside) is actually applied by us; otherwise we shall be tempted to look for an inside behind that which in our metaphor is the inside' (LPE 223). Someone may have toothache and not manifest it, may see and not say what he sees, may think and not voice his thoughts. But if he moans with toothache, describes what he sees, voices his opinion, then he has 'revealed' what is, in our metaphor, the inner. If he screams when the dentist prods his tooth, we cannot say, 'That is mere behaviour – his pain is still concealed.' If he tells us what he thinks, we cannot say, 'That is just words, but he keeps his thoughts to himself.' And if he shows us what he sees, then we too can see what he sees, without looking inside anything. For this is what is *called* 'manifesting pain', 'saying what one thinks', 'showing what one sees'. Barring insincerity, he does not leave anything behind which he keeps to himself. Insincerity and dissimulation are possible – what is 'outer' may deceive us with regard to what is 'inner' – but the evidence for such deception consists in further *behaviour*: that is, in more of the 'outer'.

One can conceal one's pain, hide one's feelings and keep one's thoughts secret. But to have a toothache, feel angry or think something is not to conceal anything. One hides one's pain when one deliberately suppresses one's groan – and one reveals it when a cry bursts from one's throat. One conceals one's feelings when one exercises self-restraint, and reveals them when one loses self-control and vents one's anger. One hides one's thoughts not by thinking them and not expressing them, but rather by keeping one's diary in code, or talking to one's wife in the presence of the children in a language they do not speak. But if the code is cracked and the diary read, or if the foreign language is understood, then one's thoughts are revealed.

It is similarly mistaken to claim that one knows only *indirectly* how things are with others, for it makes sense to talk of *indirect* only if it makes sense to talk of *direct* knowledge. But as we have seen, it is misleading to say that someone *knows* that, for example, he has toothache, or thinks this or that – for this is not a case of knowledge at all, let alone of direct knowledge. But to see another writhing and groaning after being injured *is* to know 'directly' that he is in pain – it is not an inference from the fact that he has a prescription for analgesics. Witnessing the suffering of another is not acquisition of indirect knowledge, and the sufferer does not have direct knowledge – what he has is *pain*, not knowledge. If a friend opens his heart to one, one cannot say, 'I have only indirect knowledge of his thoughts and feelings.' That would be in place if one learnt of his thoughts by hearsay, at second hand.

These misconceptions of inner and outer, concealed and revealed, direct and indirect, go hand in hand with a deep-rooted misconception of human behaviour, a misconception which characterizes both Cartesian dualism and contemporary brain/body dualism. For both conceive of behaviour as bare bodily movement caused by the inner, muscular contractions and movements of limbs and face consequent upon mental and neural events. From these externalities, we *infer* their hidden causes. We *interpret* what we see as the outward manifestation of inner events and states. But it is not like that.

> 'I see the child wants to touch the dog but doesn't dare.' How can I see that? – Is this description of what is seen on the same level as a description of moving shapes and colours? Is an interpretation in question? Well, remember that you may also *mimic* a human being who would like to touch something, but doesn't dare. And what you mimic is after all a piece of behaviour. But you will also be able to give a *characteristic* imitation of this behaviour only in a wider context . . .
>   But now am I to say that I really 'see' fearfulness in this behaviour – or that I really 'see' the facial expression? Why not? But that is not to deny the difference between the two concepts of what is perceived . . . 'Similar expression' takes faces together in a quite different way from 'similar anatomy'.
>   (RPP I §§1066–8)

The idea that we do not really see the joy, distress or humour in a person's face, but only muscular contractions, is as misguided as the idea that we do not really see the trees in the garden, but only patches of colour and shapes or only sense-data and appearances. A similar misconception attends the thought that what we hear when listening to another talking are mere sounds, which our brain then interprets as meaningful speech. Joy, distress or amusement are not hidden behind the face that manifests them, but visible on it. What we so misleadingly call 'the inner' *infuses* the outer. Indeed, we could not even describe the outer save in the rich terminology of the inner. We see friendliness or animosity in a face and do not infer its presence from the disposition of the facial muscles (which we could not even describe). Indeed, it is a mistake to think that we normally *infer* the inner from the outer:

> In addition to the so-called sadness of his facial features, do I also notice his sad state of mind? Or do I *deduce* it from his face? Do I say: 'His features and his behaviour were sad, so he too was probably sad'?
>   (LW I §767)

One might infer that someone is in pain if one knows that he is suffering from arthritis. But when one observes someone writhing in agony, one does not infer that he is in pain from his movements – one sees that he is suffering. *Pain*-behaviour is a criterion of being in pain, as *joyous* behaviour is a criterion of being joyful. If it is objected that one can see *that* he is in pain, but one cannot see his pain – *that* one must infer – the reply is that (1) he cannot perceive his pain either, and (2) one cannot see his pain only in the sense in which one cannot see sounds or hear colours.

The thought that another person can only surmise that I am in pain (whereas I *know* I am) is wrong. 'If we are using the word "know" as it is normally used (and how else are we to use it?), then other people very often know when I am in pain' (PI §246). If a philosopher objects that, all the same, another cannot know with the certainty with which I know, the reply is that 'I know', construed as the philosopher is construing it, is nonsense. True, another may doubt whether I am in pain, and I cannot – but then another may be certain that I am in pain, and I cannot. For, to be sure,

> I can be as *certain* of someone else's sensations as of any fact.
>
> 'But, if you are *certain*, isn't it that you are shutting your eyes in face of doubt?' – They are shut.   (PI p. 224)

Why are they shut? Well, 'Just try – in a real case – to doubt someone else's fear or pain' (PI §303).

Can one say:

> 'I can only *believe* that someone else is in pain, but I *know* it if I am.' – Yes: one can make the decision to say 'I believe he is in pain' instead of 'He is in pain'. But that is all. – What looks like an explanation here, or like a statement about a mental process, is in truth an exchange of one expression for another which, while we are doing philosophy, seems the more appropriate one.   (PI §303)

If it is not merely a decision to use this form of expression, then it is absurd to say that we can only attain *belief* regarding the states of mind of others:

> 'I believe he is suffering.' – Do I also *believe* that he isn't an automaton? . . .
>
> (Or is it like this: I believe that he is suffering, but am certain that he is not an automaton? – Nonsense!) . . .
>
> 'I believe he is not an automaton', just like that, so far makes no sense.
>
> My attitude towards him is an attitude towards a soul. I am not of the *opinion* that he has a soul . . .
>
> The human body is the best picture of the human soul. (PI p. 178)

MINDS, BODIES AND BEHAVIOUR

Our psychological concepts are logically connected with the behaviour that manifests the inner. For it is the behaviour of a human being that constitutes the logical criteria for saying of him that he is perceiving or feeling something, thinking or recollecting, joyful or sad. Such behaviour is not bare bodily movements, but smiles and scowls, a tender or angry voice, gestures of love or contempt, and what a person says and does. Human behaviour is not a mere physical phenomenon like the appearance of a blip on a computer screen or the movements of an industrial robot.

This runs counter both to Cartesian dualism and to brain/body dualism. It is implicitly denied by our contemporaries who contend that computers can think (or will do so soon). Wittgenstein assails the presuppositions of such views:

> 'But doesn't what you say come to this: that there is no pain, for example, without *pain-behaviour*?' – It comes to this: only of a living human being and what resembles (behaves like) a living human being can one say: it has sensations; it sees; is blind; hears; is deaf; is conscious or unconscious.   (PI §281)

Of course, one can be in pain and not show it, think and not say what one thinks. But

> one might say this: If one sees the behaviour of a living being, one sees its soul. – But do I also say in my own case that I am saying something to myself, because I am behaving in such-and-such a way? – I do *not* say it from observation of my behaviour. But it only makes sense because I do behave in this way.   (PI §357)

The subject of psychological predicates is a living creature who can and does manifest his feelings and thoughts in behaviour. A human being, a horse or a cat can be said to see or hear, be blind or deaf. But an electronic sensor neither sees nor is blind. A robot which responds to verbal instructions does not hear, and when it malfunctions it is not deaf. A computer does not become conscious when it is turned on, nor does it fall asleep when turned off.

> What gives us *so much as the idea* that living beings, things, can feel?
> Is it that my education has led me to it by drawing my attention to

feelings in myself, and now I transfer the idea to objects outside myself? That I recognize that there is something there (in me) which I can call 'pain' without getting into conflict with the way other people use this word? – I do not transfer my idea to stones, plants, etc. (PI §282)

But it is not so. We do not learn the use of the word 'pain' by identifying a certain sensation within us, which we know occurs and which we recognize as such and then name. Rather, we learn to use the sentence 'I have a pain' as an extension of our natural pain-behaviour and to ascribe pain to others when they behave likewise. There is no such thing as identifying (or misidentifying), recognizing (or misrecognizing) our own pains, and the word 'pain' is given its meaning not by naming an inner object, but by being used in expressions of pain by the sufferer and by his cry 'I am in pain' being a criterion for others to ascribe pain to him.

It seems that sensations, perceptions, thoughts, indeed consciousness itself, must be attributable either to physical things – human bodies or brains or computers – or to minds or souls, which some bodies have. Wittgenstein attacks this false dilemma with a subtle, indirect strategy:

Couldn't I imagine having frightful pains and turning to stone while they lasted? Indeed, how do I know, if I shut my eyes, whether I have not turned into a stone? And if that has happened, in what sense will *the stone* have the pains? In what sense will they be ascribable to the stone? And why need the pain have a bearer here at all?!

And can one say of the stone that it has a soul and *that* is what has the pain? What has a soul, or a pain, to do with a stone?

Only of what behaves like a human being can one say that it *has* pains.

For one has to say it of a body, or, if you like, of a soul which some body *has*. And how can a body *have* a soul? (PI §283)

Were we *per impossibile* to learn what 'pain' means by naming an inner object which we recognize, then ascribing pain to others would be problematic. One would have to imagine that some other thing *has* what one has oneself – namely *this* – in *his* body. But if *this* were in his body, that would simply mean that I felt a pain in *his body* rather than in mine.

If one has to imagine someone else's pain on the model of one's own, this is none too easy a thing to do: for I have to imagine pain which I *do not feel* on the model of pain which I *do feel*. That is, what I have to do is not simply to make the transition in imagination from one place of pain to another. As, from pain in the hand to pain in the arm. For I am

not to imagine that I feel pain in some region of his body. (Which
would be possible.)

   Pain-behaviour can point to a painful place – but the suffering person
is he who gives it expression.   (PI §302)

If one can imagine another person's having a pain *on this model*, can one
not also imagine a stone's having a pain? If I am to imagine a pain I do
not feel on the model of a pain I do feel, why should I not imagine a
stone's having one too? If I imagine turning to stone and my pain
continuing, would the stone have pain? But there is no such thing as a
stone manifesting pain. Why should the pain be the stone's at all? One
might just as well say that here there is a pain without a bearer! But that
is absurd. And it is equally absurd to ascribe pain to a stone.

   Do *I* then continue to have a pain after *my body* has turned to stone? Is
the bearer of pain then the soul or mind, the Cartesian *res cogitans*, which
belongs to the stone? So the stone has a pain in as much as *its* mind has a
pain! But this is doubly absurd. First, the possessive form of representation for pain, as we have seen, does not signify ownership; 'I have a pain'
is an *expression of pain*, and the expression of pain is *pain-behaviour* –
but stones do not *behave*. Nor, indeed, do minds or souls. Second, stones
do not have minds – it is living human beings, who laugh and cry, act and
react to the circumstances of their lives in endless ways, who have minds.
I have a body and a mind – although the possessive 'have' is again
misleading, since 'my body' does not signify a relationship of possession
between *me* and my body and 'I' does not refer to my body. *My body*,
however, does not *have* a mind. It is not the body that exhibits pain in its
behaviour, for it is not *bodies* that behave – it is not my body that cries
out and groans, grits its teeth and behaves stoically. And if I turn to stone,
the stone does not have a soul or mind.

   Look at a stone and imagine it having sensations. – One says to oneself:
   How could one so much as get the idea of ascribing a *sensation* to a
   thing? One might as well ascribe it to a number! – And now look at a
   wriggling fly and at once these difficulties vanish and pain seems to get
   a foothold here, where before everything was, so to speak, too smooth
   for it.
      And so, too, a corpse seems to us quite inaccessible to pain. – Our
   attitude towards the living and towards the dead, is not the same. All
   our reactions are different.   (PI §284)

We respond differently in innumerable ways to what is alive, and these
natural reactions are not a consequence of a theory or a foundation for

one, but constitutive of the human form of life and hence the bedrock of our language-games.

> But isn't it absurd to say of a *body* that it has pain? – And why does one feel an absurdity in that? In what sense is it true that my hand does not feel pain, but I in my hand?
>
> What sort of issue is: Is it the *body* that feels pain? How is it to be decided? What validates saying that it is *not* the body? – Well, something like this: if someone has a pain in his hand, then the hand does not say so . . . and one does not comfort the hand but the sufferer: one looks into his face.
>
> How am I filled with pity *for this man*? How does it come out what the object of my pity is? (Pity, one may say, is a form of conviction that someone else is in pain.)   (PI §§286f.)

Whether it is or is not the body that feels pain is not an empirical issue, but a logical or conceptual one. We do not say, 'This body feels pain.' We do not observe that this body must take an aspirin and go to the doctor, nor do we advise that this body should grin and bear it. Rather we speak of human beings as sufferers, not of their bodies or their minds. And the way we speak meshes with our lives, is interwoven with our behaviour, actions and reactions. We tend the injured limb, but we comfort the person who is injured and pity him. This sort of behaviour has pre-linguistic roots: 'a language-game is based *on it*, . . . it is the prototype of a way of thinking and not the result of thought' (Z §541).

Wittgenstein's argument has direct bearing on contemporary neurophysiological psychology (and on brain/body dualism), for scientists are prone to ascribe to the brain those functions which the Cartesian tradition wrongly ascribed to the mind. For example,

> we can thus regard all seeing as a continual search for the answers to questions posed by the brain. The signals from the retina constitute 'messages' conveying these answers. The brain then uses this information to construct a suitable hypothesis about what there is . . .[14]

> the brain gains its knowledge by a process analogous to the inductive reasoning of the classical scientific method. Neurons present arguments to the brain based on the specific features they detect, arguments on which the brain constructs its hypothesis of perception.[15]

But if psychological predicates make literal sense only if ascribed to the living animal or human being as a whole, and not to the body, then they can make no sense if ascribed to a part of the body: namely, the brain.

One sees with one's eyes, not with one's mind or brain, and it is not one's mind or brain that sees, but rather the living human being. It is nonsense to ascribe toothache to one's mind or brain, for neither the mind nor the brain can *logically* manifest toothache in behaviour. The firing of neurons concurrently with pain is not a behavioural manifestation of the brain's being in pain, but a concomitant of the person's being in pain, and it is the person who manifests pain-behaviour, not his brain. And if it is nonsense to say 'my brain has toothache', it is 'nonsense on stilts' to claim that the brain poses questions and answers them, constructs hypotheses or understands arguments. These predicates make sense only as applied to human beings and creatures like us, and they are applied on the grounds of sophisticated linguistic behaviour. A brain cannot talk, not because it is dumb, but because it makes no sense to say, 'My brain is talking.' I may be a chatterbox, but my brain cannot. There is no such thing as a brain using a language. Brains do not have opinions, argue, hypothesize or conjecture. It is we who do so. To be sure, we could not do so if our brain were destroyed; but then we could not have toothache or walk without a brain either – yet it is not the brain that has toothache and walks to the dentist. If one is asked what one thinks of the weather, should one say, 'My brain is thinking it over; give it a minute, and it will tell me, and then I'll tell you'?

CAN MACHINES THINK?

Wittgenstein's arguments might seem to be refuted by the invention of computers, for do we not say that these machines compute and have powerful memories? Artificial-intelligence scientists say that their machines can recognize and identify objects, make choices and decisions, think. Chess-playing machines can beat chess-masters, and computers can calculate faster than mathematicians. Does this not show that the claim that such predicates are ascribable only to human beings and to what behaves like them has been overtaken by the march of science? Wittgenstein lived before the computer age. Nevertheless, he did reflect on these questions.

> 'Is it possible for a machine to think?' ... the trouble which is expressed in this question is not really that we don't yet know a machine which could do the job. The question is not analogous to that which someone might have asked a hundred years ago: 'Can a machine liquify gas?' The trouble is rather that the sentence, 'A machine thinks

(perceives, wishes)' seems somehow nonsensical. It is as though we had asked 'Has the number 3 a colour?' (BB 47)

Today the question does *not* seem nonsensical – so accustomed have we become to our science-fiction and the jargon of computer scientists. But it is nonsense for all that. Wittgenstein approached the issue circuitously: 'Could a machine think? – Could it be in pain? – Well, is the human body to be called such a machine? It surely comes as close as possible to being such a machine' (PI §359). Science popularizers often write of the body as a 'biological machine', but even of such a 'machine' we do not say that it is in pain – for it is not my body that has a headache in its head, rather *I* do in *my* head.

> But a machine surely cannot think! – Is that an empirical statement? No. We only say of a human being and what is like one that it thinks. We also say it of dolls and no doubt of spirits too. Look at the word 'to think' as a tool. (PI §360)

The criteria for ascribing thought to a subject lie in behaviour in appropriate circumstances. But do computers not behave appropriately? Do they not behave, produce the desiderated results of calculation on their screens in response to the questions we ask them? Do we not say, as we wait for the answer to flash up, 'Now it's thinking'? Indeed – just as we say of our old car, 'She's getting temperamental.' Even if a computer were so programmed that the answers it displayed in response to the questions we typed into it were indistinguishable from the answers a human being might type (the 'Turing test'), the machine would not be behaving as a human being. It takes more, but not *additively* more, to answering a question than to make an appropriate noise or generate an inscription. The appearance of an appropriate inscription on the screen is a product of the behaviour of the programmer who designed the program, but not a form of human behaviour of the machine. The behavioural criteria in the stream of life for saying of a being that it is thinking can no more be exemplified by a computer than the number three can turn green with envy.

But does it not *calculate*? Not in the sense in which we do. The computer does not understand the results it types out, does not know what the symbols it displays mean, for it neither knows nor understands anything. It is all one to it whether it is linked to a screen which displays symbols or to a keyboard which plays notes. Does it not at any rate calculate mechanically? Only in the derivative, secondary sense in which a nineteenth-century calculating machine did. But in the sense in which *we* calculate, a being that can calculate mechanically can also calculate thoughtfully. If it can think, it can also reflect, ponder, reconsider (and there is no such thing as reconsidering mechanically). It must make sense to say of it that it is pensive, contemplative or rapt in thought. It must be capable of acting thoughtlessly as well as thoughtfully, of thinking before it acts as well as acting before it thinks. If it can think, it can have opinions, be opinionated, credulous or incredulous, open-minded or bigoted, have good or poor judgement, be hesitant, tentative or decisive, shrewd, prudent or rash and hasty in judgement. And this battery of capacities and dispositions must itself be embedded in a much wider skein. For these predicates in turn can be applied only to a creature who can manifest such capacities in behaviour, in speech, action and reaction in the circumstances of life. 'What a lot of things a man must do in order for us to say he *thinks*' (RPP I §563).

Intellectual capacities are not detachable from affective and conative ones, and these in turn cannot be severed from perceptual capacities or from susceptibility to pleasure and pain. We have invented computers to save us the trouble of computing. These machines are not thinking beings who do our thinking for us, but rather devices that produce the results of calculations without *anyone* literally calculating or thinking. What prevents the *literal* application of intellectual concepts to computers is not deficiency of computational power. Rather, it is the fact that it makes no sense to attribute to a machine will or passion, desire or pain. These are capacities of the animate; of beings that have a body – but machines have do not have bodies; of beings that have no intrinsic purpose yet adopt purposes of their own – but machines have whatever intrinsic purpose they are made for and have no purposes of their own; of beings, unlike machines, who set themselves ends, have preferences, likes and dislikes, are pleased to achieve their goals and distressed to fail. They are capacities of beings who have a good, who can flourish or flounder, who have a welfare. But while circumstances may affect the condition of a machine, be good or bad *for it*, they cannot affect the welfare or good of the machine, since it has none. What is inanimate cannot be well or do well. What is lifeless has no welfare.

Thinking is a phenomenon of life. It is exhibited in endlessly varied kinds of behaviour in the stream of life. Its forms are aspects of a form of life, of a culture. We need not fear that our machines will out-think us – though we might well fear that they will lead us to cease to think for ourselves. What they lack is not computational power, but animality. Desire and suffering, hope and frustration are the roots of thought, not mechanical computation.[16]

Frederic Raphael

POPPER

Historicism and Its Poverty

Karl Raimund Popper was born in Vienna on 28 July 1902. His parents were of Jewish origin, though they had converted to Protestantism. His father, Simon, was an intellectual and a lawyer whose library was said to contain 15,000 volumes. Portraits of Schopenhauer and Darwin hung in his study. Karl's mother, Jenny Schiff, had a passion for music, which Popper shared. He thought of devoting himself to music as a young man and, as an amateur composer, he remained dedicated to it all his life.

Popper began to grow up in the fertile decadence of the Austro-Hungarian empire. A precocious scholar, he enrolled in the University of Vienna in 1918, though he did not become a matriculated student until 1922, by which time Austria had been shrivelled, by the Treaty of Versailles, to a small republic. The consequent inflation reduced his family to something like poverty. As a university student, Popper survived through teaching (mathematics, physics and chemistry) and, for a while, as a cabinet-maker.

He also involved himself in the political activities which followed the dissolution of the empire. At first a socialist, he became a communist in 1919. After a few months, however, he was appalled by the wilful bloodshed during Béla Kun's brief régime in neighbouring Hungary and disgusted by the speciousness of Marxist arguments justifying revolutionary violence. The prospect of an Ideal State, somewhere over the capitalist horizon, could not reconcile him to a programme of human sacrifice. If he continued to consider himself a socialist, he meant nothing more doctrinaire than that he believed in social justice. Eventually, in line with the views of Friedrich von Hayek, to whose thought he displayed an unusual measure of deference, he came to regard state socialism as a form of oppression. Freedom, he then argued, mattered more than equality; if freedom were lost or abandoned, equality itself could not be maintained among those who were not free.

The collapse of the Austro-Hungarian empire did not prevent Vienna from remaining a centre of intellectual vigour. The desire for a commanding post-imperial philosophy of life was fostered by political disintegration. Freud, Adler, Einstein and the so-called Vienna Circle of positivist philosophers, led by Moritz Schlick (who was later gunned down by a crazed student), propounded hypotheses of more or less durable worth, in all of which Popper became more or less durably interested. Elsewhere, Marxism was constantly advanced as the answer to political confusion and economic turmoil. So too, quite soon, was National Socialism.

Einstein stimulated Popper's enthusiasm for physics. What distinguished Einstein from Marx, Freud and Adler was that his ideas were susceptible of test, and hence of refutation. For instance, before Einstein's Theory of Relativity could be said to be valid, a particular event had had to take place, in the Solar System, which was impossible according to classic Newtonian principles. When a star's rays were indeed seen to be bent, by the gravitational pull of the sun, Einstein's prediction was fulfilled. Relativity had survived a key test that might have led to its refutation. This single instance had not proved Einstein to be entirely right, only right*er* than the now refuted Newton. Since there were only two eligible competitors, Einstein's theory was temporarily triumphant, but not *unquestionably* or conclusively.

Popper never cared to doubt the reality or the existence of the physical world. In order for physics and science to supply reliable foundations for civilization, he maintained that we have to accept that what is 'out there' is, however complicated or improbable, real. Thus many of the obsessions of English empirical philosophy remained alien to him: neither phenomenalism nor the problem of knowledge detained him for long. What *we* know, he was disposed to think, is more important than whether or how *I* know. *Cogitamus* was more important than any *cogito*.

Popper came early to the keystone of his idea of scientific method: scientists proved their good faith by seeking the most stringent possible ways of *falsifying* their hypothesis – that is, of detecting flaws in their own work. Any idea that cannot conceivably be refuted is not scientific. It may, however, have interest-value for other reasons. In the light of this cautious generosity, Popper could argue – against the philosophical current both in Vienna and, later, in England – that metaphysics was *not* a useless subject. What he did challenge, implacably, was 'scientism', which involved metaphysicians and sociologists passing off their all-embracing theories as scientific. Metaphysic might be stimulating; it could never be prescriptive.

Scientific method implied being accessible to challenges devised by others. Hence knowledge could not be a matter of personal conviction, however sincere; nor could an untestable theory be warranted by the intuitive genius of no matter how brilliant a prophet or seer. For anything to qualify as knowledge it had to be open to examination, and to the risk of disproof, by the most rigorous possible critics. Fallibility was not evidence of the weakness of a theory; on the contrary, the possibility of refutation guaranteed engagement with reality. Theories that were alleged to be about the world, but which could never *conceivably* be falsified, were for that reason *not* about the world.

Marx and Freud, however seductive their critical or diagnostic astuteness, were revealed to be unscientific by their *systematic* inability to imagine, let alone supply, circumstances under which their ideas might be proved fallacious. If, through the elasticity of its terminology, a theory could always explain away whatever phenomena might seem to render it erroneous, it could not be scientific. Popper did not deny that Freud and Marx were *interesting* and innovatory as moralists or social critics; what he denied, fervently, was the claim, as dear to them as to their followers, that they were scientists.

The philosophers of the influential Vienna Circle – among them, Rudolf Carnap and Otto Neurath – seemed to concur with Popper. As 'logical positivists', they had argued that any proposition that could not be verified was meaningless. Positivism intended to banish metaphysics from intellectual esteem. It aimed to establish the universality of the scientific outlook. Only the propositions of natural science could be said meaningfully to be true. However, logical positivists faced a central problem, albeit an old one, concerning verification. David Hume had pointed out – embarrassingly for those who sought absolute certainty – that there was no logical reason to believe that, because the sun rose yesterday, and this morning, it would *certainly* do so tomorrow. Such arguments from induction, on which science was said conventionally to be based, could claim only that, after an indefinite number of regularities had been observed, it was irrational, although never strictly illogical, not to accept that what happened before would happen again. 'If *p*, then *q*' might express something incontrovertible in logic (depending, of course, on the values of *p* and *q*); but in the physical sciences it could never be *logically* certain that effect would follow cause. In view of this, the verification of a scientific law could never be conclusive. Popper maintained that unless the problem of induction could be resolved (and, he insisted, it could *never* be), positivism's Verification Principle had no warrant to ascribe meaning to science.

How true could scientific truth be, if it was based on nothing more secure than a series of observations and on the consequent assumption, at some indeterminate moment, that the Universe would henceforth honour its contract with science by maintaining an observed consistency? Popper proposed that the problem of scientific method, and hence of verification, be looked at in a different way. In fact, he insisted, it was not the case that scientific thought proceeded on the basis of accumulated observations of regularities. Scientific theories were *never* inductively proved by virtue of a plethora of instances that, at some moment, amounted to a law.

Absolute verification was a chimera. Fortunately, however, there was no call to remain racked by the uncertainty that induction failed to dispel. In science, the hypothesis came *first*; tests and observations followed. No heap of observed instances either prompted a theory or amounted to a proof, as inductionists implied. What lent plausibility to scientific hypotheses – which, in practice, were often proposed on the basis of no preliminary observations whatever – was their ability to survive stringent challenges that their authors or their peers devised to test them.

Science did not proceed by showing why, or that, certain things happened; it established that – if a theory were valid – certain things could *not* happen. For instance, 'One cannot carry water in a sieve' is a theory that no sane man would seek to verify by filling a succession of sieves with water and seeking to carry them to a given point. We begin to recognize something to be the case when to deny it would be to fly in the face of demonstrable facts. By the same token, science cannot 'discover' a tautology, since to deny it is merely self-contradictory. All theories, such as Marxism, which affect to be infallible can only be elaborate tautologies, protected from refutation by their circularity. For simple instance, 'What will happen will happen' is irrefutable only because, although it may *seem* predictive, no possible event or non-event in the future can prove or disprove it.

Ancillary to Popper's vision of science was that of the scientist as an honest man. Civilization and science were intimately linked in the sociology of knowledge. The personal honesty of a researcher might be admirable, but it could never supply a validation. A scientist's work had, by definition, only to be open to honest scrutiny by his peers. Such openness to challenge was integral to progress. In science there might be guesswork; there could not be privilege. Scientific method was both central to human progress and a paradigm of responsible community. No scientist could claim to have struck theoretical gold without making his findings available to public assayers. And when the alchemist was found not to have turned lead into gold, he could not save his theory by redefining his lead as a special form of gold. Genius might (as Einstein did) amaze, but it could not *by itself* certify: without the humility to endure examination, there could be no valid pride in achievement.

In pseudo-science as practised by Freud or Marx, ideology can make facts accord with anything if its terms are sufficiently elasticized (and elusive). The critics of such ideologies can be systematically dismissed by their proponents, since *in the terms of the system* they can always be accused of being, for instance, either 'in denial' or 'lackeys of the bourgeoisie'. In the same way, those who questioned the tenets or authority of the Catholic Church could be anathematized as heathens or heretics or apostates. In such totalizing world-systems, there *could* be no disinterested critic, since there was no room in their conception of the Universe for anyone to be free of their all-consuming, all-explaining logic. No Archimedes could find a platform from which to lever them from infallible omniscience.

Popper's *Logik der Forschung* (translated as *The Logic of Scientific Discovery*) unveiled his principle of fallibility. When it appeared in Vienna in 1934, it was more or less favourably reviewed by members of the Vienna Circle, to which, though never an adherent, he remained personally tangential. However, Popper's challenge to inductionism was held, by its author at least, to have killed off logical positivism. It is certainly the case that the notion of verifiability – over which A. J. Ayer was to muse, futilely as he admitted, for many years – never became a feasible measure, still less a logical determinant, of meaningfulness.

As a result of his book's success, Popper was invited to England during 1935 and 1936. If his anti-inductionism was not well received (and sometimes derided), he made literally vital contacts with the British philosophical establishment: he was soon to be offered academic posts that would enable him to remove himself from Austria. Although his parents had renounced Judaism, in which he never showed much interest, he would undoubtedly have been defined as a Jew by the Nazis. There may be no causal link between his rejection of what he was to term 'essentialism' and the racist notion that 'once a Jew always a Jew', but it would be implausible not to see some psychological connection between his personal circumstances and the urgency with which he denounced the specious logic of totalitarian doctrines.

By the time war broke out in 1939, he had already sketched out the arguments that were to appear as *The Poverty of Historicism*. However, the material was rejected by, among others, the English philosophical journal *Mind* and did not find a publisher until 1944. Popper was offered hospitality at Cambridge in 1936, but he had already applied for, and secured, a teaching post at the University of Canterbury, in New Zealand, where he and his wife, whom he had married in 1930, spent the war. While engaged in arduous teaching duties, and without the use of an adequate library, he wrote both *The Poverty of Historicism* – on which I propose to concentrate in this monograph – and *The Open Society and Its Enemies*, whose densely annotated two volumes are, to a considerable degree, amplified (and impressively ponderous) pendants to the first book.

Popper's notion of scientific method remained fundamental to the political thought that he called his war work. Although he was far from any battlefield, the peaceful seclusion of New Zealand did not calm his conscientious horror at the murderous effects of what he was to call 'historicism'. *The Poverty of Historicism* carries a dedication 'In memory of the countless men, women and children of all creeds or nations or races who fell victim to the fascist and communist belief in the inexorable Laws of Historical Destiny'.

His critics often winced at the caustic rhetoric with which Popper pressed his case (he had become a master of the English language, though no habitual user of understatement). His lack of temperance meant that his war work, like Orwell's *Animal Farm*, did not find an eager publisher. When *The Poverty of Historicism* and, in particular, *The Open Society and Its Enemies* were finally printed, the author's exaggerations were often cited as an excuse for dismissing his case. His attacks on Aristotle were held to be improperly irreverent and those on Plato – more thoroughly argued, but also more virulent – were said by entrenched Platonists to be lacking in scholarship. Popper had taught himself Greek in order to read Greek authors (Heraclitus was also the subject of his scourging admiration), but he had been somewhat reliant on translations which, in the unendowed state of the libraries at Canterbury, were sometimes not as good as they might have been. Those who wish to examine the attacks made on his readings of Plato (and his replies) will find a useful compendium in *Plato, Popper and Politics* (1967), edited by Renford Bambrough.

The publication of *The Open Society and Its Enemies* owed much to the advocacy of Ernst Gombrich and Friedrich von Hayek, who had made good their transition from Vienna to English academic eminence. With their sponsorship, Popper was soon recruited to a readership at the London School of Economics, where he later became a professor. From 1946 onwards, his life was based in England. His assimilation was celebrated by a knighthood in 1967.

Popper's marriage was both childless and, reports indicate, not particularly happy. However, his intellectual partnership with his wife was sustained until her death in 1985. In the following year, he was a visiting professor in Vienna. He continued to engage actively, and often aggressively, in philosophy and in practical politics, almost to the end of his long life in 1994. He published prolifically, on a number of topics, but his fame rested on his notion of 'the open society', even though he considered his contributions to the philosophy of science, such as *Conjectures and Refutations* (1969) of at least equal importance.

Karl Popper was not, as they say, an easy man. He was both opinionated and touchy. If he advocated public discussion, he was quick to scorn those who doubted him. In the gossip of academics, it was said that *The Open Society* had been written by one of its enemies. On one famous occasion, at the Moral Sciences Club in Cambridge, he and his fellow ex-Austrian Wittgenstein almost came to blows. Bertrand Russell is said to have stepped between them, after which Wittgenstein slammed out of the room. Freud might have ironized on what he once called 'the Narcissism of small differences', though neither man would have been likely to acknowledge that there was little to choose between their views.

Popper's intolerance of others lends comedy to his championship of the sociology of knowledge and to his advocacy of a willingness to be criticized, but it does nothing to damage the logic of his case. One of the central aspects of Popper's position, on both science and politics, is his insistence on the importance of *institutions* in the conservation of freedom and of knowledge and in creating an arena for their interdependent propagation. It was never impossible that a fool should propose a valid solution to a problem, even if it was by chance; whoever we are, your theory and mine must both be tested in the hard, even light of public scrutiny. Neither your eminence nor my obscurity could *guarantee* the wisdom or entail the folly of our ideas. However inconveniently for tidy theorists, chance too played a part in social and scientific history. As the discovery of penicillin showed, scientists often stumble on a solution before they have posed the problem.

Popper's campaign against historicism was conducted on the same principles that he declared mandatory in the advance of science. He said that he had not, at the time of their discovery, considered their application to the social sciences, in which he had yet to become interested. He claimed that this lack of preconceived purpose rendered all the more striking the relevance of scientific methodology to areas where he had not previously considered applying it. Since his demand for refutability had not been devised specifically to demolish historicist theories, he could not be accused of premeditated partiality when it happened to destroy their pretensions. Since both Marxism and Social Darwinism (on which Hitlerism relied to justify its ruthlessness) claimed to be at once incontrovertible and scientific, what was intended to prove them invulnerable was revealed to be their failing.

In view of Popper's passionate opposition to totalitarianism, it must have given him some satisfaction to live to see the collapse of both Hitler's Germany and Stalin's USSR. Each had based barbarous policies on pseudo-scientific philosophies defective alike in logic and in humanity. Since Popper regarded democracy as the only political system capable of institutionalizing knowledge *and* freedom, and since he regarded the latter as a condition for the former, it may be said – though he might not say it – that history had proved him right. The fallibility of the democracies had turned out to be a strength; the infallibility of dictators had revealed their weakness. Totalitarian systems created an illusion of frictionless cohesion and inflexible unanimity, but – by damning all dissent as treachery – such régimes lost any prospect of improvement or self-correction through constructive criticism.

THE POVERTY OF HISTORICISM

Popper was a philosophical polemicist whose battles, when he began to fight them, were of urgent significance. The success of his campaign has, perhaps, rendered his belligerence somewhat obsolete. Victory has left his enemies free to accuse him of a want of subtlety and an excess of animus. His importance, it is argued, was transitory and his time is past. There is facile optimism in this claim. The notion that we have nothing more to fear from ideology – implicit in Fukayama's Popperian book about 'the end of history' – has helped to bury Popper under garlands of obituary appreciation. However, it may be too soon to assume that uncontrolled liberalism is now and for ever the only viable (or plausible) system. It is also dubious whether Popper would have endorsed a world order in which economic might is always right.

When he challenged the inevitabilities of historicism, it was because he was convinced that he knew the correct way for scientific inquiry to be conducted (and that no theory was correct unless scientific). Recently, there has been a reaction – for example, on the part of Lewis Wolpert and David Papineau – against the idea that we need, or can sustain, a philosophy of science along Popperian lines. Whether or not this challenge is justified, I cannot judge. Fortunately, nor need I: Popper's assault on historicism loses little of its persuasive force even if (as I do not believe) he was completely wrong about scientific method.

Popper's political writing may have been fortified by his philosophy of science, just as, in another context, Bertrand Russell's opinions on morals and society seemed (in some eyes) to be certified by largely unread works of genius such as *Principia Mathematica*. In logic, Russell's views on marriage or the hydrogen bomb were in no way sustained by his mathematical brilliance, although his and the public's confidence in them was probably strengthened by it. In the same way, Popper's faith in his ideas may well have derived from the precocious originality of his philosophy of science. Certainly that faith armed, and informed, his sociological studies. But even if his conception of scientific method were to merit refutation, his criticism of historicism would not on that account alone be nullified.

In the view of his admirers, he was often right about aspects of ideology. He had few rivals (Raymond Aron is the most formidable) among intellectuals when it came to opposing the tyranny not only of tyrants, but also of their intellectual apologists. The political theorists whom Popper thought most dangerous, and wicked, based their programmes on a cluster of pseudo-scientific or pseudo-logical notions about history, its course and its supposed laws.

The view that history had an inevitable direction and an immutable final destination, which was, so to say, written in the stars, and from which it could and should not be diverted, was common to both fascism and communism. Popper termed this common factor a belief in historicism, which he defined as

> an approach to the social sciences which assumes that *historical prediction* is their principal aim, and which assumes that this aim is attainable by discovering the 'rhythms' or the 'patterns', the 'laws' or the 'trends' that underlie the evolution of history.   [PoH, p. 3]

He refers with constant derision to both historicism and historicists, not hesitating to name names (Plato, Hegel and Marx in particular), but no less often ascribing to an unspecified historicist arguments that he then proceeds to dismantle. This method opens him to the charge of fabricating accessible targets. The usual philosophical retort to the attribution of untenable pronouncements to some generalized Aunt Sally is to exclaim 'But who ever said this?' Popper's prolonged disclosure of his sources in *The Open Society and Its Enemies* responds very thoroughly to this question. In the text, he declared his *parti pris* without hesitation, but he also took honest pains to make the best possible case for historicism, with certain elements of which (though never its conclusions) he confesses his sympathy. Would he have written with such obsessive vigour had he not recognized the formidable qualities, as well as the fundamental flaws, in the intelligences with whom he engaged? In view of his days as a communist, it would not be reckless to say that it was because he understood the temptations of historicism that he considered its refutation to be so important.

Although social Darwinism, with its affectations of conformity with the laws of nature, gave certain versions of fascism a spurious underpinning of scientific plausibility, the main thrust of Popper's reasoned indignation was against Marxism, which was a worthier (and hence more dangerous) enemy of the open society. The intellectual precedents for Marx's theories had a certain respectability, assuming that Hegel was respectable. As for Marx's moral indignation at capitalism's ruthless treatment of the working class, Popper shared it. He never took the view that, because change was not inevitable, nothing should or could be changed. On the contrary, his belief in indeterminism warranted, and demanded, what he called 'piecemeal social engineering'. He did not object to social (or even socialist) experiment, in controlled doses, where its effectiveness could be measured and tested, in a properly scientific way. His steady purpose was to question the effectiveness and, finally, even the *possibility* of long-term, Utopian planning, whether or not it was said to be consistent with the inevitable course of history.

Historicists claimed, and had to claim, that

> some of the characteristic methods of physics cannot be applied to the social sciences, owing to the profound differences between sociology and physics. Physical laws, or 'the laws of nature', ... are valid anywhere and always; for the physical world is ruled by a system of physical uniformities invariable throughout space and time. Sociological laws, however, or the laws of social life, differ in different places and periods ... [Historicism] denies that the regularities detectable in social life have the character of the immutable regularities of the physical world ... They depend on a particular *historical situation*.
>
> [Op. cit., p. 5]

Popper both presents the case candidly and admits some of its plausibility. He concedes that there are good reasons for *not* assimilating social laws (e.g. those of economics) to immutable laws of physics, on the grounds that historical periods can lead to radical changes in them. Is it not true that, unlike the laws of nature, social laws are man-made and hence can be changed by human decision? While pointing out that even the 'laws' of physics are subject to variation (water does not boil at 100 degrees centigrade regardless of the altitude at which the kettle is switched on), Popper accepts that reform, change and even revolution can be practical possibilities. His regular target is not the idea of change, but the idea that there can be a *law* of changes and, above all, that such so-called laws can certify long-term predictions.

Marxism, in particular, proclaims its oracular powers, against which there can be no appeal: once history has spoken, through the uniquely prescient voices of those who have cracked the code of its immutable changes, there is nothing more to be said or done, except to prepare the way of The Future or, in Marx's phrase, to 'ease its birth-pangs'. Historicism typically emphasizes the supposed futility of the experimental method in sociology, since experiments

> are not made to advance knowledge as such but to achieve political success. They are not performed in a laboratory detached from the

outside world; rather, their very performance changes the conditions of society. They can never be repeated under precisely similar conditions since the conditions were changed by their first performance.

[Op. cit., p. 9]

Later, the historicist is credited with believing that

Even if the ordinary methods of physics were applicable to society, they would never be applicable to its most important features: *its division into periods, and the emergence of novelty.* Once we grasp the significance of social newness, we are forced to abandon the idea that the application of ordinary physical methods to the problems of sociology can aid us in understanding the problems of social development.   [Op. cit., p. 11]

The claim that (modest) social measures are futile, since they are almost certainly devised merely to win votes, was first implied by Plato's indictment of Athenian democracy. Popper points out that unrepeatability in exactly similar laboratory conditions does not prove an experiment's futility (which *can*, however, be more or less strongly suggested by its *failure*); nor is exactitude always a condition of scientifically useful testing. He insists again and again that sociology can and should observe the rules of other sciences. What he does not seem to envisage is the argument that a one-party state *might* supply conditions under which limited social experiments could be undertaken by the government without the dreaded consequences of its eviction, should even well-intentioned measures fail to produce their hoped-for dividend. It seems that Popper does not give due weight to the possibility of avoiding the ochlocracy (mob rule) that Plato deplored, without going all the way with historicist deference to long-term inevitabilities. Can we not ask whether the one-party state *has* to be run on historicist principles? Popper's answer is implicit. He advocates that sociology should be systematically aware of what he calls 'the logic of the situation'. Since the one-party state must, by definition, imply that opposition is either forbidden or repressed, the experiments conducted by its rulers, however philosophical, can never be duly monitored or challenged. Freedom and division are, it seems, inseparable.

Popper's allegiance to democracy is unsentimental; if he regards it as the best way of avoiding bloodshed when governments fail or fall, his principal reason for favouring it is that its institutions are always likely to be uniquely congenial to the scientific advances on which mankind's future happiness (or lessening of unhappiness) depends. The kind of science that Popper valued had to have room for the unprogrammed discovery, for the maverick spirit, for the theorist who finds more than he is looking for.

It was Picasso who said, 'Je ne cherche pas, je trouve', but Popper's man of science was entitled to make the same claim. Once he had found what he was not looking for, however, he had to design public tests to validate his heuristic skills. The sort of state science that endorsed, for instance, experiments in eugenics, as the Nazis did, might be acceptable to men like George Bernard Shaw, whose tendency to admire dictators sprang from his own blithe delusions of superiority, but it was not an option for a surly humanist like Popper. Shavian eugenics – which involved euthanasia – were not accidentally anti-democratic: one of the first steps had to be to disenfranchise those whose unsuitability or uselessness made them eligible for superfluousness. There is a connection, in the logic of the situation, between open societies and the legal institutions that they alone spawn. For instance, a type of state-run medicine, where the Hippocratic code is rewritten by social Darwinism or Marxism, can sponsor murderers in white coats or the strait-jacketed travesties of Soviet psychiatric hospitals.

Historicism is said to be inclined to stress the importance of prediction as one of the tasks of science. Popper agrees, up to a point: however, he does *not* believe that *historical prophecy* is (or can be) one of the tasks of the social sciences. Historicism mystifies the subject by claiming that only the expert, or philosopher-king, has the intellectual capacity for prophecy. Popper offers an instance of the inherent difficulty of such predictions:

> Suppose . . . it were predicted [in some kind of oracular register] that the price of shares would rise for three days and then fall. Plainly, everyone connected with the market would sell on the third day, causing a fall of prices on that day and falsifying the prediction . . . *exact and detailed* scientific social predictions are therefore impossible.
>
> [Op. cit., pp. 13, 14]

The particular example is open to objection. The Marxist, for instance, might limit (or expand) his prediction to say only that the stock-market would – and should – be consigned to the dustbin of history. He might also say that Popper's example was both frivolous and irrelevant. Marxism was never intended to supply an inside track for fund managers. It claims that what matters, if we wish to understand and foresee its future development, is the history of the group, its traditions and institutions. Popper is not appeased:

Such considerations strongly suggest . . . a close connection between historicism and the so-called *biological or organic theory* of social structures – the theory which interprets social groups by analogy with living organisms . . . Similarly, the well-known theory of the existence of a *group-spirit*, as the carrier of the *group-traditions*, although not necessarily itself a part of the historicist argument, is closely related to the holistic view. [Op. cit., p. 19]

'Holism' in Popper's bestiary of aberrations, is not quite as bad as historicism, but it manifestly shares the totalitarian view that there can be no effective small-scale changes in society: what holism calls for, by definition, is wholesale planning. Only by replacing the entire machinery of an obsolete or immoral society (evolutionists like C. H. Waddington tended to conflate them) can durable reforms or revolutions be made. Holism is almost synonymous with Utopianism, which is the well-intentioned, certainly idealistic (*ergo*, in Marxist eyes, impractical) version of what Marxists have in mind when they tell us what the classless society will be like after the state has withered away.

Popper's attitude to group-spirits and the traditions that they carry may indicate his scorn for Jung, whose amalgam of psychoanalysis and fanciful, unprovable theories qualifies him as a pseudo-scientist. Jungian ideas belong, if at all, in a dubious category of the knowledge accumulated in what Popper chose to call 'World 3'. He gave this uncatchy title to the whole compendium of humanly fabricated and scientifically established knowledge. Its accumulation, over the millennia, has created what mankind calls objective reality. Popper accepts (and even insists) that subjective impressions can pass over into the category of objective knowledge, provided they coalesce into testable theories. In this way, he avoids, or postpones, the Kantian issue of a metaphysical reality outside man's intellectual or sensible grasp. If appearances are our reality, then they are, since we cannot transcend them. What we cannot properly do is what intuitionists and prophets affect to do, which is to 'know' what lies beyond the limits of human knowledge. There can, and will, be additions to World 3, thanks to science, but no one can trump it with superior certainties.

An unconvinced critic might say that World 3 was merely a more solid structure that serves in much the same office as Jung's group-traditions. Be that as it may, it is perhaps less the traditions than the groups to which Popper takes individualistic exception. He would insist, however, that the price of respectable entry into World 3 has to involve the same test of refutability that no holistic theory can ever pass.

HISTORICISM AND SOCIETY

The historicist is said to claim that 'physics aims at causal explanation: sociology at an understanding of purpose and meaning'. Hence he maintains that the latter has prompt, and proper, recourse to intuition and imagination, neither of which can be expected to propound theories that can then be tested. On the contrary, their rare quality is, allegedly, to offer a privileged method of untestable theorizing – for instance, about national character or the spirit of the age. Popper's response is to list three versions of intuitive understanding, in ascending order of delusiveness.

The first asserts that a social event is understood when analysed in terms of the forces that brought it about, i.e. when the individuals and groups involved, their purposes or interests, and the power they can dispose of, are known. The actions of individuals or groups are here understood as being in accordance with their aims – as promoting their real advantage or, at least, their imagined advantage. The method of sociology is here thought of as an imaginative reconstruction of either rational or irrational activities, directed towards certain ends.

The second variant goes further. It admits that such an analysis is necessary, particularly in regard to the understanding of individual actions or group activities. But . . . more is needed for the understanding of social life . . . [A] social event . . . changes the situational value of a wide range of other events . . . demanding a re-orientation and re-interpretation of all objects and of all actions in that particular field . . . Thus in order to understand social life, we must go beyond the mere analysis of factual causes and effects . . . [and] understand every event as playing a certain characteristic part within the whole. The event gains its significance from its influence upon the whole, and its significance is therefore in part determined by the whole.

The third variant . . . goes even further . . . It holds that to understand the meaning or significance of a social event, more is required than an analysis of its genesis, effects, and situational value . . . it is necessary to analyse objective, underlying historical trends and tendencies . . . prevailing at the period in question, and to analyse the contribution of the event in question to the historical process by which such trends become manifest. A full understanding of the Dreyfus Affair, for instance, demands over and above an analysis of its genesis, effects, and situational value, an insight into the fact that it was the manifestation of the contest between two historical tendencies in the development of the French Republic, democratic and autocratic, progressive and reactionary.   [Op. cit., pp. 20–22]

It may well seem that there is a good deal of sense in these claims on behalf of intuitive understanding. Would Popper have spelt them out so elaborately if he had not recognized it? He did not think it wrong for historians to use wit and imagination in evaluating aspects of their subject. Where he became apprehensive was the point at which the fruits of imagination were wrapped in the language of science. They were then held to establish 'historical trends or tendencies [and] to a certain extent the application of *inference by analogy* from one historical period to another'. [Op. cit., p. 22]

This kind of reasoning was used, Popper recalls, in order to postulate a tendentious similarity between Greece before Alexander the Great and southern Germany before Bismarck, thus justifying as historically inevitable the latter's aggressive *Realpolitik*. Popper was eager to puncture grandiose theories with pointed ridicule. For instance, he piqued Hegel's logic of astronomy by pointing out that Hegel proved that a certain planet could not exist only shortly before its existence was established by observation. His derisive zeal disposed some philosophers to accuse Popper of vulgarity. It was, very often, the vulgarity of a man who had personal experience of the way in which murderous schemes could be derived from sublime and unchallengeable intuitions:

> the method of historical understanding does not only fit in with the ideas of holism. It also agrees very well with the historicist's emphasis on novelty; for novelty cannot be causally or rationally explained, but only intuitively grasped.   [Op. cit., p. 23]

What is offensive is the intrusion, by apparently reasonable steps, of a notion of evidence that depends only on the authority of intuition. It leads to an absolute reliance on the power to persuade rather than on the ability to demonstrate in a challengeable way. The *Führerprinzip* is an example of what happens when rhetoric supplants reason. Art may supply beauty; it does not generate truth. Applause is not a form of proof.

It does not follow that it is wrong to have enthusiasms or, indeed, intuitions. There is nothing wrong, in principle, even in guesswork. But, if he wants them to be acted upon, the honest man, typified by the scientist, has to devise ways of establishing the validity of his intuitions *in public* and in accordance with the principle of refutability. Hence what is objectionable in the historicist is his flight from reason and from reason's dull accomplice, measurement. By alleging that there is no way of measuring the qualities of states, economic systems or forms of government in *quantitative* terms, the historicist claims that the laws of the social sciences, if there are any, must be *qualitative*. And qualities, whether physical or not, can be appraised only by intuition.

On this (false) account, it appears plausible to maintain that social science can never be scientific in Popper's sense. What alarms him, however, is not the allegation that social science is not exactly like physics. (Popper claims neither that it should nor that it could be, though he does think it has important similarities to natural sciences.) The scandal, for him, was that historicists and holists alike proceeded to claim that they were still scientists, but of a different, more far-seeing brand. For Popper there could be no such category of visionaries. Scientific methodology was one and indivisible. In this respect, it is interesting – and even amusing – to observe that Popper continued to share the typically Viennese urge to discover a universal morality, or logic. Having found it in science, he had no more tolerance for deviant ideas than the prophets, such as Marx and Freud, whom he denounced.

If it would be a mistake to charge Popper with sharing the ideologue's irrationality or pre-emptive self-righteousness, he was undoubtedly as fierce for reason as a reasonable man could well contrive. At the same time, he insisted that the use of reason was a human choice, not a natural characteristic. The point had been brought home to him when he accused a Nazi of lacking sound arguments. His opponent flashed his revolver and said, '*This* is my argument.'

It is indisputable that we are always free to use brutal or unreasonable methods, in the sense that no natural embargo prevents us, but we should not then be surprised to arrive at brutal or unreasonable conclusions. However, we should be *extremely* surprised, as Schopenhauer pointed out, to arrive by these means at reasonable ones. To be reasonable requires decision and application. Within reason itself, there are important decisions to make and a choice of methods to apply, good and bad. Getting things right depends on using valid terms and arguments. We may arrive first at a conclusion, but it cannot of itself be conclusive.

Popper's quarrel with Plato begins here. The greatness of Plato was never denied; his genius had issued in a formidably persuasive lobby for ideas that were at once superbly argued and fundamentally flawed. The source of much error was what Popper called essentialism, of which Aristotle too was a towering, if somewhat less purposeful, proponent.

The source of essentialism lay in Plato's Theory of Forms or Ideas. As Popper explains in vol. I of *The Open Society and Its Enemies* (pp. 27, 28):

The Theory of Ideas demands that there should be only one Form or Idea of man; for it is one of the central doctrines of the Theory of Forms that there is only one Form of every 'race' or 'kind' of things . . . similar things are copies or imprints of *one* Form . . . In *The Republic* . . . Plato explained his point . . . using as his example the 'essential bed', i.e. the Form or Idea of a bed: 'God . . . has made one essential bed, and only one; two or more he did not produce, and never will . . . For . . . even if God were to make two, and no more, then another would be brought to light, namely the Form exhibited by those two; this, and not those two, would then be the essential bed'.

What in this antique theory was, in Popper's view, so relevant to modern political theory that it required long, polemical attention? In the context of historicism, Plato's doctrine of a single true form of everything to be found on earth supplied a noble warrant – what A. J. Ayer would call an 'argument from piety' – for a misconceived reading of social realities. The influence of *The Republic*, seconded by a perverted version of Socrates' inquisitive method, had inspired social theorists to search for, and propose, the 'real' (immutable and, for some, God-given) meaning of such crucial terms as justice, society, freedom and life. The Platonic–'Socratic' line was to claim that, until we knew what 'justice' was meant, ideally, to be, we could not contrive its equivalent on earth. Only philosophers could be relied on, by virtue of their genius, to perceive and define the *essence* of these God-given meanings and so to ensure that human institutions conformed to the heavenly plan. Such a metaphysic claims that, unless our terminology is substantiated by what George Steiner terms 'real presences', words can have no valid meaning. No reliable conclusions can be drawn, it is claimed, from arguments unanchored in metaphysical reality.

Popper was not alone in arguing for the systematic delusiveness of first defining one's terms; he pointed out that biology – the science of life – has functioned perfectly well without having to define what 'life' means. The quest for the universal or real meaning of any word or term was not merely futile but misguided. The correct attitude to words was to be found in nominalism, which regards them as 'useful instruments of description' rather than as the encrypted carriers of God's true meaning, which had to be discovered by some guild of intuitional diviners.

Popper's assault on essentialism was purposeful as well as philosophical: 'it has . . . been suggested that *while the methods of the natural sciences are fundamentally nominalistic, social science must adopt a methodological essentialism*' [PoH, p. 30]. This 'must', he maintained, is tendentious. After positing what affects to be a viable alternative to the methods of the natural sciences, the argument has insisted that the method alone is relevant to sociology. So? In the grim light of Marxism and its practice, Popper fears that the 'anti-naturalistic doctrines of Historicism' lead directly to the notion that it is possible, and important, to discover historical laws or trends. Such discoveries, although undiscoverable in Popper's view, will then be paraded as inevitably true. They will be accompanied by the assertion that it is, by definition, *morally improper*, no less than futile, to tamper with the inexorable (and inhuman) progress of history.

Having claimed that their style of political theorizing conforms to scientific principles, historicists insist on 'the importance of successful prediction and its "corroboration" '. Popper concedes that, up to this point, he has no large methodological quarrel with his opponents. What is intolerable to him is when they move on to say, for example, '*If it is possible for astronomy to predict eclipses, why should it not be possible for sociology to predict revolutions?*' [Op. cit., p. 36]

As soon as this demanding inquiry is made, it is often modified. After all, if such a possibility does exist, might it not – *should* it not? – be validated by a display of successful predictions? In order to avoid being put to specific tests, the historicist's answer is that 'qualitative' changes cannot be measured precisely. Instead of backing down, however, he takes convenient refuge in maintaining his ability to make long-term predictions or large-scale forecasts. The convenience lies in the fact that the truth or falsehood of long-term predictions lies 'over the horizon'. Vindication or disappointment is often beyond access in the lifetimes of those who are, more often than not, called upon to sacrifice themselves for the sake of another generation, which can, in its turn, be called upon for further necessary sacrifices.

Thus the coming of the classless society, like that of the Messiah, has to be taken on trust. The Marxist state of unalienated humanity lies on the unseen side of the foreseeable struggle, which must lead to the disappearance of capitalism. Because it is the nature of humanity, or at least of the bourgeoisie, to kick against the pricks, the withering away of the state and the end of alienation may be delayed, for instance, by the necessity to impose the 'dictatorship of the proletariat'. We can and must trust the evolutionary logic of history, but we have to accept that the future cannot, of its nature, be experimentally procured now.

Unfortunately for this kind of argument, Popper has a better one: the reason, he maintains, that we can *never* accurately predict the future – and this 'never' is logical, as well as practical – is that it is impossible for men to know now what they, or other men, *will* know in the future. Hence we are never possessed of the data that can allow us to make certain predictions about what may lie over the horizon of our present stock of knowledge. Marx, for instance, had no notion of modern industrial methods or energy-production, still less of the forms of economy that would be created *as the result of his own analysis of economic conditions and prospects*. Marx's predictions procured their own negation by alerting those who might have suffered from them of the measures they should take to counteract them. In this sense, he resembled the man who, by predicting that the stock market will fall at the end of the week, makes sure that, as a result of others acting on this information, it will fall *before* the end of the week.

Historicist historians are more impressive when they point out past inevitabilities than in divining them in the future. It requires no experiment to conclude that what has already happened could not not have happened. The past is not, however, a test-bed for the future. No historian's hindsight, however shrewd in its observations, cannot generate sufficient kudos to warrant putting our faith in his foresight. No intuition is required to discover that we cannot change (though we can certainly re-describe) what has already happened; this is true by virtue of a simple tautology. Unfortunately or not, no conclusions can be drawn about the predictability of the future from the fact that historians have uncovered the causes of what happened in the past. Historians, however objective they think themselves, are always selective. The choice of causes or reasons for any historical event is legion; even the event itself is an artificial construct. It is often arbitrarily defined and may well be compounded of many events (the French Revolution is an instance).

The difficulty about *why* things happen in history is that, unlike in a controlled scientific experiment, it is very difficult (not to say logically impossible) to isolate a historical event. It is even more difficult (and, as it were, *more* impossible) to determine definitively what is and is not relevant to its happening. Byron was alert to this when he remarked on the disproportionate effect of historical trifles such as the relations of Mrs Masham with her sovereign on the evolution of the Duke of Marlborough's career. Tolstoy, on the other hand, challenged the Great Man theory of history by discounting the significance of, in particular, Napoleon, but also of Kutuzow, the successfully obstinate Russian general, in turning the great tides of human change. Hegel was less decisive: when Napoleon rode in triumph through Jena, the philosopher regarded him as a 'world-historical' figure, but his veneration did not survive Bonaparte's eclipse.

Popper conceded a measure of merit to both points of view, without yielding an inch to systematic historicism, of which Tolstoy was clearly a somewhat casual adherent. When we get to programmatic systematizers, scientism leads us along a road paved with facile arguments of the following order:

> since [detailed forecasts] . . . are confined to brief periods . . . if we are at all interested in social predictions, large-scale forecasts (which are also long-term forecasts) remain . . . not only the most fascinating but actually the only forecasts worth attempting . . . [One] of the characteristic claims of historicism which is closely associated with its denial of the applicability of the experimental method, is that history, political and social, is the *only* empirical source of sociology . . . [Historicism] demands the recognition of the fundamental importance of historical forces, whether spiritual or material; for example, religious or ethical ideas, or economic interests. To analyse . . . this thicket of conflicting tendencies and forces and to penetrate to its roots, to the universal driving forces and laws of social change – this is the task of the social sciences, as seen by historicism. Only in this way can we develop a theoretical science . . . whose confirmation would mean the success of social theory . . .
>
> Sociology thus becomes, to the historicist, an attempt to solve the old problem of foretelling the future; not so much of the future of the individual as that of groups, and of the human race . . . it could thereby become the foremost instrument of far-sighted practical politics.
>
> [Op. cit., pp. 38 et seqq.]

Popper proceeds, not a moment too soon, to make a distinction between prediction and prophecy. For him, the only honest predictions are technological. Predictions of this kind (assessing the tolerances of metal, the load-bearing limits of reinforced concrete, etc.) form the basis of engineering. It is typical of Popper's roots in continental tradition that he held the 'engineer' in high esteem, even though both Plato and Aristotle, not to mention Oxbridge dons of the old school, regarded such practical men as 'banausic'. For Popper, the engineer was a paragon of the practical man: he dealt with 'designed experiment, as opposed to mere patient observation' (or absurd speculation). It was not to be denied that impracticality yielded its fruits – for instance, in astronomy – but that was because they proved germane to practical predictions: for instance, when they were of meteorological value.

Popper proceeds with occasional, and significant, wariness, before resuming his polemical course:

> I only wish to stress that historicists, quite consistently with their belief that sociological experiments are useless and impossible, argue for

historical prophecy – ... of social, political and institutional developments – and against social engineering, as the practical aims of the
social sciences ...

The kind of history with which historicists wish to identify sociology
looks not only backwards to the past but also forwards to the future. It
is the study of the operative forces and, above all, of the laws of social
development ... not the pseudo-laws of apparent constancies or
uniformities ... in order that men may adjust themselves to impending
change by deducing prophecies from these laws.

[Op. cit., pp. 44, 45]

The wariness derives, I suspect, from a certain nervousness in the
introduction of the notion of 'the engineer' as a paradigm of the kind of
practical man whose experience is not only useful, but also crucial to the
running of a social machine. 'Piecemeal social engineering' will soon be
advanced as the only proper way of tinkering with societies, purposefully
but without exaggerated expectations or immodest blueprints.

In some respects, Popper never renounced a certain idea of socialism.
His problem was to make an unbridgeable distinction between his kind of
meliorism (involving making things better, or less bad) and the ideolo-
gist's aggressive optimism (involving helping to make things as good as
they could possibly be, as God, or Marx, intended). That they shared
certain common hopes did not, he insisted, entail that he was simply less
energetic or less committed than his opponents. Differences of style *are*
differences of content: because perfection is unattainable, to sacrifice
blood in its pursuit is not only cruel but fatuous. Science can never have
an end (Popper entitled his intellectual autobiography *Unended Quest*)
and hence the question of means is capital. While art, and perhaps
Popper's beloved music in particular, need not – perhaps *must* not – care
about means (the method of procuring sublime results), politics procures
no exemption from humane procedures. Socially speaking, means are
among, and perhaps indistinguishable from, our ends. Civilization is a
matter of deciding to use reason both in the evaluation of our prospects
and in the avoiding of wars, massacres and social degradation.

The historicist scorns such amiable caution. He insists that

the real outcome will always be very different from the rational
construction. It will always be the resultant of the momentary
constellation of contesting forces. Furthermore, under no circumstances
could the outcome of rational planning become a stable structure; for
the balance of forces is bound to change. All social engineering, no
matter how much it prides itself on its realism and on its scientific
character, is doomed to remain a Utopian dream ...

> Historicism . . . does not teach that nothing can be brought about; it
> only predicts that neither your dreams nor what your reason constructs
> will ever be brought about *according to plan*. Only such plans as fit in
> with the main current of history can be effective . . . Social midwifery is
> the only perfectly reasonable activity open to us . . . based on scientific
> foresight.   [Op. cit., pp. 47, 49]

Historicism denies to human reason the power to bring about a more
reasonable world. Marx famously observed that philosophy had so far
only described the world and that what it now had to do was to *change* it.
However, the deposit of his mature theories, so Popper insists, is that a
historicist like Marx ends up by telling us that even he can only *interpret*
social development and aid it in various ways, but that *nobody can
change it*. Is there something a little glib in paying Marx back so neatly in
his own coin? Popper asserts that he is merely criticizing attempts to link
historicism with optimism or activism. If Marx and his like are right,
there is in fact nothing necessarily good to be hoped for and, in addition,
there is no way of helping to procure it. Activism, so far from being a
logical adjunct of communist doctrine, is a fifth wheel on time's chariot,
which (on Marx's analysis) has its own wings anyway.

Popper could not forget the essentialist argument advanced by German
(and other) communists who, having defined fascism as a temporary, and
necessary, stage on the road to communism, therefore did nothing to
prevent Hitler's access to power on the grounds of 'the sooner it comes,
the sooner it's gone'.

Wittgenstein once famously observed that 'philosophy leaves everything as it is'. Popper would have been justified in adding the rider that
bad philosophy is liable to leave nothing as it is. Bloody consequences
flow from embracing the wrong model for thought; neither sincerity nor
good intentions can excuse the abuse of reason. We may all be entitled to
our opinions, but it is decidedly not true that all opinions are of equal
merit.

> – the consistent historicist will see . . . a useful warning against the
> romantic and Utopian character of both optimism and pessimism in
> their usual forms, and of rationalism too. He will insist that a truly
> scientific historicism must be independent of such elements; that we
> simply have to submit to the existing laws of development, just as we
> have to submit to the law of gravity. The historicist . . . may add that
> the most reasonable attitude to adopt is *so to adjust one's system of
> values as to make it conform with the impending changes*. If this is
> done, one arrives at a form of optimism which can be justified, since

any change will then necessarily be a change for the better, if judged by that system of values . . .

The historicist's moral theory which could be described as 'moral futurism' has its counterpart in an aesthetic modernism . . .

[Op. cit., pp. 53, 54]

Comrade Pangloss is clearly in Popper's sights, but (not unusually) there is an interestingly suggestive aside, which is not followed up, about aesthetic inevitabilities. The glide from moral futurism to aesthetic (post-) modernism may owe its symmetry to a typically Viennese trope, curtly echoed by the young Wittgenstein in his *Tractatus-Logico-Philosophicus*, where he *equates* ethics and aesthetics. What deserves attention is the degree to which the cultural priority of modernism may have been foisted on us by notions of aesthetic inevitability that derive their force from the inevitability that is said, by Marxists, to belong to political development. The idea of a *single* correct aesthetic current is akin to that of a single correct political direction. Conceptualism is only the latest version of art that validates itself on the grounds of aesthetic premeditation. It is no accident, as Marxists used to say, that this puts artists under the ideological command of those – curators, journalists, dispensers of the residue from lotteries – who affect to predict which movement must be conducive to the Future of Art. Thus the avant-garde persists, albeit under new colours, when the rest of the Marxist army has been disbanded.

THE NATURE OF PROGRESS

If social change is not obligatory in the nature of things, on what grounds is it desirable and how is it to be contrived? Popper's answer to the second question is similar to the old one of how porcupines make love: very, very carefully. As to the first, need it be answered at all? If man is not perfectible, no more is he perfect, hence his situation can be improved. However, instead of wholesale plans to destroy whatever is not ideal and to begin again from scratch, Popper advocates 'piecemeal technology', made articulate by a process of critical analysis. Von Hayek had already said that 'economics developed mainly as the outcome of the investigation and refutation of successive Utopian proposals'. Such modesty seems wise, when it concerns prudent adjustments of already functioning institutions, but uneasiness sets in when Popper explores the argument that it is

> a technological problem . . . of a public character [to discover whether]
> state management of production, is compatible with an effective
> democratic control of the administration; or . . . *how to export
> democracy to the Middle East.*   [Op. cit., p. 59]

The italics are mine, and I think I am entitled to them. It probably
always was, and certainly is now, an extraordinary task to allot to a
technological engineer to find a way to export *democracy* to the Middle
East. Surely democracy and armaments cannot be packaged in quite the
same kind of vessel. If the exporting of democracy was only an example,
it remains a dubious one. How can it chime with Popper's belief,
expressed elsewhere, that the social engineer has to take his cue, and his
funds presumably, from political decision-makers, and that he himself
does not implement specifically political ideas? How should we devise an
unspecific export model of democracy that would be as purely structural
as, say, the kit for an industrial plant? Could it be sold with confidence,
or even honesty, to those unfamiliar with parliamentary processes and to
the notion of majority rule and the compromises it involves? Ernest
Gellner's studies offer evidence of the categorically undemocratic principles of Muslim societies. Can one legitimately, or honourably, insist that
democracy is always ideologically neutral?

The primacy of the West (the home of science) is implicit in Popper's
philosophy, just as it was in Marx's. I suspect that he took for granted a
decline in the political significance of religion in the post-war world. He
never discusses religion as anything but a personal choice of morality, to
which harmless notions of salvation might attach. If he can, at times,
accuse his Christian opponents of being unchristian, he means little more
than that they are failing to love their neighbours. It suggests a want of
practical imagination to insist that democracy can be 'sold' to Muslim
societies, which are, rightly or wrongly (but who is to say?), disposed to
regard it less as a panacea than as a Trojan horse containing alien and
divisive forces. In this case at least, the proposed means by which change
is to be procured cannot fall convincingly under the bland rubric of
piecemeal technology.

There is another objection. Popper would not have us ask the
essentialist question, 'What does democracy (really) mean, entail, involve?', but that will not prevent the question being posed, and with some
urgency, if democracy is to be part of an export drive. Whether or not we
choose to define it exactly, there *has* to be some consensus about what is
meant by democracy. The Stalinist coinage 'People's Democracy', like the
Nazi term 'People's Court', is laughable where it is not nauseating,
precisely because we know that the terms 'Democracy' and 'Court' were

being used in a perverted way: that is, not in accord with what we call their real meaning. Our knowledge of this is lodged, so to speak, in Popper's 'World 3'. That we cleave to these meanings as immutable is why arbitrary despots, from Robespierre to Pol Pot, excite outrage when they deform them.

On this account, the distinction between essentialism (bad) and nominalism (good) looks to be somewhat less abrupt than Popper claims. It may be the case that we do not need to define 'cricket' before we knock a ball about, but we do discover, and quite soon, that there have to be rules, and that what is against the rules is 'not cricket'. Purely verbal definitions, however strict, will never (and should never) be the means of imposing conclusions on mankind that are neither humane nor – whatever the pretence – necessary. However, rules do determine how a game is to proceed: elastic as they may be (or may be found to be), they do define – supply limits to – what constitutes playing the game, or not. We may not be able to say, ahead of time, what precise breach will dispose us to say 'it's not cricket any more', but it remains true that cricket cannot change into football and still be called cricket.

Nominalism taken beyond its (essential?) limits becomes indistinguishable, in its evasive self-validation, from the alchemy of those who can arrange never to be wrong. To talk of games and rules is not, in this context, light-hearted. Wittgenstein's question 'Can you play chess without the queen?' addressed the same topic. If the tone was playful, the issue is not. There was a kind of ghastly facetiousness in the use of the vocabulary of morals and responsibility by both Nazis and Soviet rulers, who knew very well that they were cheating. In a century of vicious parody, a sense of humour can be overused. If we mean to export democracy, we had best be clear what we mean by it.

Popper might have protested that he was advocating nothing more peremptory than the development of institutions and practices that might wean the Middle East from unsociable confrontations on the basis of previously irresoluble differences. He cannot, however, be acquitted of a programmatic complacency when it comes to the application of 'piecemeal social engineering' when the project is both large and without precedent. He observes, a little later, that

> piecemeal social engineering resembles physical engineering in regarding the *ends* as beyond the province of technology ... In this it differs from historicism, which regards the ends of human activities as dependent on historical forces and so within its province.
>
> [Op. cit., p. 64]

Respectability seems to derive from avoiding affectations of certainty in the results of an undertaking. But it is to strain an analogy to equate 'exporting democracy' with building a bridge or widening a road. Friedrich von Hayek had advanced an argument against centralized planning (and thus against large-scale social engineering) which impressed Popper. It was that 'the typical engineering job involved the centralization of all relevant knowledge in a single head, whereas it is typical of all truly social problems that knowledge has to be used which cannot be so centralized' (Hayek, *Collectivist Economic Planning*, 1935, p. 210). Popper draws the inference that 'the engineer must use the technological knowledge embodied in these hypotheses which inform him of the limitations of his own initiative as well as of his knowledge'. [Op. cit., p.64 note]

It could be argued that these limitations have been considerably broadened by the accumulation of knowledge in computers of whose power and accessibility Popper was no more prescient than Marx was of the advanced industrial methods that would make nonsense of his theory of surplus value. Does the single head model not lose some of its force when the planner can, with the aid of a computer, have two or three heads, as it were, at his fingertips? It may be said that such knowledge, drawn from elsewhere, might not be of the right kind; it might derive from unreliable, ideologically distorted sources. But Popper would not deny that scientists had a wider view when carried on giants' shoulders. Why should this not be true of planners?

Popper would probably not be fazed by this objection. For him the difference between piecemeal and Utopian engineering was that between the possible and the impossible:

> one is possible, while the other simply does not exist . . . while the piecemeal engineer can attack his problem with an open mind as to the scope of reform, the holist cannot do this; for he has decided beforehand that a complete reconstruction is possible and necessary.
>
> [Op. cit., p. 69]

Unless one defines a complete reconstruction as meaning only that *nothing* that was there before can be allowed to survive, need the distinction be as logically abrupt as Popper would have it? Haussmann's radically re-planned Paris is still, manifestly, Paris. Popper would probably find this instance irrelevant. His target is typified by the Utopianist Karl Mannheim, when he says 'the political problem . . . is to *organize human impulses* in such a way that they will direct their energy to the right strategic points and steer the whole process of development in the right direction'. This kind of project, Popper tells us, clearly discounts any possibility of testing the success or failure of the new society: 'Wholes in the [sense] holistic can never be the object of scientific inquiry' [Op. cit., p. 74]. That is reason enough for the holistic approach to merit anathema.

When Mannheim says that we must set up and direct the whole system of nature, he is telling us, so Popper insists, that we are *forced* to a logical impossibility. Hence he cannot be right. It remains an open question whether 'exporting democracy' would be any less of an attempt to 'steer the whole process of development in the right direction'.

WHAT CAN AND WHAT CANNOT BE DONE?

Popper insists, again and again, that 'not one example of a scientific description of a whole, concrete social situation is ever cited'. In today's (temporarily?) unideological climate, where non-democratic blocs do not seriously challenge western complacency, one is free to wonder whether Popper's adherence to the notion that science alone can provide a comprehensive model for human progress (towards an end we will never see and need not define) is not itself, however genially, ideological. He seeks, like any reasonable man, to discountenance false gods, but he never engages seriously with the notion of divinity. As a result, he seems hardly to notice the deep social and intellectual divisions implicit in the variety of religious response to the human condition. If we dismiss religion as dated mystification, we risk seriously misreading mankind. Whether or not we can prove, rationally, that God exists (clearly we cannot), we are still faced with Pascal's neat observation that the heart has its reasons. Neither the physical shape of the world nor the forms of human thought would be as they are, or have begun to be as they are, without the dimension of the sacred, without the fear of gods and the habit of obedience to divine ordinance. Human credulity may be a folly; religion may have done more harm than good (if such a balance sheet is conceivable); yet to strip out the spiritual and replace it only with science might be – to reverse the parable – to drive out seven demons and replace them with one. As one modern philosopher puts it, 'the remorseless secularism of those Austrians – that was what made Wittgenstein (who was one of them) come out fighting!'

Popper's own view, manifest in his sympathetic scolding of John Stuart Mill's 'psychologism', was that, since we cannot legislate for the vagaries of human nature, we do better to build social institutions in which man's diversity can be housed and honoured than to seek to rebuild man himself. Popper's notion of political rectitude was that modest social ambitions, accessible to piecemeal achievement, were better than grandiose and uncontrollable master-plans. Was there in this an element of nostalgia for the Hapsburg empire of his youth, in which, under a happily incompetent central authority, all kinds of ethnic communities agreed to differ? Austro-Hungary was written out of history by the master-plan of Versailles, an instance of grandiosely inept planning to which Popper barely refers, except to ironize about self-determination.

Popper retains a measure of faith in piecemeal experiments. He gives as an instance 'an experiment in socialism carried out in a factory or village'. Except in the case of modest 'pilot-schemes', it is hard to imagine what such an experiment could prove, or disprove. The Israeli kibbutz, for instance, was a brave experiment (although tainted, in some eyes, with Platonism), but it has, in the long run, proved only how difficult it is to sustain a cloistered social system in a larger society that has rejected its brand of Utopianism. The kibbutz movement was intended to be a model of co-operative living, and still has its proud adherents, but even its successes did nothing to justify, or prompt, imitation on a national scale (which might have involved something like the coercive nightmare of Soviet collective farming). On the simplest level of communication theory, it is impossible to argue from the viability of small communities (where votes and policies can be determined in almost daily conclave) to the virtue of organizing nation-states on similar lines. The ancient city-state *could not* expand and remain democratic, on the Athenian model, for that reason, among others. When the *demos* spoke, in Athens, they could literally be heard; when modern democratic politicians affect to listen to the people's voice, it is a rhetorical courtesy. Small ideas, when watered, cannot be relied on to grow into fertile big ideas. The dinosaur dies; the lizard lives.

Popper's determination to find only negligible differences between the methods of the natural sciences and those of the social sciences offered a trenchant method of criticizing ideology. It supplied no very convincing means of replacing it. The irony is manifest: Popper admired Marx for the sharpness of his criticisms of capitalism, but found him deficient when it came to proposing practical measures for its replacement. He might reply that it is not regrettable to lack a large scheme for organizing mankind. However, it is naive, or disingenuous, to presume that science and democracy are neutral and unaggressive ideas, which, in genial tandem, will avoid the horrors visited on humanity by unproven and unprovable certitudes such as Marxism.

Popper wants politicians to be more like scientists:

Scientific method in politics means that the great art of convincing ourselves that we have not made any mistakes, of ignoring them, of hiding them, and of blaming others for them, is replaced by the greater art of accepting the responsibility for them ... and of applying this knowledge so that we may avoid them in the future.[Op. cit., p. 88]

But was it not almost exactly with this argument, and for the same reasons, that Plato proposed the replacement of democratic crowd-pleasers, grubbing for votes, with philosopher-kings whose immunity to election would allow them to transcend vulgar expedients and so create an Ideal State? Lenin's autocracy rolled along similar lines. The incapacity of actual tyrants (such as Plato's Syracusan protégé, Dionysius II) to measure up to expectations has never deterred advocates of the closed society from arguing the theoretical benefits of communities dominated by better or more enlightened tyrants or philosopher-kings. If Plato's ideas are to be rejected for their impracticality, why should we embrace the idea of a scientific democracy, which appears little more feasible, except on the grounds that it may be morally more amiable?

Popper's answer might be that democratic institutions can and often do, in fact, enable society to detect errors. By voting them out of power, it has bloodless means of sanctioning those responsible for mistakes. When businessmen make bad decisions, their balance sheets turn red; when they make catastrophic ones, their companies may be liquidated. This is painful for them, but endurable (even perhaps salutary, marketeers will argue) for the economy at large. But when centrally planned economies go grievously wrong, the entire society is traumatized. The failures of governments and companies in democratic societies suggest that the policies they have followed have been, in some metaphorical sense at least, refuted. Thus we may not be so far from a 'scientific' community as pessimists believe.

Popper claims that modesty of scale is part of any sound scientific method:

> it must be nearly impossible for us to persist in a critical attitude towards those of our actions which involve the lives of many men. To put it differently, it is very hard to learn from very big mistakes.
>
> [Op. cit., p. 88]

If we have had enough of macro-ideologies, the world remains in need of an *attitude*, if not of a scheme, for the betterment of mankind. Popper argues that

> a *systematic fight* against *definite wrongs*, against *concrete forms of injustice or exploitation, and avoidable suffering such as poverty or*

unemployment, is a very different thing from the attempt to realize a
distant ideal blueprint of society.   [Op. cit., p. 91]

The italics are again mine. They emphasize the temptation to pass off
measures of which Popper approves as 'piecemeal', and hence feasible,
while maintaining that communists, holists and Utopianists are alike in
baying for the moon. The notion that the terms emphasized are either
easy of definition ('wrongs', for instance) or susceptible of piecemeal
treatment deserves, but does not get, the rigorous self-scrutiny of which
Popper was such an advocate. If piecemeal engineering ever had or ever
could be the instrument of a 'systematic fight', there would be no need
whatever for the holistic, Utopian schemes (or systematic fights) against
which Popper so righteously, and rightly, protested when the wrong
people were to be in charge.

Where Popper proves most convincing is in refusing to accept the
theoretical distinction between (refutable) scientific claims and the
historicist's claim to have knowledge – by infallible intuition – of the laws
of historical change. Such a distinction, if it were not false, would
discriminate in favour of historicists. But it is false.

> In the natural sciences . . . we can never be quite certain whether our
> laws are really universally valid . . . [but] we do not add in our
> formulation of natural laws a condition saying that they are asserted
> only for the period for which they have been observed to hold . . .
>
> If we were to admit laws that are themselves subject to change,
> change could never be explained by laws. *It would be the admission
> that change is simply miraculous. And it would be the end of scientific
> progress: for if unexpected observations were made, there would be no
> need to revise our theories: the ad hoc hypothesis that the laws have
> changed would 'explain' everything.*
>
> *These arguments hold for the social sciences no less than for the
> natural sciences.*   [Op. cit., pp. 102, 103]

Again the italics are mine. They emphasize a point on which Popper is
unflinching and, it seems to me, unarguably correct. There can, he
concedes, be a historicist hypothesis which holds that the task of the
social sciences is to 'lay bare the *law of evolution of society* in order to
foretell its future . . . the so-called "natural laws of succession", if only
because there can be a *hypothesis* of almost any kind'. The historicist
claim is said to be a concoction of astronomy, Darwin and millennarian
religious and metaphysical beliefs.

This [evolutionary] hypothesis is not a universal law ... It has, rather, the character of a particular (singular or specific) historical statement ... the fact that all laws of nature are hypotheses must not distract our attention from the fact that not all hypotheses are laws.

But can there be a *law* of evolution ... in the sense intended by T. H. Huxley when he wrote: '... he must be a half-hearted philosopher who ... doubts that science will sooner or later ... become possessed of the law of evolution of organic forms – of the unvarying order of that great chain of causes and effects of which all organic forms, ancient and modern, are the links ...'[?] I believe that the answer to this question must be 'No', and that the search for the law of the 'unvarying order' in evolution cannot possibly fall within the scope of scientific method, whether in biology or in sociology ... Such a process ... proceeds in accordance with all kinds of causal laws, for example, the laws of mechanics, of chemistry, of heredity and segregation, of natural selection, etc. Its description, however, is not a law, but only a singular historical statement ...   [Op. cit., pp. 106, 107, 108]

We have ... no valid reason to expect of any apparent repetition of a historical development that it will *continue* to run parallel to its prototype. Admittedly, once we believe in a law of repetitive life-cycles [cf. Vico, Spengler, Toynbee, etc.] – a belief ... perhaps inherited from Plato – we are sure to discover historical confirmation of it nearly everywhere. But this is merely one of the many instances of metaphysical theories seemingly confirmed by facts – facts which, if examined more closely, turn out to be selected in the light of the very theories they are supposed to test ...

Of nearly every theory it may be said that it agrees with many facts: this is one of the reasons why a theory can be said to be corroborated only if we are unable to find refuting facts, rather than if we are able to find supporting facts.   [Op. cit., p. 111 and note]

Here Popper is at his most characteristic and persuasive. He also reveals very clearly why the logical positivists of his youth found him congenial: his attitude to 'metaphysics' is here as dismissive as theirs. (It is not inconsistent with finding 'some' merit in metaphysics as a speculative preliminary to scientific validation or literary insight.) What matters here is the inflexible rule that 'trends are not laws'. The logic of the 'laws of history' is not a scientific logic, but it seeks to draw credibility through the scientistic pretence that it is.

Although we may assume that any actual succession of phenomena proceeds according to the laws of nature, it is important to realize that practically *no sequence of, say, three or more causally connected concrete events proceeds according to any single law of nature* . . . The idea that any concrete sequence or succession of events (apart from such examples as the movement of a pendulum or a solar system) can be described or explained by any one law, or by any one definite set of laws, is simply mistaken. There are neither laws of succession, nor laws of evolution . . .

   That [John Stuart] Mill should seriously discuss the question whether 'the phenomena of human society' revolve 'in an orbit' or whether they move, progressively, in a 'trajectory' is in keeping with this fundamental confusion between laws and trends, as well as with the holistic idea that society can 'move' as a whole – say, like a planet.

[Op. cit., pp. 117, 118, 119]

Popper pays steady tribute to Mill, as he does to Auguste Comte, the founder of positivism, for their contributions to the methodology of science. What he challenges, implacably, is a kind of enthusiasm that extends the kudos of science to various kinds of crystal-ball gazing and seems to warrant its visions. It is no accident that the result, almost inevitably, is either a kind of callous resignation, in the face of unstoppable history, or a doctrine of heartless collaboration with the inhumanity of forces that we are powerless to control or avoid.

This . . . is the central mistake of historicism . . . *its 'laws of development' turn out to be absolute trends*; trends which, like laws, do not depend on initial conditions, and which carry us irresistibly in a certain direction into the future. They are the basis of unconditional *prophecies*, as opposed to conditional scientific *predictions* . . .

   . . . we have all the time to try to imagine conditions under which the trend in question would disappear. But this is just what the historicist cannot do . . . The poverty of historicism . . . is a poverty of imagination. The historicist continuously upbraids those who cannot imagine a change in their little worlds; yet it seems that the historicist is himself deficient in imagination, for he cannot imagine a change in the conditions of change.   [Op. cit., pp. 128, 129, 130]

   . . . if we are uncritical we shall always find what we want: we shall look for, and find, confirmations, and we shall look away from, and not see, whatever might be dangerous to our pet theories. In this way it is only too easy to obtain what appears to be overwhelming evidence in favour of a theory which, if approached critically, would have been refuted. In order to make the method of selection by elimination work, and to ensure that only the fittest theories survive, their struggle for life must be made severe for them.   [Op. cit., p. 134]

Popper's furious hostility to bogus 'scientific' arguments on grand lines does not leave him blind to a certain need for sociological attention to larger issues. There is, he suggests,

room for a more detailed analysis of the *logic of situations* . . . We need studies based on methodological individualism . . . of the way in which new traditions may be created . . . our individualistic and institutional-ist models of such collective entities as nations, or governments, or markets, will have to be supplemented by models of political situations as well as of social movements such as scientific and industrial progress . . .   [Op. cit., p. 149]

It is possible, for example, to interpret 'history' as the history of class struggle . . . or as the history of the struggle between the 'open' and the 'closed' society, or as the history of scientific and industrial progress. All of these are more or less interesting points of view, and *as such* perfectly unobjectionable. But historicists do not present them as such; they do not see that there is necessarily a plurality of interpretations which are fundamentally on the same level of both, suggestiveness and arbitrariness (even though some of them may be distinguished by their *fertility* . . .). Instead, [historicists] present them as doctrines or theo-ries . . . And if they actually find that their point of view is fertile, and that many facts can be ordered and interpreted in its light, then they mistake this for a confirmation, or even for a proof, of their doctrine.

On the other hand, . . . classical historians . . . [aiming] at objectivity . . . feel bound to avoid any selective point of view; but since this is impossible, they usually adopt points of view without being aware of them. This must defeat their efforts to be objective, for one cannot possibly be critical of one's own point of view, and conscious of its limitations, without being aware of it.

The way out of this dilemma, of course, is to be clear about the necessity of adopting a point of view; to state this point of view plainly, and always to remain conscious that it is one among many, and that even if it should amount to a theory, it may not be testable.

[Op. cit., pp. 151, 152]

Somewhere behind Popper's allegiance to science (and thus to reason) there lurks an acknowledgement that it is *possible* that certain theories, even of ultimate destinations for man, might *turn out to be true* eventually. We may even all finally be hailed before God's judgement seat.

But it remains unjustifiable, not to say immoral, to impose unproved truths – and their social consequences – in terms of class or exclusion, on humanity now, on the grounds that they may be proved valid in some inaccessible future. Since what will be known then cannot logically be known *now*, those who affect to pierce the veils of time and report what the future must hold are charlatans today, *even if they turn out to have been clairvoyants, come some distant tomorrow*. No doubt, there are those who would say that Chartres Cathedral, for instance, was a consequence of a scientifically unprovable doctrine. Indeed, myth has been, in many cultures, the unquestionable foundation of both art and literature. This objection has its force, which can be turned away, at least partially, by saying that theories of divine or metaphysical truth, of the kind that sponsored religious art and architecture, cannot be protected artificially against scientific criteria that were inapplicable when they came into being. Popper always conceded that the primacy of reason in human affairs was a matter of decision, not of natural necessity. Hence we must choose (if we can) whether or not we want to be ruled by creeds and credulities whose advocates have usually relied more on coercion than on choice.

Popper's scepticism is both methodological and humane. He is an indeterminist who is determined to accept no argument that our fate is not only fixed (which in some trivial sense it is, since what will be will be), but also predictable. Progress, he insists, is no more inevitable than decline and fall, even if we take all available steps to assist science in improving life:

> we cannot exclude the logical possibility, say, of a bacterium or virus that spreads a wish for Nirvana . . . ultimately, much depends on sheer luck . . . For truth is *not manifest*, and it is a mistake to believe – as did Comte and Mill – that once the 'obstacles' (the allusion is to the Church) are removed, truth will be visible to all who genuinely want to see it.
>
> . . . the human factor is *the* ultimately uncertain and wayward element in social life and in all social institutions. Indeed this is the element which ultimately *cannot* be completely controlled by institutions (as Spinoza first saw); for every attempt at controlling it completely must lead to tyranny; which means, to the omnipotence of the human factor – the whims of a few men, or even of one.
>
> [Op. cit., p. 157, 158]

But is it not possible to control the human factor by *science* – the opposite of whim? No, because that will interfere with the diversity of individuals . . .

Even the emotionally satisfying appeal for a *common purpose*, however excellent, is an appeal to abandon all rival moral opinions and the cross-criticisms and arguments to which they give rise. It is an appeal to abandon rational thought.

. . . The mainspring of evolution and progress is the variety of the material which may become subject to selection. As far as human evolution is concerned it [viz. the mainspring] is the 'freedom to be odd and unlike one's neighbour' . . . 'to disagree with the majority, and go one's own way'. Holistic control, which must lead to the equalization not of human rights but of human minds, would mean the end of progress.   [Op. cit., p. 159]

Progress is not a certainty, but a prospect. Reason is not part of human nature, but a choice which, alone, can encourage (and *construct*) tolerance and the rule of law. As the Nazis demonstrated, man can always draw his gun and put an end to arguments, or (if the weapon is large enough) to mankind. Nothing guarantees us a happy future or a wise choice, even where we choose freely and rationally. Individuality is necessary for diversity, as are well-manned institutions for the storage and testing of the theories that individuals propose. We can neither escape the unevenness of chance nor be sure how the unloaded dice will roll. Popper sees the good news and the bad news as almost indistinguishable; man can only do so much and yet there is no set limit to what he may do. He argues for foresight against prophecy and for small steps on reliable grounds rather than for a hectic faith in pie in the sky.

It could, however, be said that Popper's datedness is made manifest by the fact that he seems to rely on the machinery of democracy now in place, in civilized society, for further improvements in the human condition. What well-manned institutions, other than the governments of nation-states, are going to be able to inaugurate schemes of piecemeal engineering grand enough to deal with global pollution, genocidal oppression of minorities and pandemics such as AIDS?

The assumption that prevailing structures could deal with curable difficulties such as poverty and unemployment was naive even in Popper's day. How can global corporations, with their overriding influence, now be controlled by nation-state legislatures (or supernational congeries of ministers responsible to national electorates)? In a state of affairs where multinational conglomerates can afford to be indifferent to local laws and enrol corrupt governments to their service, existing institutions – whether or not they call themselves democratic – seem inadequate. Global corporations render piecemeal measures effective only against companies and individuals who lack the stamina and clout for economic survival.

How, if at all, are major corporations, with transnational funds and managements, to be controlled by democratic authorities whose writs run only to their frontiers? A host of organizational questions of this sort confronts mankind in the coming millennium.

Popper's answer might be that we have no better choice than to arm ourselves with reason, to avoid fatalism and to try to make things less bad. If his advertisements for tolerance and patient effort were sometimes mocked by his personal style, it never disgraced them. Where he was right, he was magisterial; where he was wrong, he was – as in theory he might have wished – fallible.

Andrew Hodges

TURING

A Natural Philosopher

INTRODUCTION

Alan Turing dared to ask whether a machine could think. His contributions to understanding and answering this and other questions defy conventional classification. At the close of the twentieth century, the 1936 concept of the Turing machine appears not only in mathematics and computer science, but in cognitive science and theoretical biology. His 1950 paper 'Computing machinery and intelligence', describing the so-called Turing test, is a cornerstone of the theory of artificial intelligence. In between, Turing played a vital role in the outcome of the Second World War, and produced single-handedly a far-sighted plan for the construction and use of an electronic computer. He thought and lived a generation ahead of his time, and yet the features of his thought that burst the boundaries of the 1940s are better described by the antique words: *natural philosophy*.

Alan Turing's immersion in and attack upon Nature was a unity; divisions between mathematics, science, technology and philosophy in his work have tended to obscure his ideas. He was not a prolific author; much remained unpublished in his lifetime; some remained secret into the 1990s. Private communications shed a little more light on the development of his thought, a subject on which he was generally silent. We shall see, for instance, how he came to logic and computation from a youthful fascination with the physical description of mind. But we have only hints as to the formation of his convictions amidst the secrecy of wartime cryptanalysis, and suggestions of fresh ideas are lost in the drama of his mysterious death.

THE NATURE OF TURING'S WORLD

Alan Mathison Turing was born in London on 23 June 1912, and from the beginning showed a personality out of place in the upper-middle-class schooling undergone by sons of Indian Civil Service officers. Conformity to class meant unquestioning obedience to the rituals of the British preparatory and public school. But the book *Natural Wonders Every Child Should Know* opened his eyes to the concept of scientific explanation, and from then on Nature as opposed to human convention commanded his attention, as many nagging reports demonstrated. Duty, hierarchy, masters, servants, rules and games would later play a striking role in the illustration of his ideas; but while at school he was more baffled and incompetent than rebellious at the demands of the British empire, ignoring as much as possible while pursuing his own priorities. In 1925 he wrote to his mother: 'I am making a collection of experiments in the order I mean to do them in. I always seem to want to make things from the thing that is commonest in nature and with the least waste in energy.'[1]

His experimental chemistry incurred displeasure, as did poor handwriting and unconventional methods in his mathematics. He was bottom of the form in English. The headmaster wrote, 'If he is to stay at a Public School, he must aim at becoming *educated*. If he is to be solely a Scientific Specialist, he is wasting his time at a Public School' and this judgment on British ruling-class priorities was almost correct. Turing was nearly prevented from taking the equivalent of GCSEs. Thereafter, he found his level in Einstein's own exposition of relativity and Eddington's view of quantum mechanics in *The Nature of the Physical World*. But this was isolated private study, and he might never have felt the urge to communicate but for an impossibly romantic story.

Human nature brought him to life; but it was his own homosexual nature, bringing revelation and trauma in equal measure. He fell in unrequited love with Christopher Morcom, a very talented youth in the school sixth form, and his longing for friendship brought him to communicate. A brief flowering of scientific collaboration perished when Morcom suddenly died in February 1930. Turing's correspondence with the dead boy's mother gives insight into the development of his ideas in the aftermath. He was concerned to believe the dead boy could still exist in spirit, and to reconcile such a belief with science. To this end he wrote for Mrs Morcom an essay, probably in 1932. It is the private writing of a twenty-year-old, and must be read as testament to background and not as a thesis upheld in public; nevertheless it is a key to Turing's future development.

Nature of Spirit

It used to be supposed in Science that if everything was known about the Universe at any particular moment then we can predict what it will be through all the future . . . More modern science however has come to the conclusion that when we are dealing with atoms and electrons we are quite unable to know the exact state of them; our instruments being made of atoms and electrons themselves. The conception then of being able to know the exact state of the universe then must really break down on the small scale. This means that the theory which held that as eclipses etc. are predestined so were all our actions breaks down too. We have a will which is able to determine the action of the atoms probably in a small portion of the brain, or possibly all over it. The rest of the body acts so as to amplify this . . . [2]

In stating the classic paradox of physical determinism and free will, Turing is influenced by Eddington's assertion that quantum mechanical physics ('more modern science') yields room for human will. Eddington asked how could 'this collection of ordinary atoms be a thinking machine?' and Turing tries to find some answer. His essay goes on to espouse belief in a spirit unconstrained by the body: 'when the body dies the "mechanism" of the body, holding the spirit is gone and the spirit finds a new body sooner or later perhaps immediately.' Letters show he retained such ideas at least until 1933.

Turing was much more successful in undergraduate work than at school, and King's College lent him a protective ambience sympathetic to homosexuality and unconventional opinion. He was not, however, one of its élite social circle, nor in a political group. Politically, he responded briefly to the 1933 anti-war movement, but not to the Communist party as others of his close acquaintance did. Nor did Turing share the pacifism of his first lover, fellow mathematics student James Atkins.

In a similar way Turing found a home in Cambridge mathematical culture, yet did not belong entirely to it. The division between 'pure' and 'applied' mathematics was at Cambridge then as now very strong, but Turing ignored it, and he never showed mathematical parochialism. If anything, it was the attitude of a Russell that he acquired, assuming that mastery of so difficult a subject granted the right to invade others. Turing showed little intellectual diffidence once in his stride: in March 1933 he acquired Russell's *Introduction to Mathematical Philosophy*, and on 1 December 1933, the philosopher R. B. Braithwaite minuted in the Moral Science Club records: 'A. M. Turing read a paper on "Mathematics and logic". He suggested that a purely logistic view of mathematics was inadequate; and that mathematical propositions possessed a variety of interpretations, of which the logistic was merely one.' At the same time he was studying von Neumann's 1932 *Grundlagen den Quantenmechanik*. Thus, it may be that Eddington's claims for quantum mechanics had encouraged the shift of Turing's interest towards logical foundations. And it was logic that made Alan Turing's name.

THE TURING MACHINE AND THE
ENTSCHEIDUNGSPROBLEM

Then, in the spring of 1935, Turing attended the advanced lectures on the
Foundations of Mathematics given by the Cambridge topologist
M. H. A. Newman, he was not making a career move. Mathematical
logic was a small, abstruse, technically difficult area devoid of applications, and unrepresented in the undergraduate curriculum. Turing's work
was a labour of love.

Newman's lectures brought Turing to the point reached by Gödel in his
now-famous 1931 Incompleteness theorem. The underlying problem here
addressed is how we can grasp the truth of a statement about *infinitely
many* instances: such as that for all, a, b, c, (a+b)×c = a×c + b×c, or that
there is no largest prime number. An apparently reasonable response
might be that statements such as these do not in fact involve infinitely
many instances at all, but are only finite sentences with words like 'all' in
them, deduced by finitely many rules of deductive logic. Mathematical
logicians in the late nineteenth century had tried to make this argument
explicit, but Bertrand Russell, showing how finite descriptions like 'set of
all sets' could be self-contradictory, had discovered the unavoidable
difficulties that arose through *self-referential* terms. Since then the
mathematician David Hilbert had made more precise demands of any
proposed finite scheme in the famous terms: consistency, completeness
and decidability. In 1931 Gödel had shown that consistency and
completeness could not both be attained: there were statements about
numbers, indubitably true, which could not be proved from finite axioms
by finitely many rules. Gödel's proof rested on the idea that statements
about numbers could be coded *as* numbers, and constructing a self-
referential statement to defeat Hilbert's hopes.

Gödel's work left outstanding Hilbert's question of *decidability*, the
Entscheidungsproblem, namely the question of whether there exists a
definite method which, at least in principle, can be applied to a given
proposition to decide whether that proposition is provable. In a restricted
calculus there may indeed be such a method: for example, the truth-table
technique for deciding whether a formula in elementary propositional
logic is a tautology. Could there be such a decision procedure for
mathematical propositions? This question had survived Gödel's analysis
because its settlement required a precise and convincing definition of
method. Giving precise definitions is the meat and drink of pure
mathematics, but in this case, something more than precision was called
for – it had to be something unassailable in its generality, which would

not be superseded by a more powerful class of methods. There had, in fact, to be some philosophical as well as some mathematical analysis.

This, working by himself for the year until April 1936, Turing achieved; his idea, now known as the *Turing machine*, was to be published at the very end of 1936 in a paper 'On computable numbers, with an application to the *Entscheidungsproblem*.'[3] It is characteristic of Turing that he refreshed Hilbert's question by casting it in terms not of proofs, but of computing *numbers*. The reformulation staked a clearer claim to have found an idea central to mathematics. As his title said, the *Entscheidungsproblem* was only an application of a new idea, that of computability. There are no surviving drafts or correspondence relating to its formation; no later accounts of his intellectual journey; just the story he told to his later student Robin Gandy that he had the main idea while lying in Grantchester meadows. Newman only saw the work when it was fully formed.

His paper starts with the line of thought already mentioned: how can we specify the infinite in finite terms? In particular, how can we specify the infinite sequence of digits in a 'real number', such as $\pi = 3.141592653\ldots$? What does it mean to say that there is a definite method for calculating such a number? Turing's answer lies in defining the concept of the Turing machine.

> We may compare a man in the process of computing a real number to a machine which is only capable of a finite number of conditions ... which will be called '*m*-configurations'. The machine is supplied with a 'tape' (the analogue of paper) running through it, and divided into sections (called 'squares') each capable of bearing a 'symbol'. At any moment there is just one square ... which is 'in the machine'. We may call this square the 'scanned square'. The symbol on the scanned square may be called the 'scanned symbol'. The 'scanned symbol' is the only one of which the machine is, so to speak, 'directly aware' ...

Turing then specifies precisely the repertoire of action available to the imagined machine. The action is totally determined by the 'configuration' it is in, and the symbol it is currently scanning. It is this complete determination that makes it 'a machine'. The action is limited to the following: at each step it (1) either erases the symbol or prints a specified symbol; (2) moves one square either to left or right; (3) changes to a new configuration.

Slightly different versions of Turing's idea are given in different textbooks, and the precise technical form he originally gave is not important; the essence is that the action is completely given by what

Turing calls a 'table of behaviour' for the machine, dictating what it will do for every configuration and every symbol scanned. Each 'table of behaviour' is a different Turing machine.

The actions are highly restricted in form, but Turing's thesis is that they form a set of atomic elements out of which all mathematical operations can be composed. In fact, in a style most unusual for a mathematical paper, argument is given in very general terms, justifying the Turing machine actions as sufficient to encompass the most general possible method:

> Computing is normally done by writing certain symbols on paper. We may suppose this paper is divided into squares like a child's arithmetic book. In elementary arithmetic the two-dimensional character of the paper is sometimes used. But such a use is always avoidable, and I think that it will be agreed that the two-dimensional character of paper is no essential of computation. I assume then that the computation is carried out on one-dimensional paper, *i.e.* on a tape divided into squares. I shall also suppose that the number of symbols which may be printed is finite. If we were to allow an infinity of symbols, then there would be symbols differing to an arbitrarily small extent. [A footnote gives a topological argument for this.] The effect of this restriction of the number of symbols is not very serious. It is always possible to use sequences of symbols in the place of single symbols ... This is in accordance with experience. We cannot tell at a glance whether 9999999999999999 and *999999999999999* are the same.

Turing thus claims that a finite repertoire of symbols actually allows a countable infinity of symbols, but not an infinity of *immediately recognisable* symbols. Note that the tape also has to be of unlimited length, although at any time the number of symbols on it is finite. In the next paragraph note that the word 'computer' then meant a *person* doing computing. Turing's model is that of a *human mind* at work.

> The behaviour of the computer at any moment is determined by the symbols which he is observing, and his 'state of mind' at that moment. We may suppose that there is a bound B to the number of symbols or squares which the computer can observe at one moment. If he wishes to observe more, he must use successive observations. We will also suppose that the number of states of mind which need to be taken into account is finite. The reasons for this are of the same character as those which restrict the number of symbols. If we admitted an infinity of states of mind, some of them will be 'arbitrarily close' and will be

confused. Again, the restriction is not one which seriously affects computation, since the use of more complicated states of mind can be avoided by writing more symbols on the tape.

Let us imagine the operations performed by the computer to be split up into 'simple operations' which are so elementary that it is not easy to imagine them further divided. Every such operation consists of some change of the physical system consisting of the computer and his tape. We know the state of the system if we know the sequence of symbols on the tape, which of these are observed by the computer (possibly with a special order), and the state of mind of the computer. We may suppose that in a simple operation not more than one symbol is altered. Any other changes can be split up into simple changes of this kind. The situation in regard to the squares whose symbols may be altered in this way is the same as in regard to the observed squares. We may, therefore, without loss of generality, assume that the squares whose symbols are changed are always 'observed' squares.

Besides these changes of symbols, the simple operations must include changes of distribution of observed squares. The new observed squares must be immediately recognisable by the computer. I think it is reasonable to suppose that they can only be squares whose distance from the closest of the immediately previously observed squares does not exceed a certain fixed amount. Let us say that each of the new observed squares is within L squares of an immediately previously observed square.

In connection with 'immediate recognisability', it may be thought that there are other kinds of square which are immediately recognisable. In particular, squares marked by special symbols might be taken as immediately recognisable. Now if these squares are marked only by single symbols there can be only a finite number of them, and we should not upset our theory by adjoining these marked squares to the observed squares. If, however, they are marked by a sequence of symbols, we cannot regard the process of recognition as a simple process. This is a fundamental point and should be illustrated. In most mathematical papers the equations and theorems are numbered. Normally the numbers do not go beyond (say) 1000. It is, therefore, possible to recognise a theorem at a glance by its number. But if the paper was very long, we might reach Theorem 157767733443477; then, further on in the paper, we might find '. . . hence (applying Theorem 157767733443477) we have . . .'. In order to make sure which was the relevant theorem we should have to compare the two numbers figure by figure . . .

The simple operations must therefore include:

(a) Changes of the symbol on one of the observed squares.

(b) Changes of one of the squares observed to another square within L squares of one of the previously observed squares.

It may be that some of these changes necessarily involve a change of state of mind. The most general single operation must therefore be taken to be one of the following:

(A) A possible change (a) of symbol together with a possible change of state of mind.

(B) A possible change (b) of observed squares, together with a possible change of state of mind.

The operation actually performed is determined, as has been suggested [above], by the state of mind of the computer and the observed symbols. In particular, they determine the state of mind of the computer after the operation is carried out.

Turing now continues, 'We may now construct a machine to do the work of this computer' – that is, specify a Turing machine to do the work of this human calculator. Note, for its later significance, that Turing does not here raise the question of whether the mind is capable of actions which can *not* be described as computations.

Turing was very bold and untypical of mathematicians in placing this analysis of mental activity at the forefront. He added a less contentious argument:

> . . . we avoid introducing the 'state of mind' by considering a more physical and definite counterpart of it. It is always possible for the computer to break off from his work, to go away and forget all about it, and later to come back and go on with it. If he does this he must leave a note of instructions (written in some standard form) explaining how the work is to be continued. This note is the counterpart of the 'state of mind'. We will suppose that the computer works in such a desultory manner that he never does more than one step at a sitting. The note of instructions must enable him to carry out one step and write the next note. Thus the state of progress of the computation at any one stage is completely determined by the note of instructions and the symbols on the tape . . .

But note that this calls for the method to be *consciously known in every detail*, whereas the 'state of mind' argument could be held to apply to a person who can reliably perform a process without being able to describe it explicitly.

The *computable numbers* are then defined as those infinite decimals which can be printed by a Turing machine starting with a blank tape. He sketches a proof that π is a computable number, along with every real number defined by the ordinary methods of equation and limits in mathematical work. But armed with this new definition, it is now easy to show that *uncomputable* numbers exist. The crucial point is that the table of behaviour of any Turing machine is *finite*. Hence, all the possible tables of behaviour can be listed in an alphabetical order: this shows that the computable numbers are countable. Since the real numbers are uncountable, it follows that *almost all* of them are uncomputable. We can refine this idea to exhibit a particular uncomputable number. Before showing the construction, a point has to be noted: a table of behaviour may have the property of running in a loop and never producing more than a finite number of digits.

With this in mind, we again place all Turing machines in an alphabetical order of their tables in behaviour. We discard those which fail to produce an infinite series of digits, leaving only the Turing machines which produce infinite strings of digits – the computable numbers. Let us suppose that binary notation is being used, so that the digits are either 0 or 1. Now define a new number so that its *n*th digit is different from the *n*th digit produced by the *n*th machine. This new number differs in at least one place from every computable number; therefore it cannot be computable.

As Turing explains, this seems to be a paradox. If it can be described finitely, why can it not be computed? Inspection shows that the problem comes in identifying those Turing machines which fail to produce infinitely many digits. This is *not* a computable operation: that is, there is no Turing machine which can inspect the table of any other machine and decide whether it will produce infinitely many digits or not. This can be seen more directly: if there *were* such a machine, it could be applied to itself, and this idea can be used to get a contradiction. Nowadays this is known as the fact that the *halting problem* cannot be decided by a Turing machine. From this discovery of a problem that cannot be decided by a machine, it is not a difficult step to employ the formal calculus of mathematical logic, and to answer Hilbert's *Entscheidungsproblem* in the negative.

A point which Turing stressed, however, is that there is no inconsistency involved in *defining* uncomputable numbers; in modern computability theory they are the subject of rigorous manipulation and logical argument. It may even be that every digit of an uncomputable number may be calculated; the point is, however, that infinitely many different methods are required to work them out. Nevertheless the property of computability rests on mathematical bedrock: this was Turing's claim at the time and it has never since been challenged.

CHURCH'S THESIS AND TURING'S THESIS

This was a triumph for anyone, let alone an isolated graduate of twenty-three, but Turing suffered an immediate setback in a tiresomely classic case of scientific coincidence. Before he had submitted his paper, Alonzo Church, the pre-eminent American logician at Princeton, announced the same conclusion regarding the *Entscheidungsproblem*. Turing took the time until August 1936 to write an appendix relating his result to Church's. For publication by the London Mathematical Society, Newman had to make a case that Turing's argument was different from that produced by Church. In fact Turing's argument differed from Church's in a fundamental way. When the dust had settled, in 1938, he gave his own view in the self-effacing terms that in public he always used of his own work:

> A function is said to be 'effectively calculable' if its values can be found by some purely mechanical process. Although it is fairly easy to get an intuitive grasp of this idea, it is nevertheless desirable to have some more definite, mathematically expressible definition. Such a definition was first given by Gödel at Princeton in 1934 . . . These functions were described as 'general recursive' by Gödel . . . Another definition of effective calculability has been given by Church . . . who identifies it with λ-definability. The author [i.e. Turing himself] has recently suggested a definition corresponding more closely to the intuitive idea . . . It was stated above that 'a function is effectively calculable if its values can be found by some purely mechanical process.' We may take this statement literally, understanding by a purely mechanical process one which could be carried out by a machine . . . The development of these ideas leads to the author's definition of a computable function, and to an identification of computability [in Turing's precise technical sense] with effective calculability. It is not difficult, though somewhat laborious, to prove that these three definitions are equivalent.[4]

Turing here gives a view on what is now known and famous as *Church's thesis*. Although Church's thesis is nowadays given various other interpretations, in 1936 it was the claim that effective calculability could be identified with the operations of Church's very elegant and surprising formalism, that of the *lambda-calculus*. As such it lay *within* the world of mathematical formalism. But Turing offers a reason *why Church's thesis should be true*, drawing on ideas *external* to mathematics such as that one cannot do see or choose between more than a finite number of things at one time. Church's thesis is now sometimes called the Church-Turing thesis, but the Turing thesis is different, bringing the physical world into the picture with a claim of what can be done. It should not go without mention that Turing after referring to his machine definition of computability, also cited the work of the Polish-American logician Emil Post, which had also brought an idea of physical action into computation. However Post had not developed his ideas so fully.

THE UNIVERSAL TURING MACHINE

Since the modern digital *computer* is now so important to the exploration of Turing's ideas, a digression is called for to explain its relationship to this paper. It is a startling fact that 'On computable numbers' not only solved a major outstanding question posed by Hilbert, opened the new mathematical field of computability, and offered a new analysis of mental activity, but had a practical implication: it laid out the principle of the computer through the concept of the universal Turing machine.

The idea of the universal machine is easily indicated. Once the specification of any Turing machine is given as a table of behaviour, tracing the operation of that machine becomes a mechanical matter of looking up entries in the table. Because it is mechanical, a Turing machine can do it: that is, a single Turing machine may be designed to have the property that, when supplied with the table of behaviour of another Turing machine, it will do what that other Turing machine would have done. Turing called such a machine the universal machine. A technical problem arises in encoding the table in a linear form for the 'tape' and arranging working space, but these are details.

Turing introduced the universal machine as a tool in the argument described above for exhibiting an uncomputable number. As such it was not necessary to his conclusion regarding the *Entscheidungsproblem*. But Turing made the very striking concept prominent in his paper, and according to Newman's later statement, was inspired *even then* to consider practical construction. It is the universal machine which gives Turing the claim to have invented the principle of the computer – and not merely in abstract principle, as we shall see. And nowadays it is impossible to study Turing machines without thinking of them as computer programs, with the universal machine as the computer on which the programs are run. It is not difficult to turn a 'table of behaviour' into the explicit form of a modern program, in which each 'configuration' becomes a numbered instruction, containing IF conditions which dictate a writing action and the number of the next instruction.

Some care is needed here with terminology. The phrase 'the Turing machine' is analogous to 'the printed book' in referring to a class of potentially infinitely many examples. Within this class, certain Turing machines are 'universal', having sufficient complexity to interpret and execute the table of behaviour of any other Turing machine. Again, although we speak of 'the' universal Turing machine, there are infinitely many designs with this property.

Turing's own work in constructing tables of behaviour must have put him in the mind of a programmer; all the more so as Turing used abbreviated notation which amounts to defining subroutines. The mind of the programmer cannot be said to originate with Turing's paper; the axiomatic programme, and Gödel's ingenious methods, had already given rise to this way of thinking. But in Turing's work the idea is formalised in the language of instruction, to a degree that it is hard to believe that the computer was not already in existence. Yet the point should be emphasised: Turing was *not* considering the computing machines of his day. He was modelling the action of human minds. The physical machines would come ten years later.

THINKING THE UNCOMPUTABLE

Turing then studied at Princeton for two academic years, with a break back at Cambridge in summer 1937. It was a period of intense activity at a world centre of mathematics. Turing was over-optimistic in thinking he could rewrite the foundations of analysis, and added nothing to the remarks about limits and convergence given in 'Computable numbers'. (One reason for this might be the following: if x and y are computable numbers, as specified as Turing machines, the truth of the statements $x = y$, or $x = 0$ cannot tested by a computable process.) But besides wide-ranging research in analysis, topology and algebra, and the 'laborious' work of showing the equivalence of his definition of computability to those of Church and Gödel, he extended the exploration of the logic of mental activity with a paper 'Systems of logic based on ordinals'.[5]

This, his most difficult paper, is much less well known than his definition of computability. It is generally regarded as a diversion from his line of thought on computability, computers and the philosophy of mind, and I fell into this assumption in *Alan Turing: the Enigma* (see Further

Reading), essentially because I followed Turing's own later standpoint. But I now consider that *at the time*, Turing saw himself steaming straight ahead with the analysis of the mind, by studying a question complementary to 'On computable numbers'. Turing asked in this paper whether it is possible to formalize those actions of the mind which are *not* those of following a definite method: mental actions one might call creative or original in nature. In particular, Turing focused on the action of seeing the truth of one of Gödel's unprovable assertions.

Gödel had shown that when we see the truth of an unprovable proposition, we cannot be doing so by following given rules. The rules may be augmented so as to bring this particular proposition into their ambit, but then there will be yet another true proposition that is not captured by the new rules of proof, and so on *ad infinitum*. The question arises as to to whether there is some higher type of rule which can organise this process of 'Gödelisation'. An *ordinal logic* is such a rule, based on the theory of *ordinal numbers*, the very rich and subtle theory of different ways in which an infinite number of entities may be placed in sequence. An ordinal logic turns the idea of 'and so on *ad infinitum*' into a precise formulation. Turing wrote that: 'The purpose of introducing ordinal logics is to avoid as far as possible the effects of Gödel's theorem.' The uncomputable could not be made computable, but ordinal logics would bring it into as much order as was possible.

Turing's work, in which he proved important (though somewhat negative) results about such logical schemes, founded a new area of mathematical logic. But the motivation, as he himself stated it, was in mental philosophy. As in 'On computable numbers', he was unafraid of using psychological terms, this time the word 'intuition' appearing for the act of recognising the truth of an unprovable Gödel sentence:

Mathematical reasoning may be regarded rather schematically as combination of two faculties, which we may call *intuition* and *ingenuity*. The activity of the intuition consists in making spontaneous judgments which are not the result of conscious trains of reasoning. These judgments are often but by no means invariably correct (leaving aside the question what is meant by 'correct'). Often it is possible to find some other way of verifying the correctness of an intuitive judgment. We may, for instance, judge that all positive integers are uniquely factorizable into primes; a detailed mathematical argument leads to the same result. This argument will also involve intuitive judgments, but they will be less open to criticism than the original judgment about factorization. I shall not attempt to explain this idea of 'intuition' any more explicitly.

> The exercise of ingenuity in mathematics consists in aiding the intuition through suitable arrangements of propositions, and perhaps geometrical figures or drawings. It is intended that when these are really well arranged the validity of the intuitive steps which are required cannot seriously be doubted.

Turing then explains how the axiomatisation of mathematics was originally intended to eliminate all intuition, but Gödel had shown that to be impossible. The Turing machine construction had shown how to make all formal proofs 'mechanical'; and in the present paper such mechanical operations were to be taken as trivial, instead putting under the microscope the non-mechanical steps which remained.

> In consequence of the impossibility of finding a formal logic which wholly eliminates the necessity of using intuition, we naturally turn to 'non-constructive' systems of logic with which not all the steps in a proof are mechanical, some being intuitive. An example of a non-constructive logic is afforded by any ordinal logic . . . What properties do we desire a non-constructive logic to have if we are to make use of it for the expression of mathematical proofs? We want it to show quite clearly when a step makes use of intuition, and when it is purely formal. The strain put on the intuition should be a minimum. Most important of all, it must be beyond doubt that the logic leads to correct results whenever the intuitive steps are correct.

It is not clear how literally Turing meant the identification with 'intuition' to be taken. Probably his ideas were fluid, and he added a cautionary footnote: 'We are leaving out of account that most important faculty which distinguishes topics of interest from others; in fact we are regarding the function of the mathematician as simply to determine the truth or falsity of propositions.' But the evidence is that at this time he was open to the idea that in moments of 'intuition' the mind appears to do something outside the scope of the Turing machine. If so, he was not alone: Gödel and Post held this view.

TURING AND WITTGENSTEIN

As it happened, Turing's views were probed by the leading philosopher of the time at just this point. Unfortunately their recorded conversations shed no light upon Turing's view of mind and machine. Turing was introduced to Wittgenstein in summer 1937, and when Turing returned to Cambridge for the autumn term of 1938, he attended Wittgenstein's lectures – more a Socratic discussion group – on the Foundations of Mathematics. These were noted by the participants and have been reconstructed and published.[6] There is a curious similarity of the style of speech – plain speaking and argument by question and answer – but they were on different wavelengths. In a dialogue at the heart of the sequence they debated the significance of axiomatising mathematics and the problems that had arisen in doing so:

> Wittgenstein: . . . Think of the case of the Liar. It is very queer in a way that this should have puzzled anyone – much more extraordinary than you might think . . . Because the thing works like this: if a man says 'I am lying' we say that it follows that he is not lying, from which it follows that he is lying and so on. Well, so what? You can go on like that until you are black in the face. Why not? It doesn't matter. . . . it is just a useless language-game, and why should anybody be excited?
>
> Turing: What puzzles one is that one usually uses a contradiction as a criterion for having done something wrong. But in this case one cannot find anything done wrong.
>
> W: Yes – and more: nothing has been done wrong. . . . where will the harm come?
>
> T: The real harm will not come in unless there is an application, in which a bridge may fall down or something of that sort.
>
> W: . . . The question is: Why are people afraid of contradictions? It is easy to understand why they should be afraid of contradictions, etc., *outside* mathematics. The question is: Why should they be afraid of contradictions inside mathematics? Turing says, 'Because something may go wrong with the application.' But nothing need go wrong. And if something does go wrong – if the bridge breaks down – then your mistake was of the kind of using a wrong natural law . . .
>
> T: You cannot be confident about applying your calculus until you know that there is no hidden contradiction in it.
>
> W: There seems to me an enormous mistake there. . . . Suppose I convince Rhees of the paradox of the Liar, and he says, 'I lie, therefore I do not lie, therefore I lie and I do not lie, therefore we have a contradiction, therefore $2 \times 2 = 369$.' Well, we should not call this 'multiplication', that is all . . .
>
> T: Although you do not know that the bridge will fall if there are no contradictions, yet it is almost certain that if there are contradictions it will go wrong somewhere.
>
> W: But nothing has ever gone wrong that way yet . . .

Turing's responses reflect mainstream mathematical thought and practice, rather than showing his distinctive characteristics and original ideas. In 1938, it should be noted, he was an untenured research fellow whose first application for a lectureship had failed, and whose chance of a conventional career lay in the mathematics studied and taught at Cambridge. His work in logic was but a part of his output, by no means well known. His fellowship was for work in probability theory; his papers were in analysis and algebra. That year, he made a significant step in the analysis of the Riemann zeta-function, a topic in complex analysis and number theory at the heart of classical pure mathematics.

Getting statements free from contradictions is the very essence of mathematics. Turing perhaps thought Wittgenstein did not take seriously enough the unobvious and difficult questions that had arisen in the attempt to formalise mathematics; Wittgenstein thought Turing did not take seriously the question of why one should want to formalize mathematics at all.

There are no letters or notes which indicate subsequent contact between Turing and Wittgenstein, and no evidence that Wittgenstein influenced Turing's concept of machines or mind. If influence in the next ten years is sought, it should be found in the Second World War and Turing's amazing part in it.

TRIUMPH OF THE COMPUTER

It is a feature of Turing's thought, one quite untypical of a Cambridge-based mathematician, that his mathematical interests flowed not only into philosophy, but into practical engineering, and with his own generally clumsy hands. The possibilities of machines had seized his imagination. On 14 October 1936 Turing wrote to his mother that

> You have often asked me about possible applications of various branches of mathematics. I have just discovered a possible application of the kind of thing I am working on at present. It answers the question 'What is the most general kind of code or cipher possible', and at the same time (rather naturally) enables me to construct a lot of particular and interesting codes. One of them is pretty well impossible to decode without the key, and very quick to encode. I expect I could sell them to H. M. Government for quite a substantial sum, but am rather doubtful about the morality of such things. What do you think?[7]

Nothing more is known about this theoretical investigation, but at Princeton he spent time on building a machine out of electromagnetic relays which effected binary multiplication as an encoding device, with some theory of immunity to cryptananalysis. This Turing machine has not survived, nor has its theory, nor do we know the course of his moral decisions regarding its application. Incidentally, to give the flavour of Turing's personality, he was at this point highly indignant at Baldwin and the British establishment for opposing Edward VIII's marriage. ('As for the Archbishop of Canterbury, I consider his behaviour disgraceful.') However he lost sympathy with the ex-king on learning that he had behaved improperly with state papers. Meanwhile he was an astute judge of the prospect of war with Germany.

When back at Cambridge, Turing also designed and partially built another machine, which approximated by gear-wheel motion a Fourier series for the Riemann zeta-function. It was intended to shorten the hard labour of finding the possible locations of zeros – the subject of the Riemann hypothesis, which remains today perhaps the most important unsolved problem in mathematics. But Turing meanwhile had indicated his interest in cryptography, probably through King's College channels. Whatever the moral and practical means, a rational miracle came about, in which an unworldly person found a perfect application at the heart of the world crisis. In September 1938 he began part-time work on the outstanding problem facing British intelligence: the German Enigma cipher. Progress, however, depended on the Polish mathematicians' work, donated to Britain after the British guarantee to Poland in July 1939. After Hitler called this bluff, Turing began full-time work at Bletchley Park, wartime home of the cryptanalytic establishment.

Turing had substantial influence on the course of the war. In summary: (1) He took on the naval version of Enigma in 1939, when it was thought beyond hope, and found a solution. He said himself that he took up the challenge because 'no-one else was doing anything about it and I could have it to myself.'[8] The reading of U-boat communications, achieved under Turing's direction, was arguably the most vital aspect of Bletchley Park work. (2) Turing crowned the design of the machine (the 'Bombe') which was central to the analysis of all Enigma traffic, with a logical idea which had a curious echo of the discussion with Wittgenstein, as it depended on the flow of logical implications from a false hypothesis. (3) Turing created a theory of information and statistics which made cryptanalysis a scientific subject; he was chief consultant and liaison at the highest level with American work.

Practical work brought with it demands of co-operation and organisation to which Turing was unsuited, and in the early part of the war he had to fight a difficult corner on questions of strategy and resources, at one point joining with other leading analysts to appeal to Churchill over the heads of the administration. But there was another side to this uncongenial coin: war broke peacetime boundaries and gave him practical experience of technology at its leading secret edge. In peace his ideas had flowed into small-scale engineering; in war they led to the electronic digital computer of 1945.

Electronic speeds made a first impact on the Enigma problem in 1942, and thereafter in the engineering of very advanced large-scale Colossus electronic machines for breaking the other high-level German machine cipher, the Lorenz. Note, incidentally, that the Colossus was nothing to do with the Enigma, as is often lazily stated; also that Turing had no part in *designing* the Colossi, but had input into their purpose and saw at first-hand their triumph. Turing did, however, have an electronic design of his own: in 1944, he with one engineer assistant built a speech scrambler of elegant and advanced principle. It appears that in proposing the speech scrambler, not an urgent requirement, he had his own hidden agenda: to acquire electronic experience. The scrambler worked in 1945, and at the same time, Turing combined logic and engineering, pure and applied mathematics, to invent the computer.

Care with words and claims is required: the word 'computer' has changed its meaning. In 1936 and indeed in 1946 it meant a *person* doing computing, and a machine would be called an 'automatic computer'. Until the 1960s people would distinguish digital computers from analogue computers; only since then, as digital computers have swept the field, has the word come to mean a machine such as Turing envisaged. Even now, the word is sometimes applied to any calculating machine. In speaking of 'the computer', I take the salient feature to be that programs and data are alike regarded as symbols which may alike be stored and manipulated – the 'modifiable stored program' – and this is the feature implied by Turing in speaking of a 'practical universal machine', which is how he described his own idea.

Even here, however, care is required. Although the universal machine was presented in 1936 with instructions and working space all in the common form of the 'tape', the instructions only required reading, *not* manipulation or modification, so it would not matter if they were stored in some unalterable physical form. Turing recognized this and counted Babbage's Analytical Engine, on which instructions were fixed cards, as a universal machine. In practice, however, the recognition that programs and data could be stored alike in a symbolic form and could alike be manipulated, was immensely liberating. It made a clean break from the Babbage-like machines which culminated in the electronic ENIAC of 1946. In enunciating the power of the universal machine concept, Turing was far ahead of contemporary wisdom; his idea that a single type of machine could be used for all tasks was stoutly resisted well into the 1950s.

But in peace, Turing's ideas flowed also into philosophy; how did the war affect Turing's philosophy? In *Alan Turing: the Enigma* I wrote that Christopher Morcom had died a second death in 1936, meaning that the concept of spirit freed from Laplacian determinism, which had stimulated Turing in 1930, would never be heard of again. It seemed to me strikingly clear that Turing's emotionally charged fascination with the problem of mind was the key to the mystery of how he, youthful outsider, had made a definitive and fundamental contribution with the concept of computability. By modelling the action of the human mind as a physical machine, he had brought radical new ideas into the world of symbolic logic. After 1936, it seemed, it was the powerful concept of the machine that had seized his imagination; and Turing's post-war writing would support this view. But in fact, his interpretation of ordinal logics in 1938 did leave the door open for something non-mechanical in the mind, and it now seems to me that Turing's views did not shift all at once in 1936 to espouse the total power of the computable.

My guess is that there was a turning point in about 1941. After a bitter struggle to break U-boat Enigma, Turing could then taste triumph. Machines turned and people carried out mechanical methods unthinkingly, with amazing and unforeseen results. This is when there was first talk between Turing and the young I. J. (Jack) Good about chess-playing algorithms. As I described in *Alan Turing: the Enigma*, this vision of mechanical intelligence must have stimulated great excitement; I would now go further and suggest that it was at this period that he abandoned the idea that moments of intuition corresponded to uncomputable operations. Instead, he decided, the scope of the computable encompassed far more than could be captured by explicit instruction notes, and quite enough to include all that human brains did, however creative or original. Machines of sufficient complexity would have the capacity for evolving into behaviour that had never been explicitly programmed. And it was at this period that he also lost interest in logic as a tool for probing reality – although it must be said that he retained a keen interest in theoretical computability *within mathematics*, being one of the first into the field when it was yoked to algebra in the late 1940s.

Possibly it was at the same time, or within months, that he also saw the megahertz speed of electronic components, and their reliable performance in the speech scrambling system used for telephone conversations between Roosevelt and Churchill. I suspect that it was only a short step to see the possibility of building a practical universal Turing machine in electronics.

Certainly, by the end of the war, he was captivated by the prospect of exploring the scope of the computable on a universal Turing machine; and indeed he called it 'building a brain' when talking of his plans to his electronic engineer assistant.

Turing went to the National Physical Laboratory and worked on his detailed design for a computer,[9] submitting it for approval in March 1946. Turing's Automatic Computing Engine (ACE), as it was dubbed, was chronologically second to the June 1945 EDVAC report bearing von Neumann's name, but in addition to the originality of its hardware design, it was ideologically independent: for (1) it was conceived from the outset as a universal machine for which arithmetic would be just one application, and (2) Turing sketched a theory of programming, in which instructions could be manipulated as well as data.

It was an intensely exciting idea that engineering could be done once for all, so that new problems would only need paperwork. Of course, Turing had Bletchley Park as a model of how non-numerical and versatile machines might be urgently needed. Turing dramatised the range of possible operations with farsighted examples, of which the last was as follows:

> Given a position in chess the machine could be made to list all the 'winning combinations' to a depth of about three moves on either side. This is not unlike the previous problem, but raises the question 'Can the machine play chess?' It could fairly easily be made to play a rather bad game. It would be bad because chess requires intelligence. We stated at the beginning of this section [i.e. when describing how programming is done] that the machine should be treated as entirely without intelligence. There are indications however that it is possible to make the machine display intelligence at the risk of its making occasional serious mistakes. By following up this aspect the machine could probably be made to play very good chess.

This is a crucial statement of his thought, which I take to show that by 1945 Turing had come to believe computable operations had sufficient scope to include intelligent behaviour, and had firmly rejected the direction he had followed in studying ordinal logics. The puzzling reference to 'occasional serious mistakes' makes sense in the light of his later stated argument (considered below) for holding uncomputability to be irrelevant to intelligence, and proves that he must have pondered this question during the war.

For a year Turing set forth plans for the practical organisation of a modern computer centre, with a library of routines, and control from remote terminals, exuding the confidence in the collaboration of mathematics, engineering and administration acquired at Bletchley Park. But his plan though formally accepted was not pressed into action; his planned machine (with about 32kbyte storage) was thought far too ambitious. Treated as a liability rather than an asset at the National Physical Laboratory, his eagerness to speak openly of building brains was an embarrassment. In 1947 he left for Cambridge on a 'sabbatical year'.

THE TRAINING OF THOUGHT

During the year, besides training for marathon running to near-Olympic standard, Turing reflected on the 'indications' of mechanical intelligence, writing a report[10] for the National Physical Laboratory in 1948. Cambridge brought about contact with post-war biology; this and contact with 'cybernetic' thinkers probably reinforced his thesis that there was sufficient scope in the complexity of machines to account for apparently non-mechanical behaviour. But Turing's report quoted nothing from such sources; in fact its most conspicuous citation was from a book by, of all people, the religious novelist Dorothy Sayers, which encapsulated the naive notion of 'mechanical' behaviour. (It was a book he was reading in 1941.) And he argued less from biological theory than from his own life experience, in holding that modification of behaviour could be adapted from learning brain to learning machine.

> If the untrained infant's mind is to become an intelligent one, it must acquire both discipline and initiative. So far we have been considering only discipline. To convert a brain or machine into a universal machine is the extremest form of discipline. Without something of this kind one cannot set up proper communication. But discipline is certainly not enough in itself to produce intelligence. That which is required in addition we call initiative. This statement will have to serve as a definition. Our task is to discover the nature of this residue . . . and to try to copy it in machines.

The influence of the general behaviourist climate seemed to blend easily with his own public school background:

> The training of the human child depends largely on a system of rewards and punishments, and this suggests that it ought to be possible to carry through the organising with only two interfering inputs, one for 'pleasure' or 'reward' and the other for 'pain' or 'punishment' . . .

> Pleasure interference has a tendency to fix the character, i.e. towards preventing it changing, whereas pain stimuli tend to disrupt the character, causing features which had become fixed to change . . . It is intended that pain stimuli occur when the machine's behaviour is wrong, pleasure stimuli when it is particularly right.

It is often supposed that computers began with heavy arithmetic, and that with this successfully achieved, computer scientists wandered to more ambitious fields. This may be so of others, but is quite untrue of Turing, who had *always* been concerned with modelling the human mind. (Besides, no computer in the modern sense performed a single addition until 1948.) That he now invaded the behavioural sciences is not in itself surprising; more surprising is that he so vehemently embraced the view that apparently non-mechanical steps of 'initiative' were only hidden mechanism, given his own experience of inspiration, and knowledge of the subtlety of computability. I find it surprising also that he used uncritically, almost gleefully, perversely, a primitive view of education. In his actual childhood experience he had ignored social training as much as possible.

Turing's ideas could not be tried out except on a very small scale as what he called 'paper machines' – the working through of programs by hand. But they anticipated the neural net or connectionist programme of artificial intelligence research, in which what Turing called 'unorganised machines' of sufficient complexity can be trained to perform tasks for which no explicit instructions have ever been written, and where indeed the evolving logical structure is unknown to the human trainer.

His 1948 report, unpublished until 1968, made no impression on the National Physical Laboratory, from which in any case he abruptly resigned. But the ideas resurface, expressed in more general terms, in the famous philosophical paper to which we now turn.

THE TURING TEST

Turing moved to Manchester University, where Newman, professor of pure mathematics there since 1945, had secured for him a first full academic post. Turing had a difficult position as software writer for the pioneer computer, the first such in the world, that the electronic engineer F. C. Williams and his team had built after Newman gave them the principle. Press reports of the machine had already used the terminology of 'brains', which Turing's own comments in 1949 did nothing to discourage. Jefferson, a Manchester brain surgeon, attempted to dispel such talk in a 1949 lecture. Michael Polanyi, chemist turned Christian philosopher of science at Manchester, was another intellectual opponent (with whom, however, Turing was on friendly personal terms). It was probably Polanyi who suggested that Turing should present his views as a paper, which appeared as 'Computing machinery and intelligence' in 1950.[11]

Turing addressed the problem of writing for a non-mathematical readership with typical sang-froid, ignoring all conventional cultural barriers. Notably without any serious citations in philosophical or psychological literature, it stands intransigent in style as well as content.

The paper is now famous for the 'imitation game', as described below, and now often called the Turing test. But the most solid aspect of the paper is Turing's setting out of the model of the *discrete state machine*, which is the Turing machine of 1936, but more clearly thought of as being physically embodied. A careful paragraph explains first why computing machinery is discrete:

> Digital computers ... may be classified amongst the 'discrete state machines'. These are the machines which move by sudden jumps or clicks from one quite definite state to another. These states are sufficiently different for the possibility of confusion between them to be ignored. Strictly speaking there are no such machines. Everything really moves continuously. But there are many kinds of machine which can profitably be *thought of* as being discrete state machines. For instance in considering the switches for a lighting system it is a convenient fiction that each switch must be definitely on or definitely off. There must be intermediate positions, but for most purposes we can forget about them ...
>
> This special property of digital computers, that they can mimic any discrete state machine, is described by saying that they are *universal* machines.

Turing's argument is simply that the brain should also be considered as a discrete state machine. In his classic statement, made in a 1952 radio broadcast:[12] 'We are not interested in the fact that the brain has the consistency of cold porridge. We don't want to say, "This machine's quite hard, so it isn't a brain, so it can't think." The physical greyness or soft sponginess of the brain is irrelevant, and so is the mode of operation of the nerves:

> Importance is often attached to the fact that modern digital computers are electrical, and that the nervous system also is electrical ... Of

course electricity usually comes in where fast signalling is concerned, so that it is not surprising that we find it in both these connections. In the nervous system chemical phenomena are at least as important as electrical. In certain computers the storage system is mainly acoustic. The feature of using electricity is thus seen to be only a very superficial similarly. If we wish to find such similarities [i.e. significant similarities between brain and computer] we should look rather for mathematical analogies of function.

Turing's claim is that the only features of the brain relevant to thinking or intelligence are those which fall within the discrete-state-machine level of description. The particular physical embodiment is irrelevant. Not quite made explicit, but implicit in every statement, is that the operation of a discrete state machine is *computable*. We now see the definitive extension to the argument presented in 1936, the effect of the change of thought I conjecture for 1941. The post-war Turing claims that Turing machines can mimic the effect of *any* activity of the mind, not only a mind engaged upon a 'definite method'.

Turing's term 'discrete state machine' is a judicious choice. He avoids expressions such as 'logical structure' which might carry the false connotation of common parlance: logical as opposed to illogical, informal or emotional thought. There is no such dichotomy in Turing's analysis, and indeed no distinction between conscious and unconscious. Turing is clear that discrete state machines include machines with learning or self-organising ability, and makes a point of the fact that these still fall within the scope of the computable. Turing draws attention to the apparant conflict with the definition of Turing machines having fixed tables of behaviour, but sketches a proof that self-modifying machines are still in fact defined by an unchanged instruction set, ending:

> The explanation of the paradox is that the rules which get changed in the learning process are of a rather less pretentious kind, claiming only an ephemeral validity. The reader may draw a parallel with the Constitution of the United States.

If Turing's thesis about the function of the brain is accepted, then from a materialist point of view, the argument is almost complete. The behaviour of a discrete state machine can then, at least in principle, be written down in a table. Hence every feature of the brain relevant to thought can be captured by a table of behaviour, and so emulated by a computer. The only question that might remain is that of whether the speed and spatial dimensions of the brain, and the character of its physical interface with the world, are also essential to its function.

However the rest of the paper, bringing in the definition of the Turing test, does much to illustrate the idea of a brain and its function as a physical object whose properties can be examined like any other, and to suggest constructive methods by which intelligent machinery could be engineered. To do this, Turing dramatises the operational viewpoint. Instead of considering the question 'Can machines think?' Turing explains, 'I shall replace the question by another, which is closely related to it and is expressed in relatively unambiguous words':

> The new form of the problem can be described in terms of a game which we call the 'imitation game'. It is played with three people, a man (A), a woman (B), and an interrogator (C) who may be of either sex. The interrogator stays in a room apart from the other two. The object of the game is for the interrogator to determine which of the other two is the man and which is the woman.

If Turing's introduction to the problem of creative mind through a party game with camp innuendo was calculated to offend arts-educated intellectuals, it probably succeeded. Unfortunately Turing also succeeded in creating disastrous confusion. Although it was intended to clarify the picture of the brain being tested like any other physical object, for many readers the purpose of the imitation game is obscured, in fact turned on its head, by careless syntax:

> We now ask the question, 'What will happen when a machine takes the part of A in this game?' Will the interrogator decide wrongly as often when the game is played like this as he does when the game is played between a man and a woman?

I have no doubt that 'the game is played like this' means, 'the game is played between a human being and a computer pretending to be human'. But many are now the books, articles, lectures, and Webpages which assert that in the Turing test the computer must take the part of a man who is imitating a woman. This is indeed the literal meaning of the words 'a machine takes the part of A', but such an interpretation is contradicted by the sample interrogation:

> Q: Please write me a sonnet on the subject of the Forth bridge.
> A: Count me out on this one. I never could write poetry.

Q: Add 34957 to 70764.

A: (Pause about 30 seconds and then give as answer) 105621.

Q: Do you play chess?

A: Yes.

Q: I have K at my K1, and no other pieces. You have only K at K6 and
   R at R1. It is your move, What do you play?

A: (After a pause of 15 seconds) R–R8 mate.

These answers establish no impression of gender; they are meant to establish human intelligence (including – a subtle point – the incorrect addition). The point of the game is this: If a machine cannot be distinguished from a human being under these conditions then we must credit it with human intelligence.

A deeper problem is that Turing's gender-guessing analogy detracts from his own argument. In the gender game, successful fooling of the interrogator proves nothing about the reality behind the screen. In contrast, Turing wants to argue that the successful imitation of intelligence *is* intelligence. Equivalently, Turing defines the subject matter of intelligence as that which can be wholly communicated via the teleprinter link, consistent with his thesis that the brain is relevant only *qua* discrete state machine. Discrete symbols over the teleprinter link can faithfully represent all the inputs and outputs to and from a discrete state machine. As Turing puts it: 'The new problem has the advantage of drawing a fairly sharp line between the physical and intellectual capacities of a man.'

The setting of teleprinter communication is intended to separate intelligence from other faculties of the human being. 'We do not wish to penalise the machine for its inability to shine in beauty competitions, nor to penalise a man for losing in a race against an aeroplane. The conditions of our game make these disabilities irrelevant.' The conditions are intended to make qualities such as gender irrelevant; and from the point of view of clarity it is unfortunate that his iconoclastic introduction gives the opposite impression.

But if Turing's gender-game is misunderstood, he certainly courted such confusion. He painted the pages of this journey into cyberspace with the awkward eroticism and encylopaedic curiosity of his personality. Modern cultural critics have jumped with delight to psychoanalyse its surprises. The intellectual text is the austere statement of the capacity of the discrete state machine for disembodied intelligence; the subtext is full of provocative references to his own person, as if putting his own flesh-and-blood intelligence on trial.

It might be said that the 'imitation' intrinsic to the Turing test is also a distraction from the core of the argument. Subjecting 'imitation' to analysis raises questions, undiscussed in Turing's paper, such as why an intelligent machine should be expected to play a dishonest game; in my view this is overburdening Turing's illustration and missing the main point. The real claim, as I have emphasised above, is that the brain's function is that of a discrete state Turing machine, and therefore can be performed by a computer. The colour and drama in Turing's writing is secondary: it is intended to invite a wide variety of readers into constructive reflection upon this conclusion, which runs contrary to all intuition but is not at all easy to refute.

Courtroom imagery runs through the paper: not only is the Turing test an interrogation, but Turing puts himself in the dock and answers objections to his thesis. The objections differ considerably in how seriously they are set up and taken. After a sally at 'Heads in the Sand' objectors, Turing enunciates:

> *The Theological Objection.* Thinking is a function of man's immortal soul. God has given an immortal soul to every man and woman, but not to any other animal or to machines. Hence no animal or machine can think.

This is not an objection made or answered with seriousness, but used to make fun of Christianity, with a reference to Galileo's heresy as an analogy to his own. He wrote as he spoke: a proud atheist, in the habit of anti-Church remarks. A more serious response might have been aimed not just at religious dogma, but at the more general assertions made by moral philosophy that human beings have properties (e.g. responsibility, authority) that other objects are unable to possess. As it stands, the paragraph might amuse those who already shared his views, it would convince no one who did not. However there is a serious kernel in his debating society point, made to dispose of this objection, that God could give a machine a soul. From the operational viewpoint adopted, Turing need not argue about whether or not people have 'souls'; he need only address what can be observed.

Although rooted in intellectual integrity, there is an unattractiveness in Turing's easy dismissal of such questions. In the aftermath of the Second World War there were good reasons for anxiety about treating people as machines. In his personal attitudes Turing was fierce for liberty and honesty, qualities hard to fit into the setting of the imitation game. But *ad hominem* questions cause one to ask: what words of moral discourse could have been appropriate from an innocent valiant-for-truth who had lent a mastermind to the defeat of Nazism, but could never breathe a word of it? His frivolity had its own moral seriousness, the washing of hands from the evil of the 1940s. Like others of the early 1950s, Turing was impatient to see the future, having defeated Hitler's attempt to destroy it. And with its references to the place of women in Islamic theology, the cloning of human beings, and the question of animals' consciousness, one cannot accuse Turing's paper of lacking foresight for moral issues.

I now turn to the strangest passage in all Turing's writing.

> *The Argument from Extra-Sensory Perception.* I assume that the reader is familiar with the idea of extra-sensory perception, and the meaning of the four items of it, *viz.* telepathy, clairvoyance, precognition and psycho-kinesis. These disturbing phenomena seem to deny all our usual scientific ideas. How we should like to discredit them! Unfortunately the statistical evidence, at least for telepathy, is overwhelming. It is very difficult to rearrange one's ideas so as to fit these new facts in. Once one has accepted them it does not seem a very big step to believe in ghosts and bogies. The idea that our bodies move simply according to the known laws of physics, together with some others not yet discovered but somewhat similar, would be one of the first to go.
>
> This argument is to my mind quite a strong one. One can say in reply that many scientific theories seem to remain workable in practice, in spite of clashing with E.S.P.; that in fact one can get along very nicely if one forgets about it. This is rather cold comfort, and one fears that thinking is just the kind of phenomenon where E.S.P. may be especially relevant.

It is not clear how serious the statements are. The exclamation mark suggests irony, the 'overwhelming' evidence sounds literal. On balance it appears he was at that time convinced by contemporary claims for observing ESP. There are no other passages on ESP in Turing's writing or letters, although his interest in dreams and strange events was sharp. In 1930 he had a presentiment of Christopher Morcom's death at the very moment he was taken ill, and he later wrote, 'It is not difficult to explain these things away – but, I wonder!' He wondered; it was natural wonder.

There is a point made here, though left elliptical, of more general significance: namely that the discrete state machine model rests upon the brain's operation according to 'known laws of physics, together with some others not yet discovered but somewhat similar'; we shall return to this question.

Further objections are more clearly made and seriously answered, and of these I consider first what Turing called:

The Argument from Consciousness: This argument is very well expressed in Professor Jefferson's Lister Oration for 1949 ... 'Not until a machine can write a sonnet or compose a concerto because of thoughts and emotions felt, and not by the chance fall of symbols, could we agree that machine equals brain – that is, not only write it but know that it had written it. No mechanism could feel (and not merely artificially signal, an easy contrivance) pleasure at its successes, grief when its valves fuse, be warmed by flattery, be made miserable by its mistakes, be charmed by sex, be angry or depressed when it cannot get what it wants.'

This argument appears to be a denial of the validity of our test. According to the most extreme form of this view the only way by which one could be sure that a machine thinks is to *be* the machine and to feel oneself thinking. One could then describe these feelings to the world, but of course no one would be justified in taking any notice. Likewise according to this view the only way to know what a *man* thinks is to be that particular man. It is in fact the solipsist point of view ...

I do not wish to give the impression that I think there is no mystery about consciousness. There is, for instance, something of a paradox connected with any attempt to localise it. But I do not think these mysteries necessarily need to be solved before we can answer the question with which we are concerned in this paper.

Jefferson's central objection is that of commonsense repugnance to the idea of machines being credited with thought; and its burden is similar to John Searle's claim of the machine lacking human 'intentionality'. It is of interest, even if anachronistic, to guess Turing's answer to Searle's parable of the Chinese Room, itself a sort of riposte to the drama of the imitation game. Searle supposes (1) That there is an algorithm for translating Chinese to English; (2) that this algorithm is effected not by a machine but by one or many people in a room, working mindlessly. Then the Chinese is translated; but none of the translators has the faintest knowledge or understanding: a paradox. Turing's thesis is, I believe, that this if achieved would be no paradox at all, merely a dramatisation of the true state of affairs. It would reflect the mechanism of the brain, where the neurones have no understanding individually, but somehow the system as a whole seems to; and that appearance is all that matters. One might go further: the situation in Bletchley Park was uncannily like the

Chinese Room, since for reasons of secrecy people were trained to perform the cryptanalytic algorithms without knowing their purpose. Perhaps this very sight, of good judgement emerging from mindless calculation, was what positively inspired Turing to the picture of mechanical intelligence in about 1941. The drift of Turing's views is that the definiteness of consciousness is an illusion, a quality emerging from and ultimately to be explained by great complexity. His approach would not accept 'intentionality' as any better an explanation than 'soul'. For a materialist such words are a restatement of the problem, perhaps the greatest problem of science, and not an answer to it.

At this point it is appropriate to introduce the ideas of Roger Penrose, who shares the materialist dissatisfaction with explanations through souls or intentionality, but holds consciousness to be an undeniable fact. Penrose poses a physical question about consciousness, probably similar to what Turing had in mind when referring to a paradox in trying to localise it: is the intelligence supposed to emerge when the machine is run? If so, it is not the discrete state machine alone, but that *plus* its physical implementation. Or is intelligence present in the abstract table of behaviour? But if so, we could choose a notation where the number 42 encodes the table of behaviour of Einstein's brain; can 42 have Einstein's intelligence? As Turing says, his own presentation leaves such mysteries unresolved.

Turing's most positive contribution comes as a response to what he called:

> *Lady Lovelace's Objection.* Our most detailed information of Babbage's Analytical Engine comes from a memoir by Lady Lovelace. In it she states, 'The Analytical Engine has no pretentions to *originate* anything. It can do *whatever we know how to order it* to perform.'

This is the cue for a large section on learning machines, with constructive arguments for how machines might do apparently unmechanical things for which explicit programs are unknown: the first public exposition of what I have called his 1941 vision. Turing advocates two different approaches – in modern parlance top-down and bottom-up – which in fact derive from his 1936 descriptions of the machine model. Explicit instruction notes become explicit progamming; implicit states of mind become the states of machines attained by learning and self-organizing experience. Turing's positive assurance that machines are capable of all that anyone including himself had done, is illustrated in curiously masochistic self-deprecation, and one passage has a particular resonance:

The view that machines cannot give rise to surprises is due, I believe, to a fallacy to which philosophers and mathematicians are particularly subject. This is the assumption that as soon as a fact is presented to a mind all consequences of that fact spring into the mind simultaneously with it. It is a very useful assumption under many circumstances, but one too easily forgets that it is false. A natural consequence of doing so is that one then assumes that there is no virtue in the mere working out of consequences from data and general principles.

Turing could hardly have typed these words without private allusion to his own contribution ten years earlier, in another world: for his logical breakthrough into the Enigma involved the instantaneous flow of implications, as embodied in ingenious electrical circuitry. He was crediting the mechanical with the capacity for everything, including moments of world-shattering inspiration.

I come now to a raft of questions which arise through the question of how the brain interacts with the external world. Some of these Turing discusses under Jefferson's objections; others fall under 'The argument from disabilities'.

The inability to enjoy strawberries and cream may have struck the reader as frivolous. Possibly a machine might be made to enjoy this delicious dish, but any attempt to make one to do so would be idiotic. What is important about this disability is that it contributes to some of the other disabilities, *e.g.* to the difficulty of the same kind of friendliness occurring between man and machine as between white man and white man, or between black man and black man.

Just as the themes of moral philosophy are hardly met by Turing's theological response, these are somewhat throwaway remarks with which to dispose of the entire content of the social sciences, in which thought and behaviour are considered dominated by external influence. But this was not because Turing was sure of his ground in this case; rather, it is on topics involving interaction that Turing shows himself least certain, anxious about what sensory and motor organs an artificial brain will require. In the development of his thought away from the mathematical calculations of 1936, he allowed first chess, cryptography and (tentatively) languages in the 1948 report as 'topics where not too much interaction is required'. His reference to the machine being denied 'sex, sport and other things of interest to the human being' must have struck an unusual note in the archives of the National Physical Laboratory, and again in the 1948 report Turing distinguishes the concentrating and non-interacting brain from the process of interaction which allows it to learn:

> We may say then that in so far as a man is a machine he is one that is subject to very much interference . . . constantly receiving visual and other stimuli . . . it is important to remember that although a man when concentrating may behave like a machine without interference, his behaviour when concentrating is largely determined by the way he has been conditioned by previous interference.

Unless the intellectual and physical, internal and external, can be separated, the value of the discrete state machine model of the brain is questionable, for the interface with the ambient world becomes crucial, and the robotic elements need attention as well as the simulation of brain function. In the 1950 paper Turing finally loses all inhibition and throws open the machine to general conversation, but the problem of physical interaction is still an anxiety:

> Instead of trying to produce a programme to simulate the adult's mind, why not rather try to produce one which simulates the child's? . . . It will not be possible to apply exactly the same teaching process to the machine as to a normal child. It will not, for instance, be provided with legs, so that it could not be asked to go out and fill the coal scuttle. Possibly it might not have eyes. But however well these deficiencies might be overcome by clever engineering, we could not send the creature to school without the other children making excessive fun of it. It must be given some tuition. We need not be too concerned about the legs, eyes, etc. The example of Miss Helen Keller shows that education can take place . . .

These are untypical worries for a mathematician, but then Turing was more natural philosopher than typical mathematician, and the connection between thinking and doing was what had inspired his Turing machine construction in the first place.

> We may hope that machines will eventually compete with men in all purely intellectual fields. But which are the best ones to start with? . . . Many people think that a very abstract activity, like the playing of chess, would be best. It can also be maintained that it is best to provide the machine with the best sense organs that money can buy, and then teach it to understand and speak English . . . Again I do not know what the right answer is, but I think both approaches should be tried.

THE UNCOMPUTABLE REVISITED

The remaining questions concern the computable discrete state machine model itself, and are the most fundamental. Turing points out that in a theoretical discrete state machine:

> It will seem that given the initial state of the machine and the input signals it is always possible to predict all future states. This is reminiscent of Laplace's view that from the complete state of the universe at one moment of time, as described by the positions and velocities of all particles, it should be possible to predict all future states. The prediction which we are considering is, however, rather nearer to practicability than that considered by Laplace. The system of the 'universe as a whole' is such that quite small errors in the initial conditions can have an overwhelming effect at a later time. The displacement of a single electron by a billionth of a centimetre at one moment might make the difference between a man being killed by an avalanche a year later, or escaping. It is an essential property of the mechanical systems which we have called 'discrete state machines' that this phenomenon does not occur.

This perhaps needs clarification: Turing means that the small physical displacement of an electron inside a computer will not (except with an extremely small probability) affect the discrete state that the computer is representing. Hence it will not affect the future evolution of the computation.

On this basis, Turing then poses

> *The Argument from Continuity in the Nervous System*: The nervous system is certainly not a discrete-state machine. A small error in the information about the size of a nervous impulse impinging on a neuron, may make a large difference to the size of the outgoing impulse. It may be argued that, this being so, one cannot expect to be able to mimic the behaviour of the nervous system with a discrete-state system.

Turing's following remarks briefly indicate how a digital machine can imitate analogue machines, so that discreteness would be no disadvantage. On this topic, Penrose has reinforced Turing's comment, with the observation that 'avalanche' effects of instability and amplification, nowadays better understood through the analysis of chaos, are to the *brain*'s disadvantage, and no argument against the feasibility of machine intelligence.

But this brings us to Penrose's central objection, which is not to the *discreteness* of Turing's machine model of the brain, but to its *computability*. Penrose holds that the function of the brain must have evolved by purely physical processes, but that its behaviour is – in fact must be – *uncomputable*. Since it cannot be that the laws of Nature are waived for the atoms in the brain, it follows that physical law, which at present is incompletely known, must in general have non-computable aspects. Penrose sees the key in the as yet unknown rules which govern the reduction of the wave function in quantum mechanics. Turing raises no such possibility, and if we look for a discussion of what physical laws he supposes to underpin the function of the brain, we find a vagueness that is surprising considering Turing's knowledge of applied mathematics and physical theory. Apart from the remark made on ESP (raising the possibility of laws of physics different from those so far known) there is only a comment that, 'Even when we consider the actual physical machines instead of the idealised machines, reasonably accurate knowledge of the state at one moment yields reasonably accurate knowledge any number of steps later.' This can be elucidated by reference to his 1948 report; it refers *not* to quantum mechanics but to uncertainty in classical thermodynamics. The tendency of Turing's argument, though not explicitly stated, is that once the discrete state machine model is arrived at, it does not matter what exactly physical laws are. However, the ESP discussion does implicitly admit that physical law enters into the underlying assumptions. Penrose takes a completely different point of view: to discuss what the mind does, as Turing attempts, it is of prime importance to know the fundamental physical content of mental 'doing'. But fundamental physics is quantum-mechanical and at present not fully known; here according to Penrose must lie a fundamental non-computability in nature, which the brain has evolved to take advantage of.

Quite apart from Penrose's theory, it is unclear how to apply computability to continuous quantities, as Turing must have known since he had to abandon in 1937 his intention of rewriting continuous analysis. The question of the computability of physical laws, which are generally expressed as differential equations for continuous variables, remains a loose end in Turing's argument.

With computability now at the forefront, it is worth a further look at the problems of interaction between brain and external world. From Penrose's point of view these are irrelevant. If the physical world is computable, then in principle the world external to a brain can be simulated by a computer, and so all its experiences could be faithfully imitated; hence all interface questions take second place to the question of the computability of physical law. The same view is adopted by the most confident proponents of artifical intelligence, though with the opposite intent: they are happy to conceive of simulating the whole external world as well as a single brain. Turing never suggests doing this, but imagines a machine learning from interaction with the world; here his anxieties are concentrated. Penrose, regarding these problems as irrelevant, focuses attention on those questions of intelligence in which external interaction plays no role, questions in pure mathematics. In Penrose's view the impossibility of mechanical intelligence can be seen within mathematics alone: and this impossibility can be put in terms of Turing's own uncomputable numbers. How did Turing himself deal with this objection?

As I have already suggested, Turing probably decided in the 1941 period that the uncomputable, unprovable and undecidable were irrelevant to the problem of mind. In the 1950 paper, Turing exposes and responds to what he calls 'the mathematical objection', but his answer is short, and I therefore quote the fuller version he gave in a talk to mathematicians in 1947:

> It has for instance been shown that with certain logical systems there can be no machine which will distinguish provable formulae of the system from unprovable, i.e. that there is no test that the machine can apply which will divide propositions with certainty into these two classes. Thus if a machine is made for this purpose it must in some cases fail to give an answer. On the other hand if a mathematician is confronted with such a problem he would search around and find new methods of proof, so that he ought to be able to reach a decision about any given formula. This would be the argument. Against it I would say that fair play must be given to the machine. Instead of it sometimes giving no answer we could arrange that it gives occasional wrong answers. But the human mathematician would likewise make blunders when trying out new techniques. It is easy for us to regard these blunders as not counting and give him another chance, but the machine would probably be allowed no mercy. In other words, then, if a machine is expected to be infallible, it cannot also be intelligent.[13]

This is the passage which explains the 1946 ACE report claim for the 'indications' of machine intelligence at the cost of making serious mistakes. Penrose disputes Turing's argument: we do not expect intelligence in mathematics to turn upon the making of mistakes, and even if a result is mistaken, it can be reliably verified or corrected by others when communicated. Indeed the very essence of mathematical intelligence is *seeing the truth*. In the 1950 paper, Turing adds a further statement, again very brief: 'There would be no question of triumphing simultaneously over *all* machines. In short, then, there might be men cleverer than any given machine, but then again there might be other machines cleverer again, and so on.' This may be contrasted with Penrose's explicit and detailed exposition of human triumph over any Turing machine capable of partial judgements on the halting problem by an argument that is a development of seeing the truth of unprovable Gödel statements. This, in Penrose's argument, establishes that the mind is capable of the uncomputable. Turing's bald assertion, putting human and machine on a par, is no more than reassertion of his claim that the brain's function is that of a discrete state machine; it does not add any evidential weight to it.

So in the course of the war Turing dismissed the role for uncomputability in the description of mind, which once he had cautiously explored with the ordinal logics. A great body of opinion has followed Turing's example; not only within computer science, but in philosophy and the cognitive sciences. To a surprising degree the subject of mathematical logic, in Russell's time an enquiry into fundamental truth, has followed Turing's example and come to justify itself as adjunct to computer science. Yet Turing was careful to offer his conclusions not as dogma, but as constructive conjectures to be tested by scientific investigation.

> I believe that in about fifty years' time it will be possible to programme computers, with a storage capacity of about 10^9, to make them play the imitation game so well that an average interrogator will not have more than 70 per cent chance of making the right identification after five minutes of questioning. The original question, 'Can machines think?' I believe to be too meaningless to deserve discussion. Nevertheless I believe that at the end of the century the use of words and general educated opinion will have altered so much that one will be able to speak of machines thinking without expecting to be contradicted. I believe further that no useful purpose is served by concealing these beliefs. The popular view that scientists proceed inexorably from well-established fact to well-established fact, never being influenced by any unproved conjecture, is quite mistaken. Provided it is made clear which are proved facts and which are conjectures, no harm can result. Conjectures are of great importance since they suggest useful lines of research.

A notable feature of the Turing test setting is that it requires not so much a judge as a jury: not an expert, but common humanity. The democracy of Turing's thought has lasted well. As new computer applications come into circulation, the technology of the Internet will give a new spin to the futuristic drama of the Turing test. We shall all judge for ourselves.

The fifty-year figure seems to derive from an estimate of sixty people working fifty years to write sufficient code: hardly a practical research proposal, and indeed no such proposal was made. In July 1951 Turing gained the use of a more reliable machine at Manchester, but there is no trace of him using it to simulate neural networks, nor to code chess-playing algorithms. He and the small group around him published articles[14] under the heading 'Digital computers applied to games' in 1953, which mark pioneering research into machine intelligence. But this lead made no impact on the fresh start to artificial intelligence made by Newell, Simon, Minsky and McCarthy in the United States. Turing never wrote the book on theory and practice of computation which would have established his reputation. Nor was he prepared to argue and fight over strategy and practical support: he had done this successfully in 1940 over naval Enigma, he had done it unsuccessfully in 1946 for the ACE; after this he did not try again.

GROWING CRISIS

In any case, by 1950 Turing had an excited interest in a new field. Turing was interested in the body in Nature as well as the brain; his boyhood experiments had been chemical rather than mathematical, he retained the eyes to see biological structure as intensely puzzling. We recall his early fascination with determinism and his idea that 'the rest of the body amplifies' the action of the brain. His later claims for machine intelligence and the mechanical simulation of learning had directed his attention to the growth of brain cells. He now formulated some simplified problems in biological growth, and attacked them by postulating non-linear differential chemical equations. He showed how inhomogeneity could arise from homogeneous initial conditions, using a symmetry-breaking effect of chemical instability.[15] He described his philosophical outlook as countering the theological argument from design, suggesting a future Richard Dawkins of physiology. He set himself as a goal the explanation of Fibonacci patterns in plants; this was perhaps unfortunate as this problem remains unsolved, but his research, as a first user of electronic computation for serious mathematical investigation, was twenty years ahead of its time and full of potential for discovery. With hindsight we notice that the elucidation of chaotic dynamics was later to come from just such computational experiment.

This work struggled against personal catastrophe. In December 1951 he met a young man in Manchester, and told him of his work on 'the electronic brain'. An unsatisfactory affair led to indirect blackmail, exploiting the fact that all sex between men was then criminal. Resisting it by going to the police, he was arrested. Unrepentant and unashamed at his trial, he had to agree to the injection of oestrogen, supposed to neutralize his supposedly unnatural nature. The alternative would have been prison. Deemed a security risk by post-war regulations, he was stopped from the work he had continued to do from GCHQ, the Cold War successor to Bletchley Park. He found himself under watch; and other pressures may have been placed on him.

Turing complained that he lacked concentration; yet for two years he developed a mass of geometric and analytic-ideas; he also turned to new topics, or rather old ones revived. In particular, he puzzled over the standard view of reduction of the wave-function in quantum mechanics, noting the paradox that continous observation freezes the dynamics. He told Robin Gandy of his new idea for quantum mechanics: 'Description must be non-linear, prediction must be linear.'[16] Possibly he had in mind a non-linear quantum theory in which reduction would arise as did the symmetry breaking in his non-linear morphogenetic theory.

To relieve depression and anger he had turned to Jungian therapy, and found new interest in writing down his dreams. On a visit to Blackpool in early 1954 with the therapist's family, he consulted the Gypsy Queen fortune-teller, and emerged 'white as a sheet'. He remained silent for the rest of that day; nor did he leave a public word at his suicide on Whit Monday, 7 June 1954. Symbolism, in the cyanide-poisoned apple he ate, was his language. What words could have sufficed? Jokes, as perhaps in the 1950 paper, were his serious defence from the ineffable irony of the world. After his arrest he wrote:

> Turing believes machines think
> Turing lies with men
> Therefore machines do not think [17]

and shortly before he died, he wrote postcards headed 'Messages from the Unseen World' – explicitly referring to Eddington, some with schoolboy allusions, and a hymn-like relativistic verse:

> Hyperboloids of wondrous Light
> Rolling for aye through space and time

Harbour those waves which somehow might
Play out God's holy pantomime.[18]

Had an earlier agenda, the nature of spirit, resurfaced? Would he have reconsidered his philosophy, bringing quantum mechanical substrate into the discrete-state picture? In my biography I suggested that the emotional intensity and gross interference of this period might have undermined his certainty in the mechanical model of mind, but offered no evidence, for there is none. His last publication[19] was in *Penguin Science News*, written like a modern *Scientific American* article, and entitled 'Solvable and unsolvable problems'. Written vividly but from the perspective of a pure mathematician, its final words concerned the interpretation of unsolvable problems, such as the halting problem for Turing machines. They were lame: 'These ... may be regarded as going some way towards a demonstration, within mathematics itself, of the inadequacy of "reason" unsupported by common sense.' No clues are offered here.

Alan Turing's philosophy might appear the ultimate in reductionism, in its atomising of mental process, its scorn for the non-material. Yet it depends upon a synthesis of vision running against the grain of an intellectual world split into many verbal or mathematical or technical specialisms. He preached the computable, but never lost natural wonder; the law killed and the spirit gave life.

Abbreviations

Descartes

AT   C. Adam and P. Tannery (eds), (*Œuvres de Descartes*) (12 vols, revised edn, Paris, Vrin/CNRS, 1964–76).

CSM   J. Cottingham, R. Stoothoff and D. Murdoch (eds), *The Philosophical Wrings of Descartes*, Vols I and II (Cambridge, Cambridge University Press, 1985).

CSMK   J. Cottingham, R. Stoothoff, D. Murdoch and A. Kenny (eds), *The Philosophical Writings of Descartes*, Vol. III, The Correspondence (Cambridge, Cambridge University Press, 1991).

Note: 'AT' is the standard Franco-Latin edition of the complete works of Descartes. Cross references to 'CSM' and 'CSMK', the standard English edition, are given for the reader's convenience, but in a number of the passages quoted I have made occasional minor alterations in phrasing and/or punctuation. In some of the quotations, I have also put certain key words and phrases in italics to draw the reader's attention to their importance for the argument under discussion.

Berkeley

Quotations from Berkeley's writings are, with three exceptions, taken from *The Works of George Berkeley* (Edinburgh, 1948–57), A. A. Luce and T. E. Jessop (eds) in nine volumes. The three exceptions are: Berkeley's notebooks, or *Philosophical Commentaries* (Alliance, 1976), G. Thomas (ed.); Berkeley's *Manuscript Introduction* to the *Principles* (Oxford, 1987), B. Belfrage (ed.); and Berkeley's essays in Steele's *Guardian* (Kentucky, 1982), J. C. Stephens (ed.); quotations from which have been, where necessary, modernized and standardized.

PC   Philosophical Commentaries, *c.* 1706–7

MI   *Manuscript Introduction* to *Principles*, *c.* 1708

NTV   Essay Towards a New Theory of Vision (1709; 4th edn 1732)

PHK   (or *Principles*) *Principles of Human Knowledge* (1710; 2nd edn 1734)

DHP   Three Dialogues between Hylas and Philonous (1713; 3rd edn 1734)

Alc.	*Alciphron, or the Minute Philosopher* (1732; 3rd edn 1752)
TVV	*Theory of Vision Vindicated and Explained* (1733)
Works	*Works of George Berkeley* (1948–57), nine volumes.

Hume

E	*Enquiries: concerning the human understanding and concerning the principles of morals*, ed. L. A. Selby-Bigge. 2nd edn, Oxford, 1902.
D	*Dialogues concerning natural religion*, ed. Norman Kemp Smith, Oxford, 1935.
Ess	*Essays*, Oxford, 1963.
N	*The Natural History of Religion and Dialogues Concerning Natural Religion*, ed. A. W. Glyn and J. V. Price, Oxford, 1976.
T	*Treatise of Human Nature*, ed. L. A. Selby-Bigge. Oxford, 1888 and later.

Russell

Auto 1	*The Autobiography of Bertrand Russell 1872–1914*, London, Allen and Unwin, 1967
Auto 3	*The Autobiography of Bertrand Russell Volume III, 1914–1944*, London, Allen and Unwin, 1968
CPBR2	*The Collected Papers of Bertrand Russell 2*, London, Unwin Hyman, 1990
EA	*Essays in Analysis*, London, Allen and Unwin, 1973
HWP	*History of Western Philosophy*, London, Routledge, 1991
LA	*The Philosophy of Logical Atomism*, La Salle, Illinois, Open Court, 1985
ML	*Mysticism and Logic*, London, Unwin Paperbacks, 1976
MPD	*My Philosophical Development*, New York, Simon and Schuster, 1959
NEP	*Nightmares of Eminent Persons*, Harmondsworth, Penguin, 1962
POM	*The Principles of Mathematics*, London, Allen and Unwin, 1985
PM	*Principia Mathematica to *56*, Cambridge University Press, 1962
PFM	*Portraits from Memory*, London, Allen and Unwin, 1956

Wittgenstein

| BB | *The Blue and Brown Books* (Blackwell, Oxford, 1958). |
| BT | 'The Big Typescript', excerpts in J. Klagge and A. Nordmann (eds), *Ludwig Wittgenstein: Philosophical Occasions 1912–1951* (Hackett, Indianapolis and Cambridge, 1993), pp. 161–99. |

CV   *Culture and Value*, ed. G. H. von Wright in collaboration with
          H. Nyman, tr. P. Winch (Blackwell, Oxford, 1980).
LPE   'Notes for lectures on "Private Experience" and "Sense Data"',
          ed. R. Rhees, repr. in Klagge and Nordmann, *Ludwig
          Wittgenstein: Philosophical Occasions 1912–1952*, pp. 202–88.
LSD   'The Language of Sense Data and Private Experience', notes by
          R. Rhees, repr. in Klagge and Nordmann, *Ludwig Wittgenstein:
          Philosophical Occasions 1912–1951*, pp. 290–367.
LW I   *Last Writings on the Philosophy of Psychology*, Vol. 1, ed.
          G. H. von Wright and H. Nyman, tr. C. G. Luckhardt and
          M. A. E. Aue (Blackwell, Oxford, 1982).
MS 165   Unpublished manuscript number 165.
PI   *Philosophical Investigations*, ed. G. E. M. Anscombe and
          R. Rhees, tr. G. E. M. Anscombe, 2nd edn (Blackwell, Oxford,
          1958); references to Part I are by section number (§), to Part II
          by page.
PR   *Philosophical Remarks*, ed. R. Rhees, tr. R. Hargreaves and
          R. White (Blackwell, Oxford, 1975).
RPP I   *Remarks on the Philosophy of Psychology*, Vol. 1, ed.
          G. E. M. Anscombe and G. H. von Wright, tr.
          G. E. M. Anscombe (Blackwell, Oxford, 1980).
RPP II   *Remarks on the Philosophy of Psychology*, Vol. 2,
          ed. G. H. von Wright and H. Nyman, tr. C. G. Luckhardt and
          M. A. E. Aue (Blackwell, Oxford, 1980).
Z   *Zettel*, ed. G. E. M. Anscombe and G. H. von Wright, tr.
          G. E. M. Anscombe (Blackwell, Oxford, 1967).

I have occasionally changed quoted passages where the translation seemed
to me to be unsatisfactory.

Notes

Socrates

Abbreviations used in these notes:

CDP   *The Collected Dialogues of Plato*, E. Hamilton and H. Cairns (eds) (Princeton University Press, 1961)

CWA *The Collected Works of Aristotle*, J. Barnes (ed.) (Princeton University Press, 1984)

LCL   Loeb Classical Library

LOP *Lives of the Philosophers*, Diogenes Laertius, translated by R. D. Hicks (Harvard University Press, 1972)

p. 7 You are mistaken . . . Plato, *Apology*, 28b (CDP, p. 14)

p. 7 started wrestling . . . Plato, *Symposium*, 220c (CDP, p. 571)

p. 7 fell into a fit . . . ibid., 174d, 175b (CDP, pp. 529–30)

p. 8 I have never lived . . . Plato, *Apology*, 36b (CDP, p. 21)

p. 8 anyone who is close . . . Plato, *Laches*, 187e (CDP, p. 131)

p. 8 Marsyas: Plato, *Symposium*, 215b (CDP, p. 566)

p. 8–9 speaking for myself . . . ibid., 215d (CDP, p. 567)

p. 9 I've been bitten . . . ibid., 218a (CDP, p. 569)

p. 9–10 The first step, then . . . Xenophon, *The Banquet*, V (transl. adapted from E. C. Marchant and O. J. Todd, Xenophon, LCL edn, 1923, Vol. 4, p. 599)

p. 14 After puzzling about it . . . Plato, *Apology*, 21b (CDP, p. 7)

p. 14 I reflected as I walked away . . . ibid., 21d (CDP, p. 7)

p. 14 whenever I succeed . . . ibid., 23a (CDP, p. 9)

p. 14 the arguments never . . . Plato, *Theaetetus*, 161a (CDP, p. 866)

p. 15 If I say that this . . . Plato, *Apology*, 37e (CDP, p. 23)

p. 15 it has always been . . . Plato, *Crito*, 46b (CDP, p. 31)

p. 15 in obedience to God's commands . . . Plato, *Apology*, 33c (CDP, p. 19)

p. 15 I want you to think . . . ibid., 22a (CDP, p. 8)

p. 16 when it comes . . . ibid., 31d (CDP, p. 17)

p. 16 I spend all my time . . . ibid., 30a (CDP, p. 16)

p. 16 ashamed that you give . . . ibid., 29e (CDP, p. 16)

p. 16 these people give you . . . ibid., 36e (CDP, p. 22)

p. 17 Apollodorus: Xenophon, *Socrates' Defence*, 28

p. 17 to be afraid of death ... Plato, *Apology*, 29a (CDP, p. 15)

p. 17 heroes of the old days, ibid., 41b (CDP, p. 25)

p. 18 the work of ... Plato, *2nd Letter*, 314c (CDP, p. 1,567)

p. 18 All his private conduct ... Xenophon, *Memoirs of Socrates*, IV (transl. E. C. Marchant, LCL edn, p. 309)

p. 18 old prig ... Jonathan Barnes, *The Presocratic Philosophers* (Routledge, 1982), p.448

p. 19 modern scholars: particularly Gregory Vlastos, *Socrates: Ironist and Moral Philosopher* (Cambridge, 1991); *Socratic Studies* (Cambridge, 1994)

p. 19 purified, (etc.): Plato, *Phaedo*, 67c–d (CDP, p. 50)

p. 20–21 mathematics has come to be ... Aristotle, *Metaphysics*, 992a32 (CWA, p. 1568)

p. 21 our birth is but a sleep ... Wordsworth, *Intimations of Immortality* V, (1807)

p. 21 we have helped him ... Plato, *Meno*, 84b (CDP, p. 368)

p. 22 At present these opinions ... ibid., 85c (CDP, p. 370)

p. 22 I shall question him ... Plato, *Apology*, 29e (CDP, p. 16)

p. 23 sometimes, however ... Plato, *Lesser Hippias*, 372d (CDP, p. 209)

p. 23 I am full of defects ... ibid., 372b (CDP, p. 209)

p. 24 an accurate knowledge ... Plato, *Euthyphro*, 5a (CDP, p. 172)

p. 24 is what is holy ... ibid., 10a (CDP, p. 178)

p. 24–25 Those who believe that God ... Leibniz, *Theodicy* (1710), 176 (transl. E. M. Huggard, Open Court, 1985, p. 236)

p. 25 We must not limit our enquiry ... Aristotle, *Magna Moralia*, 1182a4 (CWA, p. 1868)

p. 25–26 he thought all the virtues ... ibid., 1216b2 (adapted from CWA, p. 1925)

p. 26 he is doing away with ... ibid., 1182a21 (CWA, p. 1868)

p. 26 No one, he said, acts ... Aristotle, *Nicomachean Ethics*, 1145b27 (CWA, p. 1810)

p. 27 in the strength of his character ... K. Joel, in W. K. C. Guthrie, *Socrates* (Cambridge, 1971), p. 138

p. 27 Milton: *Paradise Lost*, IV. 110

p. 27 no one would choose evil ... Aristotle, *Magna Moralia*, 1200b26 (CWA, p. 1900)

p. 27 divine naiveté ... Nietzsche, *The Birth of Tragedy* (1872), 13 (transl. W. Kaufmann, Random House, 1967, p. 88)

p. 27 wisdom full of pranks: Nietzsche, *Der Wanderer und sein Schatten* (1880), 86

p. 27 This was Socrates' ... Galen, *On the Use of the Parts of the Body*, I.9

p. 28 mutilated by . . . Plato, *Crito*, 47e (CDP, p. 33)

p. 28 nothing can harm . . . Plato, *Apology*, 41d (CDP, p. 25)

p. 28 the difficulty is not . . . ibid., 39b (CDP, p.24)

p. 28 to live well means . . . Plato, *Crito*, 48b (CDP, p. 33)

p. 28 the just is happy . . . Plato, *Republic*, 354a (CDP, p. 604)

p. 30 So there is every . . . Plato, *Gorgias*, 507b (CDP, p. 289)

p. 30 Those who say that the victim . . . Aristotle, *Nicomachean Ethics*, 1153b19 (CWA, p. 1823)

p. 30 if you are serious . . . Plato, *Gorgias*, 481c (CDP, p. 265)

p. 30 it is no ordinary matter . . . Plato, *Republic*, 352d

p. 33 A Socrates gone mad: Diogenes Laertius, *Lives of the Philosophers*, VI.54 (LOP, Vol. 2, p. 55)

p. 35 travelled around with her husband . . . *Lives of the Philosophers*, VI.96 (as transl. J. M. Rist in *Stoic Philosophy*, Cambridge, 1969, p. 61)

p. 35 wrangling Euclides . . . Timon of Phlius, in Diogenes Laertius, op. cit., II.107 (LOP, VOL.1, p. 237)

p. 36 O Stranger . . . Athenaeus, *Deipnosophistai*, IX.410E (transl. St George Stock in *Stoicism*, London, 1908, p. 36)

p. 36 Gödel's Theorem: see *Gödel's Proof*, E. Nagel and J. R. Newman (London, 1959)

p. 38 I know how to produce . . . Plato, *Gorgias*, 474a (CDP, p. 256)

p. 38 If you put me to death . . . Plato, *Apology*, 30e (CDP, p. 16)

Plato

The standard system of reference to Plato's works is by 'Stephanus' page numbers, which denote the page and column number of a given passage in the edition of Plato published in 1578 by Henri Estienne.

The translations of the quoted passages are by myself, but they are based on the translations, by various authors, in *Plato: Complete Works*, ed. J. M. Cooper (Hackett, Indianapolis, 1997).

For help in preparing the notes and bibliography, I am grateful to Casey Perrin.

1 The ancient sources are not consistent in their dating of Plato's life. Most modern accounts date his birth some time between 429 and 427 BC. For details see Kraut (1992), p. 30 n. 1 and Guthrie (1975), p. 10.

2 A. N. Whitehead, *Process and Reality: An Essay in Cosmology*, corrected edn, ed. D. R. Griffin and D. W. Sherburne (Free Press, New York, 1978), p. 39. As Kraut (1992), p. 32 n. 4 says, perhaps rather unnecessarily, Whitehead's remark should not be taken to imply that philosophers after Plato all accepted his views as their starting point.

3 As, it should be said, many still do.

4 Thirteen Letters are among a set of works attributed to Plato in antiquity by Diogenes Laertius (3.50, cf. 3.57–62) and included in the medieval manuscripts, but whose authenticity is a matter of long and still unsettled controversy among scholars. For references see Guthrie (1975), pp. 399–401. One other work that is not strictly speaking a dialogue is the *Apology*, which is a speech that Socrates might appropriately have made at his trial.

5 But he mentions himself three times (excluding the Letters). In the *Apology* (34b, 38b) he twice says that he himself was present at the trial of Socrates, and in the second passage he is said to be among those who offered to pay a fine on behalf of Socrates should the court accept that as a penalty. At *Phaedo* 59b the narrator of the dialogue reports that Plato himself was not present on the last day of Socrates' life, because he was ill.

6 On the historical Socrates see Vlastos (1991) and Gottlieb (1997). There is a harder question about the dialogues as evidence of what Socrates believed (the so-called 'Socratic question'): see below, p. 7, 9–10, 12, 32.

7 We can learn a lot from the *Theaetetus*, but the second, and still more the third, sections of it are clearly designed to provide material for further discussion. This is brought out in Burnyeat (1990).

8 A good example is the final argument of the *Protagoras*: see below, p. 13.

9 Whatever the status of the works ascribed to Aristotle (who was forty-three years younger than Plato, was his pupil and broke away from him) they are a lot nearer to the treatise in form, and display a very different temperament.

10 The school lasted, with an unbroken line of successors, till the 1st century BC; the prevailing philosophy changed a lot, and was by no means always Platonic.

11 For discussion of this dialogue, see Ferrari (1987), and of this passage, chapter 7.

12 For a concise discussion of the methods and results of stylometric studies, see Brandwood (1992). Aristotle tells us (*Politics* 1264624) that the *Laws* was written after the *Republic*; it is universally agreed to be late. In the case of some dialogues, there is evidence for their actual date of composition or their chronology relative to other dialogues. Several dialogues contain allusions to historical events which allow us to fix a date after which they must have been written. The *Symposium*, for example, alludes to the King's Peace of 386 BC (182b) and the Spartan division of Arcadia in 385 (193a). The

Theaetetus begins with a conversation that takes place very shortly before the death of Theaetetus after a battle in Corinth in 369 BC (142A–B). THE *Statesman* is taken to have been composed after the *Sophist* since it refers back to the *Sophist* on several occasions (257A, 258B, 266D, 284B, 286b). In what follows I use 'dating' loosely, to cover placing the dialogues in an order relative to one another.

13 The *Republic* is in 10 books, and some scholars take Book I to be significantly earlier than the other books. See Vlastos (1991) p. 248–51 for discussion.

14 Some scholars place the *Theaetetus* in Plato's Middle Period, but it must surely be associated closely with the *Sophist*. The *Statesman* is often known by its Latin name, *Politicus*.

15 See *Theaetetus*, 183e–184a, and various passages in the *Sophist* (e.g. 237a, 241b), where his central doctrine is rejected. The poem of Parmenides (*c.*515–*c.*450 BC) survives only in fragments. A translation of these, with commentary, can be found in McKirahan (1994).

16 Zeno of Elea (born *c.*490 BC), who invented famous paradoxes, including that of Achilles and the Tortoise, which supposedly show that the idea of movement is self-contradictory. For discussion, see Kirk, Raven and Schofield (1983).

17 It is worth saying that there is no hope of making adequate sense of the first part of the *Parmenides*, which is crucial to these debates, unless we can get a better grasp on the second part than most people claim to have.

18 Here, as on several other points, I am indebted to Myles Burnyeat.

19 One of the characters in the *Laches* is Melesias, the son of Thucydides – not the historian, but an Athenian politician who opposed Pericles and was banished from Athens for ten years some time around 440 BC. He is mentioned in the *Meno* (94b–e) (along with Themistocles, Aristides, and Pericles) as an example of a father who failed to teach his son (the Melesias of the *Laches*) virtue.

20 Ancient democracy was both more and less 'democratic' than modern systems: more, because all citizens could take part in political decisions; less, because there were no minority rights, it was based on slavery, and women were excluded.

21 See *Gorgias*, 515d–516d. Pericles (*c.*495–*c.*429 BC) was an Athenian statesman and the main influence on Athenian policy in the middle years of the fifth century. The noblest expression of Athenian democratic ideals is to be found in the Funeral Speech ascribed to Pericles in Thucydides' *History* (II.34–46). To call him an unprincipled demagogue was rather like comparing Abraham Lincoln to Senator McCarthy.

22 There were of course predecessors. The fragment of Parmenides' poem (see note 15 above) is an interesting case; the emphatic inferential structure, together with the determined charmlessness of the verse, seem designed to make the point.

23 The same technique is used in the *Cratylus*; in that case, it is shown that the method of etymology can be used with equal plausibility to produce contrary results.

24 *Meno*, 75b.

25 Pindar, fragment 133.

26 *Meno*, 86a: he knows this when he is a man and when he is not a man; he is always either a man or not a man; so he knows it always.

27 *Meno*, 97a. In a world without maps, personal experience may well be the best basis of such beliefs. There is a similar but more complex example, of a jury acquiring from a specious orator what is in fact a true belief about something they did not witness, in the *Theaetetus* (200d–201c).

28 Erotic relations between older and younger men were a standard feature of Athenian life, and carried strong educational and other values. See Dover (1989) for discussion. Details of Alcibiades' life (*c.*450–404 BC) are to be found in Thucydides' *History*, books V–VIII, and Xenophon's *Hellenica*, book I.

29 *Symposium*, 210a.

30 *Gorgias*, 474c–481b.

31 *Gorgias*, 491a–495a.

32 *Republic*, 352d.

33 *Republic*, 343c. The formulation 'justice is the interest of the stronger', *Republic*, 338c.

34 *Republic*, 358b–c; 367b.

35 In *Republic* IV, 435b–444e.

36 For Plato's discussion of the inclusion of women in the education of the Guardians, see *Republic*, 451c–457c.

37 *The Tempest* V, 1, 48–50. For the application of this to art, see Stephen Greenblatt, *Marvelous Possessions* (Oxford University Press, Oxford, 1991).

38 The same point is made, contrasting such explanations with others, in the *Phaedo* (96c–98b).

39 Pangloss is usually said to expound a 'vulgarized' version of Leibniz's philosophy, but Leibniz himself, like some other mathematical and metaphysical geniuses, but unlike Plato, was capable of being ethically very crass.

40 *Republic*, 509d–511e. The relations between the sun, the line, and the

cave have traditionally given rise to great controversy between interpreters.

41 *Republic*, 510b–511e. Plato's own phrase means a starting point which is not a hypothesis itself and does not depend on a hypothesis.

42 Certainly with regard to the top sub-section. It is controversial whether there are 'mathematical objects', distinct from Forms, corresponding to the sub-section below this.

43 *Metaphysics*, 987b1–13.

44 596a. But the Greek could mean: where there is a Form, the form and the particulars have the same name.

45 *Metaphysics*, 987a32–b1.

46 *Republic*, 596a–b, *Cratylus*, 389a–b. In the *Cratylus* passage there is nothing to imply that the Form is 'separate'.

47 *Theaetetus*, 155b–c.

48 *Phaedo*, 105b–107a. When Socrates' companion Crito asks how his friends should bury him, Socrates replies: 'In any way you like, if you can catch me and I do not escape from you' (*Phaedo*, 115c).

49 For the question whether there are Forms of mud and hair, see *Parmenides*, 130c–d; for the 'Third Man' argument, one version of the regress, 131e–132b.

50 *Sophist*, 249c–d. A related point is made in the *Philebus* (54c), where it is recognized that there can be 'a becoming into being'.

51 For a detailed discussion of two competing interpretations of the first part of the *Theaetetus*, see Burnyeat (1990), pp. 7–64, especially pp. 7–10.

52 *Gorgias*, 507 seq.

53 There is a complex Christian inheritance of this problem. It has included some heretical strains, related to Manicheanism, which took seriously the idea that it did not matter at all what happened in this life; and also the temptation, inherited by some Kantians, to suppose that what really counts as harming people is to make them less moral.

54 *Phaedo*, 118a. This interpretation, rare in antiquity, became popular in the Renaissance, and again in the 19th century.

55 *The Gay Science*, 340. Some of his other remarks about Plato are less interesting, such as *The Twilight of the Idols*, 'What I Owe to the Ancients', sec. 2, 'Plato was a coward in the face of reality.'

56 'Among School Children'; the reference is to the fact that Aristotle was the tutor of Alexander the Great. The contrast between Plato and Aristotle has had a complex history, and has by no means always meant the same thing; in the seventeenth century, for instance, one

thing Plato stood for was the spirit of the new mathematical science. I have said something about this in an article about Greek philosophy in Finley (1981).

57 *Symposium*, 215–217.
58 *The Gay Science*, 372.

Berkeley

1 R. I. Watson and R. B. Evans, *The Great Psychologists: A History of Psychological Thought* (New York, 5th edn, 1991), p. 196.
2 J. S. Mill, 'Berkeley's Life and Writings', in Mill, *Collected Works*, Vol. vii, J. M. Robson (ed.), (Toronto, 1978), p. 451.
3 See G. Ryle, Introduction to *The Revolution in Philosophy* (London, 1965), especially pp. 4–8.
4 T. Blackwell, *Memoirs of the Court of Augustus* (Edinburgh, 1755), Vol. 2, pp. 277–8.
5 See L. Kaufman and I. Rock, 'The Moon Illusion', in *Perception: Mechanism and Models*, R. Held and W. Richards (eds.), (San Francisco 1950), pp. 260–8; D. Berman, 'Berkeley and the Moon Illusions', in *Revue Internationale de Philosophie* 154 (1985), pp. 215–22. Curiously, Voltaire, who carried out similar experiments using pasteboard tubes, came to results similar to Berkeley, that the illusion persists; see his *Elements of Newton's Philosophy*, Ch. vi.
6 J. Bennett, *Locke, Berkeley, Hume* (Oxford, 1971), pp. 91–2.
7 See, for example, *Magic Eye: A New Way of Looking at the World* (Harmondsworth, 1994), no. 22, and D. Dyckman, *Hidden Dimensions* (London, 1994).
8 See D. Berman, *George Berkeley: Idealism and the Man* (Oxford, 1994), pp. 12–16, 144–8.
9 J. S. Mill, 'Auguste Comte and Positivism', *Collected Works* Vol. x, J. M. Robson (ed.), (Toronto, 1969), p. 296.
10 See 'Memoirs of the late famous Bishop of Cloyne', in *Works of Oliver Goldsmith*, A. Friedman (ed.), (Oxford, 1966), Vol. 3, p. 35.
11 For this and the following quotation, see my *George Berkeley* (Oxford, 1994), p. 210.
12 See R. A. Sorenson, *Thought Experiments* (New York, 1992), Ch. 3.
13 K. Popper, 'A Note on Berkeley as Precursor of Mach', *British Journal for the Philosophy of Science* IV (1953), pp. 26–36.
14 See G. Ryle, *The Concept of Mind* (London, 1949); D. Dennett, *Consciousness Explained* (Harmondsworth 1993).
15 On this essay, see my *George Berkeley*, pp. 75–7.
16 See F. Galton, *Inquiries into Human Faculty and its Development*

(London, 1911 edn), especially pp. 58–61, and W. James, *Principles of Psychology* (London, 1890), Vol 2, Ch. 18, where Galton is quoted at length.

17 See, e.g., *The Revolution in Philosophy* (London, 1965), especially Ryle's Introduction and the essays on Bradley and Frege (by R. A. Wollheim and W. C. Kneale), pp. 3–6, 13–15, 31.

18 See D. N. Robinson, *An Intellectual History of Psychology* (Boston, 1996), Ch. 11, especially p. 306.

19 G. Frege, *The Basic Laws of Arithmetic* (Berkeley, 1967), M. Furth (trans.) pp. 13–14.

20 W. Lyons, *The Disappearance of Introspection* (Cambridge, Mass., 1986), Ch. 1.

21 See NTV, § 127, first edition.

22 See *Diderot's Early Philosophical Works* (Chicago, 1916), M. Jourdain (trans.), p. 118.

I am grateful to Dr Bertil Belfrage, Professor William Lyons and Dr Paul O'Grady for comments on an earlier draft of the essay.

Marx

1 'Theses on Feuerbach', in Lewis S. Feuer (ed.), *Marx and Engels: Basic Writings on Politics and Philosophy* (London, 1969), p. 286.

2 *Karl Marx: Early Writings* (Harmondsworth, 1975), p. 257. All quotations from this work are taken from Marx's *Economic and Philosophical Manuscripts* of 1844. Subsequent references to this work as EW are given in parentheses after quotations.

3 Feuer, p. 283.

4 Karl Marx, *The German Ideology*, edited and introduced by C. J. Arthur (London, 1974), p. 47. Subsequent references to this work as GI are given in parentheses after quotations.

5 'The Communist Manifesto', in *Marx and Engels: Selected Works* (London, 1968), p. 38. Subsequent references to this work as SW are given in parentheses after quotations.

6 The second part of this quotation is taken from Karl Marx, *Capital*, Vol. 1 (New York, 1967), p. 178. Subsequent references to this work are given as C in parentheses after quotations.

7 Karl Marx, *Grundrisse* (Harmondsworth, 1973), p. 488.

8 Karl Marx, *The Holy Family* (London, 1956), p. 125.

9 Karl Marx, 'Contribution to the Critique of Hegel's Philosophy of Right', in T. Bottomore (ed.), *Karl Marx: Early Writings* (London, 1963), p. 58.

Heidegger

References give section number, followed by the page number of the German edition (H: *Sein und Zeit*, seventh edition, Max Niemeyer, Tübingen, 1953) and of the classic English translation (MR: *Being and Time*, translated by John Macquarrie and Edward Robinson, Blackwell, Oxford, 1962). All quotations are taken from this translation, with the permission of Basil Blackwell Ltd.

1 Epigraph, H1, MR19.
2 Epigraph, H1, MR19.
3 §32, H152, MR193.
4 Epigraph, H1, MR19.
5 §1, H2, MR21.
6 §1, H2, MR21.
7 §1, H3–4, MR22–3.
8 §1, H6, MR26.
9 §1, H4, MR23.
10 §2, H5, MR24.
11 §2, H5–6, MR25–6.
12 §7, H37, MR62.
13 §4, H12, MR32.
14 §4, H12, MR32.
15 §4, H15, MR35.
16 §4, H13, MR34.
17 §5, H15, MR36.
18 §5, H16, MR37.
19 §6, H25, MR47. ('Presence' and 'present' correspond to *Anwesenheit* and *Gegenwart* in the original.)
20 §6, H21, MR43.
21 §6, H20, MR41.
22 §5, H15, MR36, §6, H21, MR42.
23 §8, H39–40, MR63–4.
24 §9, H41, MR68; see also H41, MR65.
25 §9, H44, MR69.
26 §23, H109, MR144.
27 §15, H68, MR98.
28 §22, H103–4, MR137.
29 §23, H105–6, MR140.
30 §16, H73–4, 76; MR102–4, 107.
31 §21, H100, MR133; cf. §14, H65, MR94, §12, H59, MR86.
32 §15, H68, MR96–7.
33 §21, H100, MR133.
34 See §21, esp. H99–100, MR132–3.

35 §21, H96, MR129.
36 §21, H100, MR133.
37 §10, H46, MR72.
38 §25, H115, MR151.
39 §13, H62, MR89.
40 §26, H124, MR162.
41 §25, H115–16, MR151.
42 §25, H116, MR152.
43 §25, H117–18, MR153–4.
44 §26, H118, MR155; H124, MR161.
45 §26, H122, MR158–9.
46 §26, H118, MR155.
47 §26, H120, MR156–7.
48 §27, H127, MR164; H128, MR165–6.
49 §27, H127, MR165.
50 §27, H126, MR164.
51 §35, H168, MR212.
52 §36, H172–3, MR216–17.
53 §37, H173–4, MR217–19.
54 §38, H178, MR223.
55 H167, MR211; §38, H175–6, MR220.
56 §27, H127, MR164.
57 §29, H138, MR177.
58 §29, H136, MR175.
59 §29, H138, MR177.
60 §31, H145, MR185.
61 §31, H148, MR188.
62 §31, H144, MR184.
63 §32, H152–3, MR194–5; see also §63, H314–15, MR362–3.
64 §34, H164, MR208.
65 §38, H179, MR223; §44, H229, MR272.
66 §28, H133, MR171.
67 §41, H192, MR236.
68 §40, H186, MR231.
69 §40, H188–9, MR233.
70 §40, H188, MR233.
71 §44, H215, MR258.
72 §44, H228–9, MR271; §43, H202, MR246.
73 §43, H203, MR247.
74 §43, H204, MR248.
75 §43, H205, MR249.
76 §43, H202, MR246–7.

77 §43, H206, MR250.
78 §43, H206, MR249.
79 §44, H229, MR271.
80 §44, H214, MR257.
81 §44, H222, MR265.
82 §44, H225, MR268.
83 §44, H219, MR262.
84 §44, H220, MR262.
85 §44, H220, MR262.
86 §39, H183, MR228.
87 §21, H101, MR134.
88 §44, H226–7, MR269.
89 §34, H165, MR208.
90 §63, H315, MR363; H313, MR361.
91 §38, H179, MR224; see also §27, H130, MR168; §54, H267, 268, MR 312, 313.
92 §63, H315, MR363.
93 §55, H271, MR316.
94 §56, H273, MR318.
95 §58, H284, MR330.
96 §57, H274, MR319.
97 §48, H243, 242, MR287, 286.
98 §47, H238, MR282.
99 §48, H244, MR288.
100 §52, H258, MR302.
101 §50, H250–1, MR294–5.
102 §52, H258, MR302.
103 §51, H253–4, MR297–8.
104 §80, H414, 420, MR467, 472.
105 §80, H412–13, MR465–6; cf. §22, H103–4, MR137.
106 §65, H326–7, MR374–5; see also §61, H304, MR352.
107 §81, H421–2, MR474.
108 §72, H373, MR425.
109 §81, H424–5, MR477.
110 §81, H425, MR478.
111 §72, H374, MR426–7.
112 §65, H328–9, MR377.
113 §65, H325–6, MR373–4.
114 §65, H329, MR377.
115 §81, H422, MR474.
116 §68, esp. H346, 350, MR396–7, 401.
117 §81, H422–3, MR474–5.

118 §69, H356–8, MR408–9.
119 §3, H9–10, MR29–30.
120 §69, H362, MR414.
121 §69, H363, MR414.
122 §66, H332, MR381.
123 §78, H405, MR457; §75, H388–9, MR440–1.
124 §75, H391, MR443–4.
125 §82, H434, MR484–5.
126 'die ungeheure Macht des Negativen', see G. W. F. Hegel, *Phenomenology of Spirit*, translated by A. V. Miller, Oxford University Press, 1977, Preface, p. 19.
127 §74, H384–5, MR436–7.
128 §76, H397, MR449; H393, MR445.
129 'die stille Kraft des Möglichen', §76, H394, MR446.
130 §83, H437, MR487; §75, H392, MR444.

Wittgenstein

I am grateful to Dr H.-J. Glock, Professor O. Hanfling and Dr J. Hyman for their comments on the first draft of this book.

1 That is, all metaphysical theories concerning the necessary structure of reality, or of the human mind.
2 Hume, *A Treatise of Human Nature* I i vi, ed. L. A. Selby-Bigge, 2nd edn revised by P. H. Nidditch (Clarendon Press, Oxford, 1978), p. 252.
3 G. Frege, 'Thoughts', repr. in B. McGuinness (ed.), *Gottlob Frege: Collected Papers on Mathematics, Logic and Philosophy* (Blackwell, Oxford, 1984), p. 360.
4 Ibid., p. 360.
5 Ibid., p. 361.
6 Ibid., p. 367.
7 P. F. Strawson, *Individuals* (Methuen, London, 1959), p. 97f.
8 W. James, *The Principles of Psychology* (1890), (Dover, New York, 1950), Vol. I, p. 185.
9 Thomas Reid, *Essay on the Intellectual Powers of Man*, repr. in Sir William Hamilton (ed.), *The Works of Thomas Reid, D. D.* (Machlachlan and Stewart, Edinburgh, 1863), Vol. I, p. 442.
10 Hume, *A Treatise of Human Nature*, p. 190.
11 James, *The Principles of Psychology*, Vol. I, p. 189f.
12 The quotation 'In the beginning was the deed' is from Goethe's *Faust*.
13 Hume, *A Treatise of Human Nature*, p. 253.
14 J. Z. Young, *Programs of the Brain* (Oxford University Press, Oxford, 1978), p. 119.

15 C. Blakemore, *Mechanics of the Mind* (Cambridge University Press, Cambridge, 1977), p. 91.

16 In this book I have drawn freely on previous writings of mine on Wittgenstein's philosophical psychology. For a much more detailed treatment, see P.M.S. Hacker, *Wittgenstein: Meaning and Mind, Volume 3* of an Analytic Commentary on the Philosophical Investigations, Part I – The Essays (Blackwell, Oxford, 1993).

Turing

1 Letter to Turing's mother, Mrs E. Sara Turing, now in the Turing Archive at King's College, Cambridge.

2 *Nature of Spirit*, Turing's undated manuscript, is in the King's College Archive. Full text in *Alan Turing: the Enigma* (see below).

3 A. M. Turing, 'On computable numbers, with an application to the Entscheidungsproblem', Proc. Lond. Math. Soc. ser. 2, 42 (1936–7) pp. 230–65; correction ibid. 43 (1937) pp. 544–6. The paper is not yet available in the *Collected Works*, but is reprinted in Martin Davis (ed.), *The Undecidable* (Raven Press, New York, 1965).

4 A. M. Turing, 'Systems of logic based on ordinals', Proc. Lond. Math. Soc. ser. 2, 45 (1939) pp. 161–228. The paper is not yet available in the *Collected Works*, but is reprinted in *The Undecidable*.

5 Ibid.

6 C. Diamond (ed.), *Wittgenstein's Lectures on the Foundations of Mathematics* (Harvester Press, 1976). The quoted dialogue is extracted from lectures 21 and 22.

7 Letter to E. S. Turing, in the Turing Archive, King's College, Cambridge.

8 A. P. Mahon, *History of Hut* 8 (1945), released from secrecy by the National Archives, Washington DC, April 1996.

9 A. M. Turing, 'Proposed Electronic Calculator', National Physical Laboratory report (1946). Published in B. E. Carpenter and R. W. Doran (eds.), *A. M. Turing's ACE Report of* 1946 and other papers (MIT Press and Tomash Publishers, 1986); and again in the *Collected Works*.

10 A. M. Turing, 'Intelligent machinery', National Physical Laboratory report (1948). The edition (by D. Michie) in *Machine Intelligence*, 5 (1969) pp. 3–23 has been reproduced in the *Collected Works*.

11 A. M. Turing, 'Computing machinery and intelligence', Mind, 51 (1950), pp. 433–60; reprinted in the *Collected Works*.

12 Transcript, in the Turing Archive, King's College, Cambridge, published in the MIT Press volume (see 9, above- and again in the *Collected Works*.

14 B. V. Bowden (ed.) *Faster than Thought* (Pitman, 1953). Turing contributed the section on chess (pp. 288–95), which is reprinted in the *Collected Works*.

15 A. M. Turing, 'The chemical basis of morphogenesis', Phil. Trans. R. Soc. London B 237 (1952) pp. 37–72; reprinted in the *Collected Works*.

16 Letter of June 1954 from Robin Gandy to M. H. A. Newman, in the Turing Archive, King's College, Cambridge.

17 Letter to N. A. Routledge, in the Turing Archive, King's College, Cambridge. Reprinted in the preface to the 1992 edition of *Alan Turing: the Enigma*.

18 Postcard to Robin Gandy, in the Turing Archive, King's College, Cambridge. Reproduced in *Alan Turing: the Enigma*.

19 A. M. Turing, 'Solvable and unsolvable problems', *Penguin Science News*, 31 (1954), pp. 7–23. Reprinted in the *Collected Works*.

Bibliographies and Further Reading

Plato

I GENERAL WORKS

For a recent collection of essays on a wide range of topics in Plato see:

Kraut, Richard, ed., *The Cambridge Companion to Plato* (Cambridge University Press, Cambridge, 1992)

Perhaps the best single volume treatment of Plato's work, and one that is particularly sensitive to the literary aspects of Plato's writing, is:

Grube, G. M. A., *Plato's Thought*, with new introduction, bibliographic essay, and bibliography by Donald J. Zeyl (Hackett, Indianapolis, 1980)

Useful for historical material, summaries of scholarly debates about dating, and discussions of textual questions, though containing very little philosophy, is:

Guthrie, W. K. C., *A History of Greek Philosophy*, Vol. 4 (Cambridge University Press, Cambridge, 1975)

The starting points for any discussion of the Socratic dialogues are:

Vlastos, Gregory, *Socrates, Ironist and Moral Philosopher* (Cornell University Press, Ithaca, 1991)
—, *Socratic Studies*, ed. Myles Burnyeat (Cambridge University Press, Cambridge, 1994)

An edition of the Greek text of the *Gorgias*, the introduction and commentary to which has much of value to offer to the reader without Greek, is:

Dodds, E. R., *Plato*: Gorgias, *A Revised Text with Introduction and Commentary* (Clarendon Press, Oxford, 1959)

For a translation with philosophical commentary of the *Phaedo*, see:

Gallop, David, *Plato*: Phaedo, translated with notes (Clarendon Press, Oxford, 1975)

The best short discussions of the *Symposium* are the introductions to:

Nehamas, Alexander and Woodruff, Paul, *Plato*: Symposium, translated with introduction and notes (Hackett, Indianapolis, 1989), pp. xi–xxvi

Dover, Kenneth, *Plato*: Symposium, Cambridge Greek and Latin Classics (Cambridge University Press, Cambridge, 1980), pp. 1–14

The most philosophical stimulating introduction to the *Republic* remains:

Annas, Julia, *An Introduction to Plato's* Republic (Oxford University Press, Oxford, 1981)

Further discussion of a variety of topics in the *Republic*, including the sun, the line, and the cave, can be found in:

Cross, R. C. and Woozley, A. D., *Plato's* Republic: *A Philosophical Commentary* (St Martin's Press, New York, 1964)

Reeve, C. D. C., *Philosopher-Kings: The Argument of Plato's* Republic (Princeton University Press, Princeton, 1988)

An idiosyncratic but closely argued account is:

Irwin, Terence, *Plato's Ethics* (Oxford University Press, Oxford, 1995)

On the *Phaedrus*, see the imaginative study by:

Ferrari, G. R. F., *Listening to the Cicadas: a Study of Plato's* Phaedrus (Cambridge University Press, Cambridge, 1987)

A recent and important book-length study of the *Parmenides* is:

Meinwald, Constance, *Plato's* Parmenides (Oxford University Press, New York, 1991)

An excellent translation of the *Theaetetus* with a book-length, philosophically compelling introduction is:

Burnyeat, Myles, *The* Theaetetus *of Plato*, with a translation by M. J. Levett, revised by Myles Burnyeat (Hackett, Indianapolis and Cambridge, 1990)

2 Other works cited in the notes

Brandwood, Leonard, 'Stylometry and chronology', in Kraut (1992) pp. 90–120

Dover, K. J., *Greek Homosexuality*, updated with a new postscript (Harvard University Press, Cambridge, Mass., 1989)

Finley, M. I., ed., *The Legacy of Greece: a New Appraisal* (Clarendon Press, Oxford, 1981)

Gottlieb, Anthony, *Socrates* (Phoenix/Orion, London, 1997)

Kirk, G. S., Raven, J. E., and Schofield M., *The Presocratic Philosophers*, second edition (Cambridge University Press, Cambridge, 1983)

Kraut, Richard, 'Introduction to the Study of Plato', in Kraut (1992) pp. 1–50

McKirahan, Richard D., Jr., *Philosophy before Socrates* (Hackett, Indianapolis, 1994)

Popper

Popper, Karl, *The Poverty of Historicism* (Routledge (ARK edn.), London, 1986, reprinted 1994).

Popper, Karl, *The Open Society and its Enemies* (Routledge and Sons, London, 1945. Golden Jubilee Edition, Routledge, 1995).

Popper, Karl, *The Logic of Scientific Discovery* (Hutchinson and Co., London, 1959, revised 1980).

Popper, Karl, *Conjectures and Refutations* (Routledge-Kegan Paul, London, 1963).

Popper, Karl, *Objective Knowledge* (OUP, 1972).

Popper, Karl, *Unended Quest* (Fontana, London, 1976, revised Flamingo, London, 1986. Routledge, 1992).

Bambrough, Renford ed., *Plato, Popper and Politics* (Heffer, Cambridge, 1967).

Corvi, Roberta, *An Introduction to the Thought of Karl Popper* (Routledge, London, 1997).

Magee, Bryan, *Popper* (Fontana, London, 1977).

Miller, David ed., *A Pocket Popper* (Fontana, London, 1983).

Shearmur, Jeremy, *The Political Thought of Karl Popper* (Routledge, London, 1996).

Turing

J. L. Britton, D. C. Ince, P. T. Saunders (eds), *Collected Works of A. M. Turing* (Elsevier, 1992).

Three volumes of the collected works have appeared, with extensive annotation by the editors. The fourth, containing Turing's papers in mathematical logic (eds. R. O. Gandy and C. E. M. Yates) is still (as at 1997) in preparation.

Herken, Rolf, (ed.), *The Universal Turing Machine* (Oxford University Press, 1988), includes definitive articles on the concept of computability.

Hinsley, F. H. and Alan Stripp (eds.), *Codebreakers, The Inside Story of Bletchley Park* (Oxford University Press, 1993).

Hodges, Andrew, *Alan Turing: the Enigma* (London, Burnett with Hutchinson, 1983; New York, Simon & Schuster, 1983; new edn. London, Vintage, 1992)

Hodges, Andrew, *http://www.turing.org.uk/turing/Turing.html*. Website with updates of information and comment, bibliography, links, images, and Turing machines.

Millican, P. J. R., and A. Clark (eds.), *Machines and Thought: the Legacy of Alan Turing* (Oxford, Clarendon Press, 1996).

Penrose, Roger, 'Beyond the doubting of a shadow' (*Psyche*, electronic journal, 1996: *http://psyche.cs.monash.edu.au/volume2–1/psyche-96-2-23-shadows-10-penrose.html*) is the best introduction to the ideas developed in Penrose's *The Emperor's New Mind* (Oxford University Press, 1989) and *Shadows of the Mind* (Oxford University Press, 1994).

Acknowledgements

The authors and publishers wish to thank the following for permission to use copyright material:

Princeton University Press for excerpts from *The Collected Dialogues of Plato*, eds E. Hamilton and H. Cairns (1961), renewed 1989 by Princeton University; Cambridge University Press for excerpts from *The Philosophical Writings of Descartes*, Vols I & II, eds J. Cottingham R. Stoothoff and D. Murdoch (1985), and *The Philosophical Writings of Descartes*, Vol III, & II, eds J. Cottingham, R. Stoothoff and D. Murdoch (1985), and *The Philosophical Writings of Descartes*, Vol III, eds. J. Cottingham, R. Stoothoff, D. Murdoch and A. Kenny (1991); Thomas Nelson & Sons for material from 'Essay Towards a New Theory of Vision', 'Principles of Human knowledge' and 'Manuscripts Introduction to Principles' from *The Works of George Berkeley*, eds A. A. Luce and T. E. Jessop (1948–57); Lawrence and Wishart for material from *The German Idealogy*, Karl Marx (1970) and *Mark and Engels: Selected Works* (1968), and International Publishers Co. Inc. for material from *Capital*, Karl Marx (1967); Routledge and Bertrand Peace Foundation for excerpts from *Mysticism and Logic*, Unwin Hyman (1976), *Philosophy of Logical Atomism*, Unwin Hyman (1976), *Nightmares, Part III*, Unwin Hyman (1961) all by Bertrand Russell, and W. W. Norton, Inc. for excerpts from *Principles of Mathematics*, Bertrand Russell, 2nd edition, Allen & Unwin (1985); Blackwell Publishers for excerpts from *Philosophical Investigations*, Ludwig Wittgenstein, 3rd edition (1967), and *The Blue and Brown Books*, Ludwig Wittgenstein (1958); The Estate of Karl Popper for material from *The Poverty of Historicism*, Karl Popper, Routledge (1960); the Turing estate for quotation of passages from Turing's unpublished writings, the London Mathematical Society for extracts from his papers of 1936 and 1939, the Controller of HMSO for reports from the National Physical Laboratory, 1946 and 1948 (Crown copyright), Oxford University Press for extracts from the Mind articles of 1950, Harvester Wheatsheaf for reproduction of the Turing–Wittgenstein dialogue.

Every effort has been made to trace the copyright holders but if any have been inadvertently overlooked the publishers will be pleased to make the necessary arrangement at the first opportunity.